D1327306

An
Introduction to
The Medieval Mystics
of
Europe

An
Introduction to
The Medieval Mystics
of
Europe

FOURTEEN ORIGINAL ESSAYS EDITED BY

PAUL E. SZARMACH

STATE UNIVERSITY OF NEW YORK PRESS   *Albany*

Published by
State University of New York Press, Albany
© 1984 State University of New York
All rights reserved
Printed in the United States of America

For information, address State University of New York
Press, State University Plaza, Albany, N.Y., 12246

ISBN   87395-834-9
ISBN   87395-835-7 (PBK.)

10   9   8   7   6   5   4   3   2   1

Contents

Introduction   1
    Paul E. Szarmach

I.   Augustine   19
    Eugene TeSelle

II.   Smaragdus   37
    Jean Leclercq

III.   Neoplatonism and the Mysticism of William of St. Thierry   53
    Thomas Michael Tomasic

IV.   St. Bernard, the Canticle of Canticles, and Mystical Poetry   77
    James I. Wimsatt

V.   The Zohar: Jewish Mysticism in Medieval Spain   97
    Arthur Green

VI.   Mystic on Campus: Friar Thomas   135
    James A. Weisheipl

VII.   The Medieval Continental Women Mystics: 161
    An Introduction
    Valerie M. Lagorio

VIII.   Julian of Norwich: Writer and Mystic   195
    Ritamary Bradley

IX.   Margery Kempe   217
    Maureen Fries

X.   Meister Eckhart: An Introduction   237
    Bernard McGinn

XI. John Tauler   259
Richard Kieckhefer
XII. The *Cloud of Unknowing*   273
John P. H. Clark
XIII. Nicholas of Cusa's *The Vision of God*   293
Clyde Lee Miller
XIV. Jewish Mysticism in the Sixteenth Century   313
David Biale
Notes   331
Index   371

Introduction

PAUL E. SZARMACH

The essays in this volume are the result of an invitation to scholars and teachers in Medieval Studies and in Religious Studies to collaborate on a book introducing the important figures of medieval mysticism. We envision an audience of non-specialists or not-yet-specialists, i.e., readers who may know something about the Middle Ages or about mysticism, but who need an introduction to a figure or a set of figures in medieval mysticism. For some readers, who may already know something about mysticism, this collection may serve as a first book on medieval mysticism in the West; for others, who may know something about the Middle Ages, this collection may extend their knowledge of the period into an important area of study. Consequently each essayist seeks to provide, insofar as it is possible, a common interpretation of his or her subject and presents bibliographical suggestions for further study. In some cases the material presented here has had the benefit of student response.

Whatever the presumed audience, the subjects under consideration have also ineluctably shaped these essays. It is one thing to write an essay on Augustine, about whom so much has been written, and quite another to treat Smaragdus, about whom so little has been written; it is one thing to present the anonymous author of the *Cloud of Unknowing*, whose original language is comparatively accessible to a contemporary audience, and quite another to introduce the women mystics of medieval Germany, whose works have neither been properly edited nor translated for the reader of English. Likewise the material itself—apart from the aids or impediments of scholarship and the concerns of a contemporary reader—exists in varied forms

1

from treatises to poems to dictated memoirs, all written in various cultural and historical circumstances. Thus, no collaborative intention can reduce the medieval mystics, severally or jointly, to a formula, and the present volume reflects their variety in several of its major themes (the importance of women mystics, mysticism in later medieval England, the Dionysian and other traditions) and in some of its special emphases (the tradition of Jewish mysticism, which is often ignored in similar collaborations, and the applicability of a knowledge of mysticism to other studies). Before looking briefly at the individual essays, however, some general comments may be in order.

It must be observed at the outset that the term "mysticism" is a construct. Like any construct the term may validly and meaningfully organize human experience so as to facilitate understanding and to render value by illuminating connections between phenomena, especially those that might at first glance seem disparate and unrelated. Sometimes constructs may appear as mere labels, especially when those using them are slack in thought or merely facile in expression, or when those reading them bring hidden expectations and untested assumptions. It would be perilous to define (medieval) mysticism the way a dictionary might, as if the term signifies the static and the unchanging. Suffice it to say that the several essayists show how the figures they discuss enter into some knowing relationship with the Transcendent or establish a framework for it. The knowledge of one's own ignorance is an immediate and paradoxical result in many of these relationships.

Though the organization and focus of the essays in this volume imply that mysticism is an individual relationship, it is clear that medieval mysticism does not preclude a role for institutions. Lord Russell might have disallowed Thomas Aquinas from the ranks of philosophers because Thomas was a churchman, but it is patently unhelpful to disallow from the ranks of mystics Thomas and others who held common religious beliefs through institutions and practiced them accordingly. This aspect of medieval mysticism may confront or oppose one of the hidden assumptions a contemporary reader might have. So may another: while it may be a common belief that mysticism and ecstasy are virtually equivalent terms, medieval mysticism does not make the equivalence. In the Christian tradition there is a distinction between the active and the contemplative life, first sharply formulated by Gregory the Great, that confirms a mystical quality on the active life, i.e., the life of good works. In the Jewish tradition there is similarly a non-ecstatic mystical tradition. The construct "mysticism" is therefore a useful link for the figures treated in this volume, when properly construed.

While it is risky and hazardous to define or set limits to the term "mysticism," or to establish typologies that have tight, intellectual categories, but a deadening effect on an understanding of the mystics and their ideas (see McGinn p. 247 below), it may nevertheless be useful to describe the varieties of mystical experience discussed here. I would therefore like to suggest certain functional (albeit somewhat overlapping) contraries that may help to illustrate these varieties, but that certainly do not exhaust them. Granted that anything may be compared to anything else, the following contraries may be fruitful: philosophical vs. experiential mysticism, earlier vs. later Western medieval mysticism, private vs. public mysticism, abstract vs. functioning mysticism; or, in other terms, such distinctions as those between thought and feeling, monastic and scholastic, self and society, ideas and their applications, may serve to highlight the differences in emphasis and orientation that lead to the varieties of Western medieval mysticism. (I admit here that the emphasis on distinctions leaves me open to the charge of a scholastic or Aristotelian bias.) Let me adduce several examples from the figures discussed in this collection.

There are mystics like William of St. Thierry who provide an intellectually considered response to the question of knowing God. William sets out to develop an orderly way of approaching God from an established philosophical viewpoint, Neoplatonism. His interest is the God of the philosophers, so to speak, to whom the soul ascends by the operation of the intellect or mind. William's thought requires a logical, unambiguous, diction to attain to its object. By contrast, the mysticism of Margery Kempe derives its impact from experience and feeling. Margery offers testimony, not logical proof, and so biography is her appropriate mode of discourse and the common idiom her expression. Intellectual analysis may find deeper patterns, such as the quest, in her discourse, but the patterning is strictly literary, not philosophical. While William and Margery may serve as antithetical types reflecting distinct tendencies in the interior life, a figure such as Thomas Aquinas shows, in his achievements as a philosopher and as a composer of hymns, that both tendencies may be complementary in a single human life.

Students of the Middle Ages often draw a distinction between the monastic Middle Ages and the scholastic Middle Ages, i.e., between, in rough terms, the earlier period when contemplation was a dominant tendency, and the later period when teaching methods featured analytical questioning. The twelfth century is the approximate chronological dividing point. In this collection Smaragdus is the example of the tradition of monastic contemplation or meditation. Smaragdus is a practical theologian who emphasizes activities of prayer and fasting and, especially, their effects on the affective disposition of the inner life. The later period does not so much eliminate an interest in affective mysticism as give it a different context. Many of the later medieval mystics reflect the scholastic tendency either directly or indirectly. Aquinas, Cusa, and even William, are to one degree or another "scholastic mystics," and some argue that the strong emphasis on feeling and experience found in later medieval mysticism is a conscious reaction against the analytic mode of scholasticism. Thus, distinctions between the intellectual temper of the earlier and the later Middle Ages yield an additional dimension to the interplay of thought and feeling in medieval mysticism.

There are mystics who are out-of-this-world and mystics who are in-this-world. The recluse Julian of Norwich exemplifies the disengagement from secular affairs. After her visions of Christ, she withdrew to a cell attached to the church in Norwich from whose saint she may have taken her name. There her life was active only in giving spiritual guidance and counsel. By contrast, Catherine of Siena, Julian's contemporary, was actively involved in the crises of the fourteenth century, that era which Barbara Tuchman has described as a distant mirror to our own age of anxiety. Catherine gave more than spiritual counsel: she became involved in the Great Western Schism, in the reform of the Dominicans, and in a general effort to reduce corruption in church and state. Both women offer contrasting models of the mystic's involvement with *saeculum*, yet each has made a special and unique contribution to the spiritual life of her own and subsequent generations.

The mystic way did not exist separate and apart from the rest of life in the Middle Ages, as if in a vacuum or in a museum of archetypes. The mystics influenced the development of the Christian and Jewish religions in their external or exterior forms. The continental women mystics, for example, not only urged reform of the Church as an institution, but also promoted new devotional practices based on their ideas. There was even a secularization of some mystical values, so to speak. Bernard of Clairvaux's theology was transmuted into vernacular poetry—indeed, the relationship of carnal love and spiritual love is a general question in the study of the medieval lyric. Mysticism, then, was not separate from medieval society and culture, but rather it functioned effectively within them.

These four sets of functional contraries certainly do not provide an exhaustive framework for the varieties of mysticism discussed in this book. Some readers may prefer other, more established or current contraries, such as active vs. contemplative, or monistic vs. pantheistic, or positive vs. negative mysticism; these themes are also present in several of the essays gathered here. At this juncture it seems appropriate to turn to the essays themselves and offer a summary-analysis of their main points.

The first essay in the collection, which follows an approximate historical order, is Eugene TeSelle's overview of Augustine. There perhaps could not be a more appropriate beginning because so much of the Middle Ages, either in the first instance or in reaction or in subsequent development is Augustinian. Writing in what Jaspers has called the axial period of universal history, Augustine gave his imprint to Christianity when it was consolidating its gains as the official religion of the Roman Empire. Augustine's focus on the self, his pursuit of the happy life, and his analysis of the different kinds of vision are uniquely significant in his attempt to work through his classical education and his conversion to Christianity towards an understanding of the triune God. Augustine is the first "philosophical mystic" in the volume. TeSelle addresses the nature of philosophical mysticism, the meaning of ecstasy or rapture, and the question whether Augustine, who is the source of one major tradition of mysticism in the Middle Ages, fits the definition of "mystic." Summarizing the exact character of Augustine's views on mysticism, TeSelle goes on to explain Augustine's concern for the will and the affections, particularly as this concern manifests itself in the *Confessions*, *The Trinity*, and *On the Epistle of John*. Since Augustine was not a systematic philosopher, and indeed a consideration of his whole corpus shows changes and shifting emphases, if not reversals on many points, it is no surprise that he left no finished doctrine of mysticism. TeSelle ends his essay with a discussion of the theoretical issues Augustine left for his successors. These issues regarding the Trinity, mystical union, the nature of the mind, and the role of bodily experience, will reappear in various forms in subsequent essays.

Although the High and Late Middle Ages constitute the primary periods of interest in this collection, Jean Leclercq's essay is a reminder that the Early Middle Ages, exemplified here by the Carolingian period and Smaragdus of St. Mihiel, continued the development of Christian mysticism in a monastic context. Since there are no English translations of Smaragdus, and there is practically no secondary literature, Leclercq offers a précis of Smaragdus' teachings derived from the *Royal Crown for Monks* and the *Commentary on the Rule of St. Benedict*. These works discuss the contemplative life, or the life of prayer, whereas one of Smaragdus' earlier works, the *Royal Pathway*, had treated the active life, or the practice of virtues. Consistent with the temper of the early medieval period Smaragdus is a non-speculative thinker, who derives his teaching from Eastern and Western patristic sources, particularly Gregory the Great. Originality (in the modern sense), one may interject, was never a *desideratum* for a medieval teacher or writer. Smaragdus rather popularized the ancient monastic tradition. Leclerq, whose method is a form of close reading that pays attention to the nuances of Latin terms, explains Smaragdus' unified doctrine of the life of prayer. *Oratio* ("prayer"), or in Smaragdus' etymological analysis, *oris + ratio* or the "mouth" and its "means of expressing itself rationally," is an expression of the path of self-awareness towards God, a bursting forth of the soul, an experience of fondness for God *(affectus)*—finally, a habit of directing oneself to God throughout life. There is no clear distinction between prayer and meditation, or prayer and contemplation, but sometimes in Smaragdus prayer leads into contemplation, which appears as the goal towards which the desire for God is directed. Prayer has, among other features, a communal aspect, for it is not only the person who prays who receives the benefits, but also any other human being, an immediate community, and indeed humanity at large. Traditional practices, such as nocturnal vigils, fasting, reading Scripture, singing the Psalms, aid prayer, but conquering vice and moderating passion are necesary to create the proper inner disposition. Compunction is an essential predisposition: "We must face the fact of our miserable human condition head on, accept it, and even come to love it in a certain way." The ultimate purpose of prayer, and indeed the goal of life, is salvation and eternal life. Sometimes a seemingly unattainable ideal, Smaragdus' doctrine takes human weakness into account and finds a ground in concrete experience and daily living. This was the influential synthesis that Smaragdus gave to the Middle Ages.

William of St. Thierry, one of the important monastic thinkers of the twelfth century, offers a sharp contrast to the non-speculative mysticism of Smaragdus. As Thomas Michael Tomasic shows, William is a philosophical mystic whose Neoplatonic teaching demands precise terminology and sharp analysis. This kind of vigor gives mysticism a quality of open or public truthfulness that is quite distinct from any character of subjective, private, or experiential truth it may possess, and it allows, moreover, for the possibility of clarification and correction. The Neoplatonic paradigm may at first seem formidable to the non-specialist or the non-speculative reader, but, to use another mode of speaking, to understand the paradigm is in effect a process of initiation while the paradigm itself is the equivalent to the metaphorical ladder of ascent found in Pseudo-Dionysian mysticism. William's mysticism also requires a form of discourse using a three-valued logic where statements about God may be indeterminate, thus allowing the conjunction of such "collision statements" as "God is Being and not-Being." This form of discourse allows for "the third thing" and confers a special role on metaphor.

Within this framework the Trinity becomes an important idea as a law-like model or metaphor for the soul; it exemplifies both unity and union and prescribes the relationships within the soul. In the descent of the soul there is no break from its Source, God, but rather a continuity of Unity-*animus-anima*. The threat to this continuity comes when *anima* alienates herself from *animus*, which is the image of God, and becomes a subject to things. The goal is the restoration of this "marital union." The ascent of the soul to God is a reversal of the outward movement, which *anima* can begin by virtue of her natural love. *Anima* has the liberty to free herself from things. The doctrine of Incarnation (that the Second Person of the Trinity was made man in Jesus) provides the most important ascetical model. Jesus is the paradigm for man's union with God, while the Trinity is the highest, mystical expression of union. William thus works out Augustinian, Pseudo-Dionysian, and broadly Christian mystical themes in a tight, conceptual way, and, especially compared to Smaragdus, illustrates how any model of a "unified" Christian Middle Ages has to accommodate two radically different orientations.

William was the associate of Bernard of Clairvaux, the most significant and influential Cistercian thinker. James I. Wimsatt explains how some key Cistercian ideas, stated, as we have seen in William's philosophical terms, receive a strikingly different expression in Bernard's work and subsequently find their way into Latin and vernacular literature. Wimsatt begins with an introduction to Bernard's interpretation of the Canticle of Canticles as it appears in his eighty-six sermons. The sermon form may seem, to some contemporary readers, an unlikely vehicle for mysticism, yet Wimsatt makes the case for Bernard as a "great exegete, homilist, and mystical poet." Bernard interprets the sexuality of the Canticles as complete spirituality, ". . . a celebration of the most intense love possible, that between God and the perfected soul." Bernard shared the Pauline disdain for the corrupted body, but sees in the description of carnal union an analogy to mystical union: "No sweeter names can be found to embody that sweet interflow of affections between the Word and the soul, than bridegroom and bride . . ." Just as for William, for Bernard Christ as Incarnate Word is necessary for mystic union since, Bernard says, Christ sought to draw mankind to love His humanity and then to raise mankind to a spiritual love. Unlike the followers of the *via negativa*, who advocated the love of the crucified Christ in order to drive out other carnal loves in preparation for divine love, Bernard held that a corrected carnal love could be raised to a spiritual plane. These ideas about spiritualizing love influence Middle English poems. Wimsatt explicates "In a valley of this restless mynde" to demonstrate how this poem evokes the contemplative process. The poem contains themes and motifs found in secular lyrics, but the main source is Bernard's interpretation of the Canticles, and, as Wimsatt shows in a close reading informed by Bernard's ideas, its main elements are a meditation on the Passion, an account of the process by which this meditation becomes contemplation, and the presentation of a mystical experience. Wimsatt compares and contrasts other poems, particularly *Dulcis Iesu Memoria*, to sharpen his distinction between poems of mysticism and poems of meditation. Thus, the mystical tradition of the Canticles, which has exegetical and philosophical roots, gives the vernacular lyric affective power. Bernard's sermons are the poetic root.

While the Christian tradition was continuing its complex development in the High Middle Ages, the Jewish tradition was flourishing with equal sophistication. Arthur Green focuses on the Zohar, a product of Spanish-Jewish mysticism, but his introductory section on the origins of the Kabbalah and its cultural setting show that in the twelfth century speculation on "the inner life of the Deity" had already begun. In the Bahir, a work of biblical exegesis, the unknown writer hints at the mysterious reality beyond the scriptural word. As a document of religious vision the Bahir is without precedent in Jewish sources. It emphasizes symbolic speech and mystical prayer. These doctrines made their way from Provence to Gerona, where a Neoplatonic tendency developed in the Kabbalist circle, especially in the doctrine of the soul, and to Burgos and Toledo, where a gnostic tendency became prominent.

By the end of the thirteenth century the Zohar appeared in Castile. Its Aramaic language is a unique feature, while the question of authorship creates a set of problems matched, if not exceeded, by the structure of the work whose twenty-two units are unique in length, content, and style. Green gives examples of exegesis, which offer comparison with Bernard's interpretation of the Canticles. The author may be Moses De Leon, but whoever he was, he gave to the Zohar a poetic imagination that characteristically finds its way into discussions of God, the origin and power of evil, man, his soul, and Judaism. God is the essential subject of the Zohar. Green gives a detailed exposition of the Zohar's thinking about God, demonstrating that it is a cosmological mysticism and not an exercise in spiritual (auto-)biography. (One of the several distinctive characteristics of this cosmology is the notion of the Great Mother within God.) There are striking formulations in the problem of good and evil too; the Kabbalists saw evil as a real and active cosmic force. There is human responsibility, since the human heart can contribute its active participation. Indeed the Zohar has so strong an anthropocentric focus that it may serve as a guidebook for the conduct of human life. Man is in the image of God, and the Kabbalists see the body and the soul reflecting the divinity. Furthermore the Zohar stresses full and proper Judaic observance, which gives man his status and role in this world. Throughout his discussion of the Zohar and its antecedents Green contrasts this mystical variety of Judaism with rabbinic Judaism and by implication shows that, like the philosophical Christian mystics,the author of the Zohar tends to de-emphasize the autobiographical self.

Green suggests that one of the reasons for the development of the Zohar is a general movement against rationalism. The anti-rationalist strain in mysticism is also often cited in the discussion of the growth of Christian mysticism. Yet, James A. Weisheipl suggests that the greatest scholastic philosopher, Thomas Aquinas, would probably not have seen the matter that way. For Thomas "mysticism," i.e., "spirituality," and intelligence are compatible, and such things as visionary experiences are accidental or secondary effects of the true mystical state, viz., charity active on the soul. The mind active in the world may be accompanied by an interior life of the spirit that can encounter God. Adopting a biographical approach, Weisheipl shows how Aquinas both lived the mystical life and wrote about it. He places Aquinas in the context of his age, when the growth of cities, the development of the mendicant orders, and the rise of the universities shaped his external world and affected his internal life. Aquinas chose the life of a Dominican friar over strong family objections and, inspired by his mentor Albert the Great, followed the intellectual life so effectively that he became professor of theology at Paris. While compiling such works as the Catena Aurea, a line-by-line gloss of the Gospels assimilating the vast work of all the Fathers of the Church, Aquinas could at the same time transcend "mere" scholarship in such mystical hymns as O Salutaris Hostia and Tantum Ergo. From the biographical evidence it seems that during his university life a series of mystical experiences caused Aquinas to become increasingly absorbed in the life of a contemplative. Perhaps this transformation was helped by Thomas' growing appreciation of Augustine. In any case, it is in the famous Summa that Thomas gives his fullest treatment of the mystical life, when he explains the gifts of the Holy Spirit. He left Paris, its university life, and its disputes to organize a house of studies in Naples. He continued his intellectual and temporal work in good health, still experiencing abstractio mentis. On December 6, 1273, Thomas had an apparent physical breakdown that was connected, in some way, with mystical experience. Subsequently injured while traveling to a council, Thomas died March 7, 1274. His last few months have inspired many edifying legends, but the substantial contribution of Thomas to mysticism has real shape in his pages of clear, ordered theological discourse.

Valerie M. Lagorio introduces a major topic with her survey of continental women mystics. As in so many other disciplines during the last two decades the study of women in Medieval Studies and in Religious Studies has amplified those subjects by demonstrating relationships, influences, and achievements that were hitherto unknown or unappreciated—sometimes because of malign neglect. Lagorio gives an overview of the twelfth to fourteenth centuries, with occasional glances forward, and places the women mystics in context. Hildegard of Bingen is the first of the major figures she discusses. Hildegard, the "Sibyl of the Rhine," was a woman of many and varied accomplishments. She had a full life as intellectual, contemplative, and reformer. She wrote music, poetry, drama, exegesis, and treatises on science and mysticism, not to mention an account of twenty-six visions, while also running a monastery and conducting, in effect, a public ministry against laxity and heresy. She even received approval and endorsement from many prominent (male) contemporaries. Elizabeth of Schönau, who also had visionary gifts, was a spiritual daughter of Hildegard's, whose works were likewise widely circulated. The Cistercian house at Helfta became famous for the life and works of Mechthild of Hackeborn, Mechthild of Magdeburg, and Gertrude the Great. Mechthild of Hackeborn wrote *Liber Spiritualis Gratiae*, which was translated into Middle English, while Mechthild of Magdeburg's *Lux Divinitatis Fluens in Corda Veritatis* was rendered into later High German. Greater than either of these perhaps was Gertrude the Great, whose skillful Latin still suffers scholarly neglect. Feminine mysticism also expressed itself through the "beguine" movement, i.e., a semi-religious communal movement emphasizing poverty and spiritual perfection, and similar socio-religious movements. Lagorio considers these movements and other significant individuals, ending with more detailed treatments of Brigitta of Sweden and Catherine of Siena. These two women match Hildegard in their intellectual, active, and contemplative lives and in their significance and influence. Inspired in part by the revelations accorded her, Brigitta was active in papal and secular matters, attacking corruption and injustice and being met in turn with hostility and the accusation that she was a sorceress. Catherine of Siena also sought to influence the course of the papacy and the direction of the world, but her permanent legacy lies in the writings of her brief 33 years. Lagorio explains Catherine's *Dialogue* as an exemplary work illustrating the *via mystica*.

Feminine mysticism was also a special feature of religion in later medieval England. Ritamary Bradley introduces the first of two English women mystics in this volume, Julian of Norwich, the earliest known woman of letters in the history of English literature. There are few facts about Julian's life and education beyond what might be inferred from her works. Bradley thus concentrates on Julian's *Showings* as literature and as a mystical work. Though R.W. Chambers does not give Julian a full treatment in his important *On the Continuity of English Prose* of a half century ago (mainly because scholarship on Julian was not well-advanced then), Julian does reflect in her unique way that lively prose Chambers finds traditional in vernacular religious writing throughout the Middle English period. Julian did not, however, draw her models of discourse from the learned tradition, but rather from Scripture and common language. This is not to say that one cannot discern a rhetoric in her work, or a set of literary devices that unites with concepts and experiences, all of which appeal to a general audience. Her *Showings* relate her "bodily" visions and her "spiritual" showings. The latter form the higher part of her mystical experience. Julian uses metaphor and parable to convey this experience, sometimes drawing from the common stock of Christian metaphor (for example, the journey, light and darkness), and sometimes renewing old ones (for instance, she transmutes the Pseudo-Dionysian "divine" point into a kind of metaphorical needlepoint). One of her most striking metaphors is the Motherhood of Christ, which she develops from its original Judaic-biblical tradition into an expression covering the range of Christian mysteries. Julian's many strengths as a writer ought not to prevent consideration of her exemplary contribution, for, though no scholar or "philosophical mystic," her witness suggests that she encountered the Absolute and had those experiences that other mystics relate. In this context there is little that is strange in the *Showings* and nothing that might strike the contemporary reader as bizarre or esoteric. Indeed, her themes are close to many contemporary issues and interests: the relation of the feminine to the experience of the divine; the contribution of the woman writer to the history of prose; the role of faith in the lives of those living in a turbulent century.

Julian ranks highly as a writer and a mystic in the judgment of readers, but her contemporary Margery Kempe has inspired sometimes sharp controversy in this century just as she did in her own time. For some readers Margery's *Book* serves as an autobiographical-confessional account of mystical experience; for others the work is a document in social history; for still others it has little or no redeeming value as autobiography, as history, or as an expression of mysticism. Maureen C. Fries establishes a basis for both historical and contemporary understanding. After a brief review of the scanty extra-textual record Fries looks at the apparently formless *Book* and suggests that its structure resembles that of the quest-romance, where the narrative mode is the journey, or travel generally, and the object is not the Grail but Christ (salvation). Margery's story has a personal and a public aspect, for she is candid in confessing her many falls from grace and open, to a laudable degree, in marking the opposition she encountered from some quarters of Church and society. Her "plenteous tears" and "many boisterous sobbings," it seems, inspired anger and annoyance in many of those around her, rather than awe at her apparently great *compunctio cordis*. Nevertheless, she showed some miraculous powers and enjoyed a holy reputation—as the *Book* says with telling point: "for, though they loved not her weeping nor her crying in their lifetime, they desired that she should both weep and cry when they should die." Margery is no philosophical mystic, no especially gifted writer, and no intellectual-controversialist. Is she therefore not a mystic at all, and her *Book* a medieval case study of "hysteria," as one commentator has described her condition? Fries reviews the various scholarly estimates and opinions and the resultant "collision with tradition." It may be, Fries suggests, that a creative feminist criticism might solve some of the large problems that the *Book* poses. At least such a feminist awareness might remove some of the biased judgments surrounding Margery and her work. Margery still waits for the scholar who can offer a fair appraisal.

Because the essays by Lagorio, Bradley, and Fries form a coherent unit that ranges from the twelfth to the fifteenth centuries, they appear in this volume in successive order, and thus as a variation from a strict chronological scheme. Bernard McGinn returns attention to the late thirteenth and early fourteenth centuries in his consideration of the major tradition initiated by Meister Eckhart. The first third of McGinn's essay concerns Eckhart's historical context, and his discussion of trends, developments, controversies, and problems is also relevant as background material to the essays by Weisheipl and Lagorio. McGinn describes several features of the period—papal politics, the mendicant movement, lay piety—that explain how it was possible for Eckhart to be condemned. The lack of spirituality in a period that the twentieth-century reader casually assumes to be the height of spirituality may come as a surprise to some. It was in this vibrant world that Eckhart taught and wrote. As a Dominican trained in the teaching of Aquinas and Albert the Great, Eckhart had both an Aristotelian and Neoplatonic inheritance, which he passed on to his students. He wrote several important theological treatises in Latin, but his vernacular preaching was so effective that he earned great popularity and official suspicion. Two trials, complicated in their development and meaning, eventually led to the condemnation of twenty-eight propositions found in Eckhart's teaching shortly after he had died. What "errors" did Eckhart teach? After issuing a caveat regarding the typologies of mysticism, McGinn answers this question by contrasting Eckhart with other Christian mystics. Eckhart does not deny ecstasy or *raptus*, but rather considers important what McGinn calls "a new awareness of the 'depth dimension' of everyday human experience." Eckhart also took a different view of *imitatio Christi* through the sacramental life of the Church, i.e., he advocates no large role for the historical Jesus and the rites commemorating him. Some of these ideas, especially if partially or incorrectly understood, can lead to radical anti-institutionalism. McGinn highlights three broad themes in Eckhart's thought: the ground of union with God, the dynamics of the soul's reformation, and the mode of life that follows from union. Eckhart sees a unity-identity of God's ground and the soul's ground, which sin disturbs. "True detachment," superior to humility and charity, effects the Birth of the Word and "Breaking Through" to God. The result is a non-solipsistic new way of "living without a why," wherein the soul lives in union with God. These ideas had wide influence, for over 200 manuscripts containing Eckhart's works survive. Pseudonymous works, supporting both heretical or non-heretical positions, also emerged, but so did a succession of genuine heirs.

One of these heirs is John Tauler, Eckhart's younger contemporary, Eckhart and Tauler thus forming an intellectual pair of older-younger similar to that of William of St. Thierry and Bernard of Clairvaux. Richard Kieckhefer's overview of Tauler is derived almost exclusively from Tauler's eighty-four vernacular sermons. Kieckhefer grants that Tauler was less daring than Eckhart (he did, after all, avoid the charge of heresy), and explains that Tauler was more practical than philosophical, more pastoral than contemplative in his spirituality. Tauler's teaching is traditional in its emphasis on detachment from the world, on submission to the will of God, and on a life of spiritual activity, or devotional and charitable works. The theme of detachment means a turning away from all that is not God and a purging of all attachments to worldly notions or "images." The submission to God's will proceeds from a contrast between *wirken* ("working" or "acting") and *leiden* ("suffering" or "being passive"), which Tauler best expresses in the dictum, "If God is to speak, all creatures must be silent." More directly, Tauler's "passivity" means that one should persist in one's good intentions and spiritual exercise while waiting patiently for God to reveal his will. Devotional works such as fasting and vigil-keeping constitute the life of spiritual activity, but Tauler is wary of meaningless regimens that may actually hinder the inner life. As Kieckhefer points out, Tauler wishes to steer a middle course between Pelagianism (salvation through one's own efforts alone) and Quietism (salvation solely through God's activity). These general spiritual principles may not define Tauler as a mystic for some scholars, yet he communicates a continuing sense of God's presence within human personality and advocates contemplative prayer. For Tauler, as for Eckhart, God's entry into the soul is a birth, transforming the soul or making it godlike. In some sermons Tauler sees this birth as a special event, but holds its external manifestations to be rather inferior to the higher enjoyment of these mysteries. In a sermon for the Fifth Sunday after Trinity Tauler describes three stages in the spiritual life that parallel the teaching of other mystics, viz., a process of illumination, a "Dark Night" of the soul, and a unitive state. The ordinary work of God in the soul through grace, however, is sufficient for all human beings—in the *Grund* of each soul the true image of the Trinity lies hidden. Tauler's exuberant sense of God is unrestrained. As Kieckhefer puts it: " [Tauler's] image of God is one of unbounded beneficence, and his reaction to that insight is to submit himself totally to God's work within him, both in suffering and in enjoyment of spiritual delights."

The writings of the women mystics, Eckhart, and Tauler play their part in the late medieval process commonly called "the triumph of the vernacular," i.e., the growing use of the vernacular as a medium not only to "translate" the ideas of thinkers and scholars for the people but also to compose original works. The unknown author of the *Cloud of Unknowing* and related texts can lay claim to equality, if not preeminence, in the company of those writers using English as a vehicle for the expression of ideas. John P.H. Clark demonstrates the importance of the *Cloud*-author in terms of the general tradition of mystic writing and his chronological peers. The anonymous writer was apparently a priest, learned in patristic, monastic, and scholastic literature, who was able to make his own perceptive synthesis of traditional material. He observes the distinction between the "active" and "contemplative" life and allows for the "mixed" life, but emphasizes living from the special viewpoint of the contemplatives, whom actives may often misunderstand. He adopts the basic metaphor of Dionysian mysticism, the "cloud of unknowing," and elaborates it according to the Latin tradition and with his own special emphasis. As other later mystics do, the *Cloud*-author believes that sin prevents union with God, and he downplays exaggerated outward penance, thus aligning himself with those valuing interiority and against such "enthusiasts" as Richard Rolle. Essentially the *Cloud*-author describes ". . . no by-passing of the Christian and Trinitarian way, but a growth in simplicity within that way—a simplicity which is not superficial but costly—yet the work of grace." This simplicity is reflected in the apparently artless quality of his prose style, which is actually the fruit of a costly artistic discipline. Clark ends his essay by sketching a number of similarities between the *Cloud*-author and such figures as John of the Cross, Walter Hilton, and the German mystics.

In that complex transition-period sometimes called the later Middle Ages and sometimes the Early Renaissance, thinkers continued to try to understand how human beings could come to know God. Clyde Lee Miller explains how Nicholas of Cusa, who readily admitted that he himself had not tasted the sweetness of the Lord, establishes a mystical theology while giving a distinctively Augustinian tone to his prayerful meditation, *The Vision of God*. As all good teachers do, Nicholas focusses on the concrete to illustrate the abstract. With his treatise Nicholas originally sent along to his monastic readers an omnivoyant painted portrait to show "the seeing of God" in the objective and subjective senses, i.e., human vision or sighting of God and, alternatively, God's all-seeing gaze. The concrete *objet d'art* also enables Nicholas to draw contrasts between God's real vision and the illusive vision of the painted portrait. The portrait remains a touchstone as Nicholas explains the kind of "not knowing," which is an integral part of the mystical vision, and the mysteriousness of God, who is beyond the "coincidence of opposites." God dwells in a paradise walled round by the coincidence of opposites, the door of which is guarded by the angel of reason. The key chapter is the thirteenth, the mid-point of the work's twenty-five chapters, wherein Nicholas considers God's infinity and the meaning of that infinity. The human ramifications of this infinity lead Nicholas to say:

> It behoveth, then, the intellect to become ignorant and to abide in darkness if it would fain see Thee. But what, O my God, is this intellectual ignorance? Is it not an instructed ignorance [*docta ignorantia*]? Thou God, who art infinity, canst only be approached by him whose intellect is in ignorance. . . .

At this point Nicholas changes his intellectual-rational presentation, shifting towards the affective: reason is impotent in the encountering of God. The revealed mysteries of the Trinity and the Incarnation, on the other hand, afford mankind the paths to union. Nicholas is thus a mystic because he provides a framework for a relationship between the absolute God and the limited creation. For the contemporary reader Nicholas has appeal not so much for his striking or original doctrines as for his imaginative and moving presentation of them.

David Biale's essay on later Jewish mysticism ends this collection by showing what happens to kabbalistic thought in the sixteenth century, which can be seen as a second creative period in the development of (medieval) Jewish mysticism. The signal event in this process is the expulsion of Jews from Spain. This traumatic event gave experiential meaning to the feeling of historical exile from the land of Israel and produced an attendant desire for redemption. In this context the Kabbalah began to become "public" teaching, while commentators made even bolder speculations about the inner mysteries of God, and the theoretical mysticism began to acquire a personal aspect. Biale concentrates on two figures from the mystical schools of Safed, Moses Cordovero and Isaac Luria. Cordovero systematized the earlier Kabbalah literature and rendered judgments on various opinions, thus taking the earlier Kabbalah to its theoretical limits. Luria took Jewish mysticism into new directions. Some of his striking contributions are in creation-theory, for example, that the first act of Creation was a divine withdrawal—to afford an open, empty space—rather than an outflowing of divine energy; the emanation of divine light and its scattering in the form of sparks were subsequent steps. Biale sees the contraction of God and the scattering of sparks as myths of divine exile. Man becomes God's helper in restoring the primordial harmony, even by redeeming his own soul, which is an entrapped divine spark. Here is where following the commandments can be efficacious. In Luria's cosmic view the world has been striving for redemption since creation. The Lurianic Kabbalah spread so quickly that it became virtually a universal theology of the Jews.

The essays in this collection seek then to introduce the reader new to medieval mysticism to several significant thinkers and writers. While not disregarding some of the figures traditionally considered important, these essays also present medieval mystics heretofore known only to specialists and scholars. The new matter in some cases comes forward with new methodologies or new approaches. All the essays demonstrate that medieval mysticism is a subject for rigorous study, whatever estimates one may entertain regarding personal belief. Such a study requires a knowledge of the historical languages, not only those appropriate to "the children of the Book," but also the vernacular in its medieval (and modern) stage, an understanding of the social and intellectual context as it interacts with the individual seeking God, and a sensitivity to the unique expression of the seeker. A collection such as this should prove to be an exemplary invitation to the study of medieval mysticism.

The editor acknowledges with thanks the cooperation of the contributors. Diverse in disciplines and beliefs, they have been as one in their sustaining interest in this project. The editor also acknowledges with thanks his special debt to Alex Fischler, whose generous help assisted the work of this book. He also has a second major debt to Bernard Rosenthal, who took valuable time away from his own research to help at the eleventh hour of this process with his keen sense for detail, his witty patience, and his sustaining calm.

I

Augustine

EUGENE TESELLE

Aurelius Augustinus (354–430) was the source of much of the mystical thought of the Middle Ages. He was born in North Africa and grew up as a nominal Christian, but he reacted against the church's appeal to authority and went through a long intellectual quest from his nineteenth to his thirty-second year. He taught rhetoric in Carthage, Rome, and finally Milan, where in 386 he returned to Christianity under the influence of the bishop, Ambrose. He went back to Africa, became bishop of Hippo in 396, and wrote extensively on theological topics.

THE PROBLEM OF PHILOSOPHICAL MYSTICISM

W.R. Inge has emphasized that mysticism is, among other things, an intellectual tradition which seeks to demonstrate the mind's kinship with spiritual realities.[1] Augustine's return to Christianity was stimulated by one variety of philosophical mysticism, that growing out of Platonism. The "books of the Platonists," which he read before his conversion, certainly included some of the treatises in Plotinus' *Enneads*, and possibly some works by Porphyry as well. It is not hard to see how these writings could help an intellectual of that day to think more positively about Christianity, and might even arouse a desire for mystical union. They not only teach a "Trinity" of three divine principles, but they show the reader how to think of the human self, and of God, as "incorporeal," unlike the bodies we perceive with our senses; they emphasize the affinity of the self with

God and initiate the reader into a kind of ascent from the external world to the self and finally to God.[2]

Augustine describes his experiences on reading these "books of the Platonists" in three parallel passages in book VII of his *Confessions* (10, 16; 17, 23; 20, 26). These books, he says, directed his attention first to his inward self, then to the Light or Truth that is above it.[3] But his attention moved step by step through articulated stages. He first considered the corporeal world, then turned from it to his own self, gradually freeing himself from the use of images drawn from the realm of sense. It was only then—only after going through this sequence, having his feet firmly planted, so to speak, on one step before mounting to the next—that he looked above himself, where there was nothing between himself and the unchanging being of God. As he thinks back on it in his narrative, he describes it on the model suggested by Romans 1:20, a passage in which Paul showed how the Gentiles could have a knowledge of God even without revelation. It is important to catch the literal form of the Latin translation used by Augustine, and of Paul's Greek, for it says: "The invisible things of God, God's eternal power and divinity, are beheld clearly, being understood [intuited, known directly] through the things that are made." As Augustine interprets it, this knowledge is gained "through" visible things only in the sense that they are the first object of attention; then they fall silent and the mind rises above them, looking directly toward their divine origin.[4] In this way he succeeds in reaching an awareness of God. But he is unable to fix his attention upon God because of the weakness or impurity of his mind, and he falls back into his accustomed ways of thinking and feeling.

Let us look at the exact wording of the climactic statement in each of these passages in order to understand the character of his mystical aspirations. The first experience is described in this way:

> When I first knew you [he is addressing God, of course], you bore me up so that I could see that there was something for me to see, but that I was not yet the one to see it. Shining forcefully upon me, you beat back the weakness of my gaze; I shook with love and dread, and found myself far from you in the region of unlikeness, as though I heard your voice from on high, "I am the food of the mature; grow and you will eat of me."[5]

Looking back on it, Augustine says,

> And I was astonished how, while I already loved you and not an image in place of you, I was not stable enough to enjoy

my God, but was carried up by your beauty and immediately
was dragged away by my own weight and was thrown
groaning into these things once again; this weight is carnal
custom.[6]

But he tried again:

In an instant of trembling attention *[in ictu trepidantis aspectus]*
I attained to That Which Is. Then indeed I beheld your
invisible things, understood through the things that are made,
but I was not able to fix my gaze; my weakness driven back,
I returned to my accustomed experiences, bringing nothing
except a loving memory, as though its desire were aroused by
the fragrance of things which I could not yet eat.[7]

Finally he summarizes his experiences:

But then, having read those books of the Platonists and after
being thence admonished to seek incorporeal truth, I beheld
clearly your invisible things, understood through the things
that are made; and when I had been driven back, I realized
what it was that, because of the darknesses of my soul, I was
not allowed to contemplate. . . . Of these things I was
certain, but I was too weak to enjoy you.[8]

Just what is it that happened? These passages are sometimes taken
to report a mystical vision of God, even though momentary. But
Augustine, in several writings from the months soon after his conversion, seems to make no such claim; while he affirms the possibility
of such a vision and indicates that he has attempted it, he also states
or implies that he has not yet succeeded in attaining it, often using
the same language of being "driven back." [9] There was certainly an
aspiration toward mystical contact, aroused by the reading of Plotinus.
There may have been an attempt at vision, followed, however, by
an experience of his own inability. But he also uses the language of
hesitation, as though he was unable to look directly at the light and
only perceived it, so to speak, out of the corner of his eye. In any
case, the emphasis is upon his inability to endure its presence beyond
that single moment.[10]

What most interpreters overlook is that at this time Augustine was
not concerned chiefly with mystical "ecstasy"; he did not even use
the term. During those early months of spiritual excitement he was
aroused by Plotinus' promise of a "beatific" vision[11] and it involved
what he called the "happy life," a life led in true happiness, which
in turn meant virtue, which in turn meant wisdom—in other words,
a life in which his consciousness would be constantly bathed in the

light of this higher realm, a life led according to the divine Law shining within the self. The Light was always there, and one ought to be able, he thought, to open one's life to it on a permanent basis. It was only gradually that he altered his expectations, deferring this steady awareness first to a later time, when his mind should have become stronger,[12] and eventually to the changed state of the soul after death. The language of "ecstasy" or "rapture," which appears in his later writings,[13] is used to suggest precisely what Augustine was *not* expecting in those earliest months: that the mystical experience is intermittent and brief, and that it involves going "out" of one's ordinary mode of awareness.

The narrative clearly indicates Augustine's disappointment at his failure, and looking back he blames the Platonists for their pride and presumption in suggesting that union with God could be achieved through human efforts.[14] He had already read Plotinus in a Christian sense, under the guidance of Christian Platonists, as teaching something about the Trinity and about the destiny of the soul; but now, it appears, he was driven by his experiences of failure to appreciate other facets of Christian belief, including the incarnation of the divine Light in order to meet humanity where it is, and the offer of grace to assist it toward its true destiny.

Thus Augustine from the beginning has an ambivalent attitude toward the philosophers. On the one hand he is in basic agreement with their view of the soul, and he even continues to acknowledge the validity of their apprehension of God, since they touched, however slightly, the Light of unchanging Truth.[15] On the other hand he attacks the Platonists, with increasing intensity, for their pride in attempting to bypass incarnation and grace and faith, which are indispensable to true progress.[16] Thus we find him affirming the general human possibility of mystical experience, and honoring the aspirations toward it that he finds among non-believers, especially among the Platonists, and even acknowledging that they have achieved it, at least momentarily. But it is difficult to achieve this vision, and even when one is successful the experience is of dubious value, since it comes to an end. This is the tension, within which much of Augustine's approach to mysticism will be worked out.

THE NATURE OF AUGUSTINIAN MYSTICISM

While Augustine does not seem to claim any satisfying mystical experience on the basis of his reading of the Platonists, it is different with an event that occurred during the months following his baptism at Easter, 387. This is the "vision at Ostia," reported in the ninth book of the *Confessions.* He tells how he and his mother Monica were at the port city near Rome, awaiting passage back to Africa. As they were leaning from a window overlooking the garden, talking of eternal life and trying to understand it (a conversation, we may suppose, to which Augustine would have brought his own philosophical learning, and Monica her unphilosophical piety, but which is narrated by Augustine in his own language), their thoughts were led upward. There is the same pattern of ascent as in the earlier passages in book VII of the *Confessions:* they consider the various things that have been created, and they rise above material and changeable things, and come to their own souls; but then they pass beyond them to the Wisdom by which all things are made, and by which the people of God are fed with Truth.

> And while we spoke and longed for it, we touched it for one instant, with a total leap of the heart *[attingimus eam modice toto ictu cordis];* then we sighed and left the first fruits of our spirits bound there, and we returned to the sound of our own lips. . . .[18]

There are obvious similarities with the earlier experiences. But there are also differences in the way it is described. Here we do not find the language of being "repulsed" or "driven back" when splendor of the Light clashes with the weakness of the mind; there is only a resumption of the awareness of the passage of time. And Augustine speaks of it as a leap of the *heart*, indicating the importance of the affections, which we will consider at greater length below.

After their experience Augustine and his mother go on talking, this time in an attempt to understand what has happened. They again survey the various things in the created realm, and describe how each of them in turn, even the soul, has fallen silent, and how, subsequently, their attention has gone beyond the realm of creation. If all of these things were to become truly silent, they say, not even declaring that they did not make themselves,

> . . . and if God alone were to speak, not through them but through himself, so that we heard his Word, not through tongues of flesh or angelic voices or thunderclaps or parables, but God himself, whom we love in these things, heard by himself without these things, then, just as now we reached out and with a fleeting thought touched the eternal Wisdom which abides over all things, if this were to continue and all other awareness of things far inferior were to be removed, and this one alone seized and absorbed and enveloped in inward joys the one who beheld it, so that an endless life were to be like this one moment of understanding for which

he had longed, then would this not be that of which it was said, "Enter into the joy of your Lord"? And when, except when "all shall be raised, but not all shall be changed [i.e., mutable] "? [19]

The positive tone of the entire passage is evident, and the experience is interpreted as a foretaste of eternal life. And yet even this experience at Ostia, because of its similarities with the earlier ones, has been much debated. Was it a "vision" of God's "essence," or was it, like the others, a lesser experience? [20]

Indeed, although Augustine is the source of at least one major tradition of medieval mysticism, and although many passages in his writings have a mystical character, there has been an extensive debate over whether he was a mystic at all. The debate rests in large part upon the definition of mysticism. Since the Middle Ages notions of mysticism have varied considerably, being shaped by the Areopagite writings, by the Rhenish and Flemish mystics, and most decisively by the picture of mysticism presented by St. Teresa and St. John of the Cross. Increasingly the emphasis came to be upon the exceptional character of mystical experience, the need for infused gifts of grace, and the passivity of the soul. This one-sided view began to be questioned from within Catholic theology at about the turn of this century, when it was suggested that mysticism may be more in continuity than in contrast with the normal states and aspirations of the Christian life; at about the same time, writers like W.R. Inge and Evelyn Underhill were exploring the varieties of mysticism. With regard to Augustine, the decisive work was *Western Mysticism*, published by Abbot Cuthbert Butler in 1922, which recovered a tradition of mysticism that has been common in the West, especially in the monasteries, prior to the impact of the Areopagite writings in the twelfth century.[21] Following his lead, other attempts have been made to describe the distinctive character of Augustine's mysticism and to defend its character *as* mysticism.[22] But there have also been those who deny that Augustine was a mystic in the strict sense, chiefly because they are using the criteria that have prevailed since the sixteenth century.[23]

For our purposes it will be assumed that Augustine was a mystic in some valid sense, although he may not fit all definitions. It seems clear that he laid claim to immediate experiences of the presence of God. And yet the passages are sparse, and he seems hesitant to make great claims for himself as a "professional mystic" or an instructor in the mystical life; he seems to be one of the most humble and reluctant of the mystics, stressing not so much his accomplishments as his failures, and emphasizing that his experiences were fleeting, not the kind of sustained contact that he had hoped for.[24] Despite these frustrations he continued to affirm the possibility of mystical vision, not only on the basis of the experiences of the Platonists, as we have seen, but also from biblical authority.

Augustine's most explicit theoretical discussions of mysticism, based not on his own experience but on his interpretation of the Bible, came about 413–14, when he examined at length what it means to "see" God. He pointed out that "seeing" can be used in three ways, not only as sense but as imagination and even as understanding, the immediate experience of what is purely intelligible.[25] Then he considered two biblical figures who appear to have gained the vision of God in this third sense: Moses, the leader of Israel who fore-shadowed the Jews who would be united with Christ; and Paul, the last of the apostles and apostle to the Gentiles. When Moses asked to see God (Exodus 33:18–23), the very possibility seemed to be rejected, for he was told, "No one can see my face and live." But later (Numbers 12:6–8) it is said that Moses spoke more intimately with God than any of the prophets and saw God's "glory." Thus Augustine, following Ambrose, suggests that the statement "No one can see my face and live" does not *deny* the vision of God but rather indicates *the conditions under which it is possible*, namely through being liberated from this mortal life.[26] He finds confirmation of this when Paul states (2 Corinthians 12:2–4) that he was caught up into the third heaven, which Augustine interprets to mean that he was "carried away" *(raptus)* or "dissociated" *(alienatus)* from the corporeal and the imaginary, and when Paul adds, "whether in the body or out of the body I do not know," Augustine interprets this to mean that Paul died to this mortal life, "leaving" the body at least to the extent of directing his attention away from sense and imagination and being totally preoccupied with the vision of God.[27] Mystical "ecstasy" or "rapture" is thus linked with the Pauline theme of dying to mortality and rising to eternal life, interpreted, of course, in terms of the inward dynamics of the self.

Let us attempt now to describe the exact character of Augustine's views on mysticism.

1. We have seen that Augustine viewed mystical experience as something of which all are capable in principle, and this possibility is demonstrated, in his view, not only by Scripture but by the doctrines of the Platonists and their reported achievements.

2. He also emphasized just as strongly the difficulty of mystical union, and he laid the fault clearly upon the human self. The divine Light is always shining, inviting closer contact, showing itself attractive and desirable; but the mind is repulsed because of its own

weakness, being unable to bear the brightness, and it falls back with exhaustion, seeking out those things to which it is more accustomed.

3. Although the Platonists and the Christians may share the same experience of apprehending the divine, if only in passing, there is a fundamental rift between them, for the same experience has a different meaning for different people. In Augustine's view those who rely upon their own powers will be aware of the cessation of ecstasy as a loss; those who have faith and love will view it as a foretaste and a postponement of something to which they are destined to return later. The factor of time—or, specifically, the attitude one takes toward its passage—is central to the development of Augustine's mystical thought. At the period of his conversion, as we have seen, his expectation was that he could lead a life in happiness, bathed always in the light. He had to modify that expectation, eventually deferring any lasting vision of God, and the true happiness that comes from it, to the very different state of the soul in eternal life. His customary formula is that beatitude is found "in reality" only beyond death; in the present one has it "in hope." But it is not possessed merely in hope, for there can be a foretaste of it in the present.

This aspect of foretaste and anticipation is suggested not only in the vision at Ostia but elsewhere, especially in Augustine's sermon on Psalm 41 (42 in the Hebrew numbering), where he speaks of the soul hearing sounds from the "house of God" on high, but then goes on:

> Because, brothers and sisters, as long as we are in this body, we sojourn away from the Lord, and the corruptible body weighs down the soul, and our earthly habitation presses down our thoughts with many concerns—even though at times the clouds are somewhat dispersed and we, led by our desire, come briefly within reach of that sound, so that we are able by great exertion to catch something from that house of God—we fall back nonetheless because of the weight of our infirmity, and our attention is dispersed among these accustomed things. And just as there we found cause for rejoicing, here there will not be a lack of that which we lament.

Following the words of the psalm, "Why are you cast down, O my soul, and why do you disquiet me? " he rebukes his soul:

> Behold, we have already been gladdened by a certain inward sweetness, and with the gaze of the mind we have been able

to behold, even though briefly and hurriedly [*perstrictim et raptim*], something beyond change. . . .

But his soul answers,

I am not yet there where that sweetness is, to which I was carried up as though in passing [*quo sic rapta sum quasi per transitum*].[28]

The problem of temporality—the instability of the will, the dispersal of one's attention among a multiplicity of concerns—is also evoked dramatically in a celebrated passage in the *Confessions:*

I am divided by times whose order I do not know, and my thoughts, the inmost organs of my soul, are torn apart by the confusion of change. And so it will be until, purified and melted by the fire of your love, I flow into you. Then I shall become stable in you and be set firm in you, my true form, your Truth. . . .[29]

The momentary character of Augustine's highest experiences, followed by a relapse into ordinary life, leaving only a memory and a longing, does not necessarily cast doubt on their "mystical" character, for the sense of a gap between what one is and what one wishes to be can be a spur to more intense aspiration and preparation. And it is especially characteristic of Christianity to exhibit a striving for more than the present can offer, a tension between the "already" and the "not yet," and to regard the present as a foretaste of what can be.

4. We thus find in Augustine a fundamental reshaping or redescription of the mystic quest, but in many of its medieval and modern forms as well. On the negative side, it is not enough to have these fragmentary experience of the eternal, even when they take the form of being lifted "out of" time, since these experiences will cease. As Evelyn Underhill has put it in her paraphrase of a passage in Augustine, "the mystic need is for a Home, not for a Vision." [30] The ecstatic vision, which plays such an important role in much mystical literature as the principal goal that is sought, and also in the literature about mysticism as the chief experience that is probed to see whether it is an experience of any reality at all, is important to Augustine as well; but it is not the central issue. To him neither the reality of God nor the ability of the mind to apprehend God was seriously in question: the Light is always there, and one always has the mental eyes with which to see. The central problem is rather that the eyes of the mind must be purified by the right affections. To him the beatitude, "Blessed are the pure in heart, for they shall see God"

(Matthew 5:8) is not only a promise of *what* can occur, but a prescription of *how* it must occur if it is to occur at all. While the possibility of mystical ecstasy belongs to the very nature of the mind, its actualization depends upon the affections. It is here that we find the other center of Augustinian mysticism, of equal importance with the vision of God.

THE ROLE OF THE AFFECTIONS

A characteristic feature of Augustinian thought—and certainly the feature which had the most distinctive influence in Western mysticism—is its attention to the will and the affections, the orientation of the self toward that which has the appearance of being good or valuable, and of being good for the one who wills. When the affections are rightly ordered, this is the love of which the Bible speaks; it consists of making God the primary and overarching value in one's life and "referring" all else to this supreme value.[31]

Plotinus had already written of a journey not for the feet or chariots or ships, but an inward journey.[32] But while Plotinus thought of it as learning a new mode of *vision*, Augustine transposed it into a journey for the *affections*.[33] And Augustine, as we have seen, discovered how difficult this journey is, for the affections are captured and held by the things to which they are accustomed, and they are continually being distracted by new concerns. The pathos is evident in many of Augustine's more mystical passages, especially one in the *Confessions* which is a major expression of "affective mysticism":

> Sometimes you lead me into an affection that is entirely out of the ordinary, felt inwardly with I do not know what sweetness, and if it were to reach perfection in me I do not know what it would be, but it would not be this present life. But then I fall back into these things with their troubling burdens, and I am drawn into accustomed ways and am held there. I weep greatly, but I am held firmly. Such is the burden deserved by custom! I am able to be here, but I do not will it; I will to be there, but I am not able; in both respects I am wretched.[34]

And yet, although this yearning can find its satisfaction only under other conditions, there is also a positive confidence of being "on the way," of "tending" there under the inspiration of the Holy Spirit, God's "Gift" to human life:

> In your Gift we find our rest; there we can enjoy you. Our "place" is that in which we find our rest. Love draws us

there, and your good Spirit lifts up our lowly state from the gates of death. Our peace is found in goodness of will. . . . My "movement" is my love; by it I am borne to whatever place I am borne. By your Gift we are kindled and borne aloft; burning with your fire, onward we go toward the peace of Jerusalem. . . . There goodness of will shall so install us that we shall desire nothing else than to remain there eternally.[35]

Perhaps the most dramatic statement of Augustine's affective mysticism is found in book VIII of *The Trinity*. There we have a kind of initiation of the reader into several different ways of approaching God, beginning with the futile attempt to look on God directly, and gradually diminishing his expectations. Eventually he suggests that the best experience of God is to be found not in knowledge, which remains uncertain, but in love.[36]

In reading the First Epistle of John, Augustine encountered the statements (1 John 4:7, 16, 20) that God is Love, that love is from God, that one who loves is born of God, and that God is not loved if one does not love one's neighbor. As he attempts to put these together, he suggests that love is not merely *from* God; God *is* love, and the Holy Spirit is Love from Love. Thus if one has love, even it it merely takes the form of loving one's neighbor, to experience that act of love is to experience God, or specifically the Holy Spirit, as its source.

This statement has caused understandable confusion among theologians, beginning with Peter Lombard in the twelfth century, who shocked his contemporaries by asserting that the human act of love is somehow identical with the Holy Spirit, although he also recognized that it remains a human act which can grow or diminish. Augustine probably did not assume an identity of human love with the Holy Spirit. Rather he used the language of mutual indwelling:

Have you begun to love? Then God has begun to dwell in you. Love him who has begun to dwell in you, so that by dwelling more perfectly he may make you perfect.[37]

You dwell in God, but it is in order that you may be upheld; God dwells in you, but it is in order to uphold you lest you fall.[38]

He indicates at least two ways in which a confusion between the divine and the human can be avoided. First, he points out that in the act of loving one's neighbor one can also "love" one's own act of loving—that is, one can will it, affirm it, rest in it, as the love by which one loves the neighbor; and ultimately one recognizes that one loves "because of God" and that one's love is "in God," and therefore in loving one loves God.[39] The other line of reflection, which involves the divine Word as well as the Spirit, is that one can only truly love when the ultimate goal or rationale of one's affection is a love of the Pattern *(Forma)* of righteousness.[40] He seems to be suggesting that in both ways love is more than human, for it seems to be more deeply motivated and to have a higher rationale than other human acts.

Augustine never again repeated, in quite so direct a way, these assertions that in experiencing love one experiences God. But passages like these had considerable influence upon later "affective mysticism." They suggest at least part of what is meant by an "experiential knowledge" of God's influence within the self, or by the notion that God is understood most adequately through "sympathy" or "connaturality," a kind of harmony between the self and God which can substitute for a direct knowledge of God as an object. And they do represent one central aspect of Augustinian mysticism. The other aspect, which we examined earlier, is the possibility of an intellectual "vision" of God, if only momentarily and by an ecstasy or rapture which takes one "out" of one's accustomed realm of awareness, borne along by affections purified by love.

THEORETICAL ISSUES

Although Augustine is the source of much in medieval mysticism, he does not present either an unquestionable *achievement* in mysticism or a finished *doctrine* of mysticism. Rather we may say that he lies at the beginning of a long trajectory of development, and in many respects it is precisely his unanswered questions and his unfinished suggestions that had an impact on medieval thought. Let us explore several theoretical issues which he bequeathed to the Middle Ages.

1. *Mysticism and the Trinity.* We have seen the Trinitarian overtones of Augustine's mysticism. He regularly describes the mystical experience as a contact of the mind with the divine Light, the Word or Wisdom which is the second person of the Trinity; and if one is to endure the presence of this Light, or make steady progress toward it, one must be sustained by Love, the Holy Spirit as Gift, and this even arouses its own mystical experience, an "affective" state of delight at being loved by God and loving God.

Thinkers in the Middle Ages were not sure how to understand this. Not only were there technical problems concerning the relation of the human mind to the three persons of the Trinity. In addition, the Trinitarian doctrine stated that God is one "essence" or "substance" in three persons. When mystics spoke of seeing God's essence, did this mean going in some sense *beyond* the three persons, as Eckhart suggests?

Augustine seems to insist, by contrast, upon the thoroughly Trinitarian character of the mystical experience. For him it is an experience of God speaking, not through other things, but "through himself" *(per seipsum)*,[41] by the divine Word, God's own "self-concept"; and it is an adhering to God in the Holy Spirit, Love from Love, God's "self-gift." The human mind and affections are caught up into the inner life of God, since Augustine thinks of the Trinity as God's mutual self-relatedness, and only in this way can there be an experience of God's "essence," not beyond but in the divine persons. But there was ample room for debates and speculation about the Trinitarian aspects of mysticism.

2. *The Nature of Mystical Union.* Augustine, following Plotinus, used the language of spiritual embrace, anticipating the more elaborate medieval descriptions of "spiritual marriages," [42] and he spoke of the immediacy of the soul's union with God, "with nothing between," so that the two become in some sense one.[43] He emphasized, furthermore, the constant presence of God to the soul, "more intimate than my inmost, higher than my highest." [44] This, flowing together with similar motifs from other sources, will lead in the Middle Ages to suggestions that God is to be found by returning to the core of the soul, where there is a fundamental identity between them. In Augustine it is clear that when the two become one in an immediate union there is not a loss of selfhood or a rediscovery of identity with an undifferentiated One; he was too intensely aware of his own self and its difference from God, and even its fulfillment in union with God is seen as enhancing, not obliterating his individuality. But how difference and unity are to be described will remain a problem.

3. *The Nature of the Mind.* Augustine's mysticism was supported by his general theory of knowledge—or, conversely, his theory of knowledge was motivated by his eagerness for mystical experience.[45] With the Platonists he thought that when we truly "understand" something we are dealing not merely with our own experiences or our own concepts but with the intelligible realities themselves, and that when we make judgments we do it according to absolute norms of which we are immediately aware. Such experiences, he believed, are already a dim awareness of the divine Word, and they are in continuity with the direct knowledge of God in mystical experience (he draws an analogy with a fire, whose light can be seen at a distance, but whose full warmth can be felt only close by).[46]

During the Middle Ages this theory of knowledge was subjected to questioning, even before the impact of Aristotle and certainly after it. If, as many suggested, the activities of the mind are *not* always based upon an immediate influence of the divine Word—if, therefore, our mental operations are *not* similar in kind to the direct experience of God—then mysticism will have to develop a very different theoretical base, and this in fact was done with the elaboration of a doctrine of infused grace and special gifts which strengthen the mind to accomplish something of which is not normally capable.

On the other hand, Augustine's theory of knowledge is typical of "philosophical mysticism," which finds continuities between mysticism and all the operations of the mind. Weathering criticism, and adapting itself to it, this type of thinking has reasserted itself in Renaissance Platonism, in German idealism, and in certain contemporary types of philosophy of religion.[47] The debate, therefore, is not finished.

4. *The Vision of God.* Augustine believed that an intellectual "vision" of God is the goal of mystical contemplation. Other traditions of mystical theology flowed into the Middle Ages, however. The writings attributed to Dionysius the Areopagite developed neo-Platonism in a different direction, giving much more emphasis to the unknowability of God. Distinctions were made between various degrees of contemplation, so that the "vision" of God became rare and exceptional. And while most medieval thinkers accepted Augustine's assertion that Moses and Paul had achieved the vision of God, his interpretation of the biblical passages is open to serious question; even Abbot Butler, the one who did the most to recover the distinctive character of Augustinian mysticism, has criticized him on this point, suggesting that a whole tradition about Moses and Paul "is built upon St. Augustine's misinterpretation of a mistranslation of a Biblical text." [48] This is not to say that the Augustinian goal of an intellectual intuition of God in necessarily misdirected, and many continue to regard it as essential to mysticism. But Augustine's conception cannot be assumed to be the only valid one, and we are more aware than ever before of the varieties of mystical experience.

5. *The Role of Bodily Experience.* Was Augustine too "spiritual"? We have seen that he tried repeatedly to experience God apart from the sensory world and without the use of his own senses and imagination. While he did not simply ignore those realities—indeed, he used them as steps with which to rise higher—there is nevertheless a widespread suspicion that he set an impossible goal for himself and for others, more Platonist than Christian, and that the frustrations which he experienced, reaching a glimpse of God and then falling away exhausted, are the predictable result of attempting something of superhuman scale. Already in the Middle Ages there was a greater readiness to affirm the positive value of the world, the senses, and the life of the body, and in more recent times his views have been

widely criticized or corrected.[49] It is possible to point to passages in Augustine's own writings in which this extreme "spiritualism" is qualified and gradually modified. Thus it may not be an abandonment of Augustinianism but its further development when mystical experience is asserted to be fully human only when the body, senses and imagination are present and fully utilized.

Augustinian mysticism thus remains of interest in part because of the theoretical issues it has raised. But we should note that its most controversial features are assumptions which Augustine inherited from the intellectual climate of his day; less question has been raised about the affective mysticism that seems more central to Augustine's own experience. This may confirm the widespread impression that, while mysticism is shaped by its intellectual setting and leads to further theoretical reflection, what is central to it and remains most certain about it is the experience of the human subject.

BIBLIOGRAPHICAL NOTES

Translations of Augustine's writings can be found in the following series: *A Select Library of Nicene and Post-Nicene Fathers*, First Series *(NPNF)*; *Library of Christian Classics (LCC)*, vols. 6–8; *Ancient Christian Writers (ACW)*; and *Fathers of the Church (FOC)*.

Special attention is drawn to the following works by Augustine:

The *Confessions* can be found in many translations. Useful notes are contained in the editions by John Gibb and William Montgomery (Cambridge, 1908), and Aimé de Solignac, in the series Bibliothèque Augustinienne, vols. 13–14 (Paris, 1962).

Augustine's earliest writings include *Against the Academics (ACW*, vol. 12), *The Happy Life*, translated by Francis E. Tourscher (Philadelphia, 1937), and *Soliloquies (LCC*, vol. 6).

Two other early writings germane to his mystical thought are *The Greatness of the Soul* (esp. nn. 70–76), translated by Joseph M. Colleran *(ACW*, vol. 9), and *On Free Will* (esp. Book II, 9, 25–16, 43), in *LCC*, vol. 6, *ACW*, vol. 22, and a translation in the Library of Liberal Arts.

Later writings of special significance are the Sermon on Psalm 41 *(NPNF*, vol. 8); *The Trinity*, Book VIII *(NPNF*, vol. 3; *LCC*, vol. 8; *FOC*, vol. 18); Epistle 147 *(FOC*, vol. 11); *Homilies on the First Epistle of John*, esp. homilies 5 and 7–9 *(LCC*, vol. 8); and the *Literal Commentary on Genesis*, Book XII, of which a translation is now in process.

The classic translation of Plotinus, who influenced Augustine significantly, is by Stephen MacKenna, *The Enneads*, second edition (New York, 1957).

For comments on Augustine by the classic writers on mysticism see W. R. Inge, *Christian Mysticism* (London, 1899), pp. 128–32, and Evelyn Underhill, *The Mystic Way: A Psychological Study in Christian Origins* (London, 1913), pp. 278–303. General discussions of Augustinian "spirituality," without much analysis of Augustinian mysticism as such, can be found in the surveys by Pierre Pourrat, *Christian Spirituality from the Time of Our Lord till the Dawn of the Middle Ages*, translated by W.H. Mitchell and S.P. Jacques (Westminister, MD, 1953–55), I, 185–216, and Louis Bouyer, *The Spirituality of the New Testament and the Fathers*, History of Christian Spirituality, vol. I (New York, 1963), 467–94.

The most useful survey of the scholarly investigation of Augustinian mysticism, with extensive bibliographical citations, was prepared for presentation at an international congress in 1954 on the anniversary of Augustine's birth, collected in *Augustinus Magister. Congrès International Augustinien, Paris, 21–24 Septembre*, 3 volumes (Paris, 1954), abbreviated *AM*; see André Mandouze, "Où en est la question de la mystique augustinienne?" *AM*, III, 103–63, with discussion on pp. 163–68. A more recent survey, heavily dependent on Mandouze, is Jean-Jacques Heitz, "Une question ouverte: La mystique de saint Augustin," *Revue d'histoire et de philosophie religieuses*, 45 (1965), 314–34. See also Charles Boyer, "Augustin," *Dictionnaire de spiritualité ascétique et mystique*, II.1, cols. 1911–21, and M. Olphe-Galliard, "Contemplation," *ibid.*, II. 2, cols. 1911–21.

The modern scholarly discussion of Augustine's mysticism begins with Cuthbert Butler, *Western Mysticism: The Teaching of Augustine, Gregory and Bernard on Contemplation and the Contemplative Life*, first published in 1921; see the third edition, with "Afterthoughts" from the second edition of 1927 and a new foreword by David Knowles (London, 1967). A cautious response to this work can be found in E.I. Watkin, "The Mysticism of St. Augustine," *A Monument to Saint Augustine* (London, 1930), pp. 105–19.

Continuing in the same direction, highlighting even further the distinctive character of Augustinian mysticism, are Joseph Maréchal, "La vision de Dieu au sommet de la contemplation d'après saint Augustin," *Nouvelle revue théologique*, 57 (1930), 89–109, 191–214, reprinted in *Études sur la psychologie des mystiques*, II (Bruxelles, 1937), 145–88; and Endre von Ivánka, "Die unmittelbare Gotteserkenntnis als Grundlage des Erkennens und als Ziel des übernatürlichen Strebens bei Augustin," *Scholastik*, 13 (1938), 521–43.

For a denial that Augustine was a mystic see Ephraem Hendrikx, *Augustins Verhältnis zur Mystik. Eine patristische Untersuchung*, Cassiciacum, vol. 1 (Würzburg, 1936), a position reaffirmed in "Augustins Verhältnis zur Mystik. Ein Rückblick," *Scientia Augustiniana*, Zumkeller Festschrift (Würzburg, 1975), pp. 107–11.

The classic study of love and Augustine's "affective mysticism" is John Burnaby, *Amor Dei: A Study of the Religion of St. Augustine* (London, 1938). See also Rudolph Lorenz, "Fruitio Dei bei Augustin," *Zeitschrift für Kirchengeschichte*, 63 (1950–51), 51–132.

Discussion of the "vision at Ostia" was renewed by Paul Henry, *La vision d'Ostie. Sa place dans la vie et l'oeuvre de S. Augustin* (Paris, 1938), and continued by Pierre Courcelle, *Recherches sur les Confessions de saint Augustin* (Paris, 1950), pp. 157–67, 222–26.

Among the contributions made at the international congress in 1954 see especially Pierre Courcelle, "La première expérience augustinienne de l'extase," *AM*, I, 53–57, and André Mandouze, "L'extase d'Ostie. Possibilités et limites de la méthode des parallèles textuels," *AM*, I, 67–84.

A major scholarly contribution since the congress is Suzanne Poque, "L'Expression de l'anabase plotinienne dans la prédication de saint Augustin et ses sources," *Recherches Augustiniennes*, 10 (1975), 187–215. See also Vernon J. Bourke, "Augustine of Hippo: The Approach of the Soul to God," *The Spirituality of Western Christendom*, introduction by Jean Leclercq, edited by E. Rozanne Elder (Kalamazoo, MI, 1976), pp. 1–12.

II
Smaragdus

by DOM JEAN LECLERCQ,
translated by JOHN J. MELLERSKI

LIFE AND WORKS

Smaragdus is a ninth-century author of whom very little is now known. For the Middle Ages, he was one of the classic sources of Western spirituality, but he fell into almost total oblivion, and is only now being rediscovered, his life and his works the constant object of fresh research. Although light has not been shed on all aspects of his life, what we do know about him allows us to place his work in a biographical and historical context, and thereby to gain a better idea of where, when, and how his influence spread.

Smaragdus' country of origin has given rise to several conjectures. For a long time he was thought to be Irish, but that theory has been definitively set aside and a series of coincident indications now leads us to believe, more or less with certainty, that he was Visigothic or Spanish in origin. His Latin vocabulary and style present affinities with other Spanish authors, and he refers to several of them favorably. His name, Smaragdus, handed down to us in the textual tradition in variant forms, is rare but not altogether unprecedented. We are not dealing here with a surname that he might have received at the court of Charlemagne, but with a name that has symbolic import: the emerald (*smaragdus* in Latin) is one of the precious stones mentioned in the Book of the Apocalypse, and has been interpreted as applying to men whose faith is solid and whose doctrine is worthy of note.

Nothing is known of Smaragdus' life before he became abbot of the Monastery of St. Michael in Lotharingia in 814; but he must have had contact before that with Theodolfus, king of the Spanish Visigoths, who himself had connections with Charlemagne. In any case it was under Charlemagne (who became emperor in 800 A.D.) and then later under his son, Louis the Pious, that Smaragdus was called upon to contribute actively to the reform of several monasteries; and it was most likely Charlemagne who named him abbot of the royal monastery of Castellion, then of St. Mihiel.

Whatever the case may be, a chronological order for his principal works can be established. In 800 he composed a commentary on the work of Donatus, the Roman grammarian of the fourth century A.D. In it he reveals an interest in literary activity and shows himself to be a Christian humanist by using the literary resources of classical antiquity to serve as an expression of his faith. In 809 he drew up an account of the origin of the Holy Ghost. A controversy at the time separated Eastern Christians, who held that the Holy Ghost proceeded from the Father through the Son, from certain Western Christians who held that the Holy Ghost was generated from the Father and the Son at the same time *(filioque)*. It has been suggested that since Charlemagne himself favored the latter position and because he had had the opportunity to familiarize himself with Smaragdus' doctrinal competence, he rewarded him with a monastery and made us of his services in the reorganization of monastic life in his empire. In that same year 809, Smaragdus dedicated his manual on the proper conduct for princes, the *Royal Pathway (Via regia)*, to Charlemagne. In 812 he intervened in liturgical reform by writing a commentary on the *Book of the Companion (Liber comitis)*, a collection of epistles and gospels that was the "companionpiece" of priests celebrating the Mass. Finally, in 816, he finished his two greatest works: his manual on the conduct of monks, entitled the *Royal Crown for Monks* and his *Commentary on the Rule of St. Benedict*. He died about 830.[1]

His doctrine of mysticism—a term that can be legitimately applied to Smaragdus—can be found in these last two works, the pinnacle of his earlier writings. In the *Royal Crown*, Smaragdus takes up again what he had written in the *Royal Pathway*, which applies as much to monks as to lay people, viz. everything concerned with the practice of virtues, that very thing the ancient tradition calls the "active life." But the work forming the basis of Smaragdus' spirituality is his *Commentary of the Rule of St. Benedict*. It is therefore to this work and to the *Royal Crown* that we must turn to demonstrate his teachings on the activities of prayer, that is, the "contemplative life" and all that prepares for and follows it.[2] Smaragdus' doctrine has a universal and permanent value, but his vocabulary for the various aspects of Christian life has been modified since his era. The term "active life" came to be used especially for states of life which are given over to activities having an apostolic or pastoral nature, whereas the expression "contemplative life" became reserved for the several forms of monastic existence. It would be useful, then, to offer a chart showing how these various basic assumptions are related to one another in Smaragdus' schema:

CHRISTIAN LIFE

Contemplative Life= Prayer Activities		Active Life= Practice of Virtues		
Corporate Prayer	Intimate Prayer	For All	For Princes	For Pastors

As we shall see, the teachings of Smaragdus are practical in nature, not speculative. In point of fact, he really proposes a coherent doctrine. This doctrine is not original with him in the sense that he borrows all of its elements from numerous authors, most of whom he names. There are more than twenty of them, almost half of whom belong to the Eastern tradition. To these must be added the anonymous sources and St. Gregory the Great, whose name recurs most often. The doctrine does, nonetheless, embody a kind of unity stemming from the most frequently cited and oldest source: the *Lives* and *Words* of the monks of antiquity.

For his own time and for the centuries that followed, Smaragdus was the popularizer of the ancient monastic tradition. Manuscripts of his works and mention of him made by subsequent authors attest to his lasting influence in the West. In the ninth century he contributed to a spiritual renewal among lay people with his *Royal Pathway* and among clerics by his grammatical, theological, and liturgical writings, as well as influencing monastic reform with his *Royal Crown* and the *Commentary on the Rule*. In the tenth and eleventh centuries, these last two works were particularly widespread in Spain. At that time and later, in Spain and elsewhere, Smaragdus found his way after the eleventh century into the medieval *florilegia*, collections of selected extracts—flowers of a bouquet, as it were. As a consequence of the diffusion of *florilegia*, Smaragdus was continually read and he remains, even to this day, a viable force.

THE NATURE AND EXERCISE OF PRAYER

It is not easy to expound the ideas of Smaragdus in a language other than his own—Latin—because he is part of a linguistic tradition in which every word had already acquired a precise definition, often involving a rich and varied sense. The present essay must, therefore, proceed mainly by explaining words: not simply by translating them, but rather by attempting to render their exact nuances. This presents a certain difficulty for the reader, but it cannot be avoided.

For Smaragdus the life of a religious Christian is activated by his sole desire to get to heaven. Smaragdus repeats this basic tenet over and over. It is a matter of "reaching for a goal;" the word is *intentio*, used in its etymological sense and as such not easily translated.[3] *Intentio* involves, in effect, a dynamism that neither "intention," nor synonyms like "orientation," "tension" or "tendencies" can render exactly. At the same time, Smaragdus has in mind that posture or bearing of all human beings who are "on the road" towards the Lord as they "direct their sights" towards him and upon him. This path of self-awareness towards God which "magnetizes" man, so to speak, and draws him to God finds its most adequate expression in prayer, *oratio*. Again we are dealing here with a word whose literal translation invests it almost necessarily with a limited meaning, that of an activity: the act of praying. Smaragdus has in mind, on the other hand, not so much a particular exercise as such, but rather a permanent disposition, a state and condition of being that becomes a constituent element of one's being.

As a grammarian, Smaragdus utilizes etymology to construct a framework for his ideas about prayer. He breaks *oratio* into two words which mean "mouth" *(oris)* and its "means of expressing itself rationally" *(ratio)*.[4] At the foundation of this framework is reading, which was done aloud at the time, therefore with the mouth, but in preparation for which one mobilizes all the activity a reasonable being is capable of. Thus the term and the concept of prayer are interwoven with several other terms and concepts, and yet distinct from them. To understand fully all that Smaragdus includes in his life of prayer, it is incumbent upon us next to explain those distinctions.

Prayer as *oratio* is distinguished in the first instance from that which is called the "collect," a formulaic prayer recited aloud by a priest. The collect represents the tangible group expression in concise form of the prayer that all, bowed down in silence, have just made in their hearts after the reading or recitation of the psalms. *Oratio*, by way of contrast, is not a formula of prayer, but something of a much more personal nature, which comes from the heart and must needs be expressed by each individual spontaneously.

Oratio is also different from "meditation," which consists of reading or hearing something read, and reflecting upon that reading; only then, as a result of that reflection, does prayer gush forth. To meditate, then, is in some ways to "ruminate" on that which will be necessary to nourish prayer; it means to acquire a reflective awareness of what

God is and what man is. Through meditation that which is learned by reading is made to enter one's memory; it is a spiritual erudition. *Oratio*, on the other hand, is a bursting forth of the soul, an experience of fondness for God *(affectus)*, in which a prevailing interest is kept in his word (as contained in Holy Scripture), upon which one never stops thinking. This habit of directing oneself towards God must be maintained for an entire lifetime. To meditate is to enter oneself by means of the doctrinal and practical things one has learned and to assimilate them into one's being. From a spiritual organism nourished in that way an impulse will pour forth quite naturally and under normal circumstances. An impulse towards God: this is prayer.

It should be obvious that there is no clear line of demarcation between meditation and prayer. Emphasis shifts continually from one to the other. Even when one is engaged in corporal works, meditation must be ever-present to accomplish the dual purpose of preparing the ground for prayer while keeping untoward thoughts from gaining the upperhand. Smaragdus and the ancients were experts in that area of spiritual medicine that reveals the smallest obstacle or omission to union with God. Meditation on the truth cuts off evil thoughts; especially, it cuts off that kind of pseudo-meditation that is our spontaneous interior dialogue, which feeds on evil thoughts to the point of being surfeited and overcome by them. Meditation is, therefore, the center point from which one is directed either to good or to evil. Everything depends on one's thoughts and meditations, which should, ideally, be on the word of God, through which instinctive human impulses and spontaneous human thought are conquered.

It is not easy either to distinguish *oratio* from "contemplation," and it happens that one word is used as equivalent for the other. If it is understood, however, that prayer *(oratio)* is the spontaneous outburst of beseeching love, we see that prayer alone cannot be the ultimate stage in the whole spiritual process. Prayer erupts, as it were, into contemplation, and in this sense contemplation is the goal towards which the desire for God is directed. As we have said at the outset of this section, this desire for God is the essential part of spiritual life. Through contemplation a kind of beginning is made towards enjoyment of the joys of eternity; one is uniting himself to the eternal praise the saints render unto God. Whereas, as Scripture points out, the desires of the flesh, those spontaneous desires of human nature, find their pleasure in the contemplation of terrestrial reality, the desires of the spirit, that new ardor which the Holy Ghost implants in man, find their joy in contemplating celestial reality, which is final and conclusive. These new-born yearnings are the eschatalogical glories that are God. Reading, meditation, and prayer give rise to a taste for God. Contemplation is the savoring of that taste. It is the apogee where contact is made with the Creator through faith, hope, and love. In its own right, contemplation spreads its strength and pleasantness throughout those things which have been preparation for it and which must continue to be active.

The totality of these activities puts both the "heart" (cor) and the "mind" (mens) into action. It would be forcing the texts to attribute to the former a more palpable sense and to the latter a quality which is exclusively intellectual, for the whole being is swept along towards God. Under these circumstances we can understand the definition Smaragdus presents for basic prayer: A thing emanating from the depths of one's being and surging back upon and into the core of one's entire self. The one at prayer is "one who, uplifted by his desire for the ultimate contemplation, is given over entirely to the love of his Creator." All further explanations only clarify the content of this essential surrender of the creature, filled, animated, and uplifted by desire for the Creator.

The result of the reciprocal activity of God in humans and of human beings in God is an "active presence." God is always present in us, but we are not always present in him. Our hearts and minds wander and yearn naturally. Prayer takes them in hand, and lifts them and offers them to God, as we find in Jeremiah: "Let us lift up our hearts and hands to the Lord" (Lamentations 3:41). "Let us then lift up our hearts by prayer and our hands by labor and toil." In this entire activity every human act seems to be clothed in divine grace. If we call the Holy Spirit to us, it is because the Holy Spirit himself is urging us to call him. He is present in us so that we might become present in him by means of prayer.

This idea of reciprocal presence is expressed in various symbolic images drawn from the Bible. It is a kiss placed upon the feet of the Lord and an embrace we share mutually with him. It is represented also by a dialogue or colloquy in which we speak to God and his answer returns to us in Holy Scripture. This colloquy of love operates in the form of a secret clamor, hidden from humans but filling the ears of God; this colloquy, the fruit and nourishment of love, is, in the final accounting, a form of praise for God.

Prayer is therefore not a turning inward, but a projection forward, a bursting forth of the conscience; it is more than a simple reflection. It is that movement of the soul activated by our desire for knowing; it is a dynamism by which the soul passes quite naturally from knowledge acquired by reading and meditation to love. Yet, since we are still on the road, traveling only at the level of hope, the soul's movement is basically one of desire. The time is not altogether right for total possession, but is more a time for that alternate form of love which is desire. There is in us a "secret yearning to cry out" which only God hears and which fills him with joy: "In silence we cry out" *(Tacentes clamamus).*[5]

"Supplication" is the outcome of this desire, since prayer is not first and foremost an activity wherein we ask things of God. Prayer consists first in receiving God, then in consenting to his presence in us, and in accepting his demands. A request cannot be made to God except on this basis of love for him, and then only if the request itself is a petition asking God to give more of himself to us, and to fulfill the very desire for him that he has placed in us, so that we can desire him and receive him all the more. As we have already seen, the primary fruition of prayer is a knowledge that human beings acquire about themselves and God and of themselves in the presence of God—that is to say the awareness of oneself as sinner before him who is one and holy. That recognition we receive is none other than "humility." In the same way that humility emanates from love and leads back to it, humility itself is accompanied by what Smaragdus, following the tradition before him, calls "compunction." This latter quality is bilateral: On the one hand it is characterized by weeping and moaning, the sorrow and regret we feel over sins committed; on the other hand compunction is that desire, certainty and even the joy experienced concerning the remission of guilt. From self-knowledge, the human being was able to deduce his inability to acquire the object of his desire, which is union with God; from knowledge of God transmitted in Scripture that has been read and meditated on, he has learned to hope for everything from the mercy and forgiveness of God, whose pity is all-powerful and infinite. "When someone prays, he calls the Holy Ghost to himself." [6] Prayer is a supplication for succor which cannot help but be heard. The more yearning and desire we possess, the more we receive, and the more the Spirit of God is communicated, the more it arouses desire. Such is the foundation of supplication.

The "beneficiary" of supplication, it seems quite evident, is not only the person who prays but any other human being as well, the immediate community of which the supplicator is a part, or even humanity as a group. The Christian heart does not contain dividing walls. What a Christian petitions for himself he asks as well for others since he is a member of a large and singular body living in Christ. Smaragdus does not put any special emphasis on this communal aspect of prayer; today, we put it in the foreground, precisely because at one time it ceased to be prayer's natural and implicit foundation. Formerly, it went without saying that a Christian practiced his prayers in unison with the entire Church, and there was no compulsion to formulate theory about this essential element. However, the preoccupation with communal benefits is not altogether absent in Smaragdus in various allusions and brief statements. He often writes, for example, that prayer should steadfastly precede any monastic activity and that any monk who undertakes any sort of task (a voyage, a duty, an office) must first beg the prayers of his brothers.[7] He also insists that the monastery be viewed as a society and a fraternity. Those private prayers made in the course of a divine service spoken in common are gathered and brought together, as in a sheaf, by the priest in charge who transmits them to God by means of the "collects" mentioned above.

As far as the "modalities" of supplication are concerned, they can take as many forms as there are needs in human beings. Smaragdus uses several diverse terms to designate the variety of gradations supplication assumes as a part of interior prayer. "Postulation," as an example, would be the form supplication takes in one who knows that vice is hovering nearby and even feels himself touched by it. Two other modalities are "impetration," a refined and dignified entreaty, and "clamor," an insistent and perhaps even strident public expression of one's prayer.

Such are the only precise details we can draw from Smaragdus' work concerning the nature of prayer in its intrinsic sense. We can, however, delve farther into its general nature and underline further the considerable importance prayer holds in Smaragdus' scheme of things by considering its psychological and spiritual context. Prayer has pre-set conditions which are not any less important for Smaragdus than they would be for the Desert Fathers or for St. John Chrysostom, all of whom agree that the bond that links us to earth, whether it be a chain or thread, matters very little. No matter how fine the bond the bird cannot fly. The very existence of any attachment is sufficient to prevent movement. We must now turn to those measures that will create conditions favorable to the exercise of prayer, and we ought to keep in mind that here again Smaragdus is only the transmitter of long-held beliefs handed down within the tradition.

CUSTOMS AND PRACTICES FAVORABLE TO PRAYER

The traditional practices prepare and nourish the entire being, body and soul. The first in order of importance, "nocturnal vigils," is both an ascetic and mystical experience. In addition to preventing a person from being taken over and absorbed in sleep, prayer during night vigils is also symbolic of Christ's vigil and prayer in the garden. Since it was night when Christ himself prayed, it is during the helpful silence of the night that we have the greatest possibility of finding him. In this sense "Christ the Beloved does not share his bed with carnal desires, but with saintly works, sacred vigils, and frequent prayers. Christ is found not in the torpor of sleep but in vigilant and compulsive prayer." [8] "He who likes to sleep a lot is late for prayer." [9] In the same way that corporal relaxation and slumber symbolize a softening of the soul, so do nocturnal vigils activate the soul and sustain in it a state of readiness. Prayer, moreover, at any time constitutes a method of keeping vigil in a general sense and of maintaining a ready state in the presence of God. Whereas concupiscence of the spirit produces a relaxed state of sleep and slothfulness, the wholesome desires of the spirit refine one's being by provoking a state of readiness and prayer. As elsewhere in Smaragdus' writings and within the tradition itself, we find constant reference to the interaction of body and soul and the consequent uplifting of one by the other.

Smaragdus sometimes presents the concept of "fasting" as a direct complement to prayer. Prayers made in a state of abstinence will reach and enter heaven because "through the gift of fasting, hidden realities of heaven and the divine secrets are revealed." [10] But fasting as an end in itself has no value; for it to be meaningful and justified, the person who fasts externally must also pray internally. This conforms to the examples and teachings of Christ who warned that the attacks of the devil can be safely warded off only by fasting and prayer in combination. Experience itself puts us on guard: "The spirit oppressed by excessive voracity cannot direct pure prayers to God." [11] And yet, abstaining must be done in moderation, for without it one either completely extinguishes human energy or else relaxes it unduly. In the final accounting, fasting is inseparable from nocturnal vigils: "We cannot stand watch properly when our stomachs are weighed down by food. Too much eating leaves us prone to sleep and the benefits of vigils are lost on us." [12]

But all of this is only by way of preparation. Reading is the sole authentic source for a life of prayer. If rumination upon Scripture is tantamount to prayer, according to the etymological interpretation of the phrase *oris-ratio* already mentioned, there is still a stronger and deeper connection between reading and the word of God. "Reading bestows a double gift upon us. It instructs the soul but also separates it from the vanities of the world and leads it to love. In the shadowy reality of our life on earth, Holy Scripture becomes the light illuminating our path." [13] "What we used to ignore has become clear through reading; what we have learned we conserve by meditation; so that we may realize it, we must make it enter into us by praying." [14]

In order to pray, we must understand and appreciate the full meaning of Scripture, and we can only do that by reading the Bible assiduously. To give oneself over wholly to reading is to sharpen one's intellect by degrees. Thus, knowledge acquired through reading is the necessary companion of prayer. One enlightens the other. Prayer is above all else an appeal to the Holy Ghost who is the author of Scripture and he who holds the key to it. Hence: "To always pray one must read frequently." While outwardly we busy our hands doing manual labor, our inner life becomes sweeter by the process of meditation on the Psalms and by remembrance of Scripture.

The Psalms are more apt than any other parts of Scripture to make us pray because they come already clothed in the form of prayer. Daily repetition of their verses aids us in remembering them more easily. The practice of psalmody is therefore a very elevated kind of prayer because in it we not only express desires and supplications, but yield up to God a kind of praise that will last eternally, that same worshipful praise we associate with the angels.[15] Of course, psalmody does not merely mean the recitation of the psalms outloud, or even more the intention of the heart, as soon as the sweetness of a psalm is heard, it inclines the spirit towards attachment to God and to piety. By virtue of some unknown harmonic effect, modulation and proportional melodic measure associated with singing arouses a greater compunction in the heart. The soul is thus best disposed towards prayer.

INNER DISPOSITIONS NECESSARY FOR PRAYER

Prayer is possible only when proper preparation has been made in conquering vices and in moderating and orienting the passions. It is necessary to restore the new man by purity, simplicity, fear of God, right intentions, stability of spirit, chastity, and, above all, by charity. All the preceding qualities are only so many facets and constituent parts of charity. It is difficult to separate them out and to treat each individually because they form an inseparable whole.

Smaragdus places heavy emphasis on the pure state of the soul, which must be taken in a very large sense. Purity of soul means a complete detachment from all which is not God or has no connection with him. We must escape the net of corporal passions and alien thoughts, we must free ourselves from the traps they set for us. Nocturnal vigils, fasting, and meditative reading have already paved the way towards the necessary emancipation of self.[16] But now alien thoughts must be pursued to the very depths of the heart where they are wont to take refuge. Smaragdus goes to some lengths to point out that those who seek God on their own are more prone than anyone to the attacks of these alien thoughts. We can conclude from this that prayer demands a continual struggle. "We are truly at prayer only when we think of nothing else. When we give ourselves over to prayer, we must see to it that all carnal or secular thoughts go out of us and that our spirit considers nothing else than the object of our prayers." [17] Passions awaken themselves in us unceasingly. "Nothing helps prayer, so long as there is hatred in our breasts." [18] The pure heart is one in which exist no lies or fraud and dissimulation of any kind, but one which is ruled by purity and sincerity. One has to fly over vice just as a prudent bee does.[19]

Another predisposition essential for prayer is "compunction." Purity of heart is the removal of ourselves from anything which is not God; compunction, on the other hand, is the involvement in knowing ourselves: looking our misery in the face, accepting it, and even liking it in a certain sense. As St. Paul has said, "It is when I am weak that I am strong." Compunction is therefore already itself a pre-ordained component of prayer, that which the Bible calls "tearful and lamenting" prayer. One is healed through prayer precisely because one becomes cognizant of one's wounds during prayer. Compunction opens the wound for cleansing and prayer administers the medicine. "Compunction is further a humility of spirit: it proceeds from the recollection of sins and our fear of final judgment." [20] Like all saintly dispositions that appear in a man it is a gift. Joined to the gift of abstinence, it permits the keenness of spirit to fix its gaze with greater intensity on the mysteries of God.

To afford a glimpse at those elements which constitute the complex virtue of compunction, Smaragdus, following Gregory the Great and Isidore of Seville, distinguishes four aspects of interior movement through which our minds are overtaken by compunction, by that "beneficial state of anxiety" (taedio salubri compungitur).[21] In the first place, there is the reminder of past sins. This leads, in the second place, to the thought of eternal suffering. The Old Testament mentions quite frequently this saving "fear of God" which is not so much a true feeling of trepidation as it is an attitude of loving reverence we take in the presence of God. The third element of compunction is our consideration of the long earthly journey we must make, a pilgrimage fraught with temptations, dangers, and evils. The fourth and final aspect of compunction is also the ultimate and decisive recompense for the first three, namely, hope, our desire of attaining the eternal homeland. These four basic elements correspond to the four questions that each human must ask himself: "Where have I been? Where will I end up? Where am I now? What lies ahead in the future? " These are so many motifs for a sadness that will be truly salutary and that will cause shedding of real and fertile tears. "It is from suffering itself that the soul is uplifted and raised to the

joys of heaven." "Tears produce a powerful love that fulfills the
soul."

Put more succinctly, compunction is what humility brings to prayer.
Humility, which is the practical knowledge of the truth about us and
about God, makes us understand the love God has for us and the
need we have for him.[22] From that awakened consciousness of our
inherent poverty and from our confidence in God's rich bounty is
born prayer.

THE EFFECTS OF PRAYER

For Smaragdus as well as for the tradition he follows, the ultimate
purpose of prayer is none other than salvation and eternal life. "We
pray unceasingly that God in his goodness and benevolence will
bear us into that state of blissful hope and ineffable joy, the eternal
domain where only hope, praise and exultation exist." [23] Already, in
this life, God has given us the downpayment, as it were, on eternal
life in union with him; our downpayment consists in the benefits of
prayer.

Prayer is first of all like a lighthouse and tiller for us; it lights our
way and steers us. In the second place, it introduces order into our
lives, causing us to separate ourselves from our terrestrial nature and
pointing us in God's direction through Christ. Through prayer we
depart from our own selves as Abraham left the homeland.[24] Prayer
cleanses us and grants us pardon and purity. The man who prays
is calling the Holy Ghost, whose presence scatters the temptations
of demons.

Smaragdus is nonetheless on guard constantly against the danger
of judging the value of prayer through the instantaneity of its effects
produced: "The prayers of the just are answered belatedly; the longer
they are deferred, the greater the rewards." [25] The delay is like a
period of time during which capital is under accumulation, capital
that will bring the more as one invests. Expectation of quick satisfaction would be an illusion, and could lead to despondency. It is
the delaying that makes us progress and grow.

Compunction makes us "love these divine delays." Is it not already
much to hope for life eternal? "Those who shed tears in prayer will
reap after death the reward of their labor, which is joy forever
after." [26] And yet, even in our present lives, God has manifested his
kingdom in us. "He does not wait for our petition to come to total
fruition in eternity; from the first moment of our search he accords
us multiple benefits," [27] beginning with the presence of Christ the
Beloved in us. Christ himself is the essence of the Promised Land
in which we are already living. "Happy, nay, a thousand times happy

is he who lives in Christ and who can say in his prayers, thoughts and actions: 'Christ lives in me, and what I am living, I live in the faith of the Son of God.' " [28]

This "life in Christ" is not merely the vision of God in heaven. Always "the more one puts aside exterior reality, the more one is nourished inwardly by contemplation of revealed reality. Those who seem to be abiding sorrowfully in the valley of humility are raised up from within by contemplation." [29] Contemplation is a way of seeing through faith. It has the effect of *chiaroscuro*, but it is sure and certain, and through it the concupiscence of our spirit rests in the contemplation of eternal joys. These effects of prayer are all the more manifest as prayer itself increases in frequency to a point where it becomes uninterrupted, being no longer composed of a series of acts but becoming a veritable state of existence.

One of the effects, then, of the practice of prayer is a "continuity" of the state in which prayer places us. To be "entirely given over to love of the Creator," to be "in the continuous love of God" is to pray unceasingly. It is through the permanence of a state of detachment from ourselves and attachment to God that we anticipate eternal life and will achieve it. "The persistence of prayer assures the stability of the soul." [30] Since vices are deeply ingrained in us, the spirit must not cease to persevere in prayer—and it will overcome them only by persisting in it. "Each time one is attacked by a vice, one throws himself into prayer; frequent prayer puts an end to the battle that vices wage against us." [31] "Let us persist in prayer and the devil will flee." [32] Repetitive prayer produces in us more than the one apparently negative consideration of separating us from evil: Above all, prayer has the positive aspect of uniting us continually to God.

Human weakness being what it is, however, we can sin even by doing what is good. Pride can arise from constant prayer as one might be proud of a beautiful voice. Whereas prayer must be a continuous attitude, acts of prayer must be brief, for in prolonging them one might open the door to drowsiness or to diabolical suggestions which stir the senses and the heart. Intensity, not prolixity, is of the essence.

"Zeal" is, in fact, the ultimate and most decisive qualitative element of prayer. Prayer must be a sally towards God through which one rises to the assault more rapidly than temptations can. Life is like a race—to lose ground by slowing down is to expose ourselves to traps set along the way, demonstrating our unworthiness to be called onward by God. Slacking at only one point, be it in self-discipline (*ascesis*), prayer or work, promotes half-heartedness and lethargy in all other areas.

Human beings are quite well aware, moreover, how their natures are incapable of prolonged attention and fervor. Prayer slips away so easily into a simple meditation on ideas or even into discourse held with ourselves. A stroke of the spirit, on the other hand, a flash produced from the soul can more readily produce fire. The best strategy, it would seem then, is to make brief, but more frequent and more ardent bursts of prayer. "When we pray thus in earnestness, the Lord abides within us. We carry in us him to whom we are praying, and even more than that we are granted our request through him by whom we are borne." [34] To maintain ourselves in God's presence means necessarily we must not lose our breath, so to speak!

Such is Smaragdus' doctrine on prayer. At the same time that it is elevated to the point of sometimes seeming only an unattainable ideal, it is also realistic, concrete, and designed for daily living. Smaragdus' teaching takes human weakness into account, yet it rests on a foundation of absolute confidence in the power of God who transforms us by the Spirit of Christ.

We could not conclude more effectively than by citing a passage from Smaragdus himself which synthesizes his doctrine:

> Do not think to yourself, "The task I have set for myself is too large, and I am so small and puny. I cannot possibly persevere in this project." Beloved brother, understand what I am telling you: "If you were to travel to a faraway land, it would take you more than a single hour to cross the space separating you from it. But gradually and by degrees, day after day, you make a bit of progress, and after much time and labor you arrive in the country where you intended to go." Such is the kingdom of God, the garden of delights, the desired land and we get there through vigils and prayers. Observe all these things and fear not to venture out on the first step of that road which will lead you to eternal life. [35]

BIBLIOGRAPHICAL NOTES

The most recent and most complete work on Smaragdus is Otto Eberhard, *Via Regia: Die Fürstenspiegel Smaragds von St. Mihiel und seine Literarische Gattung* (Münster Westphalien, 1977). The study comes with a bibliography of all publications. No work of Smaragdus has been translated into English. Except for the commentary on Donatus Smaragdus' works are printed by Migne in PL 102, 14–980. The *Commentary on the Rule of St. Benedict* has been edited critically by Pius Engelbert, *Smaragdi Abbatis Expositio in Regulam S. Benedicti, Corpus Consuetudinarum Monasticarum* 8 (Siegburg, 1974). In Migne the *Royal Crown for Monks* is in columns 593–690, the *Commentary on the Rule* in columns 689–932. Migne provides no index, but a table of contents for PL 102 can perform help as a finding tool. Nearly every phrase of this study could find support in one or more references to the texts of Smaragdus.

On the *Commentary of the Rule* see now Caroline Walker Bynum, *Docere verbo et exemplo: an Aspect of Twelfth Century Spirituality*, Harvard Theological Studies, 21 (Cambridge, MA, 1979), pp. 201–03.

III

Neoplatonism and the Mysticism of William of St.-Thierry*

THOMAS MICHAEL TOMASIC

The mysticism of William of Saint-Thierry, friend and confidant of St. Bernard of Clairvaux, is an articulate restoration of the central principles of Neoplatonic philosophy in the twelfth century. Peremptorily, traditional Orthodox and Catholic mysticism originated from and was built upon the unique ontological, logical, and psychological paradigms of Neoplatonism, without which Christian mysticism might well have been historically, and probably logically, impossible.[1] Neoplatonism conferred on mysticism its catholicity and orthodoxy, i.e., its cognitivity and public confirmability, thereby guarding it from collapsing into obscurantism, emotivism, subjectivism, psychologism or unconfirmable private religious claims—which traits were construed by the Church Fathers as characteristics of heresy. Gnosticism falls into two general types: the privileged in-

---

* To grasp the critical sense of an antique text, one should gain a familiarity with, at least, key systematic terms—especially since there are no exact semantic equivalents in English for the important Greek or Latin terms. Throughout this chapter, some English approximation (though not necessarily a synonym) has been supplied for key Greek or Latin terms, so that the reader might gain familiarity with the original. Additionally, since a language-type—and mystical discourse is a language-type—supposes a system of logic (with proper axioms, tautologies, truth-tables, etc.) to guarantee significant and meaningful statements within the language-type, a modest attempt has been made to disclose the logic supporting mystical discourse.

tellectualist and the fundamentalist; both, however, make the claim of having personal, private or privileged access to divine truths, revelations, and charisms in their respective ways. The traditional Christian Neoplatonic position is that the truth of religious knowledge, theological or mystical, is not a matter of private access, but is public, not subjective, capable of being objectively tested, clarified and corrected (catholic), and subject to strict canons or rules of logic (orthodox). The immediate task is to develop the catholic elements of Neoplatonic ontology and orthodox logic which ground, and are indispensable for understanding mystical discourse, and then to place William's thought within its Neoplatonic frame.

THE NEOPLATONIC GROUND

The *Enneads* of Plotinus provides the principal and clearest map for charting one's way through the mainstreets of Neoplatonism.[2] Later developments, transformations and even deviations in Neoplatonism will require some adjustments; but familiarity with the original map will serve our present purpose.

The ontologico-psychological structure on which traditional mysticism builds is a triad composed of three "members"—the One, *Noûs* (Intellect, or *animus* in Latin), and *Psyché* (Soul, or *anima*)—which constitute a hierarchy and are called *hypóstases* (stages, sources, grounds). Relationship between them is represented schematically in two basic ways: either 1) as a vertically desending order or ordination with the One positioned topmost, *Noûs* emanating downward from, and subordinate to, the One, and *Psyché* emanating downward from, and subordinate to, *Noûs* or 2) horizontally, as a geometrically conceived outward expansion of concentric circles from a center. Plotinus provides a clear description of the latter:

> Imagine a center and about this center a luminous circle that sends off rays; then around this circle another circle equally luminous, light flowing from light; outside these two circles a third, which is no longer a circle of light, but lacking its own light, needs to be lighted by another. Imagine it like a wheel, or rather like a sphere that receives its light from the second circle to which it is nigh, and that is illuminated only to the extent that it receives this light.[3]

The center depicts the One, and the first two emanated spheres or circles depict *Noûs* or *animus* and *Psyché* or *anima* respectively. Plotinus here adds a third and outermost circle or sphere which represents the empirical order, the world of literal extension, and is not a *hypóstasis* or constituent member of interior or metaphorical space. Axiomatically, each higher level is paradigmatically what lower levels are iconically, i.e., each lower level is a more or less deviant image or icon of the level immediately above it, while each higher level is a model or paradigm for the one immediately below.

These three primal *hypóstases*—the One, *Noûs*, and *Psyché*—constitute a mapping of three levels of sacred or metaphorical space interior to each of us; more importantly, for understanding the metaphysical, epistemological and psychological ground of traditional mysticism, each *hypóstasis* has unique characteristics and operations which mark out three distinct and irreducible types of theological discourse in Christian Neoplatonism.[4] The three *hypóstases*, with their proper characteristics and functions, may be schematized vertically as follows:

Hypóstasis		Function or Activity	Characteristic	Type of Knowledge
The ONE		AGNŌSÍA (unitive)	aspatial/atemporal	None
NOÛS or ANIMUS *Gnôsis* or necessary truth)	Achronic	NÓESIS (intuitive or intellective)	atemporal, non-propositional, "spatial"	THEŌRÍA Contemplative
	Synchronic		atemporal, propositional, "spatial" (analytic)	EPISTÉMĒ Cognitive, meditative
		DIÁNOIA (discursive)		ANALOGÍA Reflective
	Diachronic		tensed-propositional, "spatial" (synthetic)	
PSYCHÉ or ANIMA (*Pístis* or probable truth)		PHANTASÍA (imaginative)	temporal/spatial images	DÓXA Perceptive
		AÍSTHESIS (perceptive, sensate)	temporal/spatial sensory images	

The One—or absolute self-sufficient Unity—is transcendent and immanent. As 'transcendent' (the characteristic attribute or name of God, indicating the Divine to be aspatial, atemporal, and beyond every finite reference range) the One is unknowable and inaccessible in principle to intellectual or psychological operations. This would mean that the Divine Unity or Identity is not even accessible to Divine knowing or intellection; it is only "known" by unknowing (agnōsía, ignorantia). As 'immanent' (a Divine attribute absolutely coextensive with 'transcendent'), the presence of the One is manifested wherever and however unity, union, mixture or blending is actualized; nevertheless, the immanence or presence of the One is *never an object* of *nóēsis* (intellection), *diánoia* (discursive reason), *phantasía* (imagination) and *aísthēsis* (perception/sensation). Thus, both 'transcendence' and 'immanence' position the One outside the range of noetic conceptualization and predication, psychologic reasoning, imagination and perception; consequently, the assertion that the One is 'transcendent' and 'immanent' is intentionally designed to block the logical possibility of making any literally true statements or utterances about God. Just for a moment, let us retranspose this vertical scheme back into the horizontal, geometric model, in order to become aware of an interesting assertion Neoplatonic mystics make. Imagine again the One as the center, the separate but proximate sphere of noetic or intellectual activities circumscribing the One, and the further sphere of *Psyché* encircling *Noûs*. In the realm of metaphorical space, all centers must coincide since there can be no spatial distance or qualitative distinction. It follows, therefore, that the center of our own self-identity coincides with the One, occupying the same "place" and would have the same characteristic and function. One's own self-identity, one's own center, must be construed as 'transcendent' and 'immanent' and be undifferentiated from the One—equally a focal point of mystical concern. 'Transcendence' and 'immanence' mark out the territory of contemplative, ascetical or mystical theology; utterances about the 'transcendent' and 'immanent,' which are formulated propositionally only at that level where propositions can be formed, i.e., on the noetic and dianoetic levels, *must be construed as metaphorical utterances.*

Noûs fixes the reference-range of strictly intellectual or noetic cognition, which occurs often in collaboration with, but is nevertheless distinct from, diachronic reasoning and from imagery. The proper functions or operations of *Noûs* are two-fold: 1) the formation of simple achronic concepts or ideas, e.g., the concept of 'circularity,' and 2) the formulation of synchronic propositions, e.g., analytically true statements. On our schematized diagram, the left set of brackets illustrates this by referring achronic and synchronic *nóēsis* to *Noûs*.

One should note that the lower end of the bracket extends to *diánoia*, or discursive intellection, and that the bracket referring to *Psyché* also touches *diánoia* at its upper end. The difference is that *Noûs* formulates only atemporal or untensed (synchronic) propositions, and that *diánoia* on this level occurs as discursive reasoning employing only tenseless propositions; but in the case of *Psyché*, *diánoia* is that discursive activity which employs tensed (diachronic) propositions. What is asserted is that the lowest operation of *Noûs* and the highest operation of *Psyché* is discursive reasoning; it is in this activity that *Noûs* and *Psyché* are in immediate contact or "mix." *Noûs* is the non-mediated possession of intelligibles or *noētá*, i.e., cognitive paradigms, law-like patterns or models (conceptual or propositional) which are eternal (atemporal, non-durational), necessary, and universal or catholic, the knowledge of which may be called either *theoría*, if contemplative, or *epistémē*, if speculative. *Noētá*, although atemporal and universal, are nevertheless finite because any determinate, intelligible *noētón* expresses a limited reference-range. Geometricals provide the easiest examples: the concept 'circularity' (understood in the Euclidean sense) is cognitively distinct from 'squareness,' and excludes from its definite boundaries other *noētá*, such as 'squareness' and 'straightness.' These *noētá* or cognitive paradigms are qualitatively, not numerically or quantitatively, distinct; they are to be construed as the real essences of, or constitutive laws or canons for understanding or constructing, particulars, e.g., an actually drawn circle. What counts for universality or catholicity is that the identically same referent, the very same 'circularity,' is known by all minds just in case they comprehend what counts for 'circularity'; thus, noetic paradigms guarantee universality, hence objectivity and public access to intelligible truth, to different and functional minds. Traditional conciliar dogmas (laws or canons), such as dogmatic formulations of the 'Trinity,' the 'Incarnation,' the 'Virgin Birth,' are paradigms expressed on this noetic level. Such doctrines establish a formula of range-fixing or theory-constitutive models which mark out the territory of speculative or dogmatic theology; their propositional expressions *should be construed as law-like or analytic*.[5]

Psyché, as shown by the lower left bracket in our diagram, has three distinguishable activities: 1) diachronic *diánoia* (discursive reason, employing temporally tensed propositions), 2) *phantasía* (imagination, internal simple or composite images) and 3) *aísthesis* (perception/sensation). Diachronic *diánoia* has both an "upward" and a "downward" motion. Its "upward" motion is a psychological *anábasis* (ascension) or "gathering up" items of imagination and perception/sensation, and calculating or reckoning up these items by comparison or reference to appropriate noetic models; its "downward" motion consists in applying noetic models to items of imagination and perception/sensation in order to intelligibilize these particulars. This bi-directional movement of *Psyché* is the exclusive location of analogical knowing. *Psyché* conceives of *Noûs* and possesses noetic models analogously; analogy, therefore, is a property of that psychologic "mixing" or "blending" which relates sensibles to intelligibles or intelligibles to sensibles, and expresses such proportional relationship propositionally. It is precisely this property that makes diachronic reasoning *Psyché's* highest activity, whereby she "comes in touch" with *Noûs*.[6] *Phantasía* involves a mixing or blending of dianoic judgment with perception/sensation (*aísthesis*) for the formation of internal images. *Aísthesis* is simply the operation of perceiving sensately. The specific and native function of *Psyché*, therefore, is to form appropriate imagery, to blend these with relevant cognitive paradigms by discursive reason, then to employ discursive reason to extend noetic paradigms to lower psychological activities. The operations of *Psyché* mark out the territory of practical or moral theology, e.g., Scriptural, parabolical, prescriptive and sacramental formulations. Since all intelligible utterances on the psychological level involve mixing of, or bridging, noetic models and particular imagery, theological propositions at this level *must be construed as analogical utterances.*[7]

MYSTICISM AND NEOPLATONIC LOGIC

Given the preceding hierarchical division of noetic and psychological activities, we can now examine the logical status of those noetic theological statements, or metaphorical utterances, proper to mysticism—statements which have as their grammatical subject 'Unity,' 'Identity,' 'One,' 'God,' or other such equivalent term which anomalously signifies a 'transcendent-immanent' referent. Traditionally, 'transcendent' means: 1) that God is 'ineffable' and 'unknowable' in principle, i.e., it would be contradictory to assert both that God is 'transcendent' *and* that literal truth-claims can be made about him; and 2) that literal truth-claims about creatures are possible without reference to God's causation precisely because assertions about a 'transcendent' cause can make neither factual nor empirically informative difference in or about a world of finite beings.[8] Thus, the transcendence doctrine blocks the logical possibility of making either literally true or analogically significant statements about God, thereby locking mystical language into a non-literal or metaphorical type of discourse. 'Immanence' means: 1) that God's knowledge of his own nature is inseparable from his knowledge of creatures (as is the case with ourselves); and 2) that the world itself is a theophany or manifestation of God.[9] It should be noted that focus is not principally on the epistemic sense of 'transcendence' and 'immanence,' but on the logical implications these terms hold for mystical language.

On the face of it, 'Transcendence' and 'Immanence' are contrary or collision terms; their conjunction in the traditional puzzle-formula, 'God is transcendent *and* God is immanent,' would constitute a contradiction, a nonsensical use of language, if the formula were taken literally or restricted to a two-valued logic. The crucial question becomes: "How are such mystical statements not contradictory? " The resolution of such puzzle-formulae surely requires not only the avoidance of contradiction or nonsense, but it also requires that some positive sense, or some reference-fixing, be made of 'transcendent predicates' and conjuncted collision terms and propositions. To achieve this, one must note two inseparably interconnected logical charac-teristics of mystical discourse: 1) the necessary employment of a three-truth-valued propositional logic, having the truth-values T (true), F (false), and M (middle, indeterminate or metaphorical), and 2) the necessarily non-literal and metaphorical status of all statements about a 'transcendent-immanent' subject.

The difference between a two-valued and a three-valued system is indispensable for understanding mysticism. A two-valued or biv-alent logic, based on the Law of the Excluded Middle, prescribes that significant propositions must be either T or F, and no three ways about it, thereby making metaphors incurably unmanageable. Thus, since 'This [bread] is My body' and 'I and My Father are one' cannot be literally T, they must be literally F. Consequently, whatever metaphors are, they cannot be metaphors in a two-valued system; the logical move, then, is to demetaphorize metaphors, either by requiring they be reduced to literal statements (that they be reducible) or by construing them as elliptical—hence literal—similes. Further-more, a two-valued logic would disallow any significant conjunction of collision statements, e.g., 'God is transcendent *and* God is im-manent' or 'God is Being *and* not-Being,' characteristic in mystical language. Since conjunctions also have a truth-value, the conjunction of an assertion and its denial must be viewed as contradictory in a bivalent system, hence analytically F.

In a three-valued system, the truth-value of an affirmative or kataphatic statement about God, e.g., 'God is transcendent,' 'God is Being,' is to be taken as metaphorical, i.e., not F literally as a two-valued system would have it, but rather 'not T, not F' in the sense of 'indeterminate' as a three-valued system requires. Understanding metaphor as the third truth-value, one then comprehends that the traditional mystic intends no logical predication of properties to God when making such assertive statements. What, precisely, is being asserted remains to be considered in the next subdivision. Negative or apophatic statements, e.g., 'God is not-Being,' 'God is not-Good,' are construed, on the other hand, as literally T.[10] If kataphatic statements are M-valued and are conjuncted with a T-statement, the truth-value of the conjunction must be M, and not F as in a two-valued system. Thus, in a three-valued system, where the assertion 'God is Being' is M-valued, it follows that the literally T apophatic statement, 'God is not-Being,' is not its contrary, does not collide, and contradiction is avoided. Such conjunctions are thereby preserved from being analytically F or non-sensical. M-valued statements and M-valued conjunctions are logically required by the Neoplatonic intensional synonymy of 'transcendent' and 'ineffable' or 'unknowable,' which effectively blocks the possibility of forming any informative concept, predicate, or making T- or F-valued assertions about God. In effect, all statements in which the word 'God' is the logical subject, even if it appears in a biblical context, must be construed as metaphorical or indeterminate, whether or not they employ imagery.

MYSTICISM AND NEOPLATONIC METAPHOR

We shall now focus attention on the logical, not epistemic, status of metaphor considered *altiora theoría* (the higher or deeper theory), which characterizes those tenseless statements formed by *Noûs* about the transcendent/immanent One. To avoid confusion, the Neoplatonic use of metaphor must be absolutely dissociated from those theories of metaphor based on a two truth-valued system; these include verbal opposition, emotive tension, iconic signification, deviant discourse,and comparison theories. The paradigmatic instance of Neoplatonic metaphor or third truth-value lies in the use of the conjunction connecting M-utterances and negative T-statements, of the type: 'God is Being *and* God is not-Being.' In a conjunction, if both components are true the conjunction is T; if either component is false, the conjunction is F; if both components are middle, or one component middle and one true, the conjunction is M. What, therefore, is really being asserted by the mystic making such puzzle-utterances is *not* a coincidence of opposites or contraries, as most secondary authors on mysticism seem to believe, precisely because the truth-value of 'God is Being' is M, the truth-value of 'God is not-Being' is T, and M-utterances and T-statements are not contraries or opposites. The purpose of the Neoplatonic use of M-valued conjunctions is to rigorously disavow all literal assertory T-statements about God, to render them logically impossible, and to effectively obviate any fatal, nonsensical collision of antithetical terms or propositions about God.

What, then, does an M-conjunction accomplish noetically? It operates, as do all other theological, theoretic metaphorical terms, as a Divine *Name*; it denotes or designates a referent, but does not connote, describe or explain. Functioning as a Divine Name, the M-valued conjunction allows for the possibility of a non-definitional, non-conceptual, non-descriptive—yet noetically meaningful or significant—mode of reference-fixing transcendent, unboundaried Union, Unity and At-one-ment. Consequently, where such a conjunction is used, the first component (the M-valued utterance) should be understood as expressing a Divine Name reinforced by the conjunctive Name ('and') referencing 'Union,' the second component (the negative T-valued sentence) should be construed as a negation of finite predicates, descriptions, and properties. Thus, in contrast to classical, two-valued predicate logic, Neoplatonic employment of Divine Names (whether expressed grammatically by singular terms, conjunctions, or sentences) does not rest upon any existential suppositions, hence such naming is free of any bound variables; consequently, Neoplatonic "free" logic is characterized by the occurrence of Names which are empty—a fact traditionally mirrored in the use of such privatives as 'Divine Dark,' 'Divine Silence,' 'Infinite,' and the work title, 'Negative Theology.' Unlike classical two-valued logic, Neoplatonic logic does not require that statements containing empty Names be false; it does require a new understanding of negation. There is simply no ambiguity or inconsistency in the mystic's considering the reference-fixing use of empty Names to be logically meaningful behavior, and yet denying that such Names imply descriptions; there is no necessary reason why a meaningful fixing of reference must be a fixing of predicable descriptive meaning. Clearly, for the Neoplatonist, mystical discourse is not a phenomenological, descriptive language, but rather a language employing Names to reference Union, Unity, Identity— a language of contact.[11]

A second and correlative use of the Divine Names consists in reference-fixing the conjunctive or syzygistic union "between" God and beings. This conjunction is sometimes called 'coincidence of opposites' by later, ambiguously Neoplatonic authors, to avoid a reductionistic monism (materialism) or pantheistic identity theory and to espouse an anomalous (nonreductionistic) monism. Given, however, the M-valued, metaphorical status of the Divine Names, no anomaly need arise. An anomaly would, indeed, arise if the Divine Names are interpreted as finite, participated properties of creatures just in case they are given an epistemological use; but this is not the primary focus of mysticism. Used mystically, the Divine Names are empty, non-predicative and non-descriptive; when borrowed to reference properties of finite beings, they deviate from their role as

Names and function as descriptive predicates involving quantification, and thus generate anomalies. Strictly and primarily, however, the Divine Names are not descriptions; they reference-fix, in effect, the simple, unpropertied conjunctive "blending" or "mixing" of God and beings—an autonomous union which can neither be a predicate nor the subject of predicates. It is this 'union' which is synonymous with 'Divine Immanence.' When, therefore, mystics refer the Divine Names ('Good,' 'Light,' 'Beauty, 'Being,' 'Jealousy,' etc.) to God *and* (conjunctively) to beings (but not as descriptive properties), they purport to reference a 'superessential' and autonomous Union, "Mixing," or *sympáthea* unquantified and unrestricted by finitude, property or difference. Thus the autonomy of the conjunctive or syzygistic Divine Names fixes the reference of an Identity preserved transcendently and immanently, which cuts across the boundaries of finites (hence is transcendent) and retains its self-sameness in each (is immanent); yet it is also asserted that Identity or Union fixes—through *thesmós* (providential law), *lógos* (immanent gathering-together) and *érōs* (conversional love)—the reference-range of each finite "participant." Using the Name "Beauty' as an example, the Pseudo-Dionysius writes:

> But the Super-Essential Beautiful is called "Beauty" because of
> that quality which It imparts to all things severally according
> to their nature, and because It is the Cause of the harmony
> and splendour in all things, flashing forth upon them all, like
> light, the beautifying communications of Its originating ray;
> and because It summons all things to *fare* until Itself . . ., and
> because It draws all things together in a state of mutual
> interpenetration. . . . It contains in a transcendent manner the
> originating beauty of everything that is beautiful. . . . From
> this Beautiful all things possess their existence, each kind
> being beautiful in its own manner, and the Beautiful causes
> the harmonies and sympathies and communities of all things.
> And by the Beautiful all things are united together and the
> Beautiful is the beginning of all things as being the Creative
> Cause. . . . And it is the Goal of all things, and their
> Beloved, as being their Final Cause . . ., and It is their
> Exemplar from which they derive their definite limits. . . .[12]

The 'Divine Names' thus reference an ontological syzygy (not a synthesis), a universal community, a sympathetic union, a self-same oneness, a conjunction that exists beyond, and is constitutive of, the finiteness of its participants. Thus the role of metaphor is ascetical or ascensionistic, leading upward, elevating *Noûs* and *Psyché* above the level of their proper cognitive and perceptual operations to real contact with transcendent Unity.

Understanding metaphorical referencing in this mystical way throws new light on the traditional meaning or function of both Scriptural and theological statements. Sayings of Jesus, where he makes reference to himself, as such 'I and My Father are one,' or 'This [bread] is My body,' and such claims as 'Jesus is both God and man,' would not be literally true; these statements neither intensionally or extensionally reference a literal conjunction, or synthesis, of quite distinct beings. What is referenced is far more important, namely, a transcendent union, communion, *sympátheia* which is the same *thesmós*, *lógos* and *érōs* of Father and Son, this bread and Jesus' body, and God and man. The union referenced, in another "place," is the ultimately and constitutively real, and it can only be touched by metaphor, since it lies absolutely outside the range of finite concepts, beyond the noetic, imaginative, sensate, and physical. To take conjunctions literally would amount to secularizing religious discourse. The Eucharist thus becomes an ascetical process; its reception is symbolic of the mystical and real union on quite a different plane.[13] Likewise, the Incarnation references a union, a *sympátheia*, a conjunction of God and man at a transcendent center.

However, metaphors do invite analogies. Metaphor is not a mere property of language, it is the constitutive and logically prior source of language. Mystical use of metaphor is bi-directional: 1) extending the specific operations of *Psyché* and *Noûs* upward by referencing a hyperessential union beyond concept, reason, imagination and sense its use is *anagogical* (leading up); 2) extending downward from *nóēsis* and synchronic *diánoia* to diachronic *diánoia*, *phantasía*, and *aísthēsis*, and on to persons and things, it becomes constitutive and transfigurative of *analogical* discourse. For example, the transcendent, Divine Union or *sympátheia*, referenced by mystical theology requires the articulation, on the level of *nóēsis* and synchronic *diánoia*, of achronic "spatial" paradigms *(noētá)* and analytic propositional formulations, respectively, of a communitarian model that exemplifies union, i.e., the Trinity. Hence, the doctrine of the Trinity exemplifies both Unity and union; Unity, in the sense of 'oneness,' union in the sense of metaphorically spatialized, interrelated persons. In effect, this complex noetic-dianoetic notion of divinity allows it to function as a law-like model, referencing an ascetical process toward union, and at the same time to provide a formula for interpersonal relations which would otherwise remain unstatable. Similarly, the concept of a circle depicts a metaphorical distance between center and circumference, and its synchronic propositional formula, or definition, expresses articulately the metaphorical positioning of constitutive elements as could never happen physically. These *noētá* and their propositional statements constitute finite reference-ranges, since *Noûs* can neither articulate nor comprehend what is unboundaried. Such *noētá* and *dianoētá* are not descriptive or explanatory accounts of transcendent Unity or union; rather, these cognitive paradigms count as the highest possible articulation of noetic activities and mark the limit beyond which *Noûs* cannot proceed. We are, at this point, left standing before images on an iconostasis, as it were, at the limit of speculative or scientific theology, and have not entered the sanctuary.[14]

The function of the Trinitarian formula (as of all noetic paradigms) is to serve as a law-like model (dogma) for the construction, organization, and transfiguration of the lower operations of *Psyché*, and of relations between persons on the social level. Its purpose is not to discover how persons do relate (descriptive) but how they ought to relate (prescriptive).[15] Law-like models or metaphors are extended noetically to transform the lower activities of diachronic reason, imagination, and sensation where, because of increasing limitations as one proceeds lower, greater degrees of deviant imaging are introduced. Proportionate and relevant similarities that adhere between law-like models, diachronic reasoning, imagination, and sensation map out the territory of analogical comparisons. Thus the concept *(noētón)* and definition *(dianoētón)* of 'circle' constitute the spatial and paradigmatic character of circularity, but all imagined, sensed, and drawn circles deviate from the model and are circles only analogously. So also human personal relations deviate from, and are analogous to, the Trinitarian model and can, by law-conforming reorientation, be brought into a more coherent and compatible imitation of the model. Statements of analogy are informative about relevantly similar, albeit different, boundaried operations within the range of *Noûs* and *Psyché*, and of their respective objects; analogy cannot, however, be extended beyond *Noûs* to provide informative discourse about God, for there is simply no relevant similarity to be referenced between the absolutely unknowable and accessible finites.

THE DESCENT OF THE SOUL

The descending internal operations from *noēsis* and synchronic *diánoia* to diachronic *diánoia, phantasía* and *aísthesis* depict the descent of the soul; hence, the earlier-considered triad (the One, *animus*, and *anima*—which metaphorically spatializes the ranges of relevant internal, non-physical operations) is the model for understanding what mystics mean by the ambiguous phrases, "Fall of Man" and "Fall of the Soul." [16] 'Fall' is ambiguous because it is used in two quite different senses by two different theologies. Primarily, the 'Fall' refers to Adam's original sin; rarely is it applied to the critical mystical notion of the soul's descent (*káthodos*—a "going down the path") from *animus* toward corporeal things.[17] The distinction between 'Fall' and 'descent'—though not always consistently employed—becomes, whenever made, a criterion for distinguishing between two very different, often opposing, conceptions of the human condition. The 'Fall' generally means a complete break, by sin, with God with the following consequences: a radical ontological dualism between God and man; the incorrigible corruption of intellect and will, such that these faculties are incapable of achieving their proper objects (true knowledge and good work) by their own natural power; and the necessity of God's causation to remedy the utterly helpless intellect and will by extrinsic revelation, illumination, and grace in order to redeem the human condition. Contrarily, 'descent,' in Neoplatonic mysticism, does not designate a complete break with God, hence: the intellect and soul retain an ontological continuity with their source; the intellect and will are not by nature incorrigibly corrupted, but do achieve their proper objects by their own power; and it is within the soul's capability, as her natural tendency, to be the effective agent of her own ascent and restoration, although God's agency is required to effect union with him.

The descent of *anima* from *animus*, and *animus* from Unity, implied an original hermaphroditic or androgynous conjunction of *animus* (male) and *anima* (female), and their primordial union with Unity itself. This descending hierarchy within interior space is neither a cause nor an effect or moral fault, but merely the normative state of affairs; nor is the embodiment of *anima* in the world an evil or a punishment for sin.[18] Moral fault occurs when the *anima* becomes voluntarily seduced by, and loses her identity to, material objects. She thereby alienates herself from her *animus* and from Divine Unity, introduces into herself an amnesia, a diminution of intellectual awareness, and involves herself in idolatry. Referring to his *anima* as his Eve, William of St.-Thierry writes:

> O good creator! How well You created me! How splendidly You formed me! In what a suitable place You located me! Lord, You created me, as Your Apostle Paul says, in good works, which You prepared in advance, so that I might walk in them. You fashioned me to Your own image and likeness and placed me in the paradise of Your delight, that I might work and keep it—work it by practices arising from good inclinations, keep it lest the animal that crawls should creep in. But the serpent did creep in. It seduced my Eve, and through her made of me a double-dealer. For this I was expelled from the paradise of unitive consciousness, and have

become an exile in a foreign land—in the region of
unlikeness.[19]

Once upon a time You created me in Your paradise, and You
gave me the tree of life as my rightful possession for ever;
You willed, or rather You permitted, me to reach out for the
fruit of the tree of the knowledge of good and evil, as though
I had lost my taste for the good within me and would
experience whatever I could outside myself with my Eve—my
flesh—in agreement with me.[20]

Keeping in mind that the difference between *animus* and *anima* is
not literal—they are not two separate substances—their metaphorical
distinction and distance serves to focus attention on the moral need,
and required ascetical procedures, to overcome internal dissociation
and regain wholeness. The task of mystical asceticism is to reestablish
the androgynous union of noetic-psychic space, to restore the marital
union or *sympátheia* between *animus* and *anima* by reversing the
directionality of *anima* from subjection to things back to greater
likeness to her *animus*.[21] Marital union and fidelity must first be
achieved on the noetic-psychic level before the higher, mystical
marriage becomes possible; the *anima* must conform herself to *animus*
because it is *animus* which is the image of God, and the place where
the highest expression of Divine Triunity occurs. By so conforming,
the *anima* also becomes conformed to the very image of God.

No exercise is more worthy and advantageous to the man
who has reason than the exercise of what is best in him,
whereby he surpasses all other things that have souls—and
surpasses even other aspects of himself; this preeminence is
mens or *animus*. Every other part of man is subject to *mens* or
animus in order to be ruled; there is nothing more worthy of
search, nor anything more agreeably found, nor had with
greater profit, than *animus*—except, of course, that which
surpasses even the mind itself, and that would be God alone.
"Yet in fact He is not far from any of us, since it is in Him
tht we live, and move, and exist." We do not exist in our
Lord God as we do in the atmosphere. We live in Him by
fidelity; we move and continue onward through hope; we are
fixed in our attention through love. In effect, the rational
animus is founded from Him and toward Him; thus its circular
path bears in His direction, so that its good is nothing else
but His own Self. The *animus* is good only from that Good
which He is; it is the *animus* which is founded to His image
and likeness. This means that, as long as we live here (on
earth), the *animus* can reach Him, to the extent that it is

enabled to draw near by virtue of its likeness; only by being unlike does it depart from Him. . . . In short, the only thing that is really great, really good, is that the *animus* looks toward, wonders at, and grasps what is above it—then it itself is great and good. The devout image rushes to adhere to its likeness. It is the *animus* which is the image of God. By the very fact that it is His image, it is enabled to understand that it may and should cling to Him whose image it is. Thus, although (while on earth) its task is to govern the body in its care, in its better role—in memory, understanding, and love— it likes always to have its conversation there where it knows it has received whatever it is and whatever it possesses, and wherein it may hope to remain forever and finally achieve full likeness with the full sight of God—inasmuch, of course, as a man may hope, i.e., on the condition that he does not fail to conform his life to genuine hope.[22]

THE ASCENT OF THE SOUL

"The path up and down is one and the same."[23] The ascent, or inward motion of the soul, takes the same path as the reverse, or outward movement. Plotinus remarks that the natural motion of the soul is like a circular motion around an interior center; it is not simply a solipsistic, individual center, however, but a communitarian Center where all other centers coincide.[24] William uses the same model, perhaps taken from Plotinus, but emphasizes the necessity of morally calibrating the circular "way of life" according to the Center which is Truth. Right orientation of the affections of *anima*, and her acquiring the character of fidelity, is crucial to mystical asceticism.

The innermost recesses. Alas! Alas! The wicked walk around in a circle; in conformity with Your great depth, O God, You have multiplied the sons of men. We grow dizzy, turning in the circle of error, and we are unable to attain the center of unconcealment, the unchanging point of unity which, in its standing permanent, gives movement to all else. This center is Truth. It is the One who said: "I am the Truth," and "Know the truth; the truth will free you." At any rate, one will get free of the circle of error. Let us see if the circle in which we move is drawn from the center of truth and determined by it. If the rotation is completed with rightness, the circle returns to its point of departure, according to the rules of the center of truth; but if the contrary be the case, error is manifest. One ought to consider one's affection and action. If one's affection is fixed on the center of truth, the curvature of the exterior act will result according to exact relations to the center. We owe all our affections to God. When one faithfully adheres to Him, whatever the movement of the circle of activities be, it cannot deflect from rightness, but rather converges with the rightness of its point of departure, and at every point equally coincides with the center of truth. The point can exist without the circle, but the circle cannot be drawn without the point.[25]

This presupposes that the mystic must first know the character of his own *anima*, assess its directionality, and orient it toward unity. It is axiomatic that the necessary condition for knowing God is first knowing oneself, since God is recognized in the nature and operations of the interior structure of metaphorical space.[26] It also presupposes that the *anima* can initiate her ascent by virtue of the natural love which she herself is.[27] William clearly states that the circular path of the soul, her erotic bent, is an implicit, thoroughly natural (not supernatural) tendency or aptitude to know God.[28] Her movement is a kind of memory; and the explicit calibration of her natural erotic course fixed to the center, by will, constitutes an ascensionist return. Since the soul is erotic by nature, her directionality is implicit or innate; but properly and explicitly clarified, properly calibrated from an ecliptic or erratic path to a consistently circular movement, which is accomplished by conforming love to truth, the curvature of *anima* space-time becomes also conformed to synchronic *animus* and thereby locates, and comes in contact with, the center of both concentric circles.

Herein lies the ascetical notion of liberty. Freedom is not the ability to choose between good and evil; rather, it must be understood in the sense of a liberation from alienation on the part of the *anima*— an alienation from her *animus* caused by her identifying herself with material objects. Freedom is the property of the ascension of the soul toward *animus* and thereby toward her center; it is therefore a liberation from a state of idolatry. The essence of truth, for the mystic, consists in this liberation, such that the disclosure of truth radically depends on the rightness of the will. Ordinary conceptions of truth do not conjoin it to freedom or liberty. We hardly ever think of the truth of will, and so it seems strange that the very essence of truth, even the rightness of a statement, consists in a rightness of will. Yet, this very rightness, this ascetical process of liberation, when it takes on the character of constancy becomes also fidelity. And it is this kind of faith, a fidelity as the constancy of liberating love, that brings *anima* into the orbit of universal and catholic truth, into the orbit of *animus*.[29]

What have been traditionally called "theological virtues" are, in effect, anagogical virtues; faith, hope, and love are ascensionist virtues which conform *anima* to *animus*, and *both* to the Divine Unity itself. Thus, they are what may be called conjugal virtues. Conformity of *anima* to *animus* brings *anima* into direct access to noetic law-like patterns or paradigms, i.e., those formulations of Divinity such as the 'Trinity,' which are the ultimate articulations of Divine Union logically possible within the range of human cognitivity. *Anima* then becomes capable of actively reflecting, as in a clear and undistorting mirror, the object of her innate love.[30]

> Of all the means of salvation which the God "of our salvation" has proposed to man for observance, as St. Paul says, "Three remain: faith, hope and charity." Mortal men, who wish to be saved, must have these three virtues. The Holy Trinity has constituted this little trinity in the faithful soul as Its own image and likeness. Through this little trinity, our inner man is constantly renewed, according to the image of Him Who created us. That is where the working of human salvation takes place, which all of divinely revealed writing takes care to construct and gather up in the hearts of the faithful. A man begins from faith. As long as we are on the way, still far from the Lord, St. Paul says that we should not forget that "Christ dwells in our hearts by faith."[31]

> Those who truly seek the Trinitarian God, strive to possess in themselves the trinity of these three virtues, and they are eager to model themselves on the teaching of this trinity. The witness of these virtues is an inner paradise of delight, overflowing with charm and with clean and holy pleasure.[32]

THE DESCENT AND ASCENT OF GOD

The Incarnation doctrine, the teaching concerning the union of God—specifically, the second Person of the Trinity, the Word, the perfect Image of the Father—and man (uniquely in the case of Jesus) exemplifies the most important ascetical model for Christian Neoplatonic mysticism. The human *animus*, as the constitutional image of God *(imago Dei)*, is thereby conceived as the *capax Dei* ("roomy enough" to receive God); there is, in effect, a kinship or kindredness, a native "coextensivity" between the *animus*, itself an image of God, and the Word, the perfect Image of the Father.[33] The conjunction of

God and man, expressed in the noetic doctrine concerning Jesus, occurs in the union of God and the human *animus;* thus the hominization of God and the divinization or apotheosis of man is accomplished simultaneously.[34] But the union is achieved on the order of metaphorical, not literal, space; the union of God and man is not physical nor analogical, but anagogical, occurring on a plane where a convergence of centers and a coextensivity of interiors is real in a way impossible physically. By this union of God and the *animus,* the human operations of *nóēsis* and synchronic *diánoia* are divinized, and by extension to *anima,* divinity extends its presence to the operations of diachronic *diánoia, phantasía,* and *aísthēsis.*

With this appearance of the divine Word in the human condition, there begins an ascetical pedagogy on the ontological, noetic, psychological, and moral levels which permits the image of God to positively and consciously enter on the path toward realizing union with God. The importance of the Christ event, for the Neoplatonizing mind, is that it provides an overwhelming paradigm for the divinization of man, outlining precisely the path toward wholeness, reintegration, at-one-ment, union.

> Since we have fallen into temporal realities, and by loving them we are impeded from eternal realities, a timely remedy was prepared for our cure. . . . Carnal forms have detained us by their love, into which we fell through consent to sin; so it is against these forms that one must strive in order to rise up. For this reason the Son of God, *Who is of the nature of God, emptied Himself to assume the condition of a slave,* that men might become the sons of God. In effect, we are not moved locally toward Him Who is everywhere present, but by good desires and good habits. And that would have been impossible for us, had not Wisdom itself decided to bear our such great infirmity, had it not given us a model of life in a man, since we ourselves are men. . . . To heal souls, God adopts all sorts of means suitable to the times which are ordered by His marvellous Wisdom; in no way has He shown more beneficial regard for the human race than when the very Wisdom of God, that is, the only Son, Who is consubstantial and coeternal with the Father, thought it befitting His dignity to assume all Man, and *the Word was made flesh and lived among us.* In effect, He thereby demonstrated to carnal men, who were not able to perceive the truth with their spirit and who were absorbed in their corporeal senses, the high place among creatures held by human nature. Not only did He make Himself visible, which He could have done by taking on

an ethereal body sufficient enough to hold the attention of our gaze, but He appeared to men in a real man.[35]

The union of God and man in Jesus is thus the unitive assumption not only of an historical individual, but of all human kind. Jesus, whose humanity is worthy of God, provides the paradigm for what lies open to every other human subject, and embraces not only all of human nature, but all that is relevant to human culture as well— bread and wine becomes subsumed into union with God in man. The paradigm of Christ is that of the restoration of union, the healing of the dichotomy between *animus* and *anima*, and even the remedial incorporation of the physical world, by construing it as sacrament, in the mystical ascent.[36] In effect, the union of God and man emphasizes that, on the level of metaphorical space, the divine center and the center of *animus-anima* are not two, but one center, and that the circles of *animus* and *anima* are coextensive with the *persona* of the divine Word. The awareness of things divine and human converge in one reality.[37]

The Incarnation doctrine asserts that the human *animus*, by reason of this union, has access, as communitarian, to the divine awareness interior to the Trinitarian life.[38]

This is why the Lord Himself appeared to men in human flesh: He took away from the world the vanity of idols and presented instead, to those thinking of God, the unity that exists among the Persons of the Trinity, and the notion of a Trinity in Oneness. With the brilliant light of His divinity, He stripped human ideas, even those inspired by faith, of empty imaginings. He showed that, for the time being, understanding of the divinity was beyond man, so He taught men His own way of thinking about God. All the actions and words of the Word of God are one word for us. All that we read of Him, hear of Him, speak of Him, think of Him—whether provoking love or inciting fear—call us, send us, to only one reality. Of this much has been said and nothing has been said, for no one can come to this reality unless it first approaches us, seeks us out, and shines the brightness of its face on us, so that in the light of its face we are able to see where we walk. God's face, as it makes itself known to the inner sense of lovers, is His will; His face is our understanding of His unconcealment.[39]

The union of the Word with *animus-anima*, a bond of love, is the path to union with God precisely because the same Person who takes up his dwelling in the *animus* is the dwelling place of the

Father. In joining himself to *animus,* the Word thus puts within man's range contact with the divine Community.

> These are the words of the Prophet Daniel: "God is in heaven." Then David says, "He lives in Jerusalem." Tell us who reach out to You, who are out of breath running after you, tell us, I beg, where do you live, Rabbi. Quickly You reply: "I am in the Father and the Father is in Me." "On that day you will understand that I am in My Father, and you are in Me, and I am in you." Finally, "I am in them, and You are in Me, that they may be completely one." Then the Father is the place where You are, and You are the place where the Father is; even more: we are the place where You are, and You are the place where we are. Since, then, O Lord Jesus, You are in the Father and the Father is in You, You are Your own dwelling place, most high and indivisible Trinity; You are to Yourself Your place, You are Your heaven; and because You have no other place where You are, You subsist completely from Yourself and in Yourself.

> When You dwell in us, we are Your heaven. . . . And You are also our heaven, where we should ascend and live. For us to live in You, or having Your dwelling place in us, is heaven for us, as it seems to me; Your heaven of heaven is Your inner presence *(aeternitas)* to Yourself, by which You are what You are in Yourself. The Father is in the Son, and the Son is in the Father; and the Unity by which You, Father and Son, are One is the Holy Spirit. . . .[40]

By this conjunction of the Son and the human *animus,* man ascends, with Christ, to the interpersonal union of the Trinity. The Trinity presents a noetic paradigm, given the union between the Word and man, of the possibilities open to the human person as the communitarian space of mutual indwelling of persons. The 'Trinity' constitutes the *highest expression or conception possible* of a union or communion aimed at in mysticism. Here again, reference is made to a constitutive metaphorical space which, while not literally formulatable, is eminently real.

> Either because of the necessity of argumentation, or because of the difficulties involved in treating or speaking [about the Persons of the Trinity], the Fathers preferred to use a plural number in regard to names used to designate the relationships there. In order to reply with one single word to the question "What are these Three? " they would say, "Three Persons."

But the phrase "Three Persons" must be understood in such a way that one does not imagine any mass, interval, any differences which would entail unlikeness, nor any sort of distinction that would imply either a separation or a confusion of Persons. One cannot even think in terms of part and whole, because the Trinity is not greater than any one Person, nor is any Person lesser than the entire Trinity. Granted that Each seems determined by the Other, nevertheless, as far as faith can make out, one must understand that these Three, called Persons, are infinite in Themselves; Each is in the Other and Each is in All; They are All in All, and this All is One.[41]

The goal of mysticism is to enter into this union of mutual, inter-personal indwelling which characterizes the oneness of God—a union which cannot be objectively or literally described, but can only be grasped by a certain *agnitio* (recognition) that arises from that likeness or conformity achieved by the compresence of the Word and *animus*. William characterizes mystical knowledge as an *agnitio* or *agnoscere*, which he construes as being the constitutive character of the person, whether human or divine.[42] *Agnitio* describes a mode of unconceal-ment or "understanding" that brings to light the hidden interior structure of the self, and grasps the self as the insinuation of another.[43]

Indeed, that awareness which the Father and the Son have of Each Other constitutes Their very Unity; and this Unity is the Holy Spirit. This mutual awareness is nothing else but the very substance by which They are what They are. By this awareness, "no one knows the Father but the Son; and no one knows the Son but the Father, and he to whom They wish to make themselves known." These are the words of the Lord. They do, in fact, reveal Themselves to some, namely, to those They will; They become known to those to whom They freely give the Holy Spirit, Who is Their common Will. Those to whom the Father and the Son reveal Each Other know the Father and the Son just as They know Themselves, for such persons possess within Their mutual awareness; they also have within themselves the mutual Unity, Will or Love of the Father and the Son, namely, the Holy Spirit.[44]

"Spirit" is the power to relate in a completely unitive way, tran-scending the frontiers of all and any "environment." What occurs paradigmatically in God is also open to man.[45] Communitarianism describes not only the object of mystical union, but the model to which man must conform himself to achieve this union.

There is a most intimate illustration William gives to describe the mystical union, employing the image of the *sponsa-Sponsus* (bride and Bridegroom) relation. The identity of sorts between the image of God and its Archetype, God, verified by the union of the Word, and elevated into the Trinity by the ascension of the same Word, is accomplished by the restoration of the right orientation of love such that it becomes understanding—*amor intellectus*. The image, the *animus*, through the actual realization of its own little trinity—fidelity, hope, love—is able to enter into mystical union. The human self becomes spouse.

> This is the place of that marvelous conjoining, that mutual enjoyment of sweetness, and of incomprehensible and unimaginable joy. . . . The joining of man to God, the joining of the created spirit to the Uncreated! When one says *sponsa* and *Sponsus*, human language is in search of words to express in some way the sweetness and delight of this conjoining, which is, in reality, nothing other than the very Unity of God the Father and the Son—Their Kiss, Their Embrace, Their Love, Their Goodness, and all which, in this infinitely simple Unity, is common to both of Them. This Unity is the Holy Spirit, God, Love, Who is both the Giver and the Gift. And there, in that little bed, it is the same Embrace, that same Kiss, Who unites Himself and His *sponsa* to Himself; and then she comes to know as she is known. Just as in the kisses of lovers, their breathing, by sweet and mutual contraction, pours out from one into the other, so also the created spirit completely pours itself out into the Spirit Who created it, and the Creator infuses Himself as He wills; man becomes one breath with God.[46]

BIBLIOGRAPHICAL NOTES

William's dates are c. 1085–1148. His works, in order of writing, and their availability in published editions are as follows:

De contemplando Deo (c. 1120). *On Contemplating God*, tr. Geoffrey Webb and Adrian Walker (London, 1955); *On Contemplating God, Prayer, Meditations*, tr. Sister Penelope, C.S.M.V., Cistercian Fathers Series 3 (Spencer, MA, 1971); *Prière, Contemplation de Dieu, Nature et dignité de l'amour*, ed. and tr. into French by Robert Thomas (Chambarand, 1965); *Guillaume de Saint-Thierry: La contemplation de Dieu; L'oraison de Dom Guillaume*, text and tr. Dom Jacques Hourlier (Paris, 1959).

De natura et dignitate amoris (1119–22). *On the Nature and Dignity of Love*, tr. Geoffrey Webb and Adrian Walker (London, 1956); see Thomas, as above; *The Nature and Dignity of Love*, tr. Thomas X. Davis (Kalamazoo, 1981).

De sacramento altaris (1128). PL 180, 205–48.

Meditativae orationes (1130–35). See Sister Penelope, as above; *The Meditations of William of St. Thierry*, tr. by a religious of C.S.M.V. (New York, 1954); *Oraisons meditées*, text and tr. Robert Thomas (Chamberand, 1964); *Meditations et prières*, ed. and tr. J.-M. Déchanet (Brussels, 1945).

De natura corporis et animae (1135–38). *De la nature du corps et de l'âme*, in *Oeuvres choisies de Guillaume de Saint-Thierry*, tr. J.-M. Déchanet (Paris, 1944), pp. 81–147; PL 180, 695–726.

Expositio in Epistolam ad Romanos (1135–38). PL 180, 547–694. *Exposition on the Epistle to the Romans*, tr. John Baptist Hasbrouck (Kalamazoo, 1980).

Expositio altera super Cantica Canticorum (1138). *Exposition on the Song of Songs*, tr. Mother Columba Hart, O.S.B. (Spencer, MA, 1970); *Commentaire sur le cantique des cantiques*, text and tr. Robert Thomas (Chambarand, 1961); *Exposé sur le cantique des cantiques*, text J.-M. Déchanet, French tr. M. Dumontier (Paris, 1962).

Disputatio adversus Petrum Abaelardum (1138). PL 180, 249–82.

Speculum fidei (1139–44). *The Mirror of Faith*, tr. Geoffrey Webb and Adrian Walker (London, 1959); *Deux traités sur la foi: Le miroir de la foi; L'énigme de la foi*, text and tr. M.-M. Davy (Paris, 1959).

Aenigma fidei (1139–44). *The Enigma of Faith*, tr. John D. Anderson (Kalamazoo, 1974); Davy, as above.

Epistola ad fratres de Monte Dei (1145). *The Golden Epistle*, tr. Theodore Berkeley, O.C.S.O. (Spencer, MA, 1971); *The Golden Epistle of Abbot William of Saint-Thierry to the Carthusians of Mont Dieu*, tr. Walter Shewring, ed. Justin McCann (London, 1930); *Lettre aux frères du Mont-Dieu*, text and tr. Robert Thomas (Chambarand, 1968).

IV

St. Bernard,
the Canticle of Canticles,
and Mystical Poetry

JAMES I. WIMSATT

In his doctrine and in his life St. Bernard of Clairvaux (1090–1153)
firmly joined the active to the contemplative life; the affirmative way
to mystical union to which his theory and practice point thereby
contrasts with the *via negativa* of medieval contemplatives who
followed Pseudo-Dionysius. Convinced of the necessity of action,
Bernard became one of the most prominent public figures of his age.
He was a great monastic reformer, a counsellor of popes and kings,
a powerful enemy of heresy, an eminent preacher and spiritual writer,
famous to later times as "Doctor Mellifluus" and "last of the Fathers."
Nevertheless, despite his public celebrity, it is most of all his mysticism—his part in that most secret and incommunicable aspect of
life—which has elevated him to an exalted place in human memory.
In the *Divine Comedy* it is Bernard, not Beatrice or Aquinas or
Bonaventure, who leads Dante the pilgrim to his final vision of God,
the ultimate contemplative experience. With Chaucer also "Bernard
the monk" is the authority *par excellence* on heaven; we must admit,
says Chaucer, that even he "ne saugh nat all."

Though Bernard probably composed little verse, the nature and
force of his writings make him in all but metrics a great mystical
poet; and in the great body of literature that his works inspired are
fine poems which reflect faithfully his mystical thought. Not surprisingly, these poems draw heavily on the Canticle of Canticles,

the biblical love song that supplied the texts for Bernard's magnificent series of sermons in which he most thoroughly sets forth his mystical theology. Much poetry, especially of medieval and renaissance times, has been classified as mystical on uncertain grounds; the category has been a catch-all, not clearly defined. Our consideration here of Bernard's sermons and of two poems inspired by them will perhaps show how mystical poetry may be more precisely conceived.

Twentieth-century interpretations of Canticles differ fundamentally from the medieval tradition of exegesis on which Bernard's sermons, despite their marvellous originality, are firmly based. For the typical modern reader, layperson or religious, Canticles is a beautiful and inspiring paean to love between man and woman. The descriptions of the love-partners and their reciprocal expressions of longing and joy combine an apparent unremitting sensuousness with an innocent candor that elevates and ennobles human sexual activity. The book's controlling images are those appropriate to erotic love poetry: the banquet, the garden, the chamber, the bed. It opens with the beloved's passionate call, "Let him kiss me with the kiss of his mouth," and it has numerous statements that to today's readers, conditioned as they are by a sex-oriented society, pertain without doubt to love-play: "I sat down under his shadow whom I desired: and his fruit was sweet to my palate" (2:3); "I sleep, and my heart watcheth: the voice of my beloved knocking: Open to me, my sister, my love, my dove, my undefiled, for my head is full of dew, and my locks of the drops of the night. . . . My beloved put his hand through the key hole, and my bowels were moved at his touch" (5:2,4). Notwithstanding modern perception of such passages, medieval Christian interpretations firmly shut out carnal applications for them. The bridegroom was seen as Christ, and the bride simultaneously or alternatively as the Church, the perfected soul, or the Blessed Virgin. The relationship depicted, then, was conceived of as wholly nonphysical.

No one is more positive about the complete spirituality of Canticles than is Bernard, whose eighty-six sermons[1] treat the opening chapters and comprise the most famous and edifying treatment of the book in the long and rich history of its interpretation. "Listen with modest ears," he says to his audience of monks, "to the sermon on love that is at hand. And when you consider the lovers themselves, think not of a man and a woman but of the Word and the soul" (61.2). He would not be occupied with Canticles, he declares, if he thought it dealt with carnal lovers (75.2). A lamentable narrowness, a reader today may think, wholly inimical to the poetic content of Canticles. Yet Bernard assimilates the text to his own spiritual experience, capitalizes on its pregnant figurative and emotive content—as well

as that of the rest of the Bible, especially Psalms and the Epistles—
and produces perhaps the most poetical work in all of the great
patristic literature. In his treatment Canticles emerges as indeed the
Song of all Songs, the most exalted of love poems, a celebration of
the most intense love possible, that between God and the perfected
soul. Throughout these sermons Bernard is a great exegete, homilist,
and mystical poet.

In his interpretation Bernard manifests a knowledge of the whole
exegetical tradition, utilizing particularly the model constructed nine
centuries earlier by Origen, who described Canticles as a marriage-
drama. "It seems to me," Origen says, "that this little book is an
epithalamium, that is to say, a marriage-song, which Solomon wrote
in the form of a drama and sang under the figure of the Bride, about
to wed and burning with heavenly love towards her Bridegroom,
who is the Word of God." [2] Bernard in turn finds a similar drama
in the text; what he sees is expressly unseen and unheard:

> It is not a melody that resounds abroad but the very music of
> the heart, not a trilling on the lips but an inward pulsing of
> delight, a harmony not of voices but of wills. . . . Only the
> singer hears it and the one to whom he sings—the lover and
> the beloved. (1.11)

Like Origen, Bernard finds that on one level of apprehension Canticles
deals with the Church, the whole body of Christian souls. On this
level the kiss for which the Bride calls is the Incarnation of Christ.
The meaning of the kiss for the individual soul is derived from, and
parallel to, this ecclesiological significance. Bernard finds this to be
the "inpouring of the Holy Spirit," a mystical contact with God such
as Paul experienced when he was caught up to the third heaven:
"Things which no eye has seen, and no ear has heard, things beyond
the mind of man, were revealed to Paul by God through his Spirit,
that is, through him who is the kiss of his mouth" (8.7). Bernard
more than Origen speaks of the action of Canticles as interior, as
"a mirror of the inner drama of the coming and going of God in
the soul." [3] For Bernard, who personally knew such coming and
going, Canticles was the veritable "book of experience" (3.1).

Since Bernard's was undoubtedly a powerful mind, one may well
ask how his transmutation of an erotic love poem into a spiritual
work may be rationalized. Several factors may be adduced. First of
all, a dispassionate reading shows that the denotative content of
Canticles, especially in the Vulgate version of the Bible, is not as
unremitting in its sensuousness as modern perception finds it. The
imagery is largely equivocal. For example, how do we interpret the
bride's statement which follows her opening call for the kiss: "Draw

me: we will run after thee to the odor of thy ointments. The king hath brought me into his storerooms. We will be glad and rejoice in thee, remembering thy breasts more than wine. The righteous love thee" (1.3)? In the light of the last sentence a spiritual interpretation is at least as apt here as a carnal one. And so it is for many passages. Nevertheless, Bernard does not sidestep the carnal implications when they are unequivocal. He accepts the poem as an epithalamium, and he knows that the *thalamus* is the nuptial bed. At the same time, he thinks of the marital images as figures provided by the Holy Ghost to sense-bound humanity, presenting analogies to the unseen and unseeable:

> But that which is unchangeable is incomprehensible, and hence cannot be expressed in language. . . . We are taught by the authority of the Fathers and the usage of the Scriptures that it is lawful to appropriate suitable analogies from the things we know. (51.7)

Thus, though Bernard as much as Paul disdains the corrupted body of fallen man, he can find in description of carnal union an analogy to mystical union. Obviating any apparent inconsistency in his view, furthermore, is the fact that Bernard saw presented by the letter of Canticles no illicit relationship, but rather the most noble form of friendship on this earth, marriage, a sacrament of the Church:

> No sweeter names can be found to embody that sweet interflow of affections between the Word and the soul, than bridegroom and bride. . . . They share the same inheritance, the same table, the same home, the same marriage-bed, they are flesh of each other's flesh. (7.2)

In marriage husband and wife become one flesh, in mystical ecstasy the Word and the soul become one spirit.

Furthermore, one must keep in mind that Bernard saw the image of marital union strictly as analogical. The Holy Spirit shows us where we may find "suitable words" to express "the ecstactic ascent of the purified mind to God, and the loving descent of God into the soul" (31.6). The carnal reference has no significance in itself, existing purely for its spiritual application.

Sexual love is not even the first rung on Bernard's spiritual ladder. Yet there is a carnal love which is needful to mystical progress as Bernard presents it, love of the body of Christ. This love is efficacious in the first place in turning man away from all other sensual affection:

> Your affection for your Lord Jesus should be both tender and intimate, to oppose the sweet enticements of sensual life.

Sweetness conquers sweetness as one nail drives out another. (20.4)

His emphasis on love for the body of Christ made Bernard a crucial figure in the medieval development of affective devotion to Christ the man, which centers particularly on his Passion. "This is my philosophy . . . to know Jesus and him crucified" (43.4). He advocates this love not only for driving out inferior sensual affections, but also as the only way to the divinity of Christ.

Bernard believes that contemplative union is the ultimate experience of love, and that it must be approached through loving. Since man of himself can only love carnally, however, he must first of all, in his approach to a spiritual experience of God, come to the love of Jesus in his human form. Indeed, this is why Christ became man:

I think this is the principal reason why the invisible God willed to be seen in the flesh and to converse with men as man. He wanted to recapture the affections of carnal men, who were unable to love in any other way, by first drawing them to the salutary love of his own humanity, and then gradually to raise them to a spiritual love. (20.6)

The Incarnation is the ultimate accommodation of divinity to man's understanding.

Because mystical ecstasy involves spiritual union with God, who is Love (1 John 4:8,16), love of Christ in his humanity is the logical way to approach God. Coming to know Jesus in his Crucifixion can lead to following him in his Ascension to Heaven, at least part of the way. And though man while in the body must always descend from such spiritual heights, the possibility of returning by the same way is ever present.

Later mystics who adhered to the mystical theology of Pseudo-Dionysius also commended affective devotion to the crucified Jesus. However, while they saw this devotion as necessary in purging the soul—in driving out other carnal loves—to them it was not a step on the road to contemplative union. For in their theory even carnal affection for Jesus had to be shut out before divinity could be approached. It was not that Bernard's ontological premises differed from theirs as regards body and spirit. He too thought of Christ in body and sacrament as radically different in kind from the divine Christ:

I too [i.e., like the angels] have the Word, but the Word made flesh, and the Truth is set before me, but in the sacrament. An angel is nourished with the richness of the wheat, is satiated with the pure grain; but in this life I have to be

content with the husk, as it were, of the sacrament, with the
bran of the flesh, with the chaff of the letter, with the veil of
the faith. (33.3)

Bernard's conception of the unitive experience itself, however, did
differ from that of the mystics of the *via negativa*. To him it was
dependent on the soul's recovery of its likeness to God effected
through devotion to the man whose likeness to God was never
corrupted. A corrected carnal love could thereby be elevated to a
spiritual plane.

Love effects contemplative union and love comprises the union:

I love because I love; I love that I may love. Love is a great
reality, and if it returns to its beginning and goes back to its
origin, seeking its source again, it will always draw afresh
from it, and thereby flow freely. (83.4)

Nevertheless, if Bernard find that this carnal love is a step on the
way to contemplation, he longs no less than other contemplatives,
to be free of the body, and even of the most holy carnal images, in
order to partake of the unmediated vision that the angels enjoy.

Most of the numerous Middle English poems that express affection
for Jesus in his Passion have been influenced in some way by
Bernard's devotional writings. Almost all of these are poems of
meditation, lacking a mystical dimension; they are designed to produce in the reader or hearer penitence and edification, but not to
evoke or imitate the contemplative process. One of these poems,
though, has a thoroughly-developed mystical dimension. It displays
beautifully the progress which Bernard postulates; the Passion meditation with which it begins turns neatly into a representation of
contemplative union. This anonymous poem, "In a valey of this
restles mynde," [4] has suffered at the hands of critics because of its
own emotional force. They have spoken of its emotional intensity
while remaining unaware of its firm intellectual conception. In a
comparable way, before Etienne Gilson analyzed and explained St.
Bernard's well-developed mystical theology,[5] the affective fervor of
his writing had obscured its doctrinal integrity and consistency for
many modern commentators.

The diverse and rich poetic materials of "In a valey" include
features of secular love poetry as well as standard elements of the
meditative lyric. Its opening is that of a secular love poem. Likewise
indebted to the secular lyrics, as well as to the meditative poems,
is Christ's appearance in the poem as complaining lover and wounded
knight. Also from the meditations are the sharp antitheses of the
"Improperia," the standard reproaches that Christ directs to man,

his crucifier. Nevertheless, while all of these materials are important, the main source for "In a valey" is Canticles and its tradition, led by Bernard, of mystical exegesis. Apart from the poem's refrain, specific echoes of Canticles are more noticeable in the second half of the work, the contemplative part; however, in the Passion meditation that the first half comprises there are indirect references to Canticles by way of the exegetes. To cite just one instance, the bloody shirt that Christ is said to wear (1. 28) is drawn from common explanations of Canticles 5:10: "My beloved is white and ruddy."

Except that the narrator's experience in the poem takes place in the valley of his mind, rather than in an objective countryside, the opening is that of a typical *chanson d'aventure*. The narrator travels over mountain and meadow to find a "trewe love," and in accord with the spirit of such poems his search is soon successful. On a hill sitting under a tree he finds a wounded knight, kinglike in appearance—clearly Christ on Calvary—complaining of the cruelty of his beloved, man's soul. Because of his love, he left his kingdom and followed her:

> "I purveide for hir a paleis precious;
> She flytt, I folowyd, I luffed hir soon,
> I suffred this peyne pitevous
> *Quia amore langueo.* (11. 21–24)

The refrain drawn from Canticles (2:5; 5:8), "For I languish with love," concludes each of the sixteen eight-line stanzas; it establishes and emphasizes the fact that spiritual love is the theme of the poem. As in Canticles the lover in the poem variously identifies himself as brother, humble suitor, bridegroom and husband of the beloved; by using other images from Canticles he also presents himself as pursuing hunter and nursing mother. In the dream realm of the poem, the transitions from one role to another are made easily; even his sudden appearance in the fourteenth stanza as the soul's mother presents no major problem of understanding.

After emphasizing in the third stanza his affection for the beloved, in the next four stanzas the knight echoes the Improperia, enumerating the proofs of his love that he has given the soul, and contrasting these sharply with what the soul has done to him. He saved her from beating, yet she has beaten him; he clothed her in heavenly grace, but she has set a bloody shirt on him:

> "I crowned hir with blis, and she me with thorn,
> I led hir to chaumbir, and she me to die;

> I brought hir to worshipe, and she me to scorn;
> I dide hir reverence, and she me vilonye."   (11. 33–36)

She gave him red gloves with which he woos her, and she has shod him with sharp nails, while in his love there was never deceit:

> "All me membres y have opened hir to;
> My bodi I maad hir hertis baite."   (11. 54–55)

These last lines, focussing on Christ's wounds, particularly the wound in his side, culminate the Passion meditation and provide a key transition to Christ's active wooing and winning of the soul in the second half of the poem. In this later part the figures of the narrator who observes and of the soul who is wooed are no longer clearly differentiated; the narrator increasingly seems a participant rather than a passive onlooker. His meditation, then, leads directly to his partaking dramatically in the union with Christ which the soul eventually gains.

The opening of his body to the beloved which Christ speaks of in line 54 prepares for the introduction of the primary image of the poem, whereby the wound in Christ's side is seen as the marriage chamber that Christ provides for the soul:

> "In my side y have made hir neste,
> Loke in! how wyde a wound is heere!
> This is hir chaumbir, heere shal she reste,
> That she and y may slepe in fere."   (11. 57–60)

The image of the wound as the marriage chamber and a place in which the soul may "nest" is particularly potent in uniting the wooing of the soul with the meditation on the Passion which occupies the first part; the wounds on which the narrator meditates are the wounds to which the soul is enticed and mystically enters. A movement from the carnal to the spiritual, from the action of meditation to the repose of contemplation, is effected.

The context of Canticles which has been present in the background of the poem from the beginning is brought to the forefront in these lines. Two verses from Canticles and their traditional interpretations provide a basis for the wording. The wound as the nest of the soul stems from Canticles 2:14, where the bridegroom addresses the spouse as "My dove in the clefts of the rock, in the hollow place of the wall." The clefts were usually interpreted as the five wounds of Christ, and the hollow place specifically as the hole in his side made by the spear of Longinus. Bernard, making particular use of Origen, finds in the wounds a place of contemplation where the perfected soul can make its nest. He desires to be "as the dove nesting in the highest point of the cleft." From this position *inside* the wound, he hopes that like Moses of Exodus 33 placed in a cleft of a rock, he "may be able to see at least the back of the Lord as he passes by" (61.6). Meditation on the body of Christ takes one within this body and thence to mystical experience.

When the poet of "In a valey" speaks of the nest of the soul and equates it with the bridal chamber, he is following in the line of Bernard's reading and is signifying a place of contemplation, or a place where contemplation is attainable. In later stanzas this compound image of nest and chamber is assimilated to other metaphors for the place of contemplation, most notably the garden and the bed. The image performs a strategic function in unifying the poem, and it effects the transition from meditation to contemplation in a way that conforms imaginatively to Bernard's conception.

In the next stanzas Christ continues to entice the soul by pointing out the benefits to man of his suffering. The cleansing and healing powers of Christ's blood remain prominent as he reproaches the soul for its present uncleanness and its indifference to the proffered bridal chamber:

"Wold she loke onys out of hir house
Of fleishli affeccioun and unclennes;
Hir bed is made, hir bolstir is in bliss,
Hir chaumbir is chosen, suche ar no moo.
Loke out on me at the wyndows of kyndenes,
    Quia amore langueo.   (11. 99–104)

The windows of nature—of "kyndenes"—through which the soul may see the bed and chamber derive from another passage of Canticles: "Behold he standeth behind our wall, looking through the windows, looking through the lattices" (2:9). "Our wall" was usually interpreted as the house of the body, the "windows" as the senses. Origen provides one potent model for this interpretation. "Forthwith, then, let the Word of God speak first to this fair and noble soul, to whom he has appeared by means of her bodily senses—that is, through her reading of Scriptures and hearing of doctrine—as it were, through windows . . . and then calling her to come out of doors and, being removed from the bodily senses, to cease to be in the flesh." [6]

The bed prepared for the soul in the poem, associated with the "little bed" of Canticles 3:1 provides another metaphor for the place of contemplation, and its location within the chamber makes it doubly suitable for mystical experience. Christ is calling the soul to look outside its fleshly body at its chosen bed and chamber "in blisse." As mystical union ever comes unexpectedly, so all at once it is accomplished, and in the next stanza the soul is on the bed within the chamber.

> "My love is in hir chaumbir—holde youre pees!
> Make ye no noise, but lete hir slepe." (11. 105–06)

The soul is sleeping the sleep of the contemplative, that of the *sponsa* (bride) in Canticles 2:7, where the bridegroom adjures the "daughters of Jerusalem" to "stir not up, nor make the beloved to awake, till she please." In commenting on this verse, Bernard states:

> This sleep of the bride, however, is not the tranquil repose of the body that for a time sweetly lulls the fleshly senses, nor that dreaded sleep whose custom it is to take life away completely. Further still is it removed from that deathly sleep by which a man perseveres irrevocably in sin and so dies. It is a slumber which is vital and watchful, which enlightens the heart, drives away death, and communicates eternal life. (52.3)

In the poem the soul's sleep clearly signifies the ecstasy of communion with God.

The mystical experience occupies but the one stanza. In the next Christ suddenly calls the soul back from its sleep to tribulation and adversity. He chides it with a question:

> "Shulde y alwey fede thee
> With children mete? Nay, love, not so!
> I wol preve thi love with adversite,
> *Quia amore langueo.* (11. 117–20)

The switch is unexpected, especially since Christ has told those around to "lete hir slepe." Nevertheless, the sequence of action in Canticles is similar and presents a comparable problem. Shortly after the bridegroom has told the daughters of Jerusalem not to disturb his beloved, he calls to her, "Arise, make haste, my love, my dove, my beautiful one, and come" (2:10). Bernard explains this summons:

> Who says this? Doubtless the Bridegroom. And is he not the one who, shortly before, earnestly forbade that his beloved be awakened? . . . Are we to think that the Bridegroom is moved by caprice, first willing something and then rejecting it? Of course not. Rather you must acknowledge here those changes that I have previously and more than once explained

to you concerning holy inactivity and essential action, how
this life does not cater to constant contemplation or prolonged
leisure, since we are impelled by the more cogent and more
immediate demands of work and duty. (58.1)

As one moves from carnal to heavenly love of Christ and then
returns, so he goes from action to contemplation and back. As a
result of the summons back to action, Bernard says, the bride feels
a desire for "good works, the desire to bring forth fruit for the
Bridegroom, for to her the Bridegroom is life, and death gain" (58.1).

The "food of children" from which the soul is called in the poem
is the contemplative ecstasy granted to one who has followed Christ's
injunction and become as a little child. Even such a soul, however,
can have this food but seldom in this life. To compensate for the
deprivation, it gains the knowledge that God always supports it and
that it will eventually gain permanent bliss, as Christ promises in
the poem's conclusion:

"In wele and in wo y am ay to supporte;
Myn owne wif, go not me fro!
This meede is markid whan thou art mort,
   Quia amore langueo."   (11. 125–28)

Bernard's further comment on the bridegroom's summons to the
bride is strictly consonant with the ending of the poem:

It is no small consolation to her that she hears "come," and
not "go," knowing from this that she is being invited rather
than sent, and that the Bridegroom will be coming with her.
For what will she reckon difficult with him as her companion?
(58.2)

To paraphrase the poet (11. 122–24), though the divine "disport"
or contemplation is more pleasant, Christ more often "reigns rife"
in the trials of active life.

In its presentation of a meditation on the Passion, of a progress
from meditation to contemplation, and of a mystical experience itself,
"In a valey" is thoroughly Bernardine. Though the poet was writing
nearly three centuries after Bernard, he probably knew firsthand
Bernard's sermons on Canticles; certainly there were many manuscripts of them available in England. There is another fine poem,
this from Bernard's own time, which even more profoundly reflects
his mystical thought in a dramatic presentation. This poem is the
famous "Dulcis Iesu memoria," [7] a Latin work which Gilson has well
explained as "a summa in which one finds condensed in rigorously

precise formula all the teaching of the abbot of Cîteaux." [8] Gilson's full analysis bears out this claim. In my briefer treatment here I point out the poem's particular filiation with Canticles and its mystical tradition of interpretation.

Unlike "In a valey," "Dulcis Iesu memoria" does not present the soul's progress from meditation on Christ's suffering to mystical experience. A meditative aspect of the work is contained in its repeated invocations and citations of the name of Jesus. This feature is Bernardine, Bernard having been an originator of the devotion to the name of Jesus, particularly through his sermon (no. 15) on Canticles 1:2, "Thy name is as oil poured out." In the poem, however, unlike the sermons, it is the resurrected rather than the crucified Jesus who is the focus of the soul's attention and longing. Reference to unrisen Jesus is found only in the opening stanza:

> Dulcis Iesu memoria,
> Dans vera cordi gaudia;
> Sed super mel et omnia
> Eius dulcis presentia.   (strophe 1)

[Sweet is the memory of Jesus, giving true joy to the heart; But above honey and everything his presence is sweet.]

Meditating on the life of Jesus—*remembering* him—is edifying; but delightful beyond compare is his *presence* in contemplative union.

In the body of the poem the soul strives for this presence. Imagery from Canticles marks stages in the mystical experience. The narrator's—the soul's—progress begins in the narrow bed of contemplation, the *lectulo* of Canticles 3:1:

> Iesum queram in lectulo,
> Clauso cordis cubiculo.   (strophe 6)

[I will seek Jesus in my little bed, in the closed chamber of my heart.]

In the next stanza the soul resolves to go with Mary Magdalene to seek Jesus at the tomb. Mary Magdalene was seen as a contemplative because she was identified with the Mary of the New Testament story who sat at Jesus' feet while Martha was occupied with preparing the meal, because she bathed and kissed the feet of Jesus, and because in John's account she was the first to see Jesus after the Resurrection. In the poem, after the soul "mentally" goes to the tomb with Mary, it embraces the feet of Jesus and begs him to remain on earth so that he may fill it with sweetness (strophes 8–10). Then the soul alternates prayers to Jesus with descriptions of the joy of union with him, using the passionate language of sensual love:

> Quocumque loco fuero
> Meum Iesum desidero,
> Quam letus cum invenero,
> Quam felix cum tenuero.

> Tunc amplexus, tunc oscula
> Quae vincunt mellis pocula;
> Tunc felix Christi copula;
> Sed in his parva morula. (strophes 24–25)

[Wherever I am I will desire my Jesus. How happy will I be when I find him; how joyful when I hold him. The embrace, then the kisses which are better than cups of honey; then the happy joining with Christ. But these pass quickly.]

The embrace, the kiss, and the consummation. These are the conventional steps in carnal love, but the experience of the soul here clearly transcends the carnal. The last line quoted emphasizes that the mystical contact is brief; this is a commonplace about contemplation that Bernard expresses repeatedly.

As the soul in the poem becomes more eager and ardent, the use of Canticles becomes more noticeable. The next stanza evokes the culmination of the bride's search, "When I had a little passed by them I found him whom my soul loveth: I held him and I will not let him go" (Canticles 3:4) and it echoes her familiar plaint, "Quia amore langueo," as all at once the soul achieves union with Christ:

> Iam quod quesivi video,
> Quod concupivi teneo;
> Amore Iesu langueo
> Et corde totus ardeo. (strophe 26)

[Now I see what I have sought; I hold what I have desired; I languish in the love of Jesus and my heart is wholly enflamed.]

For the next eight stanzas the narrator rejoices in the presence of Jesus:

> Cuius amore sic afficit,
> Cuius odor me reficit,
> Iesus in quem mens deficit,
> Solus amanti sufficit. (strophe 33)

[He whose love thus affects me, whose perfume remakes me,
Jesus in whom the mind faints, alone suffices to the lover.]

The language remains intense, but its reference is not carnal. The
experience is one of the mind, and it is the mind which faints.

Suddenly the unitive experience passes. In Canticles, after the
sponsus (bridegroom) has appeared "looking through the windows"
(2:9), he abruptly disappears. The bride cries, "Return, my beloved"
(2:17). So in the poem the soul exclaims, "Mi dilecte, revertere"
(strophe 35). And just as the disappearance of the bridegroom in
Canticles is generally interpreted as Christ's ascension into heaven,
so the soul here declares that Jesus has ascended:

> Iesus ad patrem rediit,
> Regnum celeste subiit.
> Cor meum a me transiit,
> Post Iesum simul abiit.   (strophe 41)

[Jesus has returned to the Father, entered the celestial kingdom.
My heart has passed from me and gone out after Jesus.]

At the end of "In a valey" the soul leaves the chamber of contemplation to return to the active life. In the final stanza of "Dulcis Iesu
memoria" the narrator similarly leaves behind his experience of
Christ's presence to pursue actively the celestial kingdom with prayers
and hymns (strophe 42). In Bernard's terms the soul once more,
having fallen from the state of contemplation, resorts to action. And
the permanent value of the contemplative experience, which the poet
expressed verbally in the introductory stanzas, is dramatically asserted: "Only he who has experienced it knows what it is to love
Jesus" (strophe 5). He has also affirmed earlier another mystical
precept which is implicit in the poem's ending, that union with Jesus
will leave a lasting desire for him:

> Qui te gustant esuriunt,
> Qui bibunt adhuc sitiunt;
> Desiderare nesciunt,
> Nisi Iesum quem sentiunt.   (strophe 16)

[Those who taste you still hunger, who drink you yet are thirsty;
they can desire nothing except Jesus whom they feel.]

As in "In a valey" and Bernard's characterization, even though the
mystical union terminates, union once achieved incites desire, thence
action which will eventually lead back to Christ.

"Dulcis Iesu memoria" was very well known through the medieval period. It has a rich manuscript tradition and was much imitated. Numerous Middle English poems, sometimes prefaced by the Latin title, make use of the monorhymed quatrains of the original in a repeated invocation of "sweet Jesus." But these are meditative poems in which static repetition of his name is used to comment on his love for man, as shown especially in the Passion. The following is a typical opening:

> Jhesu, swete is the love of thee,
> Noon othir thing so swete may be;
> No thing that men may heere and see
> Hath no swetnesse agens thee.
>
> Jhesu, no song may be swetter,
> No thing in herte blisfullere,
> Nought may be feelid delitfullere
> Than thou, so sweete a lovere.
>
> Jhesu, thi love was us so fre
> That it from hevene broughte thee;
> For love thou dere boughtist me,
> For love thou hynge on roode tre.[9]

The succeeding stanzas do not progress beyond consideration of the love Jesus showed to man in the Incarnation, and the necessity of man's showing him love in return. Whatever the merit of the works as meditations, their poetic merit is not great because they are static and repetitious; and they are not essentially mystical.

"Iesu Dulcis memoria" and "In a valey," on the other hand, are very effective mystical works; both rank among the best short poems of the Middle Ages. What accounts for their success? I would cite two factors. In the first place, their presentations adhere closely to the profound mystical theology of St. Bernard. Though good theology does not guarantee good poetry, in these works it surely helps. The basic doctrine provides a coherent imaginative situation (the soul desiring God) and a firm narrative structure (the soul's progress to God), and the Bernardine emphasis on the affective aspect of mystical love makes appropriate the highly-charged emotive language characteristic of the best lyric poetry. In the second place, the poets make good use of the Christian tradition of Canticles as Bernard employed and developed it in his sermons. Canticles made available to them an intimate and exciting language of love, which the tradition of interpretation rendered respectable, innocent, and meaningful.

To supplement the often-erotic materials provided by Canticles, the two poems discussed also draw on the language and conventions of secular love poetry. The analogy of carnal love with spiritual love, implicit in the interpretations of Canticles, gave the mystical poet warrant for employing secular models that supplemented the biblical love song. Thus the work of Mechthild of Magdeburg so melds the nuptial imagery of Canticles with the usages of secular love poetry that one is hard put to distinguish the two.[10] Yet her writing is none the less spiritual for her use of the courtly minnesingers.

The use of the language of love in medieval mystical works is often misunderstood, particularly when a female writer like Mechthild is in question. Poetry that applies such language to mystical experience is seen by the more tolerant as equivocal—somewhere between religious and secular—and by the less tolerant as "hysterical."Dean Inge was simply expressing a modern misapprehension when he came to characterize medieval applications of Canticles by the mystics: "A graceful romance in honor of true love was distorted into a precedent and sanction for giving way to hysterical emotions, in which sexual imagery was freely used to symbolize the relation between the soul and its Lord. Such aberrations are as alien to sane Mysticism as they are to sane exegesis." [11] The most interesting term here is "true love," which is precisely the subject of the medieval mystics, though not as the Dean understands it.

In any event, it only requires a reasonable familiarity with the medieval view of Canticles to see that the poems we have discussed, including Mechthild's, are by no means hysterical, and that moreover they are fine works of art. Other splendid mystical poems that utilize Canticles in a similar way are the eleventh century "Quis est hic qui pulsat ad ostium? ", which transforms the nocturnal search of the bride (Canticles 3:1–3) into a fleeting experience of union, and— at the end of the Middle Ages—several works of the Spaniard St. John of the Cross (1543–91), notably his "Songs between the soul and the bridegroom" and "En una nocha oscura." [12] It is significant that St. John's poems use the biblical imagery to describe experiences of the *via negativa*, markedly different from the affirmative way that the poems influenced by Bernard describe. The imagery of Canticles admirably adapts to presentation of either way. Both lead to love, and Canticles is above all a love poem.

There are, of course, other good medieval mystical poems; not as many, however, as anthologies and collections might lead one to believe. Some of the poetry of Richard Rolle and his followers, for instance, is quite good, and it sometimes makes use of Canticles. But it consists in large part of meditations on the Passion or on the Holy Name. Those of their poems whose subject is divine love sometimes aim, no doubt, at the evocation of contemplative union; however, leaving aside questions of the mystical theory, this poetry is usually more rhetorical than dramatic, more imprecatory than imagistic. As a consequence, it often lacks the vividness and excitement which mark the other works and which seem necessary qualities for successful mystical poetry.

Bernard's sermons are certainly vivid and stirring when he deals with contemplative union. The last five of the eighty-six sermons no doubt represent the summit, but there are sublime poetic flights throughout. The following characterization of union is from the fifty-second sermon, a commentary on the sleep of the bride which I have quoted from earlier. Bernard speaks of the likeness of the contemplative sleep to death:

> It is not absurd for me to call the bride's ecstasy a death, then, but one that snatches away not life but life's snares, so that one can say: "We have escaped as a bird from the snare of the fowlers." In this life we move about surrounded by traps, but these cause no fear when the soul is drawn out of itself by a thought that is both powerful and holy, provided that it so separates itself and flies away from the mind that it transcends the normal manner and habit of thinking; for a net is spread in vain before the eyes of the winged creatures. Why dread wantonness where there is no awareness of life? For since the ecstatic soul is cut off from the awareness of life though not from life itself, it must of necessity be cut off from the temptations of life. "O that I had wings like a dove! I would fly away and be at rest." How I long often to be the victim of this death that I may escape the snares of death, that I may not feel the deadening blandishments of a sensual life, that I may be steeled against evil desire, against the surge of cupidity, against the goads of anger and impatience, against the anguish of worry and the miseries of care. Let me die the death of the just, that no injustice may ensnare or wickedness seduce me. How good the death that does not take away life but makes it better; good in that the body does not perish but the soul is exalted.
>
> Men alone experience this. But, if I may say so, let me die the death of angels that, transcending the memory of things present, I may cast off not only the desire for what are corporeal and inferior but even their images, that I may enjoy pure conversation with those who bear the likeness of purity. (52.4–5)

Here Bernard builds his sublime vision largely from the imagery of Psalms rather than Canticles, the main source of poetic effect in this series of sermons. But this recourse to Psalms in commenting on Canticles—a typical recourse by Bernard to other parts of the Bible—simply emphasizes that in his sermons Canticles becomes the center of existence and experience, the history of the mystical union of Christ with his Church in the Incarnation and with the soul in contemplation. It becomes the book of the Bible to which all else may be referred.

As a poem Canticles itself is surely dramatic and exciting. Its imaginative force, together with its authority as the love poem of the Holy Ghost, made it a natural prime source for those medieval writers who combined the poet's and the mystic's sensibilities. St. Bernard of Clairvaux was the most important of these writers; he provided the necessary catalyst for the outpouring of mystical literature based on Canticles that came after him.

BIBLIOGRAPHICAL NOTES

Friedrich Ohly, *Hohelied-Studien* (Wiesbaden, 1958), is the standard survey of medieval Christian exegesis of the Canticle of Canticles (Song of Songs, Song of Solomon) up to 1200; Ohly treats Origen, pp. 17–25; St. Bernard of Clairvaux, pp. 135–56. The surviving Latin version of Origen's commentary has been translated by R. P. Lawson, *Origen: The Song of Songs*, Ancient Christian Writers, No. 26 (London, 1957); Latin text edited by W. B. Baerens, *Origenes Werke*, VIII (Leipzig, 1925). Bernard's sermons on Canticles are edited by Jean Leclercq, Henri Rochais, and Charles Talbot, *Sermones super Cantica Canticorum*, vols. I–II of *Sancti Bernardi Opera* (Rome, 1957–58); the translation I quote, based on the Rome edition, is by Kilian Walsh and Irene Edmunds, *Bernard of Clairvaux: On the Songs of Songs*, 4 vols. (Kalamazoo, 1971–80); the sermon and paragraph numbers that I cite are identical in edition and translation.

Cuthbert Butler, *Western Mysticism*, 2nd ed. (New York, 1966), situates Bernard's mysticism in the patristic tradition leading from St. Augustine and Gregory the Great. A convincing analysis of Bernard's doctrine of contemplation is provided by Etienne Gilson, *The Mystical Theology of Saint Bernard*, tr. A. H. C. Downes (London, 1940). Jean Leclercq places Bernard's own experience of the divine in the context of his theology, *Saint Bernard Mystique* (Bruges, 1948); and he deals with a number of medieval literary texts in treating the "psycho-historical setting" of Bernard's mystical thought in *Monks and Love in Twelfth-Century France* (Oxford, 1979).

For the two poems I quote from at length, I use the following editions: for "Dulcis Iesu Memoria," *Le "Jubilus" Dit de Saint Bernard*, ed. André Wilmart (Rome, 1944); for "In a valey of this restles mynde," the two manuscript texts edited by Frederick J. Furnivall as "Quia Amore Langueo," in *Political, Religious, and Love Poems*, Early English Text Society OS 15

(London, 1866), pp. 180–89. Particularly relevant works of scholarship on the poems discussed herein are Etienne Gilson, "Sur le *Iesu Dulcis Memoria*," *Speculum*, 3 (1928), 322–34; James I. Wimsatt, " The Canticle of Canticles, Two Latin Poems, and 'In a valey of þis restles mynde,' " *Modern Philology*, 75 (1978), 327–45; and Rosemary Woolf, *The English Religious Lyric in the Middle Ages* (Oxford, 1968), esp. her chapter, "Richard Rolle and the Mystical School," pp. 159–79.

In my footnotes the foregoing are referred to by author or editor. Translations of Bernard's sermons are quoted by permission of the editors of Cistercian Publications. Material from my article in *Modern Philology* is used by permission of the editors.

V
The Zohar:
Jewish Mysticism
in Medieval Spain

ARTHUR GREEN

The Zohar, the central work of Spanish-Jewish mysticism in the Middle Ages, is the product of an entirely distinctive literary and esoteric tradition. While the writings of the Kabbalists, as the Jewish mystics are called, were often composed in temporal and geographical proximity to those of Christian and Muslim mystics, they are essentially a product of the unique and separate religious teachings that the Jews carried into medieval Europe. Both the Kabbalah's enemies among later Jews and its devotees among Renaissance Christians and later occultists tried to separate Kabbalah from Judaism, seeing it as essentially Christian rather than Jewish in spirit, or viewing it as an "alien growth" on the historic body of Judaism. Nothing, as we shall see, could be further from the truth.[1]

Before approaching the Zohar, we shall have to look briefly at the origins of the Kabbalah and the cultural setting in which it originated. From there we shall move to questions of authorship and structure in the Zohar, and finally to the esoteric content of the book itself.

It was in that area of southern France called Provence, culturally akin in the High Middle Ages to northern Spain, that the speculations which led to the Zohar, the culmination of a hundred-year development, first appeared. The Provençal Jewish community in the twelfth century was one of great cultural wealth, forming something of a bridge between the spiritual legacy of Jewish creativity in Spain

in Muslim times and the rather separate world of Jewry in the
Ashkenazic or Franco-Rheinish area. Here were the great works of
Jewish philosophy, including those of Maimonides, translated into
Hebrew, so that a Jewry not conversant with the Arabic original
could appreciate them. Provence was a great center of creativity in
halakhah, religious law, and the ongoing legal discussion of the
Talmud which is ever at the forefront of literary activity among
medieval Jews. Traditional homiletics were also cultivated, and important works of Midrash, or homiletic commentary on the Bible,
were edited in Provence. But other studies were encouraged as well
in this rather "enlightened" atmosphere: biblical exegesis, theology,
and poetry all flourished among Provençal Jewry.

In this cultural area there appears, toward the latter part of the
twelfth century, a tradition of esoteric theosophical speculation, or
speculation on the inner life of the Deity, known in later literature
as Kabbalah. The origins of this literary movement are obscure and
are still much debated. We do not yet know how much of the
tradition was native to Provence and how much was imported from
elsewhere (either from pietistic circles in the Rhineland or directly
across the Mediterranean from the Near East.) Nor have scholars
ceased debating whether there is some connection between the origins
of Kabbalah and the Albigensian movement in Provence of the time.[2]
For our purposes, however, we shall trace the beginning of Kabbalah
to the appearance in Provence of a document that without a doubt
can be called the first kabbalistic text, and is indeed one of the
strangest and most fascinating documents in the long history of
Hebrew literature. This slim volume is known as *Sefer ha-Bahir*,
awkwardly renderable as *The Book of Clarity*. We first find reference
to it in Provençal works of the late twelfth century, and from that
time forward it has a continuous history as a major shaper of Jewish
mystical ideas.[3] The Bahir takes the form of ancient rabbinic Midrash,
expounding on biblical phrases, tying one verse of Scripture to
another, and constructing units of its own thought around what it
offers as Scriptural exegesis. Like the old Midrash, it makes frequent
use of parables, showing special fondness for those that involve
stories about kings and their courts, in which God is inevitably
compared to "a king of flesh and blood." In form, then, the Bahir
is quite traditional. But as soon as we open its pages to look at the
content, we find ourselves confounded:

> Whence do we know that Abraham had a daughter? From
> the verse: "The Lord blessed Abraham with all" (Gen. 24:1).
> And it is written: "All is called by My name: I created,
> formed, and made it for My glory" (Is. 43:7). Was this

blessing his daughter or was it perhaps his mother? It was his daughter. To what may this be compared? To a king who had a faithful and perfect servant: he tested him in various ways, and the servant passed all the tests. Said the king: What shall I do for this servant, or what can I give him? I can only hand him over to my elder brother, who may advise him, guard him, and honor him. The servant went to the brother and learned his ways. The elder brother loved him greatly, and called him 'beloved': "The seed of Abraham my beloved" (Is. 41:8). He too said: What can I give him? What can I do for him? I have a beautiful vessel which I have fashioned, containing the most precious pearls, the treasures of kings. I shall give it to him, and he will attain his place. This is the meaning of "God blessed Abraham with all." [4]

What is the meaning of the verse: "From the west I shall gather you" (Is. 43:5)? From that attribute which leans ever toward the west. Why is it called 'west' *(Maarav)*? Because there are the seed is mixed *(mitarev)*. To what may this be compared? To a king's son who had a beautiful and modest bride in his chamber. He continually would take the wealth of his father's house and bring it to her. She took everything and hid it, mixing it all together. After some time, he wanted to see what he had collected and gathered. This is the meaning of "From the west I shall gather you". And what is it? His father's house, as the verse earlier states: "I shall bring your seed from the east". This teaches that he brings from the east and sows in the west. Later he gathers in that which he has sown. [5]

The reader familiar with Midrash (as was the intended audience of the Bahir) will immediately notice something out of the ordinary here. The text simply does not work as Midrash. Questions are asked but not answered, or answered in such ways as only to call forth more questions. An image is proposed (that of the king), which always refers to God, and then suddenly that king turns out to have an older brother. Abraham's daughter, well known from earlier Midrash, here might be his mother. What sort of questions are these, and what sort of answers? The scholar is almost tempted to emend the text!

If one comes to the Bahir, on the other hand, with some familiarity with the methods of mystical teachers, particularly in the Orient, the text seems not quite so bizarre. Despite its title, the purpose of the book is precisely to mystify rather than to make anything "clear" in the ordinary sense. The reader is being taught to recognize how much there is that he does not know, how filled Scripture is with seemingly impenetrable mystery. "You think you know the meaning of this verse? " says the Bahir to its reader. "But here is an interpretation to throw you on your ear and to show you that you understand nothing of it at all." Everything in the Torah, be it a tale told of Abraham, a verse of prophecy, or an obscure point of law, hints at some reality beyond that which you can attain by the ordinary dialectic of Talmudic training.

As we read on in the Bahir, it becomes clear that the author (we speak of him in the singular only informally; the text is undoubtedly the product of several layers of compilation) is not merely advocating obscurantism for its own sake. He has in mind a notion, often expressed only in the vaguest terms, of what it is that lies beyond the many hints and mysteries of the Scriptural word. To say it briefly, the Bahir and all Kabbalists after it claim that the true subject of Scripture is God himself, that revelation is essentially an act of self-disclosure by God. Because the majority of people would not be able to bear the great light that comes with knowing God, however, divinity is revealed in the Torah in hidden form. Scripture is strewn with hints as to the true nature of "that which is above" and the mysterious process within divinity that led to the creation of this world. Only in the exoteric, public sense is revelation primarily a matter of divine *will*, teaching the commandments man is to follow in order to lead the good life. The inner, esoteric revelation is rather one of divine *truth*, a network of secrets about the innermost workings of God's universe.

A careful reading of the Bahir also shows it to document a religious vision not found anywhere in prior Jewish sources. Its language, to be sure, is good rabbinic/medieval Hebrew. It is written wholly from within the rabbinic world, showing complete familiarity with a wide range of earlier sources. Frequent reference is found in the Bahir to "the blessed Holy One," a standard rabbinic way of speaking about God. But it also becomes clear that this "Holy One" is not alone in the divine universe. There seem to be many potencies, all of them bearing some degree of divine description, and standing in relationship of some sort to another. Of course outright polytheism is out of the question here (though the Kabbalah has been accused of this too); what we seem to discover in the Bahir are various elements or stages of divine life, figures within the Godhead that interact with one another. No Neoplatonic flow from rung to rung is yet to be seen here; that will be added to Kabbalah only in the succeeding century. Here these entities seem to relate in a freer, more mythlike, and more complex manner. Most of the Bahir text leaves them quite undefined in order of relationship, and skips continually back from one to another. There is one passage, however, undoubtedly determinative for later Kabbalah, that enumerates the potencies as ten, setting them out as parallel to the ten utterances ("Let there be . . .") by which God supposedly created the world. We quote the first half of this passage:

> What are the ten utterances? The first is the sublime crown, blessed are His name and His people. And who are His people? Israel, as Scripture says: "Know that the Lord is God; it is He who has made us and not [consonantally: L'] we ourselves" (Ps. 100:3). Read rather "We belong to Aleph [L']—to recognize and know the One of Ones, united in all His names.
>
> The second: wisdom, as it is written: "The Lord acquired me at the beginning of His way, before His deeds of old" (Prov. 8:22). And there is no beginning but wisdom, as Scripture says: "The beginning of wisdom: the fear of the Lord" (Ps. 110:11).
>
> The third: the quarry of the Torah, the treasury of wisdom, hewn out by the spirit of God. This teaches that God hewed out all the letters of the Torah, engraving them with the spirit, casting His forms within it. Thus it is written: "There is no rock [zur] our God" (I Sam. 2:2). Read rather: "There is no artisan [zayyar] like our God".
>
> This is the third. What is the fourth? The fourth is the righteousness of God, His mercies and kindnesses with the entire world. This is the right hand of God.
>
> What is the fifth? The fifth is the great fire of God, of which it is said: "Let me see no more of this great fire, lest I die" (Deut. 18:16). This is the left hand of God. What is it? They are the holy beasts and seraphim on left and right; they are the exalted and beautiful ones unto the heights, of which Scripture says: "the higher ones above them" (Ecc. 5:7) and "Their rings were high and dreadful; the rings of the four were full of eyes round about" (Ez. 1:18). Around it are angels, around them, bowing and prostrating before them, proclaiming: "The Lord, He is God! The Lord, He is God! " [6]

One gets the impression here—though not for certain—that "God himself" is to be identified with the first of these figures, and that the others belong to him in some secondary way. This impression is not consistent throughout the Bahir, however: the passage in which the king refers to his "elder brother," for example, seems to indicate something different.

The reader will also notice by now the strong attraction of the Bahir to *symbolic* speech. This remains true of the Zohar and throughout the Kabbalah: God is best to be approached by way of symbols. Here the mystics take their stand against the long and highly developed tradition of rational philosophy among medieval Jews, especially in Spain, claiming that discursive reasoning and the language that embraces it can never reach beyond those bonds of ordinary human intellect that keep us from true knowledge of the divine world. Knowledge of God requires a breaking out of our limited ways of thinking, a reaching beyond into a level of reality (and consciousness) where ordinary language cannot accompany us. Symbols, with their pictorial richness and seemingly endless depth, with their willingness to breach contradiction (e.g. "God's fire is water"; "true being is nothingness," etc.) and their ability to penetrate arcane levels of our individual minds and our collective human memory, can alone remain of language as we use it to express these divine mysteries which, in their essence, are ever beyond words. One may define the most basic spiritual endeavor of Kabbalah, from its very beginnings, as symbol making. The thought it produces, particularly in such a work as the Bahir, is a symbolic narration of events and processes that exist in a realm higher than and prior to ours, events that without these symbols would remain utterly beyond the grasp of language. To say it in a word, kabbalistic thought is essential mythic.[7]

For several generations in the late twelfth and early thirteenth centuries, these new mystic/mythic ways of thinking were preserved in closely guarded esoteric circles. One family, that of Rabbi Abraham ben David of Posquières, himself a major legal authority, had a leading role in the transmission of these "secrets," as they were called. Members of this group are depicted, however, not merely as transmitters of literary sources. Several members of the circle are said to have had "revelation of Elijah," meaning that Elijah the Prophet had come to them while in a supersensory state and had revealed some new portion of the secret lore. The student of medieval Judaism knows, moreover, that the reference to Elijah serves to legitimate a claim to divine revelation, one which formally was not supposed to occur since the canon was sealed and "prophecy was taken from the prophets and given to children and fools." The early Kabbalists in fact made a dual truth-claim for their esoteric readings of Scripture and their boldly new speculative ideas: they claimed both that they were ancient, the secret wisdom passed down by countless generations, only now given to public reading, and also that they were new, freshly revealed by heavenly voices to the sages of immediately preceding generations.[8]

The teachings of this circle, aside from the Bahir itself, were largely centered around the act of mystical prayer. We find among the Provence mystics detailed instructions for *kawwanah* or inner direction in prayer. Here *kawwanah* does not simply mean "intentionality," as in the earlier rabbinic sources, nor does it refer to a general air of serious intensity in worship; rather, it indicates a series of very specific steps in which the text of the liturgy is related to a series of meditations on those same ten potencies, or *sefirot*, that we have seen in the Bahir. The words of prayer, either individually or in phrases, become a series of guideposts by means of which the worshipper is to rise in contemplative ascent through the higher realms. Here we have the aspect of practice that was missing from the Bahir itself; what appeared as a gnostic tradition, offering esoteric *knowledge* about the inner divine world, is interpreted here as a contemplative tradition, one in which the devotee may *participate* as he successively directs his prayers to ever higher realms within God.

Unlike the Bahir itself, some of these sources speak of a "cause of causes" or "root of roots," a hidden Godhead that lies beyond the active mythic world of divinity that is manifest in the *sefirot*. Here we see emerging for the first time a dichotomy that is to be universally accepted by later Kabbalists: the hidden God, beyond all knowing, address, and even naming, and the revealed God, the one-amid-ten of the sefirotic universe. From the viewpoint of the historian, what we also see here is the integration of the Bahir's radically different gnostic teaching into a theological mindset more familiar to medieval Jewry. The hidden God and his potencies are now *structurally* parallel (though surely not identical) either to the hidden Neoplatonic God and the intelligences emanating from him or the Aristotelian deity who is one with all his attributes.

We have yet to traverse, albeit briefly, two more steps before we are ready to speak of the Zohar itself. It was in the opening years of the thirteenth century that the doctrines of Kabbalah, still kept as closely guarded secrets, began to cross the Pyrenees and attract followers in Catalonia or northeastern Spain. This region, already long under Christian domination, contained a large and well-educated Jewish community that was linked by close ties, cultural as well as socio-economic, to the Jews of Provence. In the town of Gerona there developed a circle of kabbalistic devotees, including a number of writers who were most important for the later history of the movement. It is from this circle that the earliest major kabbalistic books, aside from the Bahir, have come down to us. The range of their subject-matter and forms typifies the writings of Jewish mystics for many centuries to come: we have commentaries on the prayer-book, a commentary on the Song of Songs, explanations of the

Talmudic legends, a polemical work against the writings of a philosopher, and a commentary on the Torah which, while by no means exclusively or even chiefly kabbalistic, contains frequent references to explanations of Scripture "according to the way of Truth." This last work, the Torah commentary of Moses Nahmanides, was an important departure in the history of Kabbalah. Nahmanides (1194–1270) was perhaps the best known and most widely revered Jewish intellectual of the thirteenth century. Respected as a conservative in theological matters (he sided with the opponents to Maimonides' philosophy), he was a widely accepted authority in Jewish legal circles, author of numerous *responsa* (legal opinions in response to queries) and commentaries on various tractates of the Talmud. The fact that a man of his stature had become a central figure in the Gerona mystical circle, and that he was willing to refer (albeit in a somewhat veiled manner) to kabbalistic secrets in a volume intended for popular distribution, clearly did much to pave the way for the acceptance of this new way of thinking.

In the Gerona school, the influence of religious philosophy has become more pronounced, and it is clear that Kabbalah has taken on a Neoplatonic hue. This first means that emanation, the flow of the *sefirot* out of the hidden self of God beyond, the infinite and unknowable, is now taken to be the most essential kabbalistic mystery. True, the identification of certain rites and terms with individual potencies in the supernal realm, the way of the Bahir in revealing secrets, continues in Gerona. This especially characterizes the Torah commentary of Nahmanides. But one has a sense in the longer works of this circle that a *system* has now developed out of the Bahir's more random symbolic identifications. The ordered flow of the *sefirot*, each from one another and ultimately all from the primal One, is now taken for granted. The relationship of these potencies, especially the uppermost ones, to their source in the hidden Godhead, remains perhaps intentionally vague in this literature, a point we shall discuss further when outlining the Zohar's version of this system.

Neoplatonism has also had a major impact on the *psychology* of the Kabbalah, its doctrine of the soul. The mystics of Gerona accepted the general medieval understanding of a sharp distinction between soul and body, the latter being merely the outer shell that contains the true person as manifest in the soul. They also learned from the philosophers the tripartite division of the soul, a notion which they combined with ancient rabbinic speculations and adapted for their own purposes. The essential point they sought to establish is that the soul has its origins in God and that the human being, body as well as soul, bears the stamp of its divine source. The ten *sefirot*, the essential building-blocks of all reality, make up the structure of the soul as well; because of this it is by turning inward, by self-knowledge at its most profound level, that a person can come to know God. This turn inward, the necessary first step in any contemplative system, also implies a rejection of things external except insofar as they are a manifestation of God's glory. The inward journey upon which one then embarks leads from the lower levels of self into a discovery of the true soul *(neshamah)*, its likeness to the divine world and its endless longing to be returned to its source. "To use the Neoplatonic formula, the process of creation involves the departure of all from the One and its return to the One, and the crucial turning-point in this cycle takes place within man, at the moment he begins to develop an awareness of his true essence and yearns to retrace the path from the multiplicity of his nature to the Oneness from which he originated." [10]

Paralleling the tendency toward a more philosophic Kabbalah in Gerona, there emerged in the same or a slightly later period another circle, the one with which the Zohar's author is most closely identified. This group, sometimes referred to by modern scholars as the "gnostic" circle, seems to have reacted, perhaps predictably, against the growing philosophical influences on Kabbalah, and sought a more direct linkage with the mythic world first so darkly hinted at in the Bahir. Their works, rather than explaining or commenting in order to make a difficult text more accessible, prefer to follow the Bahir tradition by expanding and creating the myth. Here, in the works of such figures as Moses of Burgos or Todros Abulafia of Toledo (the latter an important political leader of the Castilian community), the fantastic elaboration of a mystical cosmos is the center of kabbalistic activity. Angels, principalities, and especially demons filled the imagination of these writers; it was this school that first elaborated the notion of an "other side" opposing divinity, containing ten demonic *sefirot* of its own parallel to those in God, an idea that was to have great importance in the later history of the Kabbalah. The free-flowing mythic creativity of these Kabbalists clearly prepared the way for the Zohar, a work of inspired mystical-mythic imagination if ever there was one.[11]

The Zohar is a voluminous work, usually printed in three thick volumes along with various addenda. It is without question the apex of kabbalistic thought, a point agreed upon by traditional mystics and contemporary historians. For Jewish mystics the work attained a sort of canonical status, the only work after the Talmud of which this may be said. Pious Jews from the fifteenth century onward— including many, especially of Near Eastern origin, even today— would rank it alongside the Bible and the Talmud as a source of unimpeachable religious truth. The famous Hasidic master, Rabbi Pinhas of Korzec (1728–91) thanked God for having created him in the period when the Zohar was already known, "for the Zohar kept me a Jew." [12] Legend has it that Rabbi Pinhas' son, who owned a printing house in Slavuta, prepared for the publication of the Zohar edition by having the printing presses dipped in a ritual bath so that they, profane vessels that they are, might be fit to print so holy a text. The enchanting character of this work, whose title is perhaps best rendered as "The Book of Enlightenment," has fascinated readers Jewish and Christian, devotee and skeptic, for many hundreds of years.

The Zohar began to make its appearance in Castile during the closing decades of the thirteenth century. We speak of it in this indirect way, for it was precisely in that most appropriate manner that the work first came to be known, mere bits and fragments revealed while the rest was kept secret. A number of kabbalistic authors in that generation, including Joseph Gikatilla and Bahya ben Asher, the famous Bible commentator of Barcelona, seem to have been close to the source of these writings, but not to have betrayed their secret. As larger portions of the book became available, it was referred to not at all as one of the writings of contemporary Spanish Kabbalists, but rather as "the Midrash of Rabbi Simeon ben Yohai," the ancient and presumably long-hidden work of a famous second-century teacher. Rabbi Simeon lived in the Holy Land during the period of Roman persecution; according to later legend, surely treated as history in the Middle Ages, he and his son dwelt for thirteen years in a cave, where they lived a life of unblemished asceticism and conversed with one another on mystical matters. When in 1305 the travelling Kabbalist Isaac of Acre finally traced the Zohar manuscripts to their source and disseminator, Rabbi Moses De Leon, he was indeed told that they were copied from the works of that ancient sage. [13]

As though to buttress the claim of antiquity, the Zohar is composed not in Hebrew, the sole literary language of Jews in Christian Spain, but in Aramaic, the language spoken in the land of Israel during the early rabbinic period. In the Middle Ages this language was known only poorly, preserved insofar as was needed for comprehending the Talmud and other literary sources of late antiquity. To one who reads the original, the work is surely a linguistic marvel; its sonorous Aramaic tones lend to it a quality of arcane majesty, of a truth always veiled by being presented in a tongue just not quite fully comprehended, this all the more so because the Zohar is replete with words not to be found in any other Aramaic document, many

of these forming the essential technical terms needed for a comprehension of the text's most basic meaning.[14]

Despite the relatively concise form in which it is published, it is
difficult to think of the Zohar as a single book; it gives the appearance
of a vast literary corpus, the complete reading of which would take
years of careful study. There is no continuous narrative or single
form that embraces the entirety of the work. A breakdown of the
Zohar into its parts shows that it is comprised of some twenty-two
literary units, each of these entirely unique as to length, content,
and style. Perhaps half of the total Zohar corpus is contained in the
main body of the work, the so-called Zohar on the Torah. As the
name indicates, the text is organized (though rather loosely so) as
a series of comments and homilies following the order of the Torah,
divided in accord with the divisions of Scripture for weekly reading
in the synagogue. Rather than offering real commentary, the Zohar
will use the biblical verse as a point of departure, finding constant
occasion in Scripture to expostulate upon its own theosophical system.
We take as an example some passages from the Zohar's account of
the birth of Moses and the tale of his discovery by Pharaoh's daughter.

A MAN WENT FORTH FROM THE HOUSE OF LEVI AND
TOOK A DAUGHTER OF LEVI (Exodus 2:1). Rabbi Yose
began: "My beloved has gone down into his garden, into the
bed of spices" (Canticles 6:2). "His garden" is the Community
of Israel, for she is the "bed of spices", wreathed from all
sides, containing the fragrant aromas of the World-to-Come. In
the hour when the blessed Holy One goes down into his
garden, all the souls of the righteous are crowned and give off
their aroma. Of this the Scripture says: "The aroma of your
oils is of all the spices" (Canticles 4:10). These are the souls
of the righteous and Rabbi Isaac has said that all such souls
ever present and ever to be present in this world exist in the
earthly Garden of Eden, in the very form and image that they
have in this world. This secret has been transmitted to the
wise . . . .

"A man went forth from the house of Levi"—this is
Gabriel, of whom it is said: "The man Gabriel, whom I had
seen in a vision" (Daniel 9:21). "From the house of Levi"—
this is the Community of Israel, coming from the left side. He
"took a daughter of Levi"—this is the soul, as it is taught: in
the hour when the body of a righteous person is born in this
world, the blessed Holy One calls upon Gabriel to take that
soul from the garden and bring it down into the newborn
body; he is then given the task of guarding that soul as well.

But if you should say that the angel who guards the souls of
the righteous is called "night" [following a tradition of the
Talmud], and wonder why we have called him Gabriel, the
answer is thus. He comes from the left side, and anyone who
comes from that side will bear this name.

"A man went"—this refers to Amram. He "took a daughter
of Levi"—this is Jochebed. A heavenly voice came forth and
told him to join himself to her. The hour of Israel's
redemption had drawn near, and it was to take place through
the child born of them. The blessed Holy One helped him, for
we have learned that the divine presence (shekhinah) hovered
over their bed. Both of them desired to cleave as one to the
shekhinah, and for that reason the shekhinah never departed
from the son they were to bear. Thus Scripture says: "Sanctify
yourselves and you shall be holy" (Leviticus 11:44). When a
person sanctifies himself below, the blessed Holy One makes
him holy from above. Just as their desire was to cleave to the
shekhinah, so did the shekhinah attach itself to the one whom
they brought forth by their act . . . .

HIS SISTER STOOD FROM AFAR (Exodus 2:4). Whose
sister? The sister of the One who calls the Community of
Israel "my sister", as in "Open for me, my sister, my
beloved" (Canticles 5:2). "From afar", as it is said: "From afar
the Lord appears to me" (Jeremiah 31:3). What does this
mean? That the righteous, before they come down into this
world, are known to all above. Surely this is true of Moses. It
also means that the souls of the righteous are drawn from a
high place, as we have learned. The soul has a father and a
mother, just as the body has father and mother on earth.
Everything both above and below comes about through male
and female. This is the secret of "Let earth bring forth a
living soul" (Genesis 1:24). "Earth" here is the Community of
Israel: the "living soul" is that of Adam, as has been taught.[15]

A well-known event of the biblical narrative has been transformed
here in several ways. First it is supplied with a poetic or romantic
introduction, typically drawing upon the erotic imagery of the Song
of Songs. But this introduction also serves to change the essential
locus of the event itself. Rather than a bit of history, we have an
event replete with symbolic mystery. Levi and Jochebed, Moses'
parents, are here taken as symbols for the bridegroom and bride (or
garden) of the Canticle, reminding the reader that the true mystery
of conception takes place above, that the human soul is born of a
union within the divine realm.

From the realm of the *sefirot*, the soul is handed over to the angel Gabriel for protection and safe conduct into the lower world. The angels represent an intermediary world for the Zohar, linking the mysterious universe of inner divinity to the human world below. Only after Gabriel has the soul readied for entry into the body may the narrative turn (beginning of the third paragraph, as we have divided it here) to the realm in which Moses' parents join together to conceive a child. Here the account is essentially moralistic, and serves to remind the reader of the great rewards to be obtained by those who keep their minds turned to holy thoughts during the time of intercourse.

The advent of Moses' sister in the narrative gives the Zohar one more chance to return the scene to the upper realms. "Sister," like "bride" is a favorite term for the *shekhinah*, the last and most essentially feminine of the *sefirot*, which is also called here "The Community of Israel."

The biblical story, then, has served as an occasion to reflect upon the inner divine universe, source of the human soul and the true locus of *all* events, from the birth of a child to the redemption of Israel, that befall mankind. The lower world and its history are but a reflection of that which goes on above in the hidden inner life of God. The narrative of Israel's sacred history has, in the truest sense, been reread as myth.

Interwoven with this mythical Midrash, as it may be called, is a series of narratives, intended to provide a "natural" setting in which the various discourses of Rabbi Simeon and his companions are offered. The rabbis will be walking along the road, staying at an inn, or meeting some mysterious stranger; the tale is one of mystical wanderers ever in search of someone who can offer them a new bit of illumination. The companions will chance upon a great tree or a wise child; their inspiration may come from either the natural order or the human world, but always it will lead them back to "the world of truth," the inner universe of divine contemplation. Some of these encounters blossom forth into longer narratives, containing all sorts of fantastic tales that somehow come to be interwoven with the esoteric subject at hand. In a passage shortly following on that we have just quoted, still concerned with the origins of the soul, the following encounter takes place:

> Rabbi Eleazar and Rabbi Abba were going from Tiberias to Sepphoris. While they were on their way, a certain Jew met up with them and joined them. . . .
> [The stranger told them the following tale:] One day I was walking in the wilderness, and I saw a rare and precious tree.

Beneath it was a cave. As I approached it, aromas of all sorts
wafted from the cave. I took courage and went in, going
down some steps until I came to a place of tall trees that
gave off fragrant spices and aromas, more than I could bear.
There I saw a certain man with a sceptre in his hand. He was
seated at another entrance, but when he saw me he stood up
in astonishment. "What are you doing here, and who are
you? " he asked me. I was very much afraid, but I said "Sir, I
am one of the companions [Kabbalists]. Thus-and-so did I see
in the wilderness, and I entered the cave and came down
here." He said to me "Since you are one of the companions,
take this bundle of writings and give it to those who know
the secret of the souls of the righteous. He struck me with his
sceptre and I fell asleep. In my sleep I saw great crowds of
people following the path to that place. But that man struck
them with his sceptre and said: "Take the path of the trees! "
As they were walking they were lifted up into the air and
began to fly, I know not where. I heard a sound of many
people and did not know what it was. I awoke and saw
nothing, and was quite afraid. Then I saw that man and he
asked me if I had seen anything. I told him what I had seen
in my sleep, and he said, "The spirits of the righteous pass
by this path on their way to Eden. The sound you heard was
of those who are in Eden, bedecked in the form they take in
this world, rejoicing at those spirits of the righteous who have
just arrived. Just as the body is composed of a mixture of the
four elements and takes on form in this world, the spirit too
is formed in the garden by the four winds that blow there; it
is they who clothe it in its bodily form. Without these winds,
which make up the air of the garden, the spirit would remain
unadorned and would have no form at all. These four winds
are tied together as one; it is from the wind [or spirit] that the
spirit gets its form, just as the body is formed by the four
elements below. That is why "From the four winds come, O
spirit! " (Ezekiel 37:9): from the four winds of Eden by which
the spirit is formed. Now take this bundle of writings and go
on your way to deliver it to the companions."
    Rabbi Eleazar and the companions came forward and kissed
him on his head. Said Rabbi Eleazar: "Blessed is the merciful
One who has sent you here. Surely this is the proper
interpretation, and it was God Himself who put that verse
into my mouth." [16]
    He gave them the bundle of writings. Rabbi Eleazar took it
and opened it, but a flame burst forth and surrounded him.

He saw whatever he saw in it, and it flew out of his hands. Rabbi Eleazar wept and said "Who can stand in the treasure-house of the King! 'O Lord, who can reside in Your tent; who can dwell in Your holy mountain' (Ps. 15:1). Blessed is this path and this hour when I came upon you! " [17]

Other sections of the Zohar are composed in an entirely different, much more concise style. Here, in the so-called *matnitin* (Hebrew *mishnayot*), or *tosefta* (addenda) we find a terseness that imitates the legal codex rather than the expansive manner of fanciful homiletic works. In a few carefully chosen words, replete with the boldest of images, some secret is let out, offered with no explanation, and left to puzzle the reader. In such passages we cannot but have recourse to one of the later commentaries on the Zohar, hoping that its author was able to make sense of a passage that, however fascinating and glorious, seems to remain quite beyond comprehension.

O sublime beloveds, masters of intellect, look, O renowned rulers! Who among you has eyes to see, come with the power of that sight and know this: In the hour when there arose in the mystery of mysteries the will to come forth, three colors were joined together as one: white, red, and green. These three colors were interwoven, coupling with one another. The spade below receives its color from these, and all of them are seen in it. This is a sight to behold, the wondrous appearance of bdellium. As she is stricken within, the three colors appear surrounding her from without. The color goes forth, rising and descending. Guardians fuming with smoke (?) are present within her. The colors, joined as one, carry her upward by day and come down at night. A burning candle is seen at night, but it is hidden during the day in two hundred and forty eight worlds, all of them coming down from above for her sake, hidden below within the three hundred and sixty-five limbs. He who goes forth to seek her will break these hidden "wings" and "shells"; then will he open the gates. The one who merits to see will see with mind and intellect, like one seeing from behind a wall, except for the sublime and faithful prophet Moses, who saw with his very eyes that which is above and remains unknown. . . .[18]

Similar in style to these *matnitin* are the most esoteric portions of the Zohar, the *Book of Concealment* and the *Greater* and *Lesser Assemblies*, the sections of the work that have exercised the greatest fascination on the non-Jewish occultist traditions of the West ever since they were first "discovered" by believing humanist scholars in the Renaissance.

The question of the Zohar's true authorship has been debated almost since the work was first presented to the world. At first it was language, variety, and the sheer immensity of the work that pointed to ancient origin, at least for some part of the Zohar literature. The seemingly natural tales of the rabbis and their peregrinations around the Holy Land, the many parallels between zoharic and other midrashic sources, echoes of a spiritual allegory reminiscent of Philo's or of a Gnosticism that sounded like that of late antiquity, were all used at one time or another to support these claims. On the other side were those who suspected from the very beginning that the Zohar was the work of Moses De Leon's own hand, and that the ancient manuscript from which he was said to have copied was but another figment of his imagination. Some sought out base motives in this "forgery," while others considered it a legitimate case of pseudepigrapha, much like the attribution of the first-century apocalyptic works to Enoch, Abraham, or Moses. Such ascription allows the author to express his vision boldly, with limited fear of censorship or condemnation, since the text is to be offered to the public as the writings of an ancient and venerable sage, one whose teachings are surely beyond reproach, and must in fact occasion the re-interpretation of "later" works which do not agree with it.

In our own generation the question of authorship has finally been resolved by the painstaking historical and philological research of Gershom Scholem.[19] Scholem has argued on literary-historical grounds that the ideas of the Zohar are dependent upon the century of kabbalistic development that had preceded it, and not the other way around, as some defenders of the text's antiquity had argued. He has shown that the author was well-read in medieval Jewish philosophy, that the terminology of the book is much influenced by the literary Hebrew of the thirteenth century, and here and there, indeed, even by the Spanish that was the spoken language of Castilian Jewry. He has further shown that the author's supposed familiarity with Palestinian geography is a sham and, most convincingly, that the Aramaic in which the Zohar is written is a totally artificial language: that it corresponds to no dialect ever spoken, but is rather a hodge-podge of the Aramaic preserved in those literary sources that would have been most read by a medieval Jew in search of recovering that language. Finally, he has demonstrated a regular pattern of syntactical error in the usage of Aramaic verbs—a pattern that corresponds to the distinctive verb forms to be found in Moses De Leon's long-known Hebrew treatises. Scholem has shown that these literary and linguistic patterns are found diffused throughout the work, with the exception of two sections that he demonstrates to be slightly later imitations of the Zohar by another hand. Critical opinion is virtually unanimous in accepting Scholem's conclusions, excepting those within the Orthodox Jewish community who still consider such views to be heretical.

But the problem of the Zohar's authorship, and especially of the relationship between Moses De Leon and Simeon ben Yohai, is not yet fully solved. True, the entire Zohar was composed by one man, an individual of breathtaking imaginative scope who was surely one of the great religious authors of the Middle Ages. But *how* did he write the Zohar, and what did *he* believe was the relationship between his writing and his claim that the book was authored by Rabbi Simeon? Many a passage in the Zohar is written with such an extra measure of spiritual intensity and transcendent enthusiasm that one could reasonably believe the author had felt himself possessed by a spirit other than his own as he was writing it. Could De Leon have felt that Rabbi Simeon was speaking *through* him, that he was the mere vessel the ancient sage had chosen for the revelation of his secrets? Here we will do well to remember that the Kabbalists were believers in reincarnation, an idea that plays a major role in the Zohar itself. Could the author have seen himself as Rabbi Simeon *redivivus*? Did he believe that the soul of that earlier teacher had been reborn in him and was now seeking to reveal ancient truths that had long been preserved in silence? It is to these questions that the current generation of scholars, with their keen interest in mystical psychology, will surely turn. Here the author of the Zohar will have to be studied not only in his own cultural context, but also in tandem with such figures as Jacob Boehme or William Blake, masters of a poetic imagination so extraordinary that any attempt to account for it, either by the author himself or by his readers, seems to lead beyond theories of poetics and towards some form of prophecy or revelation.

What then do we know of Rabbi Moses De Leon, surely the greatest figure in the history of Jewish mysticism until the sixteenth century? Given his prominence, we know surprisingly little. He was born around 1240, probably in the town of Leon, lived most of his adult life in Guadalajara, and in his last years moved to Avila, all of these being towns in north-central Spain, an area containing an ancient and highly cultured Jewish community. He was a man of very considerable erudition in rabbinic literature (particularly Midrash) as well as in the esoteric sources. On the other hand, he was no great master of *halakhic* (legal) literature. In contrast to Nahmanides, De Leon was a man wholly given to the kabbalistic enterprise; all of his writings that we possess are of a mystical nature. We also

know that De Leon had at least dabbled in philosophical literature;
there is extant a manuscript copy of Maimonides' *Guide for the
Perplexed* written expressly for him in 1264. De Leon died in Arevalo
in 1305.

It appears that the Zohar's author saw himself as belonging to a
general movement of orthodox reaction to the rationalist rereading
of Judaism that had been taking place under the influence of Aristotelian philosophy, particularly as typified by readers of the *Guide*.
Philosophy had brought about a certain cynicism in matters of faith
and was leading, so some claimed, even to a laxity in religious
practice. Many were the voices raised in the thirteenth century against
these evils, and De Leon counted himself among them; this partially
accounts for his willingness to reveal so much of the "ancient" secret
lore. In one of his Hebrew writings we hear him say:

> Concerning this matter there are hidden mysteries and secret
> things which are unknown to men. You will now see that I
> am revealing deep and secret mysteries which the holy sages
> regarded as sacred and hidden, profound matters which
> properly speaking are not fit for revelation so that they may
> not become a target for the wit of every idle person. These
> holy men of old have pondered all their lives over these
> things and have hidden them, and did not reveal them to
> every one, and now I have come to reveal them. Therefore
> keep them to yourself, unless it be that you encounter one
> who fears God and keeps His Commandments and the
> Torah. . . . I looked at the ways of the children of the world
> and saw how in all that concerns these [theological] matters,
> they are enmeshed in foreign ideas and false, extraneous [or
> heretical] notions. One generation passes away and another
> generation comes, but the errors and falsehoods abide for-
> ever. And no one sees and no one hears and no one
> awakens, for they are all asleep, for a deep sleep from God
> has fallen upon them, so that they do not question and do
> not read and do not search out. And when I saw all this, I
> found myself constrained to write and to conceal and to
> ponder, in order to reveal it to all thinking men, and to make
> known all these things with which the holy sages of old
> concerned themselves all their lives.[20]

Such are the very bare essentials of Moses De Leon's life, including
most of what is known to us. While it is fair to say that of his
external life we know very little, there is available in his writings a
tremendous wealth of material that would help us draw a picture
of his inner life. This too is a task that stands before the scholar,

but is one that can be appreciated only as we turn, finally, to the actual contents of the Book of Enlightenment.

The Zohar must be viewed as a great compendium of all the kabbalistic thought that had come before it, reworked and integrated into the author's own all-embracing poetic imagination. Ideas contained in bare hints or clumsy expressions in the generations before him now spring forth, full-blown as it were, as a part of the ancient wisdom. This is true of the Zohar's notion of God, especially of its views on the origin and power of evil, as well as its speculations on man, his soul, and the religious world of Judaism. It is to these that we shall now successively turn our attention.

It may be said that God is the essential subject of all the zoharic writings. Whether ostensibly searching out one of the commandments, commenting on a seemingly non-theological verse of Scripture, or taking note of the mere "ways of the world," the Zohar is ever seeking out that which it calls "the secret of faith," the inner life of God in the world of the *sefirot*. The pattern of the *sefirot*, their infinitely complex relations with one another and their influence on all that happens in the world are a source of boundless fascination to the author's mind. It is time now for us to examine these ten manifestations so that we may understand this most basic key to kabbalistic thinking.

Of God as *eyn sof*, the boundless, undefined and indescribable One existing before and beyond the *sefirot*, the Zohar has relatively little to say. This ultimate reality exists always and remains unperturbed and inaccessible, beyond prayer and seemingly even beyond contemplation; there are but occasional hints to the contrary. Certainly *eyn sof* is not to be thought of in *personal* terms; this hidden Godhead is the source of all being, but not Father, not King, not Lord of the universe. Within the mysterious depths of "the endless" there takes place an inner stirring, a movement toward the establishment of an Archimidean point, one that will stand to define the very beginning, the primal unit out of which are to evolve all of space and time. This inward process, the first awakening of direction or will within the infinite, is identified by the Kabbalist as the first *sefirah*. Surely not yet defined as a "thing," for it precedes even that point which is to come about through it, one may nevertheless say that this rippling in the ocean of infinity bears within it, at least as the impulse to create bears the creature, all that is ever to come about in the world. This manifestation of primal will within the hidden Godhead is referred to by Kabbalists, for reasons that will be clear later, as *keter*, the crown. Because it is the catalyst of all being, but not yet a thing in itself, it is also called, in the paradoxical language of which the Zohar is so fond, "Nothing," or sometimes "the primal Nothing." This "air that cannot be grasped," to use another favorite kabbalistic term for it, lies wholly within *eyn sof*. Since it exists before and beyond time, it might be argued that *keter* is eternally present as an aspect of *eyn sof*, that within the infinite which is potentially turned toward creation. Kabbalistic history is filled with ongoing debate as to the nature of *keter* and its relationship to *eyn sof*, a debate in some ways reminiscent of the arguments about the eternity of the Second Person in early Christianity. This seems to be the Zohar's position: *keter* is eternally present within *eyn sof*, but is not to be identified with it.[21]

The primal point brought about through this movement of will is called "beginning"; it is the starting point of both emanation and creation, of the divine world and the world below. Everything that is ever to be already exists in that infinitesimal point as it emerges within God; as the first defined Being, however vague that definition, it becomes the source of all further being. The most widespread name for this point is *hokhmah* (wisdom), a usage often tied to an old midrashic reading of Genesis 1:1 as "In wisdom God created the heaven and the earth." It is in speaking of these primal movements of the first *sefirot* that the Zohar's language is most obscure and mystifying. Typical is this famous passage, which opens the Zohar's rendition of the story of creation:

> IN THE BEGINNING. As the will of the King began to come forth, He engraved signs in the uppermost pure light. Within the most hidden recesses a flame of darkness issued, from the mysterious *eyn sof*, a mist within formlessness, ringed about, neither white nor black nor red nor green, of no color at all. Only when measured did it bring forth light-giving colors. From deep within the flame there flowed a spring, out of which the colors were drawn below, hidden in the mysterious concealment of *eyn sof*.
>
> It broke through and yet did not break through the ether surrounding it. It was not knowable at all until, by force of its breaking through, one hidden sublime point gave forth light. Beyond that point nothing is known. Therefore it is called "Beginning"—the first utterance of all.[22]

The imagery of this passage, particularly that of the "flame of darkness" and the "spring," sets the tone for much that is to follow in the volume. It is in images of light and water, flashing sparks, deep wells, springs, flowing rivers, and shining stars that the Zohar most likes to talk about its secrets. In fact the conventional names given by Kabbalists to the sefirot (*keter*, *hokhmah*, etc.) are used rather rarely by its author, who seems to have the poet's instinctive sense that symbols freeze when they become conventionalized. The language of paradox is also very much to the Zohar's liking; only in this, it seems, can ordinary human speech be sufficiently stretched and distressed that it might be applied to a realm so utterly beyond the domain of language. The "flame of darkness" (Is it shining against the background of brilliant divine light?) is the instrument by which the *sefirot* are to be formed; like the workman's torch as it hews them out of an airy quarry, giving to each some measure of distance from the others in such a way that all, while remaining within God, can form a unity of One-in-ten, but not be completely absorbed into one another or swallowed back into *eyn sof.*

The spring which emerges from the flame is the third *sefirah.* From it will bubble forth, in an unending creative stream, the seven remaining *sefirot* and all the "lower worlds." In the passage below this same *sefirah* is referred to as a "palace." As soon as the first point *(hokhmah)* is defined, it is surrounded by a great light; the light that rings the primal point, also depicted as the chamber or palace in which that light comes to dwell, is the next stage of emanation. It is the crucial moment in the emergence of the divine self; this third rung is most frequently described in terms that are *maternal,* as the womb out of which the seven children are to be born, and as the loving one to whom all will return and be set aright at the end of time.

In fact, as we examine the symbols of this next passage, we will see that the relationship between *hokhmah* and *binah* (literally: "understanding," as this third *sefirah* is often called) has been described here in erotic terms. The light of *hokhmah* is also its "seed," entering into *binah* in an explosion of light that certainly also bears the marks of sexual climax.

> In the most hidden concealment a mark was made—unseen, not revealed. That mark was made and not made; neither persons of intellect nor those whose eyes are open can grasp it. Yet it is the existence of all. That mark is so tiny it cannot be seen or discovered; it exists through the will and gives life to all, taking what it does from that which has no marks or even will in it, from that which remains deeply hidden. The mark longed to cover itself, so it made a certain palace in which it might hide. It brought that palace out from within its own self, stretching it forth vastly in all directions. It decorated the palace in splendid draperies, and opened fifty gates which lead into it. Inside the palace that mark kept itself recondite and hidden. But once it was hidden there, as

soon as it entered, the palace filled up with light. From that
light are poured forth other lights, sparks flying through the
gates and giving life to all. . . .[23]

As *binah* is womb or mother, *hokhmah* turns out here to be father
and progenitor, the indeed hidden source whence all birth is to come.
This primal pair, existing in eternal and undisturbed union, are the
first stations in the boundless flow of divine energy that emerges
beyond them, first as the seven lower *sefirot*, aspects of the divine
persona, and then as *shefa'*, the flowing bounty of divine presence
that brings life to all the worlds below.

The earliest Kabbalists were fascinated with questions of the divine
name, and mystic lore assigned each of the names or terms for God
in the Bible to one of the *sefirot*. This allowed for a rather easy key
to kabbalistic exegesis, whereby the name of God employed in a
verse would tell the reader which *sefirah* was its secret subject. In
this context the name *elohim*, the generic term for "god" in Hebrew,
was attached to *binah*. Since this is the word used in the opening
verse of Genesis, the Zohar offers a radical new twist to that verse:
"God" is now object rather than subject of the verse; Genesis 1:1
is here taken to mean: Through *hokhmah* He (or It, a hidden subject)
created "God"! Such an understanding, utterly opposed of course
to the plain meaning of Scripture, is precisely the sort of reading
that would have been considered arch-heresy by the early rabbis,
positing as it does a realm higher than that of "God." In the kabbalistic
apologetic, of course, it is always emphasized that *eyn sof* and all
the *sefirot* are one, and therefore that no such charge is appropriate.
In fact, however, the personal God of rabbinic Judaism has been
reduced by several notches, assigned in the Zohar to a combination
of several *sefirot* below *binah*, as we shall see presently.

Here we must interrupt our outline of the *sefirot* to deal with a
question that by now may be troubling the reader. What has all this
to do with *mysticism*? If by that term we mean a religion that turns
on inner experience, building on the heart's strivings toward unifi-
cation with the One, the question is indeed legitimate, though we
have not yet seen the end of the sefirotic system. The point is that
we find very little in kabbalistic literature that speaks directly and
confessionally of religious experience. "The Kabbalists, however, are
no friends of mystical autobiography. They aim at describing the
realm of divinity and the other objects of the contemplation in an
impersonal way . . . they glory in objective description and are
deeply adverse to letting their own personalities intrude into the
picture."[24] In a larger sense, however, we may say that the Zohar
is precisely mystical in origin. The descriptions offered are not the

result of speculation in the casual sense, but rather a mirroring onto the cosmos of stages and states that the adept has known in his own inner life. The *language* of Kabbalah is cosmological. Hence, as our experiences are structured by the language system within which we work, the Kabbalist envisions his inner reality as the unfolding of universal life out of the Godhead; his chief preoccupation is the cosmos, not 'merely' his own soul. In our day, when mystical cosmology seems so distant and our shared language is rather that of psychology and inner experience, we might speak of these primal stages of emergence out of the depth in terms of the mystic himself rather than in terms of God or the cosmos. "Having been sunk completely into the unity of all things," we might say, "beyond all separation and self-consciousness, the mystic feels stirring within him that first impulse toward a reawakening of individual consciousness. That impulse, transforming him and not transforming him, taking him from the oneness of God and yet leaving him wholly within God, brings him in an eternal instant to utter silently the words: I am. This is his new birth, his first beginning."

Thus might a Kabbalist of our own period express what the Zohar says in the passages quoted. The difference between these two remains great, as vast as the difference between any two mystical texts composed in divergent religious contexts. But it is essential for the reader to understand that the choice of cosmological language does not mean that the Zohar is any less "truly mystical" for it. The task of the sensitive reader is in part (and cautiously!) to translate the Zohar's projected metaphysic back into those terms of inner enlightenment and successive states of transformed consciousness in which he can best comprehend it. The kabbalistic authors, cautious for their own reasons, do not do this for us.

Out of the womb of the Great Mother within God, or out of the spring that flows atop the deep well, if you prefer, there are born (issue forth), six children (streams), each of them having a particular function and character, and all of them uniting once again in the last of the ten *sefirot*, the bride (sea or garden). This last potency too is part of God, flowing from *hokhmah* as the end is the fulfillment of the beginning. But in relation to the six above her she occupies a passive role, that of bride receiving the affections of her beloved (the six combined as one), as sea taking into herself the multiple streams of water, or as moon receiving the reflected light of the sun, then giving it to her children, those who dwell in the lower worlds.

The six *sefirot* that intervene between mother and bride are often taken as a single figure, a "male" potency that stands between the female who is his origin and the one who is his mate. It is this figure with whom the rabbinic person-God is identified, Father of

all the lower creatures, to be sure, but "son" when viewed from the
perspective of that which stands above:

> Rabbi Simeon lifted up his hands and rejoiced. He said:
> This is the time to reveal—a full revelation is now required! It
> is taught: In the hour when the holy Ancient One, the hidden
> of all hidden, sought to be established [i.e. revealed]. It
> arranged all as male and female. Having been joined together,
> male and female no longer exist except in further
> configurations of male/female. *Hokhmah*, containing all, came
> forth shining in male/female form as it emerged from the
> holy Ancient One: since *hokhmah*, as it spread forth, brought
> out *binah* from within itself, it is in male/female form.
> *Hokhmah* is father, *binah* is mother: *hokhmah* and *binah* are
> equally balanced, male and female. Because of them
> everything exists as male/female; otherwise none would
> exist.[24]
> This beginning is father of all, father of all the patriarchs;
> they are joined to one another and give light to one another.
> When they are joined they have offspring, and faith [the
> sefirotic world] spreads forth. In the narrative of Rav Yeva's
> school it is taught: What is *binah*? When *yod* and *heh* [the first
> two letters of God's name, *hokhmah* and *binah*] are joined
> together, she becomes pregnant and gives birth to *ben*
> [literally: "son"].[25]
> Therefore is she called *binah*, the son of *yod heh*, the
> fulfillment of all. The two of them join together with the son
> between them in their form. Total fulfillment: father, mother,
> son, daughter. These words were given to be revealed only to
> the saints above, those who have come in and gone out, who
> know the ways of God and do not turn aside right or left. Of
> them it is said: "The ways of the Lord are straight. The
> righteous shall walk in them, but sinners shall stumble in
> them" (Hos. 14:10).[26]

These six figures taken as a unit are also identified with the six
days of the week, flowing into the Sabbath, and the six directions
of space (the four compass points, up and down). Taken individually
they form two triads, the lower chiefly a reflection of the higher.
This upper triad is often symbolized by the three patriarchs, Abraham
personifying the love of God, Isaac the fear of God, and Jacob
embodying peace, or the resolution of these two religious attitudes
into one. Abraham, placed on the right side of the sefirotic diagrams
(more on these below), signifies the right hand of God, the boundless
and freely given love God has for his world. Isaac, the left side,

stands for justice, the limitations God has to place on that love in order to be an effective ruler. This tension between the "aspect of mercy" and "aspect of justice" within God is part of the Kabbalists' legacy from older rabbinic Judaism. Here that tension is taken to an extreme, and the demonic is said to arise from the impulse within God to act as Judge. Only as these two forces are synthesized in Jacob, the sefirotic rung most often identified with "the blessed Holy One" or the God of rabbinic Judaism, is this tension resolved; the struggle between these two poles within God is a frequent theme of concern in the Zohar. The right and left sides of God, or *hesed* and *din* as they are conventionally called, each has a lower manifestation, bringing its particular power to bear in God's conduct of the universe. The lower form of "Jacob" (*tif'eret* or glory in the conventional terminology) is the ninth *sefirah*. This element is designated variously as Joseph, as the great "pillar," the "sign of the holy covenant," or simply "the righteous." All of these names may in one way or another be shown to refer to male potency; this *yesod* is seen as the "foundation" of the sefirotic universe. All the powers of the upper sefirot are concentrated together in it for their great flow into the tenth *sefirah*, bride or sea, moon or garden, to which we have referred above.

Rabbi Hiyya opened by saying: "A song of ascents, to Solomon. If the Lord build not a house, in vain have its builders worked on it; if the Lord guard not a city, in vain does the watchman stand" (Ps. 127:1). Come and see. At the time when it arose in God's will to create the world, He brought forth a mist from the darkened spark. It shone forth in the darkness, remained above and went below. That darkness was lighted with a hundred paths, lanes narrow but great, and the house of the world was made.[27]

That house is at the very center of all; it has many chambers and entrances all about it, holy sublime places. There the birds of heaven nest, each according to its kind. From the midst of the house there comes forth a great and mighty tree, having many branches and abundant fruit; there is food for all in it. That tree rises to the clouds of heaven and is hidden between three great mountains. It comes forth and rises from behind these mountains, goes upward and comes down. The house is watered by it, and it hides within itself sublime treasures which are not known. Thus is the house built and completed. That tree is revealed during the

day but hidden at night; the house rules at night but is
hidden in the daytime.[28]

Our understanding of the last sefirah will be enhanced if we look
briefly at some of the names by which it is called in the kabbalistic
sources. As *malkhut*, it is the *kingdom* of God, that over which the
King has dominion and in which he takes pleasure, sustaining and
protecting her as the true king takes responsibility for the sustenance
of his kingdom. At the same time it is this potency that is charged
with the rule of the lower worlds; the biblical personage with whom
it is associated is David (surprising, given its usual femininity), the
symbol of kingship. While *malkhut* receives the flow of all the upper
sefirot, it is usually held that she has some special affinity for the
left, the side of *din* or judgment. In this way she is called "the aspect
of gentle judgment," though several Zohar passages paint her in
portraits of seemingly ruthless vengeance in the punishment of the
wicked. A most complicated picture of femininity appears in the
Zohar, ranging from the most highly romanticized to the most bizarre
and frighteningly demonic.

The last *sefirah* is also called by the term *shekhinah*, an ancient
rabbinic term for speaking of the divine presence in the world. It
appears that in later midrashic literature, well before the Zohar, this
figure of speech has already become hypostatized as a winged angel-
like being, though the attribution of feminine character to it is an
innovation of the Kabbalah.[29] This symbol considerably alters our
view of the Kabbalists' theology. Insofar as she is *malkhut*, ruler of
the world, the system is quite theistic, i.e. God and his created
universe remain quite distinct from one another. But *shekhinah* had
always been a term for the indwelling presence, that which filled
the Temple, which spoke to Moses, and so forth. If the *shekhinah*
is in the world, however, (or the world in the *shekhinah?*) the Zohar
seems to veer closer to pantheism, a religious tendency common to
mystics throughout the world. In fact it is impossible to define the
Zohar as either theistic or pantheistic: though its God seems to relate
to the world in an essentially theistic manner, we are never sure,
either with regard to *eyn sof* or in connection with the *shekhinah*,
quite what it means to say that the world is "outside" God. It is
clear, however, that the *shekhinah* is to be found in this world, and
that such was God's intent in creation: the *shekhinah* would continue
the life-giving flow of emanation onward from the sefirotic world,
down through realms of palaces and angels, countless realms of
heavenly light, and into the natural and human orders. Originally
centered in Eden, the *shekhinah* followed man into his life as a mortal,
and took up residence amid the patriarchs and the people of Israel.

When they went down into Egypt, the *shekhinah* was with them, and thus she accompanies Israel in all their exiles, the earthly state of the people bearing witness to the *shekhinah*'s own condition as a hapless wanderer through history, her fate subject to the vicissitudes of human virtue or misdeed. Only with the final redemption and the rebuilt Temple will she again take up residence in Jerusalem, linking the world to God in joy and harmony as it was when the smoke of the holy altar rose and reached to heaven. Nonetheless, something of the *shekhinah* still abides, however mournfully, in her sacred home, for the rabbis long before the Zohar had taught that "the *shekhinah* has never departed from the Western Wall."

Another name given to this rung of divinity will again complicate our picture of the relationship between God, *shekhinah*, and world. She is called, very frequently in the Zohar, by the name *kenesset yisra'el*, Community of Israel. That term, always reserved in rabbinic writings for the Jewish people itself, is now chiefly applied to *malkhut*, and the people Israel are *kenesset yisra'el* only as her beloved children. Accompanying the redefinition of this term in the early Kabbalah is a new reading of the Midrash on the Song of Songs, long a basic document of Jewish devotional life as well as theological self-understanding. The old midrashic sources had always read the Song as a dialogue of love between God and the people Israel, his chosen bride whom he had brought forth as a poor slave-girl from Egypt and wed as his beloved at Mount Sinai. The liturgical poetry of earlier ages is replete with echoes of this reading. While many sources had sought to "purify" this love poem of its original erotic context, allowing in it only references to matters of history and law, there existed also in ancient esoteric reading of the Song, one highly anthropomorphic in its view of God and shocking to many a later reader.[30] Now the Kabbalists, following certain developments in medieval philosophical exegesis, elevate the Canticle to an entirely new plane. The love of which King Solomon speaks in fact takes place wholly within the divine world. Rather than God and his people calling out in affection to one another, we now find male and female, bridegroom and bride, *within* God as the subjects of the Song. Israel the folk are now relegated, along with the angels, to the status of "daughters of Jerusalem," those who witness the great romance, or even facilitate it by their hymns and praises, but are not quite part of the heavenly embrace. Using the full force of its mythic imagination, the Zohar depicts the Canticle in cosmic terms, "heaven" calling to "earth" or deep to deep, the words of the Song betokening the ultimate profundities of the love and eternal longing that exist within God, of which human longing is but a pale shadow.

Here the Zohar contrasts the Song of Songs with the Song of Moses at the Sea and the Psalms of David:

> Come and see. The song that Moses sang does refer to higher matters, not to things below. But he did not offer song like King Solomon; there was never a human being who rose so high in song as Solomon. Moses ascended in song and praise, giving thanks to the supreme King for having saved Israel, and for performing miracles and wonders for them in Egypt and at the sea. But King David and his son Solomon spoke another sort of song. David worked at preparing the maidens, adorning them for the Queen so that She and Her maidens might appear in beauty. It was this that he was striving for in his songs and praises, until finally he had prepared and adorned them all, Queen and maidens. When Solomon came he found the Queen fully adorned and her maidens beautifully arrayed. He sought to bring her to the Bridegroom, and brought the Bridegroom to the wedding canopy along with His Queen. He then spoke words of love between them so that they be joined as one, that both of them be as one whole, in love fulfilled. In this Solomon rose in sublime praise above all others. . . . There had been no man, since the creation of Adam, who had brought about love and affection through words of coupling above, until King Solomon. First he brought about their union above, then he invited the two of them together into the house that he had prepared for them.[31]

The Zohar's views on the question of evil and its origins are hardly less innovative than its view of God. Here too we are dealing with a mythic universe, a fantasy life richly nourished by the speculations of those Castilian Kabbalists who had preceded the author, and also more generally by the fascination that the forbidden demonic universe held for many a medieval mind.

Given the rather narrow range of possibilities open to Western theology in confronting the problem of evil and the sufferings of the righteous, the Zohar opts for a limited dualism. Content neither to deny the reality of evil, as Neoplatonism generally had, nor to ascribe evil to God himself, thus compromising his goodness and justice, the Kabbalists spoke of a real and active cosmic force of evil in the world, but one given vital support only by the moral and ritual defilement of human sin.

The cosmic powers of evil are not totally unknown to Jewish thought before the Kabbalah. Particularly in popular religion, demons and evil spirits are attested to in a great many sources, the formal theology of Judaism notwithstanding. The figure of Satan, known from but meager references in the Bible (the tale of Job and a single prophetic verse), lives on in rabbinic literature and already there is associated, as accuser, with the "evil urge" within each person that tempts humans into sin. The female aspect of the demonic world, headed by Lilith, also has roots that reach back into Babylonian antiquity. All these earlier sources are drawn upon by the Zohar, which both augments their ranks and systematizes them in a way that had never been done previously.

Since there is nothing in the world that does not ultimately have its roots in *eyn sof*, a myth of the origins of evil was essential to any explanation. Evil does not have its root in God, according to the Zohar, but is a negative by-product of the process of emanation. The dominant form this myth takes has to do with the necessary tension that exists as the fourth and fifth *sefirot*, *hesed* and *din*, emerge from *binah*. *Din*, the force of divine rigor or judgment, resents being tied to *hesed*, the unmitigated flow of love. In the very moment of its emanation it broke forth from the sefirotic system, saying, in the words of the Zohar "I shall rule! " The measuring rod of the *sefirot*, the flame of darkness, used the power of *eyn sof* to quickly force *din* back into line, but in that moment of escape some portion of its power was released that could not be retrieved. That portion of *din*, now turned against God, began its own sefirotic emanation in mocking imitation of the divine world. It too has ten emanated rungs, and in the union of Samāel and Lilith it represents the cosmic acting out of illicit sexuality.[32]

The moral lessons to be learned from this choice of myth are especially interesting. The Zohar sees evil as originating in justice itself, when that justice is not tempered with compassionate loving-kindness. The force of *din* within God has a legitimate role, punishing the wicked and setting out to limit the indiscriminate love-flow of *hesed*, which itself can be destructive if not held in proper balance. But once *din* has escaped the demands of love, it is no longer to be trusted. It then becomes a perversion of God's justice, one that would use his punishing powers to wreak destruction without cause. It is also interesting to note that images of the feminine and of sexual union are fully as prominent here as they are in discussions of the divine world. The Zohar represents an extreme case of the generally bipolar view of sexuality among medieval Jews: the same human drive represents the most sublime of mysteries and the most debased of sins.

The existence of an independent realm of evil was theologically problematic for the early Kabbalists. Even a demonic force somewhat lesser than the divine left them open to charges of dualism. Could God abolish the demonic powers, complete with the serpents, sea-monsters, and spirits that did their bidding? If not, he would be somehow less than God, and if he could, why had he not done so? The Zohar seems to answer apologetically that the forces of evil are a weapon God uses in the punishment of the wicked; in this sense *din* and the evil side are not clearly separate, it would seem, in the author's imagination. But the real answer to this question lies else-where: God has chosen to abdicate his responsibility for the destruc-tion of evil so that man be tested, so that the righteous themselves be given the task of combatting evil in the name of God. In fact the existence of an independent realm of evil creates a much more serious theological dilemma than that we have mentioned. If evil comes from *sitra aḥra*, the "other side," as it is often called, and not from man himself, how is the person to be held morally accountable? How can there be punishment for human sin, or reward for righ-teousness, for that matter, if evil is the result not of human choice but of the influence of outside forces?

The Zohar deals with this problem by positing a delicate balance between the forces of cosmic evil and those of moral evil stemming from within the human heart. *Sitra aḥra* is allowed by God to exist, but is given no share in divine power. As it was cut off from the sefirotic world, it lost its access to the life that flows from *eyn sof*, the vital force that allows for existence. It therefore exists only as dead matter, and would have no power at all were not man to arouse it by his evil deeds. Thoughts and act of sin give strength to the forces of evil, just as we shall see that good thought and deed energize the world of the *sefirot*. Once evil is aroused, it tempts man into further sin, requiring his sins for its own very sustenance. All it can do is tempt, however, for man is never released from the responsibility for his own actions. Of course the temptations offered by an old friend are more enticing, and the Zohar, a work that has significant moralistic intent, is filled with dire warnings to those who become too familiar with the forces of evil.

The question of evil has brought us to the threshhold of the more general question of man, his nature, and the meaning of human life. The myth of the Zohar is a highly anthropocentric one, and while the text seems much preoccupied with God and the upper realms, it can as well be read as a guide-book for the conduct of human life, and one that places squarely on man's shoulders full respon-sibility not only for his moral life but for the very survival of God's universe.

The notion that human beings are created in the image of God has a long and varied career in the history of Judaism. The Bible offers no explanation of the phrase (Genesis 1:27), but its original meaning was probably quite literal, and had as much to do with bodily form as it did with qualities of mind or spirit. The old Aramaic translation of the Bible preserves this meaning when it translates "image" (*zelem*) in that verse by the Greek loan-word *ikon*. Rabbinic sources seem divided on the question of the body's part in that likeness, a few remaining close to that literal meaning while most, possibly in fear of ascribing corporeality to God, veer toward the sense that the soul alone is in the divine form. Medieval Judaism outside the Kabbalah, with its general tendency to spiritualize the Bible far beyond what the rabbis had done, was quite unanimous in its view that soul alone was in God's image, the body serving as its temporary home, formed from dust and returning to dust. The belief in the bodily resurrection of the dead at the end of time does not seem to have mitigated this position.

Overlapping this discussion of the divine image was the question of the origin of the soul, particularly once its separateness from the body and its own inner three-part structure became the common understanding. Again, the dominant voice that emerged from rabbinic tradition, especially as refined in the Middle Ages, said that the soul was of divine origin, the body from earth. For the Zohar it was important to go beyond these claims. It insisted that the soul was not only divinely *bestowed*, but that its actual origin was in the upper world. The "home" for which it longed and which it, when un-impeded, sought to imitate, was the universe of the *sefirot*. It bears within it the stamp or "memory" of that primal union which formed it: kabbalistic learning is, in good Platonic fashion, an education to recall that which had been known to the soul eternally but forgotten in birth. The secret lore of the Kabbalist is thus seen not as alien and bizarre to the one who truly learns it, but as the hidden truth of his own soul. The highest portion of the soul is of the same "substance" as the *sefirot*. In a sort of "spiritual genetics," if you will, the Zohar therefore teaches that it too bears the sefirotic structure, that the hidden flow out of *keter*, the tensions of *hesed* and *din*, and the union of *tif'eret* and *malkhut* are all replicated in each person who bears a divine soul. This aspect of the mystical psychology of the Zohar becomes especially important for later Kabbalah and is of dominant interest to Hasidism in the eighteenth and nineteenth centuries.

Theories of exactly how the birth of the soul comes about, its life before it comes into the body, and the precise manner in which it is related to the sefirot all abound in early Kabbalah; quite a variety of these is found even within the Zohar. It is especially here that we sense the unsystematic character of the work and its role as compendium for the many views that its author had learned, and perhaps the varied visions of these matters he encountered in his own mystical life. In what is perhaps the dominant view, human souls (like the *sefirot* themselves) are conceived in *binah*, the highest possible source. Thence they are carried into *malkhut*, which serves as a treasure-house of souls, bestowing them to newborns as bodies are conceived in the lower world.

This emphasis on the divine nature of the soul should not give us the impression, however, that the Zohar sees the handiwork of God in soul and not in body. The Kabbalists are dramatically unusual in the medieval West in finding that body as well as soul reflects the inner structure of divinity. This was clearly one of the notions in the Zohar that later occultists most favored, and as a result it is among the best-known—and most often distorted—ideas of the Kabbalah.

Among the many images used for the ten *sefirot* and the patterns of relationship in which they stand to one another is that of the human body. The upper nine *sefirot*, as they are mother, father, and offspring, or as they are well, spring, and flowing streams, or roots, trunk and branches of a great inverted tree, are also depicted as limbs of a cosmic ideal "body." This is not to say that God is corporeal, or that man is wholly divine, but rather that the form of the human body is a copy in matter of the sublime and spiritual mystery of the *sefirot*. The charts that depict the *sefirot* in this way[33] see the first three *sefirot* as constituting a head, sometimes with *keter* as crown or forehead and *hokhmah/binah* as the two eyes. *Hesed* and *din*, as already indicated, are the two "arms" of God, their actions united in *tif'eret*, the trunk of the bodily form. *Nezah* and *hod* are then the two hips of the form, and as they receive the flow from above they pass it into *yesod*, the phallus and the final channel of divine energy. We should add here that this structuring in part accounts for the tremendous emphasis the Kabbalists placed upon purity and chastity in sexual matters: all sexual activity below aroused either divine or demonic energy above. From the "sign of the holy covenant" (i.e. circumcision) divinity flowed into *malkhut*, the female counterpart of this form, waiting to give the fruit of its seed to the lower world.

This view of the body and its limbs as created in the ideal holy form gives to the "image and likeness" of God a new lease on quasi-literal meaning. It also bespeaks the great ambivalence we see in the author's mind toward the human body and its passions. He was typical of his age in depicting the body as made of coarse matter, its drives and passions often at odds with the right goals of the pure soul, and as the element in man that kept him from the purity needed to unite with his Creator. But he also had a vision of the body that transcended all this, one that saw the whole person, body and soul, as capable of *imitatio Dei*, or even of *participation* in the divine process, in an utterly uncompromised manner. This is especially to be found in certain passages dealing with sexual union, in its proper setting:

> Come and see: It is written "Six days shall you labor and do all your work", and the seventh day is a Sabbath to the Lord your God" (Exodus 20:9). "All your work"—those six days are devoted to human labors. Because of this the companions do not have intercourse except at that time when there is nothing to be found of human labor, but only the work of God. What is His work? Uniting with the Queen, so that holy souls will be brought forth into the world. Therefore on this night the companions are sanctified with the holiness of their Lord and direct their hearts. Good children come forth [from such a union], holy children who turn aside neither right nor left, children of King and Queen. Of these Scriptures says: "You are children of the Lord your God" (Deuteronomy 14:1); "the Lord your God" indeed [the two names indicate] these are His children, children of King and Queen. It is to this that the companions put their mind; those who know this secret cleave fast to it. That is why their children are called God's children, and it is for their sake that the world survives. When the world is being judged, God looks at these children and has mercy for their sake. Of this Scripture speaks in saying: "All with true seed" (Jeremiah 2:21)—"true seed" indeed, for "truth" is the holy and perfect seal, as it says: "Give truth unto Jacob" (Micah 7:20) and all is one. That, indeed, is the "true seed." [34]

Here the mortal union of the companion and his wife parallels the union of the blessed Holy One and *shekhinah* above, each a priest in his Temple serving the ultimate mystery of the Godhead, souls and bodies born at once in their sublime and co-ordinated rites.

Such a vision of body and soul united in God's service, the most human of acts performed with the most divine of intent, has a particular contextual meaning within Judaism. The general tendency toward spiritualization in mysticism encountered certain limits in the Kabbalah, given the very real commitment of Judaism and its all-embracing legal system to the realm of this-wordly action. A pious Jew lives within the domain of the Torah and its commandments. These require the action of the limbs as well as commitments of mind and heart. *Halakhah* serves as a constant reminder to the Jew that he lives bound by certain physical restraints: what he eats, what he wears, where he goes, how he speaks, and many more areas of daily life are governed by the Law. We will recall that the Zohar was much concerned with full and proper observance, and was written partly as a defense of tradition against rationalist incursions. It remains, then, for us to describe the link between the self, body and soul, and the God in whose image that self is so fully made. That link, for the Zohar, is the wondrous and infinitely mysterious world of the Torah. The inner structure held in common by the divine and human selves is also to be found in God's word, the Torah. Both the written Torah and its centuries-long accompanying tradition of oral commentary and expansion are the means God offers Israel for self-fulfillment and approach to divinity. The text itself is alive with mystery, and all the intellectual talents of the Kabbalist must be directed toward the penetration of its secrets.

Rabbi Simeon said: If a man looks upon the Torah as merely a book presenting narratives and everyday matters, alas for him! Such a torah, one treating with everyday concerns, and indeed a more excellent one, we too, even we, could compile. More than that, in the possession of the rulers of the world there are books of even greater merit, and these we could emulate if we wished to compile some such torah. But the Torah, in all of its words, holds supernal truths and sublime secrets.

See how precisely balanced are the upper and the lower worlds. Israel here below is balanced by the angels on high, concerning whom it stands written: "who makest thy angels into winds" (Ps. 104:4). For when the angels descend to earth they don earthly garments, else they could neither abide in the world, nor could it bear to have them. But if this is so with the angels, then how much more so it must be with the Torah: the Torah it was that created the angels and created all the worlds and through Torah are all sustained. The world could not endure the Torah if she had not garbed herself in garments of this world.

Thus the tales related in the Torah are simply her outer garments, and woe to the man who regards that outer garb as the Torah itself, for such a man will be deprived of portion in the next world. Thus David said: "Open Thou mine eyes, that I may behold wondrous things out of Thy law" (Ps. 119:18), that is to say, the things that are underneath. See now. The most visible part of a man are the clothes that he has on, and they who lack understanding, when they look at the man, are apt not to see more in him than these clothes. In reality, however, it is the body of the man that constitutes the pride of his clothes, and his soul constitutes the pride of his body.

So it is with the Torah. Its narrations which relate to things of the world constitute the garments which clothe the body of the Torah; and that body is composed of the Torah's precepts, *gufey-torah* [bodies, major principles]. People without understanding see only the narrations, the garment; those somewhat more penetrating see also the body. But the truly wise, those who serve the most high King and stood on mount Sinai, pierce all the way through to the soul, to the true Torah which is the root principle of all. These same will in the future be vouchsafed to penetrate to the very soul of the soul of the Torah.[35]

Like many of his medieval contemporaries (in Christianity and Islam as well as Judaism) the Zohar's author knows of a multileveled truth to be found in Scripture. It is essential to his exegesis that the literal level, including the legal meanings derived by the rabbis, remain in force, while the mystical truth of his own reading is added to the Torah's meaning. At the same time, this and other passages make no secret of the fact that it is this esoteric reading that he considers "most" true or significant; here is where the heart of the Torah lives. The Torah is the ultimate corpus of secrets, pointing in every way to the "world of truth," a well of profundity never to be fully fathomed. In addition to the ongoing commandment to constantly study that profundity, man may embody the Torah's mysteries by the kabbalistic fulfillment of the life of the commandments.

Rather little in the realm of ritual life is innovated by the Zohar. The commandments to be performed are those of the Torah, as understood by the Zohar in common with all of rabbinic Judaism; only occasionally is there a minor addition or change of custom. But the *meaning* of this life of religious action is entirely transformed. No longer are the commandments either the arbitrary will of the Creator, intended to show one's faithful discipline, or the wise and educating law of the noble Monarch. Rather they are the secrets of the universe itself, each mysteriously locked inside a particular act which the devotee is to perform, and which he only partially fulfills until he fathoms its secret meanings.

We have already seen the imitation of God as a motif in the religious life, exemplified in the Kabbalist who directs his thoughts to heaven as he fulfills "be fruitful and multiply," the first commandment to be mentioned in the Bible. We have also seen that this is a particular kind of "imitation," one that reaches beyond the separateness of imitator and imitated and points toward the participation of man in the inner life of God, which is the fulfillment of his own inner life as well. As in this act he is able to bring forth holy souls by right deed and contemplation, so in other *mizwot* can he affect the condition of his own soul, defeat his own evil urge, cause encampments of angels to dwell about him and protect him, and in various ways save himself from those demonic powers that are all too ready to hold sway over him should he do wrong. The mythic mindset of the Zohar's author is at times also a superstitious one, if such a term can be used without pejorative intent. His universe is so peopled with flying demons and ill-intending spirits that the build-up of protection against them becomes a major motif in his religious life. At the same time, the accretion of merit for one's good deeds is not only a defense against evils; the more good the soul does, the higher the rungs of soul-life it is allowed to attain, and the closer it will come to that life of *zohar*, enlightenment, which the Zohar ever preaches: the life in which the soul adheres to God.

The goal of all religious life, for the Zohar as for other mystic works, is the return of the soul to God. The great mystery of existence is two-fold: how the world of multiplicity came out of the One, and how it may be returned there in a way of fulfillment that lies short of destruction. The Zohar has responded to (though hardly answered) the first question in speaking of *sefirot;* its response to the latter question comes in its understanding of *mizwot*, the sefirot as embodied in the commandments of the Torah. In giving the Torah to Israel, God has placed his own self within human access. Here, through the subtlety of symbolic language, divinity, human actions, and even the objects required for human action have become one. As the worshipper binds together the four species of plant used for the celebration of the *Sukkot* festival, he is actually drawing together, in his very hands, *hesed* and *din, tiferet* and *malkhut*. As the householder lifts his two loaves of bread for the Sabbath blessing, he holds in his hands the union of Jacob and Rachel, sun and moon, heaven and earth. As he holds them, so is he held by them, and the soul that contemplates the mysteries of these moments and their deeds is transported into a realm where the *sefirot* acting upon him and his acting upon them are processes not separable from one another. At the same time, the objects he has used in such rites, palm-branch and citron, loaves of bread, or whatever, are transported with him to that higher realm. Not only his soul is uplifted and transmuted, but the lower material world as well, through those symbolic objects that have achieved the transcendence of sanctification. The essential religious task becomes one of *attachment* and *uplifting*, the soul seeking adhesion to God, but doing so through the commandments in order that the corporeal world be raised up and transmuted with it.

The emergence of the universe out of God has been a graduated, step-by-step, process. The *shekhinah*, standing at the lower end of the sefirotic world, is at the head of a myriad of palaces, throne-rooms, antechambers and angelic choruses. Beneath those lie the spheres with their varying degrees of corporeality, ending in this world of coarse matter and its temptations. On the other side of this world lie as many realms of evil, "shells," mythical beasts, and demons that reach down into the mouth of the great pit. The human being, and especially the Jew who has that Torah which allows for the presence and fulfillment of his divine soul, stands at the very center of this universe. Something of him reaches down into its depths, but the roots of his soul extend to the uppermost heights. With the life of Torah as his guide, his task stands before him. He is the one who can draw the entire universe upward, raising matter to the level of spirit, spirit to the level of soul, soul to the level of *shekhinah*, reaching ever higher until his inner concentration effects that great *yiḥud* or union that allows the *shekhinah* herself to transcend her exile, to be united fully, through him, with God beyond, allowing the flow of divine life to abound through all the worlds, the joy of divine light to shine with undimmed brilliance. Only man can do this, for the Torah was given to him alone; his and his alone is the ecstatic task and the staggering responsibility of restoring the world to God.

> Happy is the man who goes in and out, who knows to contemplate the mysteries of his Lord and to cleave to Him. By these secrets a person is able to adhere to God, to attain full wisdom, the most sublime of mysteries. When he serves God in prayer, willingly and with a direction of heart he attaches his will to God like the flame to the coal. By this he unites the lower rungs in a holy manner, crowning them with a certain one of the lesser names. Thence he proceeds to unify the higher and innermost rungs, making them all one with that highest heaven that stands above them. Even while his mouth and lips are yet moving he should direct his heart and his will higher, higher, uniting all with that mystery of mysteries, the root of all thought and desire, the mystery that dwells within *eyn sof*. Every day he should have this intent in each of his prayers. In such worship will all his days be crowned with the mystery of those supernal days.[36]

BIBLIOGRAPHICAL NOTES

The text of the Zohar to the Torah has been translated into English and published by the Soncino Press: *The Zohar*, tr. Harry Sperling and Maurice Simon with introduction by J. Abelson (London, 1933) and various reprints. This translation, while quite readable in itself, is sorely lacking in reference to the Zohar's symbolic language and sefirotic structure, so that it is essentially incomprehensible without some prior preparation. An anthology of Zohar selections, edited by the late Gershom Scholem, is published by Schocken Press under the title *Zohar: The Book of Splendor* (New York, 1963). A new and larger selection, translated in poetic form and supplied with an excellent commentary, has been prepared by Daniel Matt for the *Classics of Western Spirituality* series of the Paulist Press. Also scheduled to appear, through the Litman Library in London, is Isaiah Tishby's monumental *Mishnat ha-Zohar*, itself a classic of modern Hebrew letters, in which passages from the Zohar are topically arranged and offered with lengthy introduction and commentary.

For further modern readings on the history of Kabbalah, the reader must consult the works of Gershom Scholem, the great master of contemporary scholarship in this field. His *Major Trends in Jewish Mysticism*, rev. ed. (New York, 1965) is the basic study in the field. Less detailed and perhaps more accessible to the general reader are his volumes of collected essays *On the Kabbalah and Its Symbolism* (New York, 1965) and *The Messianic Idea in Judaism* (New York, 1971). Scholem was given a chance to update his opinions on many questions in this ever-developing scholarly field by means of the articles on Kabbalah for the *Encyclopedia Judaica*. These articles have been reissued in a single volume simply entitled *Kabbalah* (Jerusalem, 1974), recommended only as a complement to *Major Trends* or as a reviewing survey.

Scholem writes within a modern Western historical-academic tradition. Some will seek writings on the Kabbalah that take a more traditionally pious tone, or else a more universally mystical orientation, without distorting the original meaning of the kabbalistic sources. For the former, a rather traditional Jewish view of the mystical spirit, the reader would do well to begin with Abraham Joshua Heschel's essay, "The Mystical Element in Judaism," published in Louis Finkelstein's anthology, *The Jews* (New York, 1960), pp. 932–53. Others of Heschel's writings, though modern in cast, are much influenced by the kabbalistic/Hasidic spirit. The books by Rabbis Alexander Safran (*The Kabbalah* [New York, 1975]) and Ben Zion Bokser (*The Jewish Mystical Tradition* [New York, 1981]) are also recommended for the non-specialist. In a more contemporary vein, Leo Schaya's *The Universal Meaning of the Kabbalah* (London, 1971) has the Western seeker in mind, but does not falsify the Kabbalah in presenting it. *The Thirteen-Petalled-Rose* (New York, 1980) by Adin Steinsaltz, is another such responsibly written introduction in a contemporary context. The same cannot be said of a great many other works that purport to teach Kabbalah, and the reader is duly warned.

VI

Mystic on Campus: Friar Thomas

JAMES A. WEISHEIPL, O.P.

Mystics are rarely found today on university campuses. Perhaps that is why it comes as a surprise to learn that mysticism not only can survive academic life, but can even thrive on it. There is no reason why intellectuals cannot be saints and mystics. It is easier for intellectuals to be saints than for saints to be intellectual. The great Fathers and Doctors of the Church were both saints and intellectuals, although not all of them flourished in universities and academies. But there were at least three Doctors of the Church who did survive campus life: Albert the Great, Bonaventure, and Thomas Aquinas; and this at the very beginning of university life as we know it today, the thirteenth century. The most interesting of them all is Friar Thomas d'Aquino, because he thrived on it.

The dichotomy we commonly find between intellectuals and the spirituals is not a necessary condition of mankind. It is only because the intellect and the will are two distinct faculties that it is possible to have intellectuals on one side and mystics on the other. The intellect by its very nature brings everything to its own level, exalting things below it and limiting things above it. The will, on the other hand, like all appetitive powers, is totally brought to the level of its object, exalted by the good that is greater than itself and demeaned by the good or apparent good that is beneath it. But even love of one like to itself, another human being, expands the soul and gives it a life it never had before.

135

To be clear and accurate in our understanding of the terms "mystic" and "mysticism" we should note that for St. Thomas these terms derived from Greek were equivalent to Latin terms derived from "spirit," like "spiritual" and "spirituality." Thomas would not find it paradoxical to encounter a "mystic on campus"; there is nothing incompatible between intelligence and mysticism, just as there is nothing incompatible between reason and faith, or between nature and grace. Thomas had a far richer and truer notion of "mysticism" than that which is our common inheritance from the sixteenth century. We tend to think that "mystics" are an odd group of people conspicuous for their "ecstasies," "visions," prophecies, levitations, miracles, mystical marriages, and the like. A saint may have all these things (as did Thomas), but if he has not charity, he is nothing, no matter how mystical and saintly his reputation may be. These phenomena, by which we tend to distinguish "mystics," were for St. Thomas accidental and secondary effects of the only true marks of sanctity, namely grace and the virtues, principally "charity" (or love of God above all things and one's neighbor as one's self) active in the soul. On this score true contemplation of God in this life (or mysticism) is the normal development of grace in the soul of a baptized Christian. But this contemplation is so interior and personal that it is hidden from the eyes of the spectator in this world. No one ever need know that an individual has experienced numerous purifications of soul and body, the dark night of the spirit, the workings of grace and the Holy Spirit, or true contemplation. True mysticism has to do with the interior life of the spirit in its encounter with God.

One of the fundamental convictions of all medieval theologians was that "grace does not destroy nature, but perfects it." [1] That is to say, while grace cannot take the place of nature, it cannot do without it. There must first be a nature, even fallen nature, for grace to elevate. There must be an intellect that can be brought to the heights of truth, there must be a will that can be drawn by the highest love, and there must be a human body that can be glorified. Even the emotions in man are there to be sanctified. In other words, man has an intellect that can know many truths naturally; it can know many more truths supernaturally by accepting on faith all that God has revealed. Man has a will and human affections that can love much and do much good; we can be heroic in our love and extraordinary in our works by giving back the love God gave us. This is what is meant by grace perfecting nature, raising it beyond itself without destroying the true nature God had made. It is the same God who made nature and grace.

The uniqueness of St. Thomas is that he was an outstanding intellectual in every sense of the term and a most unusual mystic, whose mysticism, instead of driving him away from the campus, made him stay right there until the end. Albert the Great left the campus to become a bishop; St. Bonaventure left the campus to become Minister General of the Franciscans and then Cardinal. But Friar Thomas refused to leave, because that is where he saw his apostolate needed most. That is because his apostolate was thoroughly intellectual and his intellectualism was thoroughly spiritual. His personal mysticism was a theological spirituality, wherein there is no break between the grace of baptism and the glory of heaven. Moreover, for him, there is no break between the spirituality of the pilgrim and the experiences of the mystic. The whole life of the spirit is the life of grace, lived with greater or less intensity—a difference of degree only, not of kind.

Undoubtedly the integral unity of St. Thomas' mystical life stemmed from his conviction that the whole of *sacra doctrina* is a single habit of mind that is both speculative and practical.[2] This *sacra doctrina* is called "faith" by the believer; it is called "theology" by the academic. Theology, for Thomas, may be thoroughly academic and scientific, but it is no whit greater than faith. Theology, as every medieval professor knew, is nothing more than the human mind trying to grasp exactly what God has revealed to be believed. This was commonly expressed, in the words of St. Augustine and St. Anselm, as the idea that theology is "faith seeking understanding" *(fides quaerens intellectum)*. This did not mean that the theologian understands or can demonstrate the mysteries revealed. It is not that the theologian knows more about God than the simple believer does; rather, his belief is clearer.[3]

A second factor in the unified vision of mysticism for St. Thomas was his conviction that the whole spiritual life from beginning to end is a single reality. All we can have of Christian perfection in this life is grace, which is a personal sharing in the intimate life of God. But this very grace is in fact the seed of glory. *Gratia est semen gloriae* was a fundamental conviction of all medieval theologians, and of St. Thomas in particular. This grace is normally received in baptism, even in the baptism of a child; it is increased or replaced through the sacraments, and can grow with every act we perform through Christian love, which is called "charity." As St. Thomas sees it, this tiny seed can and should grow to full perfection in heaven; in the process of living, this initial grace can and should pass through all the stages of Christian perfection, earthly contemplation of God through the gifts of the Holy Spirit, and can and should even experience the various aspects of mysticism before reaching the joys of heaven.[4] Thus what is called "mystical contemplation" is, for Thomas, a normal and important stage along every Christian's road to heaven. It is not an esoteric phenomenon reserved for the few. That it is relatively rare does not make it any less "normal" within the operations of grace; mysticism is indeed impossible within nature, but it is an essential companion of grace in the domain of supernature. Thus, for St. Thomas, "the light of grace (lumen gratiae) directs the mind and inflames the heart" so that every Christian man, woman, and child can be a saint (and mystic) in this life and one of the blessed in the next.[5]

This dual unity of sacra doctrina, of course, is not the common view today. It is not common today to think of all theology as having the unity of one faith; nor is it common today to think of all grace as necessarily (in the sense of "normally" and "properly") leading to mystical sanctity and eternal beatitude. The two-fold tragedy of the sixteenth century was that Christianity itself was fragmented by the Reformers, and that the unique habit of theology was fragmented by the university professors. Since the sixteenth century, and especially since the seventeenth, professors have sought to multiply chairs for themselves in the growing universities by creating specialties like dogmatic theology (speculative), moral theology (practical), biblical theology (Scripture), mystical and ascetical theology (special course), fundamental theology (apologetics), positive theology (sources), and further chairs in Church history, homiletics, and pastoral theology. The crucial error in the study of mystical theology is the assumption that mystical theology is essentially different from "grace," and as such can be studied either by the professor of dogma or the professor of morals.

This situation creates a problem for the historian who wishes to present a brief picture of Thomas the mystic. St. Thomas himself wrote no work that could properly be termed "mystical." There is no special part of his Summa theologiae, intended to be a summary of the whole of sacra doctrina for beginners, that can be called "mystical" or even "spiritual." The whole of his theology is spiritual and mystical. Since, however, his type of spirituality was that of a theologian on campus, it can be called a "theological spirituality."

Since, for Thomas, the sole measure of spirituality is supernatural charity and its intensity in loving God and neighbor, and not such "mystical phenomena" as prophecy, visions, ecstasy, levitation, and the like, we must seek the spirituality of St. Thomas in his daily life. That such phenomena were present in the life of Thomas is certain, but they are not the measure of his spirituality.[6] The primacy of love in the theology of St. Thomas is clear throughout his Summa.[7]

Without this love, no thought, word, or deed is meritorious of heaven, but with it all of one's labors are sanctified.[8]

Presenting Thomas the mystic in his medieval milieu is not the same as presenting "mysticism" according to the teaching of St. Thomas. Of the latter, there are many excellent examples. Of the former, the earliest is the *Hystoria* of blessed Thomas by the Dominican William of Tocco, who had seen Thomas at Naples in 1272–73 and who was appointed official promoter of the cause of his canonization in 1317. For many years he had been collecting family stories and facts for the purpose of getting Thomas canonized (in 1323). In Tocco's *Hystoria* many "mystical phenomena" are mentioned, but examples of Thomas' heroic virtue are also to be found. The biggest obstacle to canonization presented by the Devil's Advocate was that Thomas worked no miracles, or very few, during his life! This was eventually disposed of by a second process of inquiry at Fossanova to list the miracles after his death.

For the sake of simplicity we will concentrate on the growth of charity in Thomas' daily life as a professor on various campuses and houses of study. We will examine this growth as he worked through three crucial periods in his brief forty-nine years (1225–74): the problem of his vocation when he was nineteen, the problem of his theological apostolate when he was thirty-five, and the most trying of all, a crisis of soul that came toward the end of his life when he was close to fifty.

Since the academic milieu in which Thomas lived is so relevant to the story and perhaps cannot be taken for granted in modern readers, a word should be said about the thirteenth century context in which he lived.

THE SPIRITUAL CONTEXT OF THE AGE

For the sake of simplicity, we should recall three transforming movements that made the thirteenth century the unique century it was. The fundamental movement that transformed society was undoubtedly the urbanization of Europe. Already in the twelfth century there was an expansion of trade and commercial routes that saw the growth of new cities along waterways, like Paris, Cologne, London, Koblenz, Toulouse, Bologna, Florence, and Venice. Earlier centuries were largely rural, with religious life organized around such centers as Chartres, Sens, Laon, Canterbury, and York. Power tended to be localized in castles, fortified towns, and monasteries on hills (Benedictine) or in quiet valleys (Cistercian). Now people flocked to the new cities bringing new needs with them. Urbanization of society brought with it two other movements that made up the context of Thomas' life.

The second movement was uniquely spiritual in that it met the spiritual needs of city people, who were merchants, pilgrims, scholars, and even rulers. They wanted desperately to hear the word of God and they longed to see true piety and evangelical poverty. This need gave rise to new religious orders of mendicant friars *(fratres)*. These friars thought of themselves as returning to the life and work of the Apostles. That is, they freed themselves from manual labor in order "to concentrate on prayer and the ministry of the word" (Acts 6:4). In common with the tradition of monasteries the friars sought contemplation in community life, the three vows of poverty, chastity, and obedience, and in the daily choral office. But by an active apostolate, they sought to give to others the fruits of their contemplation. The earliest group of friars to be recognized by the Holy See were the Order of Preachers (Dominicans), founded by St. Dominic, and the Order of Friars Minor (Franciscans), founded by St. Francis. Before the end of the century many other mendicant orders were founded, such as the Carmelites, Augustinians, Trinitarians, Servites, Crosiers, Crutched Friars, and Friars of the Sack, many of which were later suppressed or amalgamated.

The special characteristic of the Dominicans, whom St. Thomas joined, was the active apostolate of preaching the Word of God, the Gospel *(Evangelium)*. Because of this preaching apostolate, originally among the Albigenses, St. Dominic added the special obligation of "assiduous study of divine truth." This obligation and its principal purpose, evangelical preaching, was particularly important for Thomas' religious vocation.

The third movement, intimately associated with the growth of cities and the orders of mendicant friars, was the organization of learning in new centers such as Bologna, Paris, Oxford, Cologne, Montpellier, and Toulouse.

This organization of students and teachers was called a *universitas*, a coming together of teachers and students in various faculties (departments): arts and philosophy, theology, law (both civil and ecclesiastical), and medicine. In 1215 the earliest charter for the guild of scholars in Paris was signed, sealed, and delivered by the Papal Legate. One year before this, a royal charter was given to Oxford masters and students. Later other organized centers, called *studia*, or houses of study, were established and confirmed. In the first dispersal of the Preaching Friars in 1217, Dominic sent seven friars to Paris, and four to Spain, while he and his companions went to Bologna. Just as the university of Paris became the foremost center of Christian thought in the thirteenth century, so the Dominican house of St.-Jacques in Paris became the most important in the Order.

These points are important for the life and spirituality of Thomas d'Aquino. Although he was born in a castle on a mountain top called Roccasecca, he spent all of his adult life in the cities. Although he was set aside by his parents to be a monk in the Abbey of Monte Cassino, he determined to be a begging friar. Although most brilliant men of the century hoped for high ecclesiastical office, he insisted on staying on campus as a mendicant friar in the big city.

A PROBLEM OF VOCATION

Thomas was born around 1225 in the castle of Roccasecca between Rome and Naples in the territory of Emperor Frederick II.[9] He was the ninth child in the d'Aquino family, headed by his father Landulf, a Lombard knight, and his wife Theodora from Naples. All of Thomas' older brothers were soldiers in the service of the Emperor, but he was offered to the Church as a monk in the famous abbey of Monte Cassino with the firm expectation that he would eventually be its Abbot. At the age of five Thomas was offered (*oblata*) to the abbey where he learned the ways of monastic life, study, and prayer. But when Thomas was fourteen years of age, the fortress abbey of Monte Cassino was occupied by the troops of Frederick II, lest it be occupied by the papal forces of Gregory IX in one of the many wars between pope and emperor. As it was unsafe for young students, Thomas and companions were sent to Naples to complete their study of the liberal arts at the university which Frederick had established as a rival of Bologna.

In the bustling harbor city of Naples young Thomas saw for the first time Dominican Friars as they begged for food, preached to the citizens, and offered the liturgy in the priory named after their founder San Domenico. He became particularly fond of a certain Friar John of San Giuliano, who "loved him dearly" and "encouraged him along the way."[10] Thomas was fascinated both by the studies he found so rewarding and by the begging friars, intent on God and the things of God. When Thomas was about nineteen, even before finishing his university course, he determined to become a Dominican, that is, a Preaching Friar who was a beggar and contemplative. Toward the end of April 1244, Thomas was clothed in the white habit of St. Dominic at the priory in Naples. He certainly was old enough to make a free choice, and he was not yet a Benedictine monk, although his parents fully intended that he should do so. His new Dominican superiors decided to send Thomas to Bologna in the north for his novitiate and theological studies, since they were aware of the objections that might be raised by a wealthy family to one of its sons becoming a begging friar. It so happened that the Master General of the Dominicans, John of Wildeshausen, was going to Bologna with some companions for the annual General Chapter of the Order opening at Pentecost, May 22.

But the Dominicans had not reckoned with the resourcefulness of the d'Aquino family, whose fortunes lay in the hands of Donna Theodora, since Landulf had died the previous December. On learning of Thomas' reckless action, Theodora sent an urgent message to her son Rinaldo, who was with the army of Frederick II encamped at Aquapendente just north of Rome, to bring Thomas home at all cost. Rinaldo and his military escort (with the connivance of Frederick) intercepted the group of Dominicans traveling by foot not far from Rome. Thomas naturally refused to return or to take off his new Dominican habit. Rinaldo then "violently separated his brother from the Master General, and forcing him to mount a horse, sent him off with a strong guard to one of the family castles in the Campagna called Montesangiovanni." [11] This castle was in papal territory and served as a stopping off place for the night en route to Roccasecca. Thomas' patience was finally exhausted when Rinaldo procured a harlot, "a very beautiful girl seductively dressed who would incite him to sin." [12] Feeling that this last indignity was worse than the first, Thomas drove the prostitute from his room with a firebrand, charred the sign of the cross on the door, broke into tears, and fell into slumber. It was commonly said and believed by all of Thomas' biographers that from this incident on Thomas never again experienced the least movement of lust. Even Reginald of Piperno, who later became Thomas' constant companion, claimed to have learned of this from Thomas himself.[13] The later Confraternity of Angelic Warfare took its inspiration from this incident, when two angels were said to gird Thomas with a cord of angelic purity.

On the following day the soldiers arrived at Roccasecca with their hostage. Theodora tried to reason with him for the good of the whole family. For almost a year Thomas was restricted to the castle while his mother and sisters tried to change his mind about his vocation. One sister, Marotta, tried to convince Thomas to obey his mother; instead Thomas convinced her to become a Benedictine nun. His friend Friar John of San Giuliano "was allowed to visit him frequently and bring him changes of clothing by the expedient of coming fully clothed in two habits, one of which, as soon as they were alone, he would take off and give to Thomas." [14]

This was a difficult year (1244–45) for young Thomas as he passed his twentieth birthday. He became all the more determined to live a life of absolute purity, poverty, and obedience to a new calling.

He was determined to be a begging friar and a contemplative intent on giving to others the fruits of his contemplation. Theodora finally gave up her hopeless task when Emperor Frederick II was finally deposed by the First Council of Lyons on June 17, 1245. Deposition at that time meant that no one had any obligations to him at all. Thomas was allowed to throw in his lot with the beggars. For Theodora, this was a complete loss to everyone: herself, the family, even the Church. For Thomas this meant freedom to study, to pray, and someday to preach. The authorities decided to send Thomas to Paris "to get him further away from his family and the Roman curia!" [15]

Friar Thomas arrived in Paris in time to hear St. Albert the Great lecture as a Master in Theology on the mystical theology of the exceptional Dionysius, the supposed disciple of St. Paul in Athens. When Thomas heard Albert, he found what his heart had always desired, and he "began to be more than ever absorbed, more than ever assiduous in study and devout in prayer." [16] When he went to Cologne as one of Albert's students in the new *studium generale* that Albert established, he really found the secret of the intellectual life as a Dominican: complete absorption in the intellectual and spiritual life. His silence in Cologne and his conspicuous size prompted his classmates to call him "the Dumb Ox." It is true that Thomas never learned German or French, although he lived in Cologne and Paris a good number of years. Under Albert's guidance he quickly learned the new philosophy of Aristotle, the spiritual theology of pseudo-Dionysius, and the profound doctrine of St. Augustine. Thomas even served as Albert's teaching assistant in Cologne.

In the summer of 1252 the position of the mendicant friars at Paris came under fire by other professors at the university. In particular it was a secular priest from Burgundy named William of St.-Amour who aroused most of the university and Parisian populace against the mendicant orders. William was not entirely unjustified, since some of the Franciscans proclaimed themselves the new prophets in the new age of the "Eternal Gospel" preceding the final coming. William denounced them as the precursors of anti-Christ. To him the new mendicant orders were an aberration, a travesty of religious orders, and a threat to Christian society.

For the Dominicans, who had two chairs of theology in the university, it was crucial to have the best professors available to argue the case. As matters turned out, Albert had his way and Thomas was ordered to Paris to begin four years of teaching as an assistant (bachelor of the *Sentences*). His graduation, or "inception," in the spring of 1256 was marked with considerable hostility, public violence in the streets, and unacademic behavior instigated by followers of

William of St.-Amour. Young Thomas, enthusiastic for the life of a mendicant contemplative on the campus, wrote *An Apology for the Religious Orders* against William's arguments, but it played no role in the condemnation of William's book that very same year on October 5. William was exiled by the king, the mendicant orders were defended by the pope, and tranquility returned to the campus where Aristotle was all the rage, even for theologians.

As a full professor of theology at Paris, Thomas had the usual functions of lecturing on the Bible, disputing current theological questions, and preaching to the academic community on certain days. His days were entirely full, his spirit was completely absorbed in prayer, study, teaching, and writing. Apart from his academic apostolate, Thomas agreed to write a handbook for preachers in Muslim countries called a *Summa contra Gentiles*. He began this work in Paris and completed it four years later in Italy; it was an arsenal of arguments "against the gentiles" and in support of the Christian view, requested by St. Raymond of Pennafort (1185–1275) for use in his "House of Arabic Studies" in Barcelona. Even then Thomas looked to the wider field of ecclesiastical needs for his theological apostolate. Shortly after beginning this *Summa*, the young master was appointed to a Dominican commission of five masters to draw up guidelines for study in the Order. This commission, under the chairmanship of St. Albert, emphasized the importance of philosophy in the Dominican apostolate.[17]

After seven years in Paris, Thomas returned to his home priory of San Domenico in Naples where he had received the Dominican habit fifteen years earlier. He was assigned a younger confrère, Friar Reginald of Piperno, to be his constant companion *(socius)* and secretary. Much of our knowledge of Thomas' private life comes from him. Some of the visions, raptures, and inspirations narrated by William of Tocco date from this period; these seem to have been more or less continuous until Thomas' death fourteen years later. During the next ten years in Italy, he was given two important assignments that must be noted here because of their influence on the theological spirituality of St. Thomas as an intellectual engaged in the academic life.

First, Thomas was assigned to Orvieto as lector in the Dominican priory (1261–65). Shortly after his arrival there, while he was commenting on the Book of Job to the brethren, Pope Urban IV took up residence in that papal city. He became very friendly with Friar Thomas. Among other things, the pope requested a line by line gloss on the four Gospels from all the Fathers of the Church that were known. This exceptional gloss was popularly known as the *Catena Aurea* ("the Golden Chain"); because of its pioneering effort to assimilate the Greek Fathers of the Church, the whole gloss was translated by some of the leaders of the Oxford Movement in the nineteenth century. At the request of the same pope, Thomas composed an exceptional liturgy, Office and the Mass, for the new feast of Corpus Christi, established for the universal Church in August 1264. The two hymns commonly sung at Benediction in church, the *O Salutaris hostia* and *Tantum ergo*, are taken from this liturgy. Some people find it difficult to imagine that these hymns were written by an academic, and an intellectual. They express nothing more than what Thomas would eventually incorporate in the third part of his *Summa Theologiae*. Devotion to the real presence of Christ's Body and Blood in the Eucharist is one of the main centers of his theological spirituality, that is, his entire spiritual life.

Orvieto was Thomas' first real encounter with many new works of Greek theology. He tells us that for the *Catena Aurea* he procured translations of special works previously unknown. He found in the papal library a Latin translation of all the early Councils of the Greek Church. And he even encouraged a Flemish confrère, William of Moerbeke, a Greek scholar then at the papal court, to check and revise all of the Latin Aristotle then known. Greek theology and Greek spirituality, called "mystical" in Greek, complemented Latin spirituality in many ways. The Greeks emphasize in a most special way the role of the Blessed Trinity in theology and mysticism; for Thomas this became the principal subject of his *sacra doctrina*. They also focused on the Incarnation of the Word, since the early Councils of the Church were primarily concerned with the two natures in Christ. What the Greeks called "mystical," the Latins called "spiritual"; both terms refer to what is beyond the literal, the material, the evident, and not to "exceptional phenomena" of any sort. That is why St. Thomas would find the modern notion of "mystical theology" an aberration and misconception of true theology, as he understood it.

The second important assignment in Italy was to teach beginners in theology at the Dominican priory of Santa Sabina in Rome. This assignment came in the fall of 1265, after the death of his dear friend Urban IV. Very quickly Thomas realized the need of a simple summary of theology that beginners could assimilate on the side, while the teacher expounded the Sacred Scriptures in class and held public disputations. Here he conceived the idea of a theological *Summa* of "sacred doctrine" for beginners, eliminating unnecessary questions, simplifying traditional arguments, and proceeding in an orderly fashion like the Creed with first things first and all things covered.[18] After two years the first part of the *Summa Theologiae* was published, in 1268. This dealt with the one God, three in persons, who created all things that exist: angels, the universe, and man made in the image of God with an incorruptible intellect and a free will. Simply speaking, the whole first part deals with the coming-forth *(exitus)* of all things from God. The rest of the *Summa* would focus on the *reditus* of all things back to God. The precision, clarity, and brevity of the first part of the *Summa* placed Thomas well above his illustrious contemporaries, even above St. Albert the Great, St. Bonaventure, and above the future Blessed Innocent V (Peter of Tarantaise). The only disputable characteristic of this first part is that it is highly metaphysical and Aristotelian throughout.

In the very first article of the first question on the nature of *sacra doctrina*, Thomas shows his respect for human intelligence while demonstrating the need for supernatural revelation. Although human intelligence can come to a knowledge of God's existence, some attributes of God, and man's natural obligations, God in his mercy decided to reveal even these natural mysteries, because so few philosophers have come to these truths, often after many years of searching, and even then with admixture of error. An essential part of St. Thomas' theological spirituality is his respect for human intelligence while leaving the last word to God. The relation between faith and intelligence, for Thomas, is a special case of the relation between grace and nature: neither can be denied or dismissed without serious consequences.

The basic mysteries of the Triune God, the Incarnation, and the reality of Christ's Body and Blood in the Eucharist can in no way be discovered or demonstrated by natural intelligence. These are the strict domain of faith. For Thomas these three mysteries happened to be the main centers of his personal spirituality. But in fact these three are so intimately related that they form a single center of his entire mystical experience.

Basically St. Thomas was an optimist. Wherever he looked he saw the good, and all goodness comes from God. Whatever real evil there is in the world comes from the hearts of men; but even the hearts of men are good, because they are created by God.[19] Unlike St. Bonaventure, who easily saw the evils of pagan philosophy, St. Thomas looked and easily saw the good that was there. Similarly, no philosophy is so erroneous as to have no truth whatever, and no person is so bad as to have nothing good about him at all. G.K. Chesterton aptly described Thomas as a "fighting optimist," meaning that Thomas fought everyone who would deny the goodness that belongs to God and his creation, much as St. Dominic fought the Albigenses who denied the good that God had made.[20]

Despite the tremendous accomplishments Thomas achieved by the time he was thirty-three, the best was still to come. Despite the heights of sanctity Thomas reached, with all of its rumored conversations with Saints Peter and Paul, reported levitations and absorption in prayer, the deepest purifications were yet to come.

A WIDER THEOLOGICAL APOSTOLATE

While Thomas was laboring on his *Summa* in Italy, anti-mendicant feeling was revived in Paris by the secular theologian Gérard d'Abbeville, a personal friend of the exiled William of St.-Amour. For Gérard the very existence and activity of all the mendicants in France was corrosive of traditional values and the stability of the social order. All the old issues were again brought up that had lain dormant since the papal condemnation twelve years earlier. What occasioned this renewal of hostilities was the death of Pope Clement IV in November 1268 and the prolonged vacancy in the Holy See. The situation became so serious in Paris that St. Bonaventure, Minister General of the Franciscans, moved his headquarters there; and Blessed John of Vercelli, Master General of the Dominicans, ordered Thomas d'Aquino and Peter of Tarantaise (the future Pope Innocent V) to return to Paris and resume their previous professorships. This was a drastic move on the part of the Dominican for it held up the creation of new Masters in Theology.

In unquestioned obedience Thomas and Reginald, his companion, arrived in Paris early in the new year of 1269, well after the academic year had begun. The situation in Paris was far more complex than Thomas could have imagined. For him it was a three-sided battle within the university. Secular professors of theology were attacking the rights of all mendicant orders, especially the Dominicans and Franciscans, who had chairs in the university. Secular professors and Franciscans were attacking the use of Aristotle in theology, meaning Thomas and Albert especially. And all the theologians, secular, Franciscan, and Dominican, were deeply disturbed by the heterodox Aristotelianism coming from the Faculty of Arts, especially from Siger of Brabant and Boethius of Dacia.

Throughout the hectic five years that followed Thomas worked with incredible zeal and energy. Yet he retained a serenity and inner absorption that amazed everyone. Even in the heat of controversy Thomas never lost his temper or his cool logic against the angriest of opponents. During these five years Thomas' vision of his own theological apostolate underwent a transformation by being widened. Most of the "mystical experiences" mentioned by William of Tocco belong to this period. They consisted mainly of absorption in contemplative prayer, shedding of tears at Mass, reported levitations, and visions. None of these things as such appears in his writings.

All of these writings—well over half of his publications—have the clarity of a syllogism, the acuteness of a rapier, and the magnificence of truth.

It is not entirely clear exactly what was involved in this expansion and transformation of his theological apostolate. The late I.T. Eschmann used to be amazed at the qualitative difference between the first part of the Summa and the rest, the earlier being more rationalistic, metaphysical, and abstract, the latter being more sensitive, realistic, and original.[21] R.A. Gauthier, discussing a significant change in Thomas' docrine of continence—placing this virtue in the will instead of in the intellect, as he had previously—claims that Thomas was induced "to mitigate the excessive intellectualism that he had earlier displayed." [22] Dom Odo Lottin also noted a change of this kind when he examined the question of free will in Thomas' teaching from this time on, but he attributed this change to the condemnation of certain Averroist theses in December 1270.[23] But this too could be attributed to his deeper understanding of Augustine. Santiago Ramirez, studying the problem of faith and the gifts of the Holy Spirit in the second part of the Summa, also noted an over-all development in thought and attributed it to the growing influence of St. Augustine.[24] In other words, while the young Thomas saw clearly what had to be rejected in the Augustinianism of his contemporaries, the older Thomas came to appreciate much more what was true in the authentic Augustine.[25] What the above-mentioned authorities say about the second part is even truer of the third part of the Summa where the Incarnation and the Eucharist are discussed.

Perhaps the simplest way to characterize this transformation is to see it as somehow more apostolic. During the five crucial years between 1269–73 Thomas certainly labored as an apostle, indefatigably and relentlessly with the aid of Friar Reginald and a team of secretaries. We are told that he ate little and slept less, devoting all of his energies to writing, dictating, teaching, studying, and praying. His actual accomplishments during these five years at Paris and Naples defy imagination and imitation.

Like the young Macedonian in St. Paul's vision, who beckoned Paul to come to Macedonia to help his people (Acts 16:9), young students, both Dominican and non-Dominican, beckoned Thomas to come into their world to help them. The Summa Theologiae was begun for beginning students in theology; the task became even more urgent as he entered the new frontiers of virtues and vices, nature and grace, the Incarnation and the sacraments. Seeing for the first time the desperate need for an accurate understanding of philosophy, Thomas undertook a detailed expositon of Aristotle's major texts used in class by young professors beginning their careers. Similarly

to enable young men to become mendicant friars with a clear conscience, he engaged in the re-heated attack on the mendicants for
enlisting mere "boys" and pretending that observing the three vows
is better than obeying the ten commandments.

Since these three apostolates are essential to Thomas' mature vision
of the spiritual life, we will treat each of these three areas briefly.
Each one contributed to Thomas' theological mysticism on campus,
a mysticism that was deeply personal and intellectual.

First, the revived controversy against the mendicants had to be
faced, since that was the very reason for his return to Paris. This
renewal of verbal hostility occurred during the two year vacancy of
the Holy See after the death of Clement IV. Gérard d'Abbeville had
always remained faithful to the exiled William of St.-Amour, and he
had many followers. They maintained that manual labor, not begging
or teaching, was proper to religious; that wealth, not poverty, is the
heritage of the Church since Constantine's donation to Pope Sylvester;
that perfection consists in obeying the precepts (ten commandments)
rather than the counsels (poverty, chastity, and obedience); and that
the so-called "privileges" of mendicants infringe on divine "rights"
given to bishops and parish priests. What was worse, these arguments
were presented to young "boys" lest they be snatched by the mendicants.

On New Year's day 1269 Gérard preached a sermon in the Franciscan church in Paris on the question of poverty, so dear to the
Franciscans. In the congregation were St. Bonaventure, John Pecham,
his successor in the Franciscan chair at the university, and Thomas
of York. Gérard pointedly attacked the favorite Franciscan claim that
Christ and the Apostles had nothing of their own, even in common.
Gérard further fanned hostility in academic disputations, incendiary
pamphlets, and in other university sermons. Each of the Franciscans
mentioned replied with writings of his own.

Friar Thomas also replied in writing and in university disputations.
Toward the end of 1269 he wrote a short but important work entitled
On the Perfection of the Spiritual Life. While this is a polemical work,
it presents Thomas' view in a concise manner on a limited number
of points: (i) the essential nature of spiritual perfection, (ii) the manner
of acquiring perfection, and (iii) activities compatible with the religious
state.[26]

As for perfection strictly so-called, "the spiritual life consists principally in charity, without which one is considered spiritually a
nothing [*nihil*]" in the sense St. Paul meant it in 1 Corinthians 13:2.
"The perfection of the spiritual life, then, consists in being perfect
in love (charity)," and not being perfect simply in kindness, mercy,
humility, or some other particular virtue, much less in poverty, which

is not even a virtue. Since God is the most lovable of all things, man's beatitude consists in loving him above all things always and actually; this is the perfection of the spiritual life in heaven. In this life we are commanded to love God with our whole heart (i.e. intent), our whole mind (i.e. knowledge), with our whole soul (i.e. affection), and with our whole strength (i.e. words and actions). This kind of love of God above all things is a universal precept binding on all creatures, without which there is no salvation. And the second is like to this: "Love your neighbor as yourself." Thomas is most emphatic in saying that love of neighbor is not a virtue distinct from love of God; it is by one and the same formality that we love God and neighbor, because the motive for loving neighbor, self, and God is one and the same, namely God himself.[27]

One acquires perfection by withdrawing from the things that hold us from loving God as intensely as possible. "Therefore all the counsels by which we are invited to perfection have to do with turning the spirit of man away from temporal affections, so that his mind can more freely tend toward God by contemplating him, by loving him, and by fulfilling his will." [28] These are the counsels of poverty, chastity, and obedience by which we turn away from temporal goods (poverty), sexual pleasures (chastity), and self-will (obedience). Discussing chastity, Thomas shows the importance of this virtue for every type of intellectual and spiritual life.

In showing how the religious can engage in any activity not contrary to the rule and constitutions, Thomas notes in particular studying, teaching, hearing confessions, and the care of souls. To the repeated quotation from St. Jerome, "The duty of a monk is to weep, not teach," Thomas simply says, "It is not in virtue of being a monk that one teaches, for then there would be as many teachers as there are monks." [29] He could also have said that friars are not monks, but clerics.

In the summer of 1271 Thomas directly faced the arguments of *Those Who Prevent Young Men from Entering Religious Life*. This strongly worded reply ends on a polemical note:

> These are the points that occur to me at present that must be made against the erroneous and pestiferous doctrine of those who would turn men away from entering religion. If anyone disagrees, let him not prattle before boys, but let him write and present his writing in public, so that what is true can be judged by intelligent people and what is false refuted by the authority of truth.[30]

This controversy raged on in university circles until the death of the two principal spokesmen. The important point is that for St. Thomas the sole criterion of sanctity (perfection, spirituality, mysticism) is the intensity of charity.

The primacy of this charity forms the backbone of the entire second part of the *Summa,* which he composed during his second professorship in Paris (1269–72). Unlike other manuals for confessors *On Virtues and Vices,* the second part of the *Summa* is structured around the ultimate goal of redeemed man (heaven) and the means necessary to attaining eternal happiness. It is the return *(reditus)* to God corresponding with the first part *(exitus).* Instead of viewing these means as simply observance of the ten commandments, Thomas views them as the life of virtue, theological and moral, regulated by the New Law of grace lived in some state of life, married or celibate, lay or religious. For St. Thomas, the highest form of life on earth is the contemplative state, but he knew perfectly well that not everyone is called to be a monk or a nun. But all are obliged to observe the law of love and seek contemplation as befits the chidlren of God redeemed by Christ.

Objectively speaking, for Thomas, the strictly contemplative life is more perfect than the active life. But there are two kinds of "activity," the kind that flows over from contemplation, like teaching and preaching, and the all-consuming kind that can be a means to contemplation, like tending to the sick and dying. Just as the contemplative life is more perfect than the active, the life that consists in contemplation and giving to others the fruits of that contemplation is more perfect than the purely contemplative, "for just as it is better to illumine than merely to shine, so it is greater to give to others the fruits of one's contemplation than merely to contemplate." It is not surprising that Thomas should think of his own Dominican Order as one of the best, consisting in contemplation ordered to teaching and preaching.[31]

In the *Summa,* I-II, qq.68–70, Thomas develops most fully his doctrine concerning the gifts of the Holy Spirit. Infused contemplation, the principal characteristic of the mystic, is that state of mind and heart wherein the Holy Spirit himself takes control. In the Latin tradition (Isaiah 11:2) there are eleven gifts listed, although in the Hebrew only six are named: understanding, knowledge, wisdom, counsel, fortitude, piety, and fear of the Lord. One would expect these to be higher than the virtues they accompany. Not so. For Thomas, all of these gifts are mere modalities of the fundamental virtues whereby the Holy Spirit can operate through them *modo divino* (in a divine manner). That is to say, a virtue is by definition an habitual way of doing what is right *modo humano* (in a human manner). The theological virtue of faith is an infused habit of freely believing everything that God has revealed. When a person decides to make an act of faith, he is making a voluntary supernatural act—assent of the mind motivated by grace *modo humano*. In this act of assent there is a vast complex of ideas, words, images in the imagination, feelings in the body, and perhaps satisfaction. This is the normal situation. But when the Holy Spirit decides to refine the virtue of faith, he darkens the consolations of sense, purifying the senses in what can be called the "dark night of the senses," and later the "dark night of the intellect." In this state, of varying duration and intensity, the soul sees the whole of created reality as nothing but emptiness; fleetingly the soul is overwhelmed by the allness of God and the nothingness of self. St. Thomas calls these acts of the mind the gift of understanding *(intellectus)* moved by the Holy Spirit *modo divino*. This modality or ability to be moved by the Spirit belongs to the gift of faith; it is not something in itself, a "thing" that can be higher than faith itself. For Thomas each one of the gifts is nothing more than an ability of the virtues to be moved, so that the life of the Spirit in the soul is really a heroic state of a virtue, whether it be wisdom, piety, fortitude or fear of the Lord.[32] Frequently in Thomas' own life, particularly from 1269/70 until his death in 1274, he was frequently in that state called "abstracted from the senses" by his early biographers.[33] But what St. Thomas wrote down in his own hand or dictated to secretaries was clear scholastic scholarship in strict syllogistic form, and quoting all the best authorities on a theological or philosophical point. Despite the originality of the second part of his *Summa*, it was still intended for beginners, who ought to see the whole of "Sacred Doctrine," since it is both speculative and practical, as a collection of truths to live by from baptism to eternal glory. Thomas clearly took beginners seriously, and he gave them his fullest attention.

The third apostolate undertaken by Thomas in Paris was to young professors of philosophy in the Faculty of Arts. Theirs was the task of explaining the philosophy of Aristotle to undergraduates. St. Thomas himself never taught philosophy, but he fully appreciated its importance for the faith. All the professors in the Arts Faculty were secular clerics; even if they intended to go on into theology, law, or medicine, each one was obliged to teach for a certain number of years to qualify. All the works of Aristotle are difficult to understand and he was, after all, a pagan who lived 400 years before Christ. It was natural that young professors use the explanations of others to help them in their teaching. The most convenient guide for some of the books was the Commentator Averroes (1126–98), who came into the Latin West from around 1230 on. St. Albert the Great had tried to assist beginners, both Dominican and non-Dominican, by paraphrasing all of Aristotle's writings and some then mistakenly attributed to Aristotle; Albert began this monumental task around 1250, completing it by 1270. But by 1269 young professors like Siger of Brabant, Peter of Auvergne, and Boethius of Dacia wanted more than a paraphrase. They wanted to understand every tortuous phrase in the Latin Aristotle, translated from both Greek and Arabic. The problem with Averroes, whose commentaries on the *Physics*, *De anima*, and *Metaphysics* were available in Latin from the 1240's, was that he was a Muslim, who tended to see certain things differently from Christians, especially such topics as the eternity of the world, one intellect for all men, and denial of personal immortality and responsibility. By 1265 these views were widely discussed and taught at Paris by young teachers of philosophy using the Commentator.

Never before did such an apostolate strike Thomas as desperately urgent. Parisian professors of philosophy called Thomas to come into their world and help them. To scotch the viper, Thomas wrote a treatise *On the Unicity of the Intellect Against the Averroists* in 1270, and *On the Eternity of the World* sometime earlier. In December 1270 the bishop of Paris condemned the two Averroist propositions which Thomas attacked and eleven more that followed from them.[34] But more than attacks and condemnations were needed to show young professors how Aristotle could and should be understood in a way consistent with the truth. Better and more accurate commentaries on the text of Aristotle were needed, and for this purpose Thomas used the most accurate texts available, usually those elicited from his Flemish confrère, William of Moerbeke. These literal commentaries (or *Sententiae*) on the major works of Aristotle were begun at Paris in 1269 and continued in Naples; many were left unfinished when he ceased writing in December 1273. In this demanding apostolate to young professors in philosophy, Thomas undertook to provide exactly what was needed at that time. His solicitude won their deepest admiration and affection. Their affection can be seen in the poetry these young men wrote on hearing of his premature death, and in the moving letter they wrote to the Dominican general chapter meeting in Lyons at Pentecost 1274.[35] The philosophical apostolate undertaken by Friar Thomas was left unfinished at the time of his death, and there really was no one around to continue it.

These three major apostolates, we must remember, were all over and beyond his regular duties as a university professor in Paris. To tell the truth, only one of these was successfully completed: the polemic against those professors who would have had the mendicant orders completely suppressed. This polemic was effectively resolved by the end of 1271; it was terminated by the death of William of St.-Amour in September 1272, and of Gérard d'Abbeville in November of that same year. The other two apostolic projects, namely the

Summa theologiae and the Aristotelian commentaries, were left incomplete at the time of Thomas' death, March 7, 1274.

A CRISIS OF SOUL

Since the anti-mendicant polemic was resolved and the internal troubles of the Arts Faculty were more or less settled by the spring of 1272, after Easter, 24 April 1272, Thomas and Reginald left Paris before the end of the academic year and began the long journey back to Naples, passing through Florence as the General Chapter of the Order was in session at Pentecost. The Provincial chapter that followed immediately entrusted Thomas with the establishment of a suitable priory for theological studies in the Roman province of Dominicans. Thomas chose to organize the house of studies, an expected *studium generale* like Oxford and Cologne, at San Domenico in Naples, his home priory.

From all that can be gathered, Thomas was in the best of health when he began the academic year at Naples toward the end of September. Thomas' health always seems to have been extremely good, despite the incredible exertions during his four years at Paris, and now another at Naples. Besides lecturing on the Bible as a university professor paid by King Charles of Naples, he fulfilled all his other duties as well as working on the Third Part of the *Summa* and more Aristotelian commentaries. He was then also engaged in various temporal affairs for his relatives, replying to numerous queries by letter, and in preaching to the citizens of Naples. But even when Thomas was in the best of health, he was always "abstracted" or "absorbed," whatever the company. His *abstractio mentis* became legendary.[36]

Toward the fall of 1273 Thomas finished his dictated or written discussion of the Eucharist in his Summa III, qq.73–83, and, as the story goes,[37] placed the manuscript on the usual altar at San Domenico. He asked the crucified Savior to destroy all he had written if it contained anything improper, badly stated, or erroneous. According to Bernard Gui, the crucifix said, "You have written well of me, Thomas. What reward will you have? " And Thomas is supposed to have answered, "None, but yourself, O Lord." This incident, immortalized in art and literature, may very well have been literally true. But the important point is that Thomas' entire productivity was the outpouring of an apostolate so Pauline in mind and Dominican in spirit, that every fiber of his mind and body was expended.

It is most probable that Friar Thomas enjoyed moments of infused contemplation from early in his second Parisian professorship onward. In St. Thomas' own theology infused contemplation is associated with the gift of the Holy Spirit called wisdom *(sapientia)*, which is produced in the intellect by heroic charity, and so belongs to the virtue of love.[38] Perhaps the simplest way to describe this gift, this mobility of charity in the hands of the Holy Spirit, is to call it a temporal vision of the scorching produced in the human soul by the burning of divine love. It is intellectual, pertaining to both faith and love, caused by the working of the Holy Spirit in affection that belongs to the will. Nevertheless this vision of God within the soul is not the beatific vision of God face to face, which is proper to eternal beatitude. These moments of infused contemplation can vary in intensity and duration. But in no way did they hinder Thomas from producing highly technical, abstruse, and scholastic writings ranging from commentaries on Aristotle to explanations of the Bible, from answering highly practical questions put by higher authority to encouraging young novices along the way.

At that time in Naples Thomas was in the best of health and fully expending all of his intellectual and spiritual abilities in an apostolate that was heroic in its determination and superhuman in its production. Thomas' routine at this time was as it had been for years: rising early in the morning to confess his sins to Reginald, celebrating his Mass daily, attending the Mass of Reginald, beginning his morning class of "Prime" (without breakfast), writing and dictating until dinner and siesta, continuing until Vespers, more dictation, writing, and studying even after Compline until bedtime. He still had only one meal a day *(Manducabat semel in die)*, and slept very little, accomplishing more by prayer than study. In class he was lecturing on the Psalms, in the *Summa* he was in the middle of the third part discussing the sacrament of penance; as for Aristotle he was simultaneously in the midst of *De Caelo, De Generatione,* and the *Metheora,* and some personal replies and summaries for Friar Reginald.

Suddenly on Wednesday morning, 6 December 1273, the feast of St. Nicholas, something happened to him during his private Mass at the side altar in the priory of San Domenico in Naples. He was suddenly seized *(commotus)* by something that radically affected him and transformed him entirely *(mira mutatione)*. He suffered, in fact, a physical break-down of nerves and muscles throughout his entire body. "After this Mass he never wrote or dictated anything." As his first biographer put it, "He hung up his instruments of writing" (an allusion to the Jews who hung up their instruments during the exile) "in the third part of the Summa, in the treatise on Penance" (III, q.90). When Reginald realized that Thomas had altered entirely his routine of more than fifteen years, he asked him, "Father, why have you put aside such a great work which you began for the praise of God and the enlightenment of the world?" To which Thomas an-

swered simply, "Reginald, I cannot *(non possum)."* But Reginald, afraid
that Thomas was mentally unbalanced from so much study, insisted
that it would be better for him to continue his writing and return
to his former routine at a slower pace. But the more Reginald insisted,
the more impatient Thomas became until he replied, "Reginald, I
cannot, because all that I have written seems to me like straw." [39]
Reginald was mystified at this reply, but the fact was that Thomas
was physically and emotionally unable to continue. The only recourse
he had was to prayer for himself, and acceptance of his inability to
work. Acceptance of an inability to do anything for so worthy an
apostolate constitutes the greatest cross any intellectual can bare.

That this was not merely a mystical experience, but a physical
break-down as well, is attested to by everything narrated about
Thomas from this time until his death three months later. Mystical
experiences, even in Thomas' own theology, do not incapacitate an
individual, but rather drive him on to even greater tasks. The physical
breakdown that Thomas experienced on December 6 rendered all
intellectual productivity impossible. It was not at all the case that
he had what today is called a "nervous breakdown." Rather it was
simply the fact that he had a physical breakdown from overwork
which rendered creativity impossible, at least for the highly cerebral
apostolate in which he was engaged. He was an intellectual who
suddenly found reasoning futile, impossible, and beyond even grace,
because grace can only perfect nature.

Late in December or early in January, Thomas expressed a desire
to visit his sister, the Countess Theodora of San Severino.[40] In the
company of Friar Reginald, Thomas "hastened there with great difficulty; but when he arrived and the countess came out to meet him,
he could scarcely say a word." Thomas was like this, "dazed," for
the three days he remained in San Severino. According to the witness
Bartholomew, the countess was "very much alarmed," and asked
Reginald, "What is wrong with Friar Thomas? He is completely out
of his senses *(totus est stupefactus)* and has scarcely spoken to me."
Reginald answered, "He has been in this state since about the feast
of St. Nicholas, and from that time onward he has written nothing."

Shortly afterward, the order came that Thomas was to attend the
Second Council of Lyons, called by Pope Gregory X. It was to begin
on Monday, 7 May 1274, at Lyons, the temporary residence of the
pope in southern France. Around the beginning of February, Thomas
set out for Lyons with Reginald and an attendant named Friar James
of Salerno. At Teano north of Capua, they were joined by William,
dean of Teano and his nephew Roffredo. Bartholomew of Capua
narrates the story briefly: "Going down from Teano to Borgonuovo,
Thomas accidentally struck his head *(percussit caput)* against a tree

that had hung across the road, and was half stunned and hardly able to stand *(ita quod fere stupefactus quodammodo fuit)."* [41]

To make a long story short,[42] after a few hours travel, Thomas became exhausted and asked to stop at the castle of Maenza, where his niece Francesca lived. Lent had already begun, that is, it was after February 14. At Maenza Thomas became increasingly ill; a few Cistercians from neighboring Fossanova visited him and remained for four or five days, during which time Thomas got steadily worse and spent more time in bed. Toward the end of February, Thomas felt that his end was near, so he asked to be taken to the Cistercian abbey of Fossanova. He could not have been there, in the second floor guest room, for more than a week, as he died on Wednesday morning, 7 March 1274, having completed his forty-ninth year and begun his fiftieth. The story of his last days is full of edifying descriptions and quotations, most of them legendary.

Much has been made of the experience of December 6 and the cause of Thomas' death on March 7. The immediate rumor of poisoning by King Charles is typical of cases in which the cause of death is unknown. Père L.H. Petitot[43] interpreted the experience of December 6 as the most extreme case of mystical ecstasy known to spiritual writers, an intellectual facial vision of divine light, which, he says, was the true cause of death three months later. According to Père Petitot, it was "a vision of light rather than a vision of love," similar to the vision given to Moses and St. Paul," far superior to the ecstasies given to saints like Dominic or Catherine of Siena." For Petitot the cause of death was the facial vision of God, experienced on December 6, that took him on March 7. The only difficulty is that neither Moses nor Paul died of their ecstasies, however facial they were.

There is no doubt that the experience of December 6 was connected with mystical experience in some way. But rather than seeing it as the spirit affecting the bodily disorder of stupor, daze, impairment of dexterity and gait, one could see it as a physical breakdown that affected his always sensitive spirit. It would have been the height of torture not to be able to work *(Non possum)*, especially in an intellectual apostolate so necessary for the Church. Thomas could do nothing but pray for himself and for courage to accept his own inability. The natural inwardness of Thomas could not help but make of this experience the ultimate purification of soul, the final crisis of an intellectual who is a saint used to mystical experiences and ecstasies. Thomas could truly say, "The only thing I want now is that as God has put an end to my writing, he may quickly end my life also." [44] What had been written by him was "like straw," insipid and lifeless, compared to the desolation of spirit now facing him. In any case, the experience of December 6, whatever its nature, would not have killed him. The cause of his death must have been the head injury suffered on the road to Borgonuovo that resulted in a clot on the top of the brain (subdural hematoma) that was ingravescent, growing larger and larger every day for about two weeks. Natural causes in no way derogate from the workings of God in the spiritual life; Thomas would have been the first to see the Spirit working in nature to the ultimate plan of the Father. The main point to emphasize here is that the ultimate sacrifice was demanded of Thomas: his own intellectual life whole and entire. That sacrifice was far greater than anything he had ever written in his life and no way comparable to previous sacrifices he had endured.

The canonization of Friar Thomas d'Aquino by Pope John XXII on Monday, 18 July 1323, was a commendation not only of the life of this angelic professor, but also a commendation of the writings of this "Common Doctor" of the Middle Ages: "He worked as many miracles [in his life] as questions he had determined." [45] In 1567 Pope Pius V declared him a "Doctor of the Church," and in 1880 Pope Leo XIII made him patron of all Catholic universities. The greatest mystic of the Middle Ages also happened to be the greatest theologian.

BIBLIOGRAPHICAL NOTES

Life and Works: most of the basic sources have been published by D. Prümmer, O.P. and by M.-H. Laurent, O.P. in *Fontes Vitae Sancti Thomae Aquinatis,* originally published as supplements to *Revue Thomiste,* 1911–34, in seven major parts. Of these three of the more important sources (William of Tocco's *Hystoria,* Bernard Gui's *Legenda,* and the Naples *Processus canonizationis*) were reprinted in *S. Thomae Aquinatis Vitae Fontes Praecipuae,* ed. A. Ferrua (Alba, 1968). What is badly needed is a critical edition of William of Tocco's life and an English translation with notes. An English translation of Bernard Gui's "Life" with annotations and selections from other sources is contained in Kenelm Foster, *The Life of Saint Thomas Aquinas: Biographical Documents* (London and Baltimore, 1959). A highly illuminating presentation of Thomas' life and wisdom is Vernon Bourke, *Aquinas's Search for Wisdom* (Milwaukee, 1965). The most extensive recent biography with bibliography is James A. Weisheipl, O.P., *Friar Thomas d'Aquino: His Life, Thought, and Works* (Garden City, 1974; Oxford, 1975)

Spiritual life and Mysticism: Despite a highly imaginative and romanticized life of Thomas, an insightful analysis of his "Spiritual Life" can be found in L.H. Petitot, O.P. *The Life and Spirit of Thomas Aquinas,* tr. Cyprian Burke (Chicago, 1966). A more sober and historical account of Thomas' spiritual life is presented by Martin Grabmann, *The Interior Life of St. Thomas Aquinas,* tr. Nicholas Ashenbrener, O.P. (Milwaukee, 1951). For an understanding of the mysticism of St. Thomas the following works are of utmost importance: A. Gardeil, O.P., *La structure de l'âme et l'expérience mystique* (Paris, 1927); D. Joret, O.P., *La contemplation mystique d'après saint Thomas d'Aquin* (Lille, 1923); L. Lavaud, "Notes distinctives de la sainteté," *La vie spirituelle,* 8 (1923): "Saint Thomas, Docteur mystique," 348; R. Garrigou-Lagrange, O.P., *Christian Perfection and Contemplation,* tr. Sister M. Timothea Doyle, O.P. (St. Louis, 1942); *idem, The Three Ages of the Interior Life: Prelude of Eternal Life,* tr. Sister M. Timothea Doyle, O.P., 2 vols. (St. Louis, 1947, 1948). Especially important are M.-D. Chenu, O.P., *St. Thomas et la Théologie,* in the series "Maîtres Spirituels" (Paris, 1959); Jean-Pierre Torrell, O.P., "Théologie et sainteté," *Revue Thomiste,* 71 (1971), 205–21.

VII
The Medieval Continental Women Mystics: An Introduction

VALERIE M. LAGORIO

In her assessment of the mystical continuum of Western Christianity from the patristic era onward, Evelyn Underhill states:

> The great periods of mystical activity tend to correspond with the great periods of artistic, material, and intellectual civilization. . . . It is always as if [the mystic] were humanity's finest flower; the product at which each great creative period of the race had aimed.
> It [the thirteenth century] has many saints but not many mystics, though they increase in number as the century draws on. The fourteenth century is filled by great contemplatives, who lifted this wave of activity to spiritual levels, and brought the intellectual vigour, the romance and passion of the mediaeval temperament to bear on the deepest mysteries of the transcendental life.

One may add that the great mystics are not isolated phenomena, but are related to one another. Each receives something from predecessors; each by his or her personal experiences enriches this legacy, and hands it on to the future.[1]

Given this cumulative power of the past on the mystical tradition, the mystics must be considered from an historical rather than a strictly biographical perspective. In this regard, Ruth Dean, along with Hope Emily Allen, has noted the need for a history of medieval women mystics, treating not only their lives and works, but also the dissemination and influence of their writings.[2] There is, moreover, room for more research on the national scale, locating the mystics in their own country and period. A concomitant desideratum would be critical editions and modern English translations of their writings.

In treating the Continental women mystics of the Middle Ages, one must also consider what the terms masculine and feminine might mean in the psychology of the inner life. In answering this question, Wendy Wright holds: "The masculine principle of agency [within an individual] prepares the way for and then relinquishes its place to the feminine principle of receptivity." She continues that it does not follow that a woman "is not more suited for the contemplative life, by nature already attuned to the receptivity that that life requires."[3] Furthermore, according to Elizabeth Petroff, the medieval woman mystic ". . . was representative of a sizeable group of medieval women with religious vocations, for whom their fantasies—their visions—were the signal to others that they were women of power. Visions were the necessary credentials for a medieval woman whose abilities and strengths demanded that she take an active role in a larger world. . . . Her power was used to improve the human condition and to encourage others in their paths of self-hood and union with the divine." Such women transcended cultural restrictions on their behavior, self-image, and influence, despite their lack of books, rudimentary education, or illiteracy, and, often, spiritual advisors who were unfamiliar with the *via mystica*.[4]

Synthesizing these historical, cultural, and spiritual considerations, Lucia of the Incarnation acknowledges women's inferior position in the society and culture of the Middle Ages, discounts the shibboleth of male superiority in intellectual and creative pursuits, as well as in the spiritual life, and offers the following balanced apologia for women's achievement in the Western spiritual tradition:

> When we turn now to the direct contribution of women, we are struck by the fact that, whenever she left her vast kingdom of silence and revealed her genius in a more outstanding way, it was almost always in the religious sphere; and here her contribution bears more characteristically that of a charismatic vocation than in the case of man. She does not speak on her own account, but as an instrument: in this way, again, profoundly true to her nature. But in so doing, each time she reveals her unmistakable individuality.[5]

This study will consider the leading Continental women mystics nationally and chronologically, assessing, albeit briefly, their responses to their historical and cultural milieux, and endeavoring to emphasize their individuality, their varying involvement in both the active and contemplative lives, and their contribution to the medieval and ongoing mystical continuum. This approach will not only reflect the period in which the mystic lived, but also her mental, emotional, and spiritual capacities, since these factors are inseparable from the mystic's idiosyncratic account of her contemplative and unitive experiences.

I. GERMANY

Twelfth- and thirteenth-century Germany produced five women mystics of extraordinary powers and influence: the two Benedictine abbesses Hildegard of Bingen (1098–1179) and her contemporary Elizabeth of Schönau (1138–65), and three mystical religious from the Cistercian house at Helfta: Mechthild of Hackeborn (1241–99), the beguine Mechthild of Magdeburg (1217–82), and Gertrude the Great (1156–1211). They were followed in the fourteenth century by the Dominican nuns on the German/Swiss borders and St. Dorothea of Prussia.

Hildegard of Bingen lived in and responded to the twelfth-century Renaissance, an age rich with political, religious, and intellectual tensions. Receiving divine visions from the age of five onward, she joined the Benedictine house at Disibodenberg three years later, becoming abbess in 1137 after the death of Jutta of Sponheim. In 1147, overcoming ecclesiastical objections, she founded the convent of Rupertsberg, near Bingen, and a daughter house at Eibingen in 1165. Hildegard was a Renaissance woman of genius and charisma, fulfilling roles as abbess, visionary, seer, natural scientist, poet, musician, and activist in the cause of Church and societal reform. Despite her many accomplishments, Hildegard's formal education is uncertain—she categorized herself as a *homo simplex*, a mouthpiece for the *Verbum Dei* which she did not supplement—but as a Benedictine nun, she was familiar with the liturgy, Scriptures, and patristic writings. In company with all of the medieval women mystics, she dictated her works to a secretary, who also served as her spiritual director, and who subsequently translated the work into Latin. Hildegard's first two secretaries were Godfrey of St. Disibodenberg and the monk and learned theologian Volmar, with both of whom she exercised a measure of editorial control. Her third secretary, Gilbert de Gembloux, was given more stylistic freedom in his transcription and translation.

In addition to her duties as foundress and abbess, she was active in the convent infirmary, treating nuns and the neighboring sick, and wrote two scientific and medical treatises, the *Liber Simplicis Medicinae*, and herbal and *materia medica* which was also called *Subtilitatum Diversarum Creaturarum* or *Physica*, and the *Liber Compositae Medicinae* or *Causa et Cura*, dealing with disease and human physiology. Her 77 individual songs, written for her nuns, were collected around 1150 into a lyrical cycle entitled *Symphonia Armonie Coelestium Revelationum*, which, according to Peter Dronke, contains "some of the most unusual, subtle, and exciting poetry of the 12th century." [6] Hildegard's music shows an affinity with chant, but, like her poetry, is very freely constructed and beautiful, meriting consideration of her as one of the most important composers of the Middle Ages. [7] As further evidence of her tremendous creative range, her liturgical drama, *Ordo Virtutum* (1141–51), which ends her mystical and prophetic *Scivias*, is not only the earliest known morality play, but a dramatic work of great originality and merit.

Her greatest fame in her own age rested on her visionary writings and apostolic missions. The greatest of the visionary works is the *Scivias* or *Scito Vias Domini*,[8] written at divine behest between 1141 and 1150, and recounting twenty-six visions, based in the shadow or cloud of the living light *(lux vivens)*, which fuse the macrocosm (Creation), Microcosm (Man), and Transcosm (God) into what Rufus Jones has termed a "cosmic vitalism." [9] Defending both her visions and the divine command to make them known to the world of men, Hildegard writes in the Preface of the *Scivias:*

> Again I heard a voice from heaven, saying to me: Speak of these marvels and write down what you have learned and say: In the year 1141 of the Incarnation of the Son of God, at the age of 42 years and 7 months, a flaming light of great brightness from the open heaven completely flooded my brain, heart, and breast like a flame that does not burn but warms, raising in me such a warmth as the sun does on all on which it sheds its rays. Immediately I was illuminated with a complete understanding and exposition of books like the Psalter and other Catholic tomes, both of the Old and New Testament. . . .

Like all of her sister mystics, Hildegard carefully delineates how she experienced these visions:

> I did not perceive these visions in dreams or sleeping, or in a trance, nor with exterior ears of man or in hidden places, but by God's will, beheld them wide awake and clearly, with the mind, eyes, and ears of the inner man.[10]

While the entire *Scivias* is concerned with salvation, the thirteen visions of the first two books are imaginative, symbolic, and allegorical, yet so descriptive and detailed that thirty-five miniatures were executed in her own scriptorium under her direct supervision. This fortuitous combination of inspired vision and accompanying illumination is exemplified by her description of the Trinitarian processions in Book 2:

> And then I saw a most beautiful light in which was a human form which shone with a most loving and gentle fire, and that beautiful light permeated the gentle fire and the fire permeated the lovely light, and both fire and light permeated the human form, all together manifesting one light, one virtue, and one power.[11]

This is illustrated by a silver circle enclosing a circle of gold, representing the Father and Holy Spirit, and both circles surrounding the human form of Christ. His arms are uplifted in supplication and blessing, and the whole figure is painted a brilliant sapphire, thus depicting his redemptive and intercessory powers and his glorified body, now imbedded in the Trinity. Other visions and illuminations feature the figure of *Sapientia*, a fact frequently noted by modern feminist critics.[12]

The eleven visions of the third book are apocalyptic denunciations of evils in the temporal and spiritual spheres. Similar chiliastic and prophetic leitmotifs and a Jeremiad tone permeate her *Liber Vitae Meritorum*, written between 1158 and 1163, and her final work, *Liber Divinorum Operum Simplicis Hominis* or *De Operatione Dei*, a profound cosmology-cum-theodicy, composed between 1163 and 1173, which stresses the ultimate triumph of good over evil.[13] In addition to these three mystical treatises, Hildegard wrote an *Explication of the Rule of St. Benedict, Lives of St. Rupert and St. Disibode, Exposition on the Gospels, Explanatio Symboli Sancti Athanasii, Solutiones Triginta Octo Quaestionum*, and the enigmatic *Lingua Ignota*, concerning a secret language of 700 words and a 25-letter alphabet, and thus is one of the most prolific among the women mystics.

Hildegard's apostolic endeavors, which, with her prophetic powers, earned her the epithet "Sibyl of the Rhine," resulted in journeys throughout Germany and France, instructing religious, preaching publicly, exhorting against the laxity and worldliness of the Church, and condemning Cathar heretics. Pilgrims flocked to her convent, and her intercession and advice were sought by popes, emperors, and kings, as well as by many lay and religious figures in lower walks of life, resulting in a sizeable number of letters of counsel, warning, and theological disquisition. Despite all these demanding activities, Hildegard continually remained the instrument of God, transmuting her life of prayer and contemplation into action in behalf of God and her fellow Christians:

> The love of God and our neighbor . . . are not to be separated. Those given corporally to the world, nevertheless continually serve God in the spirit, neither do they, on account of being detained in the world, forget those things which are of the spirit in communing with God.[14]

This strong sense of social responsibility was shared by all of her sister mystics.

Hildegard's influence was felt not only in Germany, but also elsewhere on the Continent, and especially in the Low Countries. Her apostolic and mystical vocations were strongly affirmed by St. Bernard of Clairvaux, Pope Eugenius III, and her spiritual daughter Elizabeth of Schönau. Nothwithstanding this widespread medieval acclamation, Hildegard was neglected by scholars until the late nineteenth and twentieth centuries, which have witnessed a renascence of interest in this great German mystic, which, it may be hoped, will result in critical editions and translations of all her writings, as well as scholarly studies.[15]

Like her contemporary Hildegard, Elizabeth of Schönau (1129–64) was held to be a prophetic and evangelical visionary. She entered the Benedictine double monastery at Schönau, near Trier, at the age of twelve, took the veil at eighteen, and in 1157 became *magistra* of the nuns, under Abbot Hidelin. Her visions and ecstasies occurred between 1152 and 1160, following a grave illness which was to recur throughout her life. She recorded and annotated these experiences with great reluctance, a disinclination shared with other *mulieres sanctae* of the Middle Ages; and, at Hidelin's advice, she gave them to her brother, the priest Eckbert, who edited and translated them into Latin. The question of Eckbert's influence on Elizabeth and her writings, especially after his arrival at Schönau in 1155, has received much critical attention, and, indeed, he has been cast as a Svengali by some scholars. As a result of her prophetic pronouncements against moral corruption in the Church and secular society, Elizabeth suffered ridicule, disbelief, and calumny, especially on the part of the clergy, a fate shared by many of the women mystics. She wrote to Hildegard about these difficulties, and received the following affirmation of her prophetic powers and mission of divine admonition:

> I, a poor earthen vessel, say these things, not of myself but through the Living Light. . . . Those who desire to do the works of God should always remember that they are fragile,

earthen vessels. They should put on the breast-plate of Faith and be humble and poor, living as He did, the Lamb Whose trumpet-sound they are. . . . O daughter! may God make thee a mirror of Life! [16]

The Schönau mystic's works include three books of *Visiones*, containing accounts of her visions and colloquies with Christ, the Blessed Virgin, and the heavenly host, which are closely linked with liturgical feasts; *Liber Viarum Dei*, modelled on Hildegard's *Scivias*, and consisting in visions and warnings to prelates, clerics, and lay persons, which are attributed to the Angel of the Lord; the *Visiones de Resurrectione Beatae Mariae Virginis*, which confirmed the Assumption of the Blessed Virgin, and which accordingly was welcomed by ecclesiasts; and the highly popular legend of St. Ursula and her holy band of 11,000 virgins martyred at Cologne. Elizabeth's works were widely disseminated, both in Latin and various vernaculars, throughout Europe, and enjoyed an early and continuing popularity in England, thanks to the redaction of Roger of Ford in the 1170's.[17] As with Hildegard, there is a need for critical editions and translations of Elizabeth's canon, so that, in C. C. Martindale's words, we will not misconstrue and undervalue "those allegedly 'Dark Ages' which contained personages of such fascinating psychological worth, and of so high a spiritual value." [18]

Concerning the three Helfta mystics, strong Dominican influence, joined with the older Benedictine, Cistercian, and Bernardian spirituality, prevailed at the convent of Helfta in the thirteenth century, which, under the forty-year administration of Abbess Gertrude of Hackeborn, was an intellectual, spiritual, and mystical center, dedicated to a balanced life of *ora et labora*.

Mechthild of Hackeborn, younger sister of Abbess Gertrude, assisted her with convent administration, and was also charged with directing the choir, for which she was called "God's nightingale," training novices, and teaching in the convent school. Additionally she was a counselor and friend to the nuns and to many outside the convent, and a close friend of Gertrude the Great. It was Gertrude who compiled Mechthild's seven-part *Liber Spiritualis Gratiae*, describing her visions and the graces of contemplation, and marked by a joyful spirit of love and praise of God.[19] A typically vivid and beautiful description of a heavenly visitant reads:

> The King of glory once appeared in indescribable splendor in the fullness of his joy, wearing a golden robe embroidered with doves and covered by a red mantle. This garment was open on two sides to indicate that the soul has free access to God. The red mantle symbolized the Passion. . . . The doves

represented the simplicity of the divine Heart, whose dispositions are unchangeable although the creature so often fails in fidelity to him.[20]

Mechthild not only participated in the general themes and topoi of medieval mystical writing, such as meditation on Christ's life, passion, and death, mystical inebriation, the soul's dance, the salvific agon, numerical and color symbolism, contemporaneous criticism of social and ecclesial injustice, and the theological and symbolic use of zoology, botany, and mineralogy.[21] She also belonged to the *braut-mystik* school of mystical writings which stressed the love affair between Christ and the soul, colored by incursions from the chivalric and *minnesang* cultures. And, with other Helfta nuns, she promoted the cult of the Sacred Heart of Jesus, to be sanctioned by the Church in 1673 with the revelations of St. Margaret Mary Alacoque. Following her death in 1299, after a life of penance, prayer, and great physical suffering, she and her *Liber* enjoyed a wide popularity on the Continent and in England, where it was called *The Booke of Gostlye Grace* or the *Maulde Boke*.[22]

Mechthild of Magdeburg, the second great Helfta mystic, left her aristocratic family in 1233 to live as a beguine, and later as a Dominican tertiary under the direction of the Dominican theologian Henry of Halle, a pupil of Albert the Great. She is thought to have lived at the Convent of St. Agnes in Magdeburg, and to have served as abbess in 1273. This possibility is supported by her practical comments on the duties of a prioress, and also by her allegory "The Ghostly Cloister." After years of asceticism and prayer, she suffered a serious illness in 1281, following which she was impelled by God's love to write her mystical experiences. Mechthild's reluctance to record her visions can be seen in the following protestations:

> Ah! Lord God! Who has written this book? I in my weakness have written it, because I dared not hide the gift that is in it. Ah! Lord! What shall this book be called to Thy Glory? It shall be called The Flowing Light of My Godhead into all hearts which dwell therein without falseness.[23]

> I cannot write nor do I wish to write—but see this book with the eyes of my soul and hear it with the ears of my eternal spirit and feel in every part of my body the power of the Holy Spirit. (IV/13, p. 108)

Her spiritual director Henry of Halle also encouraged her:

> Then went I, poor trembling wretch that I was, in humble shame to my confessor and told him all this and asked for

guidance. He said I should go joyfully forward; God Who had called me would look after me. Then he commanded me to do that for which I often weep for shame when my unworthiness stands clear before my eyes, namely, that I, a poor despised little woman, should write this book out of God's heart and soul. This book therefore has come lovingly from God and is not drawn from human senses. (IV/2, p. 98)

Mechthild recorded her spiritual autobiography on loose sheets in her Low German dialect, and these sheets were subsequently collected, edited, and rearranged by Henry into six books, called *The Flowing Light of the Godhead (Das fliessende Licht von Gottheit)*.[24] Like Hildegard of Bingen and Elizabeth of Schönau before her, Mechthild strongly denounced abuses in the Church, for which she was persecuted—she called her detractors "my pharisees"—and was even accused of heresy. This charge was especially ironic as she was constantly condemning the Free Spirit and allied heresies, and was, above all, unquestionably faithful to the Church, despising only those who were its unworthy ministers. As she so eloquently states in the following exemplary diatribe:

Alas! O crown of Holy Church, how dim art thou become! . . . Alas! for the fallen crown of the priesthood! . . . If anyone is ignorant of the way to Hell, let him look at the depraved priesthood . . . hastening without let to the nether regions. (VI/21, p. 189)

As a consequence of her persecution, she took refuge at Helfta around 1285, and, although blind, dictated a seventh part of her book to the Helfta nuns. Soon after her death in 1297, Henry translated her work into Latin, calling it *Lux Divinitatis Fluens in Corda Veritatis*, a translation which evinces his difficulty in rendering Mechthild's poetic flights and amatory *minnesänger* language into scholastic Latin.[25] A later High German version by Henry of Nördlingen was widely circulated among the Friends of God in Basle and Bavaria, as well as the Waldschwestern eremites at Einsiedeln.

Mechthild's *Flowing Light* is prophetic, contemplative, devotional, admonitory, and ecstatic, combining its central theme of God's love with the sorrows and torments which accompany the soul's striving for union with God. This theme is beautifully articulated in the following allegorical dialogue, a form often used by the *Minnesänger*, entitled "God asks the soul what it brings":

God: You hunt eagerly for your love,
        What do you bring me, my Queen?

Soul: Lord! I bring you my treasure;
       It is greater than the mountains,
       Wider than the world,
       Deeper than the sea,
       Higher than the clouds
       More glorious than the sun,
       More manifold than the stars,
       It outweighs the whole earth!

God: O! Image of my divine Godhead,
       Ennobled by my humanity,
       Adorned by my Holy Spirit—
       What is your treasure called?

Soul: Lord! It is called my heart's desire!
       I have withdrawn it from the world,
       Denied it to myself and all creatures.
       Now I can bear it no longer.
       Where, O Lord, shall I lay it?

God: Your heart's desire you shall lay nowhere
       But in my human breast.
       There alone will you find comfort
       And be embraced by my spirit. (I/39–43, pp. 19–20)

Like Hildegard and Mechthild of Hackeborn, Mechthild of Magdeburg wrote as an inclusivist, encompassing all of creation in her cosmic visions, and, according to James Franklin, adapted essentially Hellenic elemental and cosmological theories which coalesced with orthodox medieval theology.[26] In addition to her influence on the later Friends of God in southern Germany and Switzerland, Mechthild may have influenced Meister Eckhart's thought on the mutual craving between God and the soul.[27]

St. Gertrude the third Helfta mystic, is given the epithet "the Great" because of the theological and mystical complexity of her writings. She came to the convent at the age of five, and devoted herself to intellectual pursuits until 1281, when she suffered a spiritual crisis, and Christ called her to the *via mystica*. Not long thereafter, Gertrude prayed for and received the invisible stigmata (no visible external wounds, but all other manifestations of this phenomenon), like Catherine of Siena, and seven years later, the wound of divine love (a heightened manifestation of the love-union with God; an ineffable ecstasy resulting from a special grace), which would also be experienced by Teresa of Avila. At Christ's command, she recorded her mystical experiences in the *Messenger or Herald of God's Loving*

Kindness (Legatus Divinae Pietatis or *Insinuationes)* [28] and seven as-cetical-mystical *Spiritual Exercises,*[29] a treatise on the conduct and the goals of the spiritual life written for her community. A florilegium, entitled *Preces Gertrudianae,* and composed by an anonymous Jesuit of Cologne in 1670, reflects the spirit but not the content of Gertrude's own writings. Unlike the majority of other women mystics, Gertrude was a skilled Latinist and wrote her works in Latin. It must be remembered, however, that only Book 2 of the *Herald* was actually written by Gertrude. The first book was a posthumous tribute to the saint, while it is believed that she dictated the last three books on the soul's relation with God, liturgical feasts, and a *memento mori* section on the Helfta community.

While following the contemplative way, Gertrude continued her active involvement in convent life, translating Scriptures, teaching and counseling her sister nuns, caring for the sick, performing varied household duties, and conducting her apostolate with the laity and clergy beyond Helfta's walls. Thus, along with many of the great women mystics, Gertrude exemplified *libertas cordis,* the liberty of spirit found only in the highest mystical states.[30] The balance between the active and contemplative lives was not easily achieved by the women mystics, but the demarcation for Gertrude was clearly stated by Christ:

> A mighty emperor is not contented merely to have ladies-in-waiting richly attired in his palace, but he has also men-at-arms, officials fit for various services and always ready to carry out his orders. So I do not find my pleasure merely in the interior exercise of contemplation, but also in various exterior and useful works which are directed to my honor; these too invite me to live among the children of men and find my delight in them. Furthermore, it is by manual works that men find occasion to practice charity, patience, humility, and other virtues.[31]

Gertrude's mystical doctrine was basically Christocentric, incor-porating *brautmystik* elements, an emphasis on the Mystical Body of Christ, and a strong core of Marian piety. Along with the two Mechthilds, she promoted devotion to the Sacred Heart, following in the footsteps of Lutgarde of Aywières and other ecstatics of the Low Countries. Her eminence as a religious and a mystic is attested to by a vision granted to Mechthild of Magdeburg:

> . . . she saw Gertrude's heart under the image of a firm bridge walled on one side by the divinity, on the other by the

humanity of Christ. He said to her, 'Those who come to me by this bridge will not fall nor wander from the right way.' [32]

The rarity of manuscripts, editions, and translations of Gertrude's works reflects the undeserved neglect which has surrounded this great mystic since her death in 1301/2.

In addition to the illustrious Helfta trio, the late thirteenth and early fourteenth centuries witnessed a great flowering of women mystics in Switzerland and southwestern Germany, which can be ascribed to two major influences: the Dominican *cura monialium* and the Friends of God movement.

As will be discussed below, the Cistercian and mendicant orders were charged with the spiritual direction of semi-religious communities, as well as with the care and guidance of cloistered religious. At the beginning of the fourteenth century, many noble, well-educated nuns were cloistered in over 70 Dominican convents, several of which were famous mystical centers: Töss near Winterthur (which in 1350 had over 100 religious), Katharinental by Diessenhofen, Ötenbach near Zurich, Engeltal and Maria-Medingen near Nuremburg, Adelhausen in Freiburg, Kirchberger near Sulz, Weiler by Esslingen, and the Alsatian house at Schönensteinbach.

The Friends of God *(Gottesfreunde)* were a distinct socio-religious phenomenon in the fourteenth century, espousing a practical mysticism based on the following tenets: self-renunciation, or a ceding of self-will to God's will; the action of the Spirit in all believers and the feasibility of the *unio mystica* between God and man; the essential equality of lay and religious, with no distinction of rank or sex, while acceding to the necessity of the institutional Church. Leaders of the *Gottesfreunde* included Meister Eckhart, John Tauler, Henry Suso, Jan van Ruysbroeck, the anonymous author of the *Theologica Germanica*, Henry of Nördlingen, as well as such laypersons as Rulman Merswin and his wife Gertrude in Strasbourg, and Nicholas, Catherine, and Margaret of the Golden Ring in Basle. With regard to the impact of the *Gottesfreunde* on the Dominican nuns, Elsbeth Stagel, spiritual daughter of Henry Suso at Töss, Margaret Ebner at Maria-Medingen, closely linked with Henry of Nördlingen, and Christine Ebner and Adelheid Langmann of Engeltal all belonged to the Friends of God, and advocated its mixed life of action and contemplation.

The Dominican women mystics followed a life of intense ascesis, penance, prayer, and charitable activities, with a special devotion to the Infant Jesus, Christ crucified, the Blessed Virgin, and the poor souls in Purgatory. Because of their austerities and penitential sufferings, as well as some instances of highly subjective and erotic accounts of the mystical life, this group of religious women has been singled out rather unfairly by later critics, and described as "hysterical," "pathological," "repressed," or, at best, "uninspired," [33] which may account in some measure for their neglect by scholars. Their literary productivity was varied and usually collaborative. Margaret Ebner (d. 1351) not only exchanged numerous German letters with Henry of Nördlingen, but, at his insistence, wrote her *Revelations (Diarium)*, recounting her mystical life from 1312–48. Henry's correspondence with Margaret and her contemporary mystics represents the first collection of letters in the German language, and affords illuminating insights into the historical and religious events of the age. Christine Ebner (d. 1356), following God's command and encouraged by her confessor, worked on her *Revelations (Von der gnaden Überlast)* from 1317 to 1324, and her younger colleague Adelhaid Langmann (d. 1375) wrote her *Offenbarungen*, which record her mystical experiences. The most illustrious of these cloistered nuns was Elsbeth Stagel, who, as important in Henry Suso's life as Clare was to Francis of Assisi, encouraged him to write his *vita*, collected his letters to his spiritual daughters, and helped to translate some of his Latin works into German.

Another important written legacy from these Dominican cloisters are the *Vitae Sororum (Schwesternbücher)*, which were collections of the spiritual and mystical biographies of the sisters. They were composed by Anna von Munzingen, Elsbeth Stagel and Katherine of Gebweiler, among others, as edifying exemplars for the later nuns at Adelhausen, Töss, Engeltal, Unterlinden, Weiler, Katharinental, and Ötenbach, and represent a distinct genre of religious writing.[34] Although these chronicles have been derogated as pedestrian and derivative in language and content, a close examination reveals that such criticisms are unjust, and that they have made a definite contribution to the core of mystical language of the later Middle Ages.[35]

Our final medieval German woman mystic, St. Dorothea of Montau (1347–94), Patroness of Prussia, was greatly influenced by Birgitta of Sweden, whose mortal remains passed through Danzig in 1374, enroute to burial at Vadstena. Like Birgitta, Dorothea was married, widowed, made many pilgrimages, and simultaneously led an intense mystical life. Her experiences were recorded later by her spiritual director, John of Marienwerder (1343–1417), in her *Vita*, the *Septilium* or *Seven Graces* received by Dorothea, and the *Liber de Festis*, recounting her liturgically-related visions. In the last two years of her life, she was enclosed in the cathedral wall at Marienwerder, where she, like many of her sister mystics, gave spiritual advice to visitors, both lay and religious, and continued her life of expiation, prayer, penance, and contemplation. Her spirituality has been compared with that of Birgitta and Catherine of Siena, and, according to Hope Emily

Allen and, more recently, Ute Stargardt, may have been an informative influence on Margery Kempe of Lynn, England.[36]

II. The Low Countries

With the waning influence of Benedictine monasticism and the
corresponding rise of the Cistercian and mendicant orders in the later
twelfth and thirteenth centuries, there appeared a growing number
of *mulieres sanctae* in the Low Countries, Germany, and elsewhere
in Europe, who either allied themselves with the Cistercian and
mendicant nunneries, or who, because the order-affiliated houses
were limited as to size and number, and possibly because of a
preference for a different spiritual lifestyle, became beguines.[37] The
origin of the name "beguine" is open to question. Some say it derives
from "Albigensian," thus associating it with heretical movements,
since the heresy of the Free Spirit flourished in these semi-religious
groups. Others ascribe it to Lambert de Béges (d. 1177) around whom
several groups of pious women formed in Liège. Still others point
to the German verb "beggen," to beg and pray.

Many studies have been written on the various results of the
Frauenfrage—the problem caused by the excessive number of single
women in the Middle Ages; on the *Frauenbewegung*—"that great and
victorious revolt of pious women, everywhere in Europe, against the
reactionary traditions that would have condemned them in the cloisters, as well as in the world, to a role of subordination and silence,
which would have withheld from them the benefits of literacy or
an active part in the great spiritual revivals and innovations of the
early thirteenth century";[38] and on the strictures imposed on the *cura
monialium*, which, in turn, resulted in an increasing number of beguines. However, a more spiritual basis for the growth of the beguines
and their male counterparts, the beghards, was the emphasis on
apostolic poverty and evangelical perfection, in the spirit of *Imitatio
Christi*, upheld by the Franciscans and Dominicans, an emphasis
which anticipated the Friends of God, Brethren of the Common Life,
and *devotio moderna* movements of the fourteenth and fifteenth
centuries.

The beguines represented all social classes and feminine occupations. They lived in semi-religious, communal houses, usually in
urban areas, took no permanent vows, and fulfilled the two objectives
of chastity or continence and renunciation of worldly possessions,
in order to become *pauperculae Christi*. These women followed the
via media, combining intense spirituality with living a life of earning
a living and charitable service in the world. Thus, while they led
lives of prayer, they did not beg. Additionally, according to R. W.

Southern, ". . . the solitary religious figure, never indeed wholly submerged in the organizational zeal of the intervening centuries, once more emerged as a force in society," and, as contemplatives and mystics, critics and reformers, stood somewhat apart from the organized religious society around them.[39]

The women mystics of the Low Countries, with vocations as pious lay persons, nuns, recluses, and beguines, were especially notable: Mary of Oignies (d. 1213), Christine of St. Trond, called "the Admirable" (d. 1224), Yvette of Huy (d. 1228), Ida of Nivelles (d. circa 1231), Margaret of Ypres (d. 1237), Lutgarde of Aywières (d. 1246), Hadewijch of Antwerp, Alice of Schaarbeek (d. 1250), Juliana of Cornillon (d. 1258), Ida of Leeuw (d. 1260), Eve of St. Martin (d. 1265), Beatrice of Nazareth (d. 1268), Ida of Louvain (d. 1300), Christine of Stommeln (d. 1312), Elizabeth of Spalbeek (d. 1316), and Gertrude of Oosten (d. 1358). The exceptional spirituality of their lives and writings can only be touched upon in this study.[40] Mary of Oignies, who was closely associated with the noted ecclesiast Jacques de Vitry, exemplified the *vita apostolica* of these holy women, and furthermore was the *pia mater* of a zealous circle of religious and laity. Christine of St. Trond, visionary and seeress, led a life of severe penitence for the salvation of sinners and the poor souls in Purgatory, according to her *vita* by Thomas of Cantimpré, the Dominican prior of Louvain. Lutgarde of Aywières, who like Mechthild of Magdeburg and Gertrude of Helfta, experienced the mystical "exchange of hearts," and Alice of Schaarbeek championed the cult of the Sacred Heart. Together with Mary of Oignies, both were strenuously involved with anti-heretical campaigns. Juliana of Cornillon, along with Eve of St. Martin and Mary of Oignies, promoted the feast of Corpus Christi, which was established in Liège in 1246. Christine of Stommeln, whose life was written by the Dominican friar Peter of Gothland or Dacia, was the center of an ecstatic religious/laic group which had ties with Sweden. And, in keeping with the prevalent *conformatio* or *configuratio* with Christ crucified, Mary of Oignies, Ida of Louvain, Christine of Stommeln, Elizabeth of Spalbeek, and Gertrude of Oosten received the stigmata. As further evidence of their reputation for sanctity, the lives of Mary of Oignies, Christine the Admirable, and Elizabeth of Spalbeek were translated into Middle English.[41]

Perhaps the best known of this Low Countries group are Beatrice of Nazareth, a Cistercian nun, and the beguine Hadewijch, both exponents of the *brautmystik* tradition, which combined Bernardian mysticism with a Christianized *minne*. Beatrice authored a spiritual autobiography, translated into Latin by William of Afflighem, and a treatise, actually a chapter from the Middle Flemish version of the autobiography, *The Seven Ways or Degrees of Love (Van Seven Manieren van Heiligher Minnen)*.[42] Describing the ascent of the soul to God, this work is important for the history of Low Countries spirituality, especially in its delineation of theopathic soul states.[43] Very little is known about Hadewijch, who at one time was erroneously identified with the heretical Bloemardinne of Brussels (d. 1336). She lived around the middle of the thirteenth century and left thirty-one *Letters* addressed to an anonymous young beguine, forty-six *Stanzaic Poems* which are adjudged by many as her greatest work, fourteen *Visions*, and sixteen *Poems in Couplets*.[44]

Hadewijch's Christological and Trinitarian spirituality reveals her reliance on Augustine and other Church Fathers, the Victorines, and the Cistercians, especially Bernard of Clairvaux and William of St. Thierry. She, in turn, influenced the great Flemish mystic Jan van Ruysbroeck (1293–1381). In her writings, she was not only a conscious and inspired prose artist, as seen in her *Letters* and *Visions*, but her lyrics, which fused the poetry of courtly love, Latin sequences from the liturgy, and love mysticism, represent a new genre of medieval religious poetry. Her literary versatility, emotional range, and deep spirituality can be seen in the following four excerpts from her works on the subject of the soul's union with God: In Letter 9, "He in me and I in Him," Hadewijch writes:

> Where the abyss of his wisdom is, he will teach you what he is, and with what wondrous sweetness the loved one and the Beloved dwell one in the other, and how they penetrate each other in such a way that neither of the two distinguishes himself from the other. But they abide in one another in fruition, mouth in mouth, heart in heart, body in body, and soul in soul, while one sweet divine Nature flows through them both (2. Pet. 1:4), and they are both one thing through each other, but at the same time remain two different selves— yes, and remain so forever. (p. 66)

This theme is iterated in Stanzaic Poem 20 on love's sublimity:

> When Love thus draws the soul in resemblance to her,
> And the loving soul shows love to Love,
> I know not how, for it remains unspoken
>   And also past understanding;
> For no comparison is adequate for this—
>   How Love can embrace the loving soul. (11. 61–66, p. 182)

In Vision 12, entitled "The Perfect Bride," Hadewijch describes union in terms of the spiritual marriage of the purified soul and the great Bridegroom:

> And in that very instant I saw myself received in union by the One who sat there in the abyss upon the circling disk, and there I became one with him in the certainty of unity. . . . In that abyss I saw myself swallowed up. Then I received the certainty of being received, in this form, in my Beloved and my Beloved also in me. (p. 296)

And in her poem "Love's Seven Names," the union of the soul and God is beautifully expressed in the language of the *brautmystik:*

> Calm reigns at last,
> When the loved one receives from her Beloved
> The kisses that truly pertain to love.
> When he takes possession of the loved soul in every way,
> Love drinks in these kisses and tastes them to the end.
> As soon as Love thus touches the soul,
> She eats its flesh and drinks its blood.
> Love that thus dissolves the loved soul
> Sweetly leads them both
> To the indivisible kiss—
> That same kiss which fully unites
> The Three Persons in one sole Being. (11. 113–24, p. 355)

Hadewijch's writings, along with the works of her sister mystics, contributed to the large body of vernacular religious literature which was finding an increasing audience among the clergy and literate laity.

It should be mentioned that the spiritual reawakening among the *mulieres sanctae*, both lay and religious, was not restricted to the Low Countries, as witnessed by the lives of Douceline of Provence (1214–74), the Humiliati in Italy, and Agnes Blannbekin, a beguine in Vienna. Surely this whole phenomenon deserves scholarly attention which will concentrate on the lives, writings, and influence of these holy women, rather than the demographic and socio-economic focus that has prevailed in the past.

III. FRANCE

There is little written evidence of women contemplatives in France during the early Middle Ages. Assaying female monasticism and asceticism in the Frankish kingdom from the sixth to the ninth centuries, Suzanne Wemple notes:

> Christianity initiated a new era not only in the history of monasticism but also in the history of feminism. Accepted as fully equal to men in their spiritual potential, Christian women could transcend biological and sexual roles and seek fulfillment in religious life.[45]

Nevertheless, only St. Liutberga of Wendhausen (d. 860?) is singled out as an exemplary contemplative in the Merovingian and Carolingian eras. This apparent dearth of information also extends to the later medieval period, with only one French mystic receiving any significant notice. Marguèrite d'Oingt belonged to an old noble family of Beaujolais, and entered the Carthusian convent of Poleteins near Lyon, where she became prioress and remained until her death in 1310. While she, like her mystical consorores, declared herself uneducated, she produced several works, first at the behest of Christ, and, later, of her spiritual director. The Pagina Meditationum consisted of Latin meditations on God's love manifested through Christ's Passion, on sin, on hell, on the graces received by Marguèrite and her will to serve God, and on the Motherhood of Christ, a theme she shared in particular with Julian of Norwich. Her Speculum, Life of St. Béatrix d'Ornacieux, and five letters were all written in Provençal. The Speculum recounts her visions of Christ, the Trinity, and Heaven, while the Life reveals many concordances with Marguèrite's own spirituality.[46]

IV. ITALY AND SWEDEN

The late thirteenth and fourteenth centuries also produced three of the leading women mystics of the Middle Ages: Angela of Foligno and Catherine of Siena in Italy, and Birgitta of Sweden. It should be noted that both Catherine and Birgitta were canonized by the Church as was Gertrude the Great, but the majority of the women visionaries were not, although they eventually were included in the Roman Martyrology.

Blessed Angela of Foligno (1248–1309) was one of a group of more than 100 mulieres sanctae who lived in Italy between 1200 and 1500. Born within thirty years of Francis of Assisi's death, Angela, according to her spiritual autoboiography, was a busy matron and mother, but a vain, lukewarm Christian. In 1285, following a vision of St. Francis, she made a general confession to Father Arnaldo da Foligno, OFM, who subsequently became her spiritual director and scribe. This marked the beginning of her spiritual conversion to a life of poverty, asceticism, and contemplation, coupled with heroic duty at the leper hospital in Foligno. After the death of her husband, children, and mother, Angela entered the Franciscan Third Order in 1291, and, in that same year, experienced a mystical revelation of the Holy Spirit, who said: "I will do great things through thee in the sight of all people; thou shall be known and glorified, so that many shall praise my name in thee," according to the account in the *Memoriale de fra' Arnaldo.*[47] This record of her experiences from 1285 to 1296, dictated by her in Italian and translated word for word into Latin by Father Arnaldo, contained her thirty steps to perfection, patterned on the hidden years of Christ's life, instructions on the mystical life, and numerous visions and consolations. As a testament to her orthodoxy and sanctity, her work was approved by eight Franciscan theologians in 1297 and by Cardinal Giacomo Colonna in 1310. In her later years, her energies were directed into her spiritual maternity to a true cenacle of souls in Italy and elsewhere. This activity resulted in her *Istruzioni Salutifere* and letters of spiritual counsel, as well as frequent condemnations of the Free Spirit heresy. Of the priests under her direction—a ministry which earned her the title of "Mistress of Theologians"—the best known was Ubertino da Casale, whose *Arbor Vitae Crucifixae Jesu* contains a glowing encomium to his *pia mater.*

Angela's spirituality represents a totally Franciscan *Imitatio Christi*, with its emphasis on Christ's Passion, poverty of spirit, true humility resulting from self-knowledge and knowledge of God, and charity translated into action for one's neighbor. Also manifest is her devotion to the Eucharist, the Blessed Virgin, and the Trinity. Her view of the *via mystica* is capsulized in the following excerpt on the transformation of the soul:

> Now this transformation is a threefold one: the soul is transformed in the will of God, sometimes with God, and sometimes within God and God within it. The first transformation is when the soul uses all its endeavor to imitate the life of Christ crucified, for herein is made manifest the will of God himself. The second is when the soul is united to God and loves God; not only because it so wills but because it has great knowledge and joy of God, the which, however, it is able to explain and set forth in words. The third is when the soul is so entirely made one with God and God with it, that it knows and enjoys with God the most high things, which cannot possibly be set forth in words nor imagined except by him who feels them. (pp. 123–24)

Angela was given far more to intellectual rather than corporeal visions, as exemplified in Vision 7, which speaks of seeing God darkly and secretly, a pseudo-Dionysian motif possibly derived from Jacopone da Todi:

> There was a time when my soul exalted to behold God with so much clearness that never before had I beheld Him so distinctly. But love did I not see here so fully; rather did I lose that which I had before and was left without love. Afterwards I did see Him darkly, and this darkness was the greatest blessing that could be imagined, and no thought could conceive aught that would equal this. . . . for now do I see so clearly that what I see can neither be told by the mouth or imagined in the heart. . . . Here, likewise, do I see all Good. (pp. 181–82)

Perhaps the greatest divine consolation in Angela's life occurred when she was dying, and Christ presented her to his Father, who spoke these words:

> 'Oh bride and fair one, oh you who are beloved in me with perfect love, of a truth I would not that you should come to me with these exceeding great sufferings, but I would you should come with the utmost rejoicing and with joy unspeakable, even as it is seemly that the King should lead the bride whom he has loved so long, and clothed the royal robe.'
>
> And he showed me the robe, even as the bridegroom shows it to the bride whom he has loved a long time. It was neither of purple, nor of scarlet, nor of sendal, nor of samite, but it was a certain marvelous light which clothed the soul. And then he showed me the Bridegroom, the Eternal Word, so that now I do understand what thing the Word is and what it means—that is to say, this Word which for my sake was made flesh. And the Word entered into me and touched me throughout and embraced me, saying, 'Come, my love, my bride, beloved of me with true delight—come, for all the saints do await you with exceeding great joy.' And he said again to me, 'I will not commit you to the charge of the blessed angels or other saints that they should lead you to me, but I will come personally and fetch you and will raise you to myself, for you have made yourself meet for me and pleasing to my majesty.' (pp. 262–63)

Admired in her own age, Angela's life and writings influenced St. Teresa of Avila, Father Augustine Baker, St. Francis de Sales, St. Alphonse Liguori, and other later contemplatives, while her *Memoriale* ranks with the *Fioretti* of St. Francis and Catherine of Siena's *Dialogue* as a classic of Western Christian mysticism.

It seems fitting to incorporate St. Birgitta of Sweden (1303–73) with the Italian women mystics, since she is so often linked with St. Catherine of Siena, possibly because both strove and suffered for the same causes: the moral reform of the Church and secular governments, and the end of the Babylonian Captivity.

Of noble birth and pious childhood, Birgitta at fourteen married Ulf Gudmarsson, who was subsequently appointed as *lagman* (governor) of Nericia. After their marriage, both became Franciscan tertiaries. A model wife, mother of eight children, and, for several years, grand mistress of the Swedish royal court at Stockholm. Birgitta also led an ascetic life under the spiritual direction of Master Matthias (d. 1351), canon of Linköping Cathedral and foremost theologian in Sweden. After their pilgrimage to St. James of Compostella, Ulf entered the Cistercian monastery at Alvastra and died in 1344. From 1344 until 1346 Birgitta, released from all earthly ties, lived a life of austerity and meditative prayer at Alvastra, where her intense mystical life and revelations began. These revelations resulted in Birgitta's strong denunciation of the Swedish court's worldliness, and in Christ's command to found a new religious order, a vineyard in which Birgitta was to be the "finest vine":

> I will plant a new vineyard, from which many other vineyards shall arise. I will send watchmen who will not sleep in the night. I will fence it round with my love. I will let the roots of the vine, which are the good will of men, grow so deep that the devil, that mole, cannot scratch them up. I will let the vine plants flourish and make their grapes sweet. And thou, Bridget, shalt plant the young vines, but have a care to put them in a good place, sheltered from the cold and frost, protected from heat and drought. Stand firm therefore and love me with all thy heart. Flee from pride, live in humility. Guard thy lips and all thy members in My honor. Obey My commandments. Examine thy conscience every hour whether thou hast sinned and in how much. If thou fallest, then rise again immediately. Take no heed of the honor or friendship of the world—thou hast Me. And if thou givest Me all thy love, everything that is of the world will become bitter like wormwood to thee.[48]

Dedicated to the honor of the Blessed Virgin, Birgitta's "vineyard" was to consist in convents, each with sixty nuns, and an adjacent house for twenty-five priests and laybrothers, analogous with the thirteen apostles and seventy-two disciples.

Subsequently, at Christ's order, she went to Rome in 1349, accompanied by her confessor Peter of Skänninge, her secretary the Cistercian Peter of Alvastra, and two other priests, arriving in time to celebrate the Jubilee in 1350. Her Roman mission was to work for the reform of the Church and society, to effect the return of the pope from Avignon to Rome—the longed-for *santo passaggio*—and to establish her Order of St. Savior. Toward these ends, and constrained by her revelations, Birgitta intervened in papal, ecclesiastical, and secular affairs, attacking the widespread corruption in the Church and the worldliness and injustice of European rulers, thereby incurring humiliation, hostility, and even accusations of being a sorceress. Yet she was sustained by God:

> Hearken well to what I speak and speak what thou hast heard. Let honor and dishonor be indifferent to thee—care not for those who praise thee, nor for those who blame thee. If thou art praised then take not pride therein, if thou art blamed, let it not anger thee. . . . I speak to thee, because it pleased Me so that all may know how sin must be atoned for, punishment lessened. . . .[49]

Birgitta's prophetic mission received further divine sanction in Book VIII, Chapter 48, of her *Revelations*, which records her vision of a heavenly tribunal, in which three kings are standing before a marvelous pulpit of three shining colors, with a book on it. The voice of the Justice of God identifies the Pulpit as the Trinity, the book as the Book of Life, and extols Birgitta as God's voice on earth, and therefore to be heeded by earthly rulers.[50]

Although familiar with Latin, Birgitta wrote or dictated her *Revelations* in Swedish, the two Peters translated them into Latin, and the saint then carefully reviewed their work. Around 1369, she met the learned Bishop of Jaen, Alphonse of Pecha, who became her confessor, counselor, collaborator, and editor of her *Revelations*. After her death, he was the leading force for her canonization.

After various pilgrimages to Italian sanctuaries and cities, and Urban VI's approval of her order in 1370, Birgitta was divinely directed to journey to the Holy Land, where, during a four-month stay, she experienced many revelations about the lives of Christ and the Blessed Virgin, as, for example, the Nativity, Christ's Passion, and the Assumption.[51] While in the Holy Land, she fell seriously ill, returned to Rome in 1372, and, surrounded by her loyal circle of family, priests, and friends, died in July, 1373. Her remains were translated to the Motherhouse of her order at Vadstena, Sweden, in 1374.

Immediately after her death, her daughter Katherine, who was the first superior at Vadstena, the two Peters, the English Cardinal Adam

Easton, and, above all, Alphonse of Pecha promoted her canonization, based on her holy life and her *Revelations*. As Edmund Colledge has shown, Alphonse's *Epistola Solitarii ad Reges* (1379) was an especially effective apologia for the validity and divine inspiration of her visions.[52] Yet, despite her canonization of 1391, and its reaffirmation in 1419, Birgitta remained a controversial figure, strongly attacked at the Council of Constance by John Gerson's *De Probatione Spirituum*, which not only questioned her visions and the abilities of her spiritual directors, but also her ability as a woman to be a contemplative. A second attack, Matthias Döring's *Probate Spiritus*, occurred after the Council of Basle. However, bolstered by Alphonse of Pecha's *Epistola*, Adam Easton's *Defensorium* (1390), and Cardinal John Torquemada's *Defensiones*, Birgitta's cause prevailed.

Birgitta's major writings include her 700 *Revelations* or *Liber Celestis*,[53] the *Rule of St. Savior*, and the *Sermo Angelicus*, or lessons of the Night Office of the Birgittine nuns.[54] Her spirituality was an orthodox admixture, evolving from her rapport with the Franciscans, Dominicans, and Cistercians, which had as its epicenter the crucified Christ and his compassionate Mother. She was not a theologian like Catherine of Siena, but, like her, was an inspired visionary and ardent reformer. In many ways her earthly mission was a failure, since, as with the Avignon popes, many of her warnings were unheeded. Yet her importance as a moral and spiritual force in her own time cannot be denied, nor can her major achievement—the establishment of the Birgittine Order, which flourished throughout Europe, with major houses at Vadstena, Lübeck, and Syon Abbey, founded by Henry V at Isleworth, England, in 1415.

The *Revelations* were known and popular in late fourteenth and fifteenth century England, promoted in part by the marriage of Philippa, daughter of Henry IV, to Eric XIII of Sweden in 1406, and also by the involvement of English prelates in the great conciliar movements of the early fifteenth century at Constance and Basle. Those revelations which dealt with prophecy, the spiritual life, and the lives of Christ and Mary were often incorporated into English devotional compilations and meditational works, such as the *Contemplations of the Love and Dread of God*, William Flete's *De Remediis*, the *Pore Caitif*, *Speculum Devotorum*, *The Fruyt of Redempcyon* by Simon of London Wall, and the Bodley *Meditations*.[55] Her famous pronouncement supporting the English over the French in the Hundred Years War, was paraphrased in Thomas Hoccleve's *Regimen of Princes*, while an English translation of her *Sermo Angelicus* and her *vita* has been attributed to Thomas Gascoigne, Chancellor of Oxford, and patron of Syon Abbey. An encomium, *Salutacio Sancte Brigitte*, written by John Audelay, and the *Fifteen O's of St. Bridget*, a series of prayers on Christ's Passion, are representative of various popular devotions inspired by Birgitta.[56] The order was dispersed following the Reformation, but an active Birgittine order was established by Sr. Maria Elizabeth Hesselblad (d. 1957) with houses in Rome, the United States, India, and Vadstena. What is truly remarkable is that, in an unbroken tradition since 1415, the original contemplative Birgittine Rule is observed today at Syon Abbey, South Brent, Devon.[57]

St. Birgitta remains an exemplar of the mixed life, fulfilling her duties as wife, mother, counselor, and prophetess, while leading the contemplative life—in other words, successfully combining the activity of the human spirit with the Divine Will of God. Her influence on art and iconography is evident in medieval and later representations of Christ's Nativity, the founding of the Order of St. Savior, and the angel dictating the *Sermo Angelicus* to the saint. Her *Revelations* were greatly admired by St. Alphonse Liguori, who incorporated their doctrine into his *Glorie di Maria*, and have also achieved an honored place in Swedish *belles lettres*. Although work is proceeding on critical editions of the Swedish and Latin versions of the *Revelations*, there is no modern English translation, a lack which prevents a larger audience from knowing about this extraordinary mystic and her writing.

Like her predecessors Hildegard of Bingen and Birgitta of Sweden, Catherine of Siena (1347–80) combined the highest reaches of the mystical life with active participation in the world, as a teacher, reformer, counselor, and apostle. Like St. Teresa of Avila, Catherine, although untutored, possessed an unusual intelligence, enriched with infused wisdom, a dynamic personality, a compelling sense of her divine mission, and a gift for leadership. At 16 she became a Dominican tertiary, or *mantellata*, devoting her life to asceticism, penance, and contemplation, combined with care of the poor, incurably ill, and the condemned. Her sanctity and zeal occasioned calumny and persecution from her critics, both religious and lay, but also attracted to her a group of disciples from all classes of society, known as the *bella brigata*, or *Caterinati*, of the *dolcissima mama*. One member of this group was the noted English Augustinian recluse William Flete. Others were the learned Dominicans Tommaso della Fonte, Bartolomeo di Dominici, and Raymond of Capua, who served as her confessors, her three secretaries Barduccio Canigiani, Stefano Maconi, and Neri di Landoccio de' Pagliaresi, and Tommaso d'Antonio Nacci da Siena, known as Caffarini, who promoted her canonization. In 1368, at the age of 21, she was mystically espoused to Christ, and later received the stigmata, which remained invisible at her request.

Catherine's roles as spiritual advisor, peacemaker, and admonitory counselor to secular and ecclesiastical rulers, and, like Birgitta, leader in the *santo passaggio* cause, were accomplished by her direct intervention or by her numerous letters. Influenced by Catherine's mission to Avignon, Pope Gregory XI returned to Rome in 1376, but, much to Catherine's anguish, the papacy returned to Avignon in 1378, resulting in the Great Western Schism. Catherine and her *brigata* also undertook the reform of the Dominicans, in order to stem the corruption in the Church and in the secular world.[58] In her last years, she remained in Rome, where she became a close friend of Birgitta's daughter Katherine, and where she continued to pray and do strenuous penance for the causes of her earthly mission. Spent from her reforming activities and ascetic life, and afflicted with a serious illness, Catherine died in Rome in 1380, at the age of 33, surrounded by her grieving disciples.

Catherine's works include her 382 *Letters*,[59] twenty-six *Prayers*, and the *Dialogue*, a colloquy between her soul and God, which she called simply *Il Libro*, but which is also known as the *Book of Divine Doctrine* or *Book of Divine Providence*.[60] All of her writings reveal the multiple influences on her spirituality—Augustine, Cassian, Gregory the Great, Bernard of Clairvaux, Francis of Assisi, Thomas Aquinas, Ubertino da Casale, and Dominic Cavalca—and reflect the essential core of her mysticism: Christ crucified; the salvific nature of the Precious Blood; the Trinity and Trinitarian exemplarism; devotion to the Sacred Heart, culminating in the mystical exchange of hearts, like Lutgarde and the Helfta mystics; and Divine Love, experienced in contemplation and translated into active service of one's neighbor. Pointing to her ecclesial spirituality, Sr. Lucia of the Incarnation states:

> With Gertrude before her and Teresa after her, she had a deep sense of the Church. All three emphasized the redemptive value of prayer and holiness of life which until then had been little stressed, even by theologians. . . . St. Gertrude was the first to be imbued with this awareness, Catherine brought it into the open, and Teresa of Avila was to found a whole Order on this basis.[61]

Catherine's influence on the Dominican Order is seen in the reform movement implemented after her death by Raymond of Capua, in his capacity as Master General of the Order, and is still in process today. Her *Dialogue* and Raymond of Capua's *Legend* of her life[62] were widely disseminated on the Continent and in England, where a Middle English version of the *Dialogue*, entitled *The Orcherd of Syon*, was specifically translated for the Birgittines at Syon Abbey.[63] She was canonized in 1461, and, as final and fitting accolades, the Church proclaimed her as Patroness of Italy, an honor shared with

Francis of Assisi, in 1939, and, in 1970, she and Teresa of Avila became the first women Doctors of the Church.

Catherine can well be the spokeswoman for her sister mystics, as her *Dialogue* with God expounds so clearly many of the central precepts of the mystical life.

The opening lines articulate the soul's eager response to God's call of love, reminiscent of Augustine's restless heart longing to rest in God, and encapsulating the content of the entire book. For the response encompasses the three stages of purgation, illumination, and union which comprise the *via mystica*, and stresses the life of *Imitatio Christi* and of prayer, which leads to an increasing knowledge of self and God, and love of God. Significantly, the mystic asks nothing for herself, but is concerned with honoring God and helping humanity:

A soul rises up, restless with tremendous desire for God's honor and the salvation of souls. She has for some time exercised herself in virtue and has become accustomed to dwelling in the cell of self-knowledge in order to know better God's goodness toward her, since upon knowledge follows love. And loving, she seeks to pursue truth and clothe herself in it. But there is no way she can so savor and be enlightened by this truth as in continual humble prayer, grounded in the knowledge of herself and God. For by such prayer the soul is united with God, following in the footsteps of Christ crucified, and through desire and affection and the union of love he makes of her another himself. (p. 25)

Catherine's petitions to God are for herself, as God's instrument for good in the world, for the reform of the Church, and for the whole world in general, but especially for the peace of Christians who are rebelling against the Church. Catherine's first request is selfless, in that she wants to be perfected in virtue only so that she can serve her neighbors by teaching, example, and prayer:

You ask me for suffering to atone for the offenses my creatures commit against me. And you ask for the will to know and love me, supreme Truth. Here is the way, if you would come to perfect knowledge and enjoyment of me, eternal Life: Never leave the knowledge of yourself. Then, put down as you are in the valley of humility you will know me in yourself, and from this knowledge you will draw all that you need. No virtue can have life in it except from charity, and charity is nursed and mothered in humility. (p. 29)

Catherine comments further on self-knowledge:

As the soul comes to know herself, she also knows God better, for she sees how good he has been to her. In the gentle mirror of God she sees her own dignity: that through no merit of hers but by his creation she is the image of God. And in the mirror of God's goodness she sees as well her own unworthiness, the work of her own sin. (p. 48)

Her next petition for Church reform emphasizes the importance of the sacramental life, which is a leading characteristic of the mystics:

She found herself eager for the next day's Mass . . . because in communion the soul seems more sweetly bound to God and better knows his truth. For then the soul is in God and God in the soul, just as the fish in the sea and the sea in the fish. (p. 27)

She upholds the centrality of the Church, Christ's Mystical Body, for salvation. Hence, the insistence of the mystics on reform, with Catherine joining Hildegard and Birgitta in active campaigning against the widespread abuses in the Church:

. . . I would satisfy your anguished longings by reforming holy Church through good and holy shepherds. I will do this, as I told you, not through war, not with the sword and violence, but through peace and calm, through my servants' tears and sweat. I have set you as workers in your own and your neighbors' souls and in the mystic body of holy Church. In yourselves you must work by example and teaching. And you must offer me constant prayer for the Church and for every creature, giving birth to virtue through your neighbors. (p. 159)

Catherine's ardent commitment to Church reform is especially manifest in "The Mystical Body of Holy Church" (pp. 205–76), invoking God's justice against worldly clergy and their sinful practices.

Catherine's third petition reveals the mystics' all-consuming service to their neighbors, for the mystic does not withdraw from the world, but rather is immersed in it, and, unified with God, becomes his instrument for good on earth:

I would have you know that every virtue of yours and every vice is put into action by means of your neighbors. If you hate me, you harm your neighbors and yourself as well (for you are your chief neighbor), and the harm is both general and particular. I say general because it is your duty to love your neighbors as your own self. In love you ought to help them spiritually with prayer and counsel, and assist them spiritually and materially in their need—at least with your good will if you have nothing else. (p. 33)

The saint's discourse with God also concerns some of the prime requisites of the mystical way:

1) Discernment, rooted in knowledge and love, and resulting in true judgment of spiritual stirrings:

> Discernment is that light which dissolves all darkness, dissipates ignorance, and seasons every virtue and virtuous deed. It has a prudence that cannot be deceived, a strength that is invincible, a constancy right up to the end, reaching as it does from heaven to earth, that is, from the knowledge of me to the knowledge of oneself, from love of me to love of one's neighbors. . . . By this gentle glorious light the soul sees and rightly despises her own weakness; and by so making a fool of herself she gains mastery of the world, treading it underfoot with her love, scorning it as worthless. (pp. 44–45)

2) The continuous and ever-deepening life of prayer:

> Now I have told you how the soul arrives at mental prayer, that is, by practice and perseverance, and by abandoning vocal prayer for mental when I visit her. I have also told you about ordinary prayer and about ordinary vocal prayer apart from appointed times, and the prayer of a good and holy will, and prayer both in itself and in the form of [service to] your neighbors done with good will apart from the scheduled time for prayer. Courageously, then, should the soul spur itself on with prayer as her mother. And this is what the soul does when she has attuned the love of friendship and filial love, and shuts herself up in the house of self-knowledge. (p. 127)

3) Holy fear:

> Love, joined to holy fear . . . is enough, for the Law is built on love and holy fear. The law of fear was the Old Law that I gave to Moses. It was built on fear alone: Whoever sinned suffered the penalty. The law of love is the New Law given by the Word, my only-begotten Son. It is built on love. The Old Law was not dissolved by the New, but fulfilled. This is what my Truth said: 'I have come not to destroy the Law but to fulfill it.' He thus joined the law of fear with that of love. The imperfectness of the fear of suffering was taken away by love, and what remained was the perfectness of holy fear, that is, fear simply of sinning, not because of personal damnation

but because sin is an insult to me, supreme Goodness. So the imperfect law was made perfect by the law of love. (p. 112)

4) The counsel and guidance of an experienced spiritual director:

She saw that God's servants are called to him—and in particular eternal Truth had called and chosen her spiritual father, whom she brought before the divine goodness, asking God to light within him a lamp of grace by which he might in truth pursue this truth. (p. 57)

One of the major trials of the mystical life is the everpresent danger of the devil, tempting or seeking to delude the mystic, necessitating a stringent discernment of spirits on the part of the soul and her spiritual director. God so counsels Catherine:

For the devil gives whatever he sees the mind disposed to desire and receive. So when he sees the mind gluttonous, with its desire set only on spiritual visions and consolations . . . then, I say, the devil presents himself to that mind under the appearance of light. He does this in different ways: now as an angel, now under the guise of my Truth, now as one or the other of my saints. . . . And should you ask me how one can know that the visitation is from the devil and not from me, I would answer you that this is the sign: If it is the devil who has come to visit the mind under the guise of light, the soul experiences gladness at his coming. But the longer he stays, the more gladness gives way to weariness and darkness and pricking as the mind becomes clouded over by his presence within. But when the soul is truly visited by me, eternal Truth, she experiences holy fear at the first encounter. And with this fear comes gladness and security, along with a gentle prudence that does not doubt even while it doubts, but through self-knowledge considers itself unworthy. (pp. 133–34)

A second trial experienced by all of the mystics is the spiritual aridity and desolation resulting when God has withdrawn his presence from the soul, which, as God explains, is a loving chastisement:

. . . sometimes, to exercise them in virtue and to lift them up out of their perfections, I take back my spiritual comfort and let them experience struggles and vexations. I do this to bring them to perfect knowledge of themselves, so that they will know that of themselves they have neither existence nor any grace. I want them, in time of conflict, to take refuge in me by seeking me and knowing me as their benefactor, in true humility seeking me alone. This is why I give them these troubles. And though I may take away their comfort, I do not take away their grace. (p. 113)

When, however, the soul attains perfect love—the love of friendship and filial love—God rewards the soul:

I relieve them of this lover's game of going and coming back. I call it a 'lover's game' because I go away for love, and I come back for love—not really I, for I am your unchanging and unchangeable God; what goes and comes back is the feeling my charity creates in the soul. (p. 147)

For the mystic, suffering is not primarily for purgation of the soul or penance, but is a positive expression of love for neighbor and God. And, in the higher reaches of perfect union, the soul achieves the mystical spirit of suffering, even to renouncing the joy experienced as a result of union with God:

She [the soul] receives strength upon strength until she no longer merely suffers with patience, but eagerly longs to suffer for the glory and praise of my name. . . . [These souls] want to be of service to their neighbors in pain and suffering, and to learn and preserve the virtues while bearing the marks of Christ in their bodies. . . . To such very dear children as these, suffering is a delight and pleasure is wearisome, as is every consolation or delight the world may offer them. And not only what the world gives them through my dispensation . . . but even the spiritual consolation they receive from me, the eternal Father . . . It is not, however, the consolation, my gift and grace, that they scorn, but the pleasure their soul's desire finds in that consolation. (pp. 144–45)

The ineffable experience of union not only far exceeds the capacity of finite language to express it, but, inebriating the spiritual senses, makes the soul long for death in order to know the fullness of God's love:

All the members are bound and busied with the bond and feeling of love. By this bond they are subjected to reason and joined with the soul's emotion so that, as if against their own nature, they all cry out to me the eternal Father in one voice, asking to be separated from the soul, and the soul from the body. (pp. 147–48)

But because love, while in the mortal body, does not perfectly possess what it loves, it suffers. Once, however, the soul is separated from the body, her longing is fulfilled and so she loves without suffering. (p. 149)

God realizes that not all can follow the *via mystica*, and advises Catherine that those leading the mixed life of action and contemplation are also pleasing to him, albeit less than his servant mystics:

I am not a respecter of persons or status but of holy desires. In whatever situation people may be, let their will be good and holy, and they are pleasing to me. . . . It remains true that it is more perfect and more pleasing to me to rise above all this world's good in fact as well as in spirit. But those who feel that their weakness will not let them reach such perfection can travel this ordinary way according to their own situation. (pp. 97–98)

Ultimately, Catherine's message, like that of all the mystics, both women and men, concerns the wonder of God's love for humanity:

O immeasurably tender love! Who would not be set afire with such love? What heart could keep from breaking? You, deep well of charity, it seems you are so madly in love with your creatures that you could not live without us! Yet you are our God, and have no need of us. Your greatness is no greater for our well-being, nor are you harmed by any harm that comes to us, for you are supreme eternal Goodness. What could move you to such mercy? Neither duty nor any need you have of us . . . but only love! . . . My heart is breaking and yet cannot break for the hungry longing it has conceived for you! (p. 63)

Notwithstanding all of her accomplishments, Catherine of Siena should be viewed within the continuum of great women mystics that extends from the patristic *Vitae Matrum*, through the Middle Ages, down to our own time. These outstanding women mystics deserve to be more widely known, not only because of their courageous and inspiring lives, but also because they speak with knowledge, hope, and love to the central concerns of the human condition.

BIBLIOGRAPHICAL NOTES

General Works on the Women Mystics

Lina Eckenstein, *Women Under Monasticism* (Cambridge, 1896); Michael Goodich, "The Contours of Female Piety in Later Medieval Hagiography," *Church History*, 50 (1981), 20–33; Rufus M. Jones, *The Flowering of Mysticism: The Friends of God in the Fourteenth Century* (New York, 1939); Valerie M.

Lagorio, "New Avenues of Research on the English Mystics," in *The Medieval Mystical Tradition in England*, ed. Marion Glasscoe (Exeter, 1980), 234–49; Valerie M. Lagorio and Ritamary Bradley, *The 14th-Century English Mystics: A Comprehensive Annotated Bibliography* (New York and London, 1981); Lucia of the Incarnation, "The Western Spiritual Tradition," *The Way*, Suppl. 16 (1972), 15–23; Lucy Menzies, *Mirrors of the Holy. Ten Studies in Sanctity* (London and Milwaukee, 1928); Elizabeth Petroff, "Medieval Women Visionaries: Seven Stages to Power," *Frontiers*, 3 (1978), 34–45; Ray C. Petry, "Social Responsibility and the Late Medieval Mystics," *Church History*, 21 (1952), 3–19; Wolfgang Riehle, *The Middle English Mystics* (London, Boston, and Henley, 1981); Anna Groh Seeholtz, *Friends of God: Practical Mystics of the Fourteenth Century* (New York, 1934); Evelyn Underhill, *Mysticism: A Study in the Nature and Development of Man's Spiritual Consciousness* (London, 1911; rpt. New York, 1961); Evelyn Underhill, *The Essentials of Mysticism* (New York, 1920); Kenneth Wapnick, "Mysticism and Schizophrenia," *Journal of Transpersonal Psychology*, 1 no. 2 (1969), 49–67; Richard Woods, *Mysterion: An Approach to Mystical Spirituality* (Chicago, 1981); Wendy M. Wright, "The Feminine Dimension and Consciousness," *Studia Mystica*, 3 (1980), 33–45.

Works and Articles on Leading Women Mystics

Hildegard of Bingen: C.C. Martindale, " 'Shadow of Living Light' : Two Medieval Mystics," *Month*, 185 (1948), 77–82; Bernhard W. Scholz, "Hildegard von Bingen on the Nature of Women," *American Benedictine Review*, 31 (1980), 361–83.

Mechthild of Hackeborn: Theresa A. Halligan, ed. *The Booke of Gostlye Grace of Mechthild of Hackeborn* (Toronto, 1979).

Mechthild of Magdeburg: Odo Egres, "Mechthild von Magdeburg: *The Flowing Light of God*," in *Cistercians in the Late Middle Ages*, ed. E. Rozanne Elder (Kalamazoo, 1981), 19–37; Lucy Menzies, tr. *The Revelations of Mechthild of Magdeburg (1210–1297) or The Flowing Light of the Godhead* (London, New York, and Toronto, 1953).

Gertrude the Great: Mary Jeremy, *Scholars and Mystics* (Chicago, 1962); St. Gertrude, *The Exercises of Saint Gertrude*, ed. A Benedictine Nun of Regina Laudis (Westminster, MD, 1956); St. Gertrude, *The Life and Revelations of Saint Gertrude*, ed. Member of Order of Poor Clares (London, 1856; rpt. Westminster, MD, 1952).

Beatrice of Nazareth: The Seven Steps of the Ladder of Spiritual Love, tr. F. Sherwood Taylor (Westminster, MD, 1943).

Hadewijch: Frances Gooday, "Mechthild of Magdeburg and Hadewijch of Antwerp: A Comparison," *Ons Geestelijk Erf*, 48 (1974), 305–62; Hadewijch, *Writings*, ed. M. Colomba Hart (New York, Ramsey, and Toronto, 1981); M. Colomba Hart, "Hadewijch of Brabant," *American Benedictine Review*, 13 (1962), 1–24.

Birgitta of Sweden: E. Colledge, "*Epistola solitarii ad reges*: Alphonse of Pecha as Organizer of Birgittine and Urbanist Propaganda," *Mediaeval Studies*, 17 (1956), 19–49; William P. Cummings, ed. *The Revelations of Saint Birgitta*, EETS OS 178 (London, 1929).

Angela of Foligno: The Book of Divine Consolation of the Blessed Angela of Foligno, tr. Mary G. Steegmann (London and New york, 1909; rpt. New York, 1966).

Catherine of Siena: The Dialogue, tr. Suzanne Noffke (New York, Ramsey, and Toronto, 1980); *I, Catherine: Selected Writings of St. Catherine of Siena,* ed. and tr. Kenelm Foster and Mary John Ronayne (London, 1980).

VIII

Julian of Norwich: Writer and Mystic

RITAMARY BRADLEY

Julian of Norwich is the first known woman of letters in English literature, and one is hard-put to find prose superior to hers in the Middle English period. She belongs, by right, to the mainstream of studies in literature and culture. This survey article undertakes to show that Julian deserves to be rated as a distinguished prose stylist and recognized as a gifted mystic. In support of this reading and in the light of emerging scholarship, I will examine Julian's *Showings*, first looking for its literary qualities, and then to its ideas and the account of Julian's experiences as they relate to mysticism. As background I will summarize what is known of Julian's life, and in an afterword take note of some signs of her influence among writers in modern times.

Julian's Life

Since Julian's book is practically the only source for reconstructing her life, it is scarcely a digression to begin with a short biography. (The only other sources are mentions in a few wills, a single contemporary witness, and what little is known of her surroundings and the life style of the anchoress, for whom there were specific rules.) [1] Julian was born in 1342 and died sometime after 1416. In her youth she heard the legend of St. Cecilia, the same story which Chaucer adapted in the Second Nun's Tale. Inspired to seek a deeper knowledge of the Passion of Jesus, Julian meditated on pictures and images of the crucifixion. In a prayer of petition she asked for three gifts from God: to understand his Passion, to suffer physically while still a young woman of thirty, and to have as God's gift three wounds. The first two prayers she left to God's will, but to the third she attached no condition:

> I developed a strong desire to receive three wounds, namely, the wound of true contrition, the wound of genuine compassion, and the wound of sincere longing for God. There was no proviso attached to this third prayer.[2]

After she had forgotten about the first two prayers, she fell into a sickness so severe that she seemed to be at the point of death. Surrounded by her mother and friends, probably in her home, she was visited by a priest who counselled her to look upon the crucifix. This became the occasion for fifteen showings, which included visions of the Passion of Christ. At the end of the day she said to another priest that she had raved and been in delirium. But when the priest took seriously her mention of the visions, she was ashamed that she herself was doubting them. During the night she experienced what seemed to be an attack of the fiend. She survived the ordeal, her illness subsided, and in a final vision she became certain that her experiences were genuine and to be believed. She ascribed to them a threefold meaning:

> The first quality is the literal meaning of the words as I then received them; the second is the inner significance that I have discovered since; the third is the whole revelation itself, which, from beginning to end—covering the contents of this book—God in his goodness brings to mind, often and freely.[3]

Sometime after the revelations she became an anchoress living in a cell attached to the Church of St. Julian, Norwich, from which she is thought to have taken her name. (It was customary for anchoresses to take the name of the Church where they were enclosed.) It is probable that she was guided by a rule for anchoresses, such as the thirteenth-century *Ancrene Riwle*.[4] As an anchoress she wrote two accounts of her revelations, the second after some twenty years of reflection on what had occurred, moving from a position of insecurity in writing the Short Version, to meditative certainty in the Long Version.[5]

She also became a spiritual guide as a result of her life as an anchoress. Visitors could speak with her through one of the small windows of her room. (The other window opened into the Church, so that she could follow religious services.) One account of her spiritual counsel has survived, in the *Booke of Margery Kempe*. Margery, who sought out Julian in distinguishing the stirrings of grace from the deceptions of the devil, reports that the "anchoress was expert in such things and could give good counsel." [6] There is also internal evidence in the *Showings* that Julian meant to serve as a spiritual guide to others. She explains that "it is truly love which moves me to tell it to you, for I want God to be known and my fellow Christians to prosper. . . ." [7] And in another place she says: "I am not trying to tell the wise something they know already, but I am seeking to tell the uninstructed, for their peace and comfort." [8]

JULIAN IN ENGLISH LETTERS

Transmission of the Text: But it was not to be easy for Julian's book to reach the audience she envisioned. She herself was aware of one obstacle she faced in making her message known—that, as a woman, she was not likely to be considered expert in theological matters. Scholars are uncertain about the extent of her education, but she pleaded to be heard, against any objections that might arise:

> I am a woman, ignorant, weak and frail. But I know very well that what I am saying I have received by the revelation of him who is the sovereign teacher. . . . But because I am a woman, ought I therefore to believe that I should not tell you of the goodness of God? . . .[9]

The general disregard accorded the writings of women may have worked to keep Julian obscure, since she herself felt she must offer such a defense of her authority.

But another reason for the long delay in giving Julian her rightful place in English letters is rooted in the sparse manuscript tradition, and the difficulties the few remaining copies of her work present to scholars. Only six manuscripts have been located, and of these only two—Amherst (BL Addit. 37790) and the Westminster Cathedral copy of selected chapters—date before the sixteenth century. The short text exists only in Amherst, dating from around 1450. Westminster was not discovered until after World War II, in 1955, and only in the 1960's did the Upholland manuscript, containing excerpts from the *Showings*, come to light. It originated in the seventeenth century and is copied in four different hands. There is also a short quotation from Julian in Colwich Abbey MS 18. Long text copies are preserved in Sloane I (BL Sloane 2499), Paris (BN Fonds Anglais 40) of the seventeenth century, and Sloane II (BL Sloane 3705), judged to be an eighteenth century imitation of a fifteenth century scribal hand. At this time there is still not firm agreement as to which manuscript should be considered the primary one for the long text, and hence there are problems over contested passages. Scholars generally agree though that the short text was written first, closer to the actual experience of the visions, and that the long text, while being faithful to the same facts, adds the insights gained from some twenty years of reflections.[10]

Those primarily responsible for transmitting Julian's text were the English Benedictines, exiled to the continent after the dissolution of the monasteries. The chaplain of the Benedictine nuns in exile at Cambrai, Father Augustine Baker, wrote back to England to Sir Robert Cotton, asking for a share in his rich library of spiritual writings known "in the olde tyme." [11] This request was in large part for the benefit of Dame Gertrude More, great-great granddaughter of Sir Thomas More, martyred chancellor under Henry VIII. These English Benedictines, it is believed, copied the complete versions of the long texts of the *Showings* that have been preserved. In addition, there is evidence that Julian's work was in the nuns' libraries of both the Cambrai and Paris foundations. From the exiled Benedictines also came the first printed text of the *Showings*, in 1670, edited by Dom Serenus Cressy, successor to Father Baker.

For two centuries this printed edition was virtually the only source of information on Julian's work. Then in the twentieth century many learned of Julian through the excellent translation made in 1901 from Sloane I by Grace Warrack, from Edinburgh, "who, suddenly, at the age of 46, produces this amazing book: a solid piece of independent research with excellent footnotes and cross references, a lucid introduction, and, above all, a wonderful feeling for the strengths and rhythms of Julian's prose." [12] Even now Warrack's edition stands as "an excellent introduction which has well stood the test of time, and has been used (not always with due acknowledgement) by many later writers." [13] Through the Cressy and Warrack texts many Catholics, Anglicans, and Protestants rediscovered Julian in the nineteenth and twentieth centuries, and for different and sometimes contradictory reasons, she began to gain an international audience.

The first major university research devoted to Julian is a Leeds University dissertation by Sister Anna Maria Reynolds, who produced a critical edition of the *Showings* in 1956, from all known manuscripts, with introduction, critical notes, and glossary. She edited the short and long version, including the Westminster chapters, and later published the short version in book form.[14] In 1978 Fathers Edmund Colledge and James Walsh completed a critical edition at the University of Toronto. (See bibliographical notes.) In recent years translations of both versions have begun to appear in English, French, German, and Italian.[15]

Language of the Showings: Since Julian was not a scholar she did not have, as Chaucer did, models of discourse drawn from Latin, French, or Italian. True, as has been mentioned, she probably knew the *Ancrene Riwle*, but that work does not provide the theological terms she needed. There is no evidence that she drew to any significant degree on the mystical writings of her time. Instead, she drew on the Scriptures directly, and on the everyday language of Norwich. For example, this is the way she described her vision of the bleeding head of Christ:

> Great drops of blood rolled down from the garland like beads, seemingly from the veins; and they came down a brownish-red colour—for the blood was thick—and as they spread out they became bright red, and when they reached his eyebrows they vanished. . . . They were as fresh and living as though they were real: their abundance like the drops of water that fall from the eaves during a heavy shower, falling so thickly that no one can possibly count them; their roundness as they spread out on his forehead were like the scales of herring.[16]

Certain commonly-used alliterative expressions occur in the *Showings*, but these do not point to any borrowings or specific influences. Among these expressions are "meke and mylde," "wele and wo," and "doubtefull drede." These same alliterative expressions occur in such medieval writings as *The Wohunge of Ure Lauerd, Hali Maidenhead*, and *Sawles Warde* of the thirteenth century, and in the *Lives* of St. Katherine, St. Margaret, and St. Juliana.[17]

Even without extensive knowledge of works in Middle English, however, the reader will find few difficulties in Julian's language, though a few words require defining. "Sensuality and substance," for example, designate, respectively, the human mental structure—all that depends on the body—and the spiritual structure—that which shares in the life of God. These terms relate to the history of humanity: sensuality and substance were broken off from one another by sin, leaving a state of disharmony, but they can achieve unity again through Jesus Christ, who was fully human, and took sensuality, while remaining grounded in the Trinity. "Ground" is used to identify this unity of Christ in the Trinity, in this sense meaning also the ultimate base whereby humanity is linked to God. The "ground of being" is that which knits the human soul to Christ and is therefore the soul's deepest center, the mystic's point of contact with God.

"Kind" or "kindly" is used with overtones from the modern sense, to connote compassion; and with dependence on the medieval sense, to denote an individual species or nature—though it must be remembered that "unmade kind" is God. "Homely" is paired with courtly to suggest familiar, hospitable, being at home with, and is thus in tension with attributes of dignity and restraint associated with knightly conventions. Julian perceived these characteristics as co-existing in God's revelation of himself to his creatures.

Terms used in Christian catechesis, such as the Trinity, the Incarnation, grace, and contrition, occur throughout the text, in senses close to those used in Langland's *Piers Plowman* and other contemporary medieval writings. But Julian taught a specific form of Christian theology, and therefore used some words with a special sense. For example, Adam means, in different contexts, the historical Adam of the Genesis account; Christ as the eternal Adam, first-born of all creatures, and the one in whom all humanity will be recapitulated; and even the total Adam, which is all humanity. And the word sin is used, not generally in a moral, but in an existential sense, connoting, in different parts of the *Showings*, non-being, a turning away from God, the consequence of not seeing God, a monstrosity contrary to human nature, a void where God is not, and all that is not good. Metaphorically sin is named a blindness, diverting one's sight from God, or a sickness. Once defined, these special terms, in their varied senses, add richness to Julian's text, without detracting from its unity of theme.

Rhetoric in the Showings: Julian used the common rhetorical devices employed by her contemporaries,[18] but of first significance is the overall rhetorical focus of her work, which distinguishes her from others of her time. Her text is set apart from other mystical tracts, not so much because of the person speaking, of whom so little is known, but because of the audience addressed. The practice in Julian's time of carefully ranking persons by profession, position in religious orders or in the Church, or title in society frequently carried over into the life of devotion. The devout tried to achieve measurable progress, labeled by distinct degrees, as in William Langland's *Piers Plowman*, which uses the allegory of Do-Well, Do-Bet, Do-Best. But Julian spoke to all Christians. She spoke to all who are to be saved, men and women, without mention of grades, degrees of holiness, or hierarchical rank. The *Cloud of Unknowing*,[19] by contrast, has for its audience a young man spiritually advanced above the ordinary. Furthermore, the author of that tract cautioned that his book is only for those who have forsaken the active life and have espoused the contemplative life, given over primarily to prayer. Likewise, Richard Rolle's *Fire of Love* is for a special class of exercitants, all of whom must renounce the love of women.[20] But Julian's *Showings* are not alone for anchoresses, but for the whole Church—all who make up the invisible and corporate body whose members will reach heaven (for those of the devil's party she has no revelation). She spoke to the person who had turned to God for one day of service or for a lifetime—all will share the bliss of heaven. This concept of equality, of universal love, permeates the treatise.

Furthermore, she meant by "all who are to be saved," not just individuals, no matter how numerous, but humanity corporately and collectively: all are one through their bond in the first-born of all that has been made—Christ—who is, in turn, grounded in the Trinity. Thus Julian is distinguished among her contemporaries by the audience she envisioned for her work.

Julian's treatise lends itself to literary as well as rhetorical analysis. One scholar has discovered, for example, that a musical dialectic pervades the treatise, stemming from concepts of looking, seeing, and beholding.[21] In whatever way one approaches the structure of the *Showings*, it becomes clear that literary devices bond with the underlying concepts and experiences. The most remarkable of these literary devices is an original parable added to the Long Version— the parable of the Lord and the Servant.

JULIAN AS MYSTIC

The beginning reader of the *Showings* might do well to start with a study of this central parable of the Lord and the Servant and the attendant explication (chaps. 51–54). The total book might then be read in normal sequence. Repeated readings will unveil the essential ideas in Julian's mysticism. The text gives guidance as to the three ways in which Julian received her mystical knowledge:

> All this blessed teaching of our Lord was shown in three ways: by physical sight, by words formed in my intellect, and by spiritual sight. With regard to the physical sight I have related what I have seen as truthfully as I can. For the words I have repeated them exactly as our Lord showed them to me. About the spiritual sight I have already said a fair amount, but I can never describe it fully. So I am prompted to say more about it, if God will give me grace.[22]

In the following section of this paper, then, I will deal: (1) with what Julian relates directly about her bodily visions and the words formed in her understanding; (2) with the metaphors and parables she employs, including the parable of the Lord and the Servant; and (3) with the overall question of Julian's mysticism.

The Experience of the Showings

Julian presents herself as one being continually taught by Christ, the divine teacher.[23] She learns progressively by attending to the bodily showings, by using her reason—sometimes to question, sometimes to relate one part of the revelations to another part—and also by opening her heart with desire and trust to the mysteries she cannot understand. This seeking, which sometimes breaks out into a beholding of divine wisdom and love, is sustained by persevering prayer.

In bodily visions Julian saw five phases of the Passion of Christ: his head bleeding from the garland of thorns; his face undergoing changes of color; his flesh marked with the scourging and the consequent profuse bleeding; his body drying from lack of moisture as it neared the moment of death; and the cloven heart, from which flowed an abundance of blood. These were only appearances, she insisted, for had the flow of blood been real, it would have saturated the bed. She also saw Christ transfigured in a glorified state.

The words formed in her understanding and the reflections and spiritual showings she reports are integral to all the sixteen showings. In the first revelation (Chap. 1–9), though visually she focuses on the crown of thorns, Julian understands in an interior way that the one who suffers is God and that he endures his pain for all God's people. Further, she knows that it is the Trinity which fills her heart with mystical joy. She thinks of this time of comfort as strength fortifying her for the hour of purifying struggle which she foresees may come. God Incarnate and the Trinity seem to her both homely and courteous. As an example of homely loving, she perceives that God enwraps us—clothes us—in his goodness. In fact, God is the goodness which is in all things as they touch and serve us. More comprehensively, in the vision of a little thing the size of a hazelnut, she sees that God is at work in all things that exist, making them, loving them, sustaining them. She arrives at the truth which Augustine had stressed in the *Confessions:* no one will be at ease or at rest in heart and soul, by seeking sufficiency in things that are made. Only God is rest. Her first explicit teaching about prayer comes also in this showing: prayer is cleaving to God's goodness—that which rightfully moves our desires. This goodness is at work for us in the lowliest of human needs and reaches to the true knowing of God himself.

Perhaps the most important line in the first revelation is: "For where Jesus is spoken of, the Blessed Trinity is always to be understood, as I see it" (Chap. 4).[24] Julian's mysticism takes its character from this belief:

> . . . For Julian the Incarnation "manifests" the Trinity: that is,
> the relationship between the divinity and the humanity of
> Christ, in which the Godhead dwells bodily in Christ,

manifests the in-dwelling relationship of the Persons of the
Godhead to one another. . . . The divine Love which
impresses Julian in this vision is . . . evident in the presence
of the whole Trinity to humanity, in the person of Christ.
This is the Love which brings God to man . . . his self-
revelation, such that Julian herself is able to see the glory of
God "without any intermediary." [25]

Yet God's love for us is beyond our knowing: there is no creature
who can grasp this immeasurable divine love. The effect of the vision
on Julian is that her compassion and charity for all her fellow
Christians expands while she seems very little in her own sight. This
effect is strengthened by a sight of Mary, the mother of God, as she
was as a young girl. Then in a spiritual sight Julian sees in part the
wisdom and truth of God reflected in Mary's soul. But even this
highest of God's creatures remains entirely other than God himself.

In the second showing (Chap. 10), Julian contemplates the bruised
face of Christ and reflects on the love which moved him to take on
our broken, helpless condition in order to restore us to the divine
likeness: his fair face was bruised and blackened so that our face,
wounded by sin, might become fair with God's own likeness. In a
section that echoes the spirit of Psalm 68, she sees herself in the
depths of the sea, but she finds hope there in the sight of "hills
and green dales." These are symbols that God is everywhere, leading
to safety and providing sustenance for all those who trust him,
however limited their experience of seeeing the glory of God.

Then—in the third revelation (Chap. 11)—Julian sees that God
does all things, that all his works are good, ordained to a purpose,
undisturbed by chance, and all is rightly accomplished, though, from
our perspective, his purpose may seem blocked by evil. At this point
she does not see the workings of creatures but only of God; and as
for sin, she concludes that it has no substance or positive reality—
"no being in kind."

Among the good deeds which God does (fourth revelation, Chap.
12) is giving us the plentiful waters of the earth for our service and
bodily comfort. But it is his blood—which is a human substance—
that by its power purifies from sin. It is poured out in a cleansing
stream on all sinful creatures of good will, bursting the hellish bonds
of the fiends, and in Christ's glorified body, praying for us to the
Father. Christ's blood is an image for his life, and for his power to
give and restore life.

In the fifth revelation (Chap. 13) Julian sees how this power of
God frustrates the malice of the fiend, who is, in fact, powerless. (It
was this malice of the fiend she had feared would mislead her at

the hour of her death). But all the woe and tribulation he has occasioned will be turned into an increase of joy for Christ's lovers.

That joy will reach its fullness in heaven, as the sixth showing portrays (Chap. 14). All service of God will be rewarded eternally. Heaven is like a great feast to which God welcomes all his friends, moving among them in intimate communion, but with a royal demeanor. His fair face is the music of this feast, filling heaven with "a marvellous melody of endless love."

In revelation seven (Chap. 15), Julian finds this heaven in her own soul, which was flooded with gladness and peace, emanating from God's presence. She is thereby taught that even when the absence of God does not result from sin, the pain of that absence must be endured patiently in faith. There are prayers which are appropriate to these alternating states of comfort and desolation. While in peace she protests like St. Paul "that nothing shall separate me from the love of Christ"; and in desolation she cries out with St. Peter, "Lord, save me, I perish."

In the eighth and ninth showings (Chap. 16–23), she learns to choose Jesus for her heaven, even when she sees him only in his suffering state. The highest reality of the Passion is to realize that it is the work of the whole Trinity. Though "only the maiden's son suffered," it is God who suffered: the one-ing with the Godhead gave strength to the humanity of Christ to travail without measure out of love. Since in the Incarnation the Son of God took upon himself all mankind—human nature, body and mind, physical and spiritual humanity—and since he is the "remaking" of that humanity in his Passion, he has lifted human lives into the being of God.[26] He continues to suffer in the people who are one with him. As a further consequence of his bond with humanity, all those whom he leads to heaven are the sign of his victory—his crown. That is the meaning of the second garland of dried blood formed over the crown of thorns: it is his eternal triumph. Under those perspectives Julian continues to contemplate the Godhead in its manifestation in Christ and in its bonding with humankind. About the one-ing with humanity she says: "The whole Trinity was involved in the passion of Christ, giving us an abundance of virtue and grace by him. . . ." (Chap. 23).

Elsewhere Julian speaks of this whole work of the Trinity as nature (the Father), mercy (the Son), and grace (the Holy Ghost):[27] Pelphrey explains how this mystery affects human lives:

> . . . nature, mercy and grace work together, as the
> expressions of the Father, Son, and Spirit in our lives. In
> "nature" our capacity for God is established; in "mercy" this

capacity is made an actuality, in the person of Christ; by "grace" it becomes true of ourselves . . . for Julian, nature itself turns toward God (for example, in the needs of our bodies, or in fear). In "mercy" God comes to meet humanity as a human being; and in "grace" we are enabled to respond to God.[28]

In the tenth, eleventh, and twelfth showings (Chap. 24–26), Christ further assures Julian of his love for mankind, whom he wills to bring to everlasting peace. Again, he relates to her not only courteously, but as a friend—as brother, savior, parent. As an example of full response to God Mary is shown again, this time not in bodily likeness but as a mirror of the Trinity, which is truth, wisdom, and charity (Chap. 25). The twelfth revelation is a profound mystical experience of Christ glorified.

Then the showings take a somewhat different turn. Revelations thirteen and fourteen (Chap. 27–63) deal with the obstacles on the human side for responding to mercy and grace, namely sin. These same revelations also treat of the means which open the way for receiving grace and comfort, especially prayer.

The problem of sin baffled Julian greatly—her own sin, the sin of mankind collectively, the sin of Adam, the sin of those to be damned. She put many troubling questions to herself and presented them in her prayer: Why was sin allowed? Why did she herself fall again and again? Why was not Adam's sin forestalled? How can it be that God's love never wavers, yet people are often alienated from him by their sin? If God loves us even in our sin, why do we blame ourselves, if he is not angry with us? How could anger be compatible with compassionate love? Even when reassured by the repeated promise that "all will be well," she asked how, then, there can be a hell for the damned, as her Church taught?

The words in her understanding let her comprehend that "sin is behovable"—that is, necessary. The key to the conflict, she learned, is in the first great secret, by which she means a mystery. The first secret is that all men are one man and one man is all men, with all that such a union implies. Our nature is wholly in God. The higher part is grounded and rooted in the Trinity; God is knit to the lower part in the Incarnate Word.

The meeting point of this union makes it possible for God always to love humanity, since he thereby loves Christ. Furthermore, in the perspective of eternity, he loves all that human beings will become, though we see them as they are in moments of time. Though sin is not to be taken lightly, there is no wrath in God—that is, no shifting, unpredictable, human-like displeasure. There is rather loving compassion, which is like what we know in human parents and marriage partners—father, mother, husband, wife.

This secret, though a mystery for us, has been made known for our belief. But there is a second great secret, which is a deed yet to be accomplished, and it will resolve the seeming impossibilities raised in her remaining questions. In some way, yet unknown, all that is good will be transformed—nothing will be lost or left behind—for God is the highest, the lowest, the all:

> God was revealing that he himself would do it: this deed with all its qualities already mentioned. . . . But what this deed was going to be was kept secret from me.[29]

In this context Julian heard again that all will be well, for he who made the greatest evil to be well—that is, Adam's sin—can make all else well. All manner of things will be well, and she herself, and her co-Christians, will see for themselves that all will be well (Chap. 27).

She is counseled not to try further to probe the hidden things of God in this regard. Instead, she is to heed the lesson she learned in the first revelation, that God himself is sufficient for her:

> And as long as we are in this life, whenever in our folly we turn to behold the reproved, tenderly our Lord toucheth us and blissfully claspeth, saying in our soul: "Let be, my love, my most dear child, and attend to me (for I am enough to thee), and take joy in thy Saviour and thy salvation.[30]

This passage also relates to what Julian teaches about prayer in the context of the fourteenth revelation. It is in harmony too with the awareness Julian develops that Christ is mother. This metaphor, along with the parable of the Lord and the Servant which unveils the first secret, are communications which she calls spiritual sights. There is more in them than bodily visions or reason can comprehend.

The fifteenth and sixteenth revelations (Chap. 64–86) present Julian confronted alternately with comfort and with fear. She acknowledges that such is the human condition, as long as we are in this life:

> The more clearly the soul sees the blessed face by grace and love, the more it longs to see it in its fullness.
> Notwithstanding that our Lord lives in us, and is here with us; notwithstanding that he is nearer to us than tongue and heart can think or tell, the fact remains that we shall never cease from sighs, complaints, or tears—or longing—till we see clearly his blessed face. In that precious, blessed sight, no grief can live, no blessing fail.[31]

Julian's account closes with the final teaching of the *Showings,* received as a spiritual sight:

From the time that these things were first revealed I had often wanted to know what was our Lord's meaning. It was more than fifteen years after that I was answered in my spirit's understanding. "You would know our Lord's meaning in this thing? Know it well. Love was his meaning. Who showed it to you? Love. What did he show you? Love. Why did he show it? For love. Hold on to this and you will know and understand love more and more. But you will not know or learn anything else—ever." [32]

The Spiritual Sight in Metaphors and Parables: The spiritual sights are at times described in direct discourse and dialogue. More often they are conveyed through metaphors and parables, or at least amplified by such means.

Some of the metaphors in Julian's work are common to medieval writings, and to mystical writings generally. Among these well-known metaphors are the journey, to signify the spiritual life on earth, spiritual blindness, the ground of being, light and darkness, the city of the soul. Julian also develops concrete analogies from nature, with references to water, blood, rain, thirst, dryness, the seabed, the garden to be cultivated by God's servants, and the treasure hidden in the earth, which stands for humanity in its capacity to grow and flower into something greater than the seed of its common status.

But Julian adds metaphors of her own to this familiar list. Among these is the well-loved reference to the little thing in the palm of her hand, about the size of a hazelnut, which stands for all that has been made. Though this experience teaches her the littleness of creation, it also helps her see that nothing that has been made is to be despised, for it reveals God's goodness. In taking such a position Julian differs from many medieval writers, such as Walter Hilton, who often seemed to despise the flesh.

Julian further affirms how near God is to his creation by images of cloth and clothing. The torn flesh of Christ resembles a cloth about to fall into shreds; and the Church, considered as the body of Christ, because sorrows afflict it, is like a cloth shaken in the wind. Clothing images also amplify the parable of the Lord and the Servant: Julian describes the garments of both Lord and Servant and explains what they signify, both as to kind and color.[33]

Julian also uses familiar metaphors in a new way. An important example is the likening of God to a point:

. . . I saw God in a point . . . by which I learned that he is
in all things . . . at this time the working of creatures was
not shown, but only the Lord God in the creature; for he is
the mid-point of all things and of all that he does . . . "See:
I am God. I am in all things. I never lift my hands from my
works, nor ever shall, without end." [34]

Some writers have used the symbol of the point as if it related
to a geometrical figure:

. . . all the radii of a circle are concentrated into a single
unity in the center, and this point contains all the straight
lines brought together within itself, and unified to one
another, and to the one starting point from which they
began. [35]

The concept in this form is as old, at least, as the writings of the
Pseudo-Dionysius and occurs widely. Dante, for one, sees a point
of light—the starting point in God's mind of all that is—radiating
out into all that exists. [36] Father William Johnston describes still
another variant on the metaphor, which he calls the "still point." It
involves:

. . . vertical thinking, a process in which the mind goes
silently down to its own center, revealing cavernous depths
ordinarily latent and untouched by the flow of images and
concepts that pass across the surface of the mind. It is that
mysticism in which one descends to the "still point" or to the
ground of the soul, thus finding a type of knowledge that is
supra-conceptual and therefore ineffable, a species of super-
thinking whereby one grasps the unity of all things. . . . [37]

But Julian's metaphor of the point suggests a more concrete reference
than either the geometrical or super-conceptual figures of these others.
For her, God is the central point of all, and human life is only a
point in him. This concept extends to the idea that God is present
to the lowest parts of human needs, even including the body's
eliminative functions, for which the body is suited like a fine purse. [38]
She may be thinking, then, of needle- or lace-point, which anchoresses made. In such a structure each point (or stitch) is everywhere
the same, yet each is really distinct from the pattern which arises
from the points. Also this pattern pre-exists in the mind of the
worker, who, for a perfect work, never lifts his hands from what he
makes. Such a metaphor conveys Julian's teaching that God is in all
things, as maker and keeper, yet is really other from what he sustains
in being:

To the same blessed power, wisdom, and love by which he made them are all things being continually led, and our Lord himself will bring them there. In due time, we shall see. . . . The reason for this was shown in the first revelation, and more clearly in the third, where it was said: "I saw the whole Godhead concentrated in a single point." [39]

The metaphor which contains Julian's most intricate theology—those mysteries which she herself struggled with for nearly twenty years—is the great parable of the Lord and the Servant. This story conveys Julian's insights about the first Adam, the cosmic Christ, the Trinity, and the unity of all who are to be saved. [40] The one great reality in the parable is the person of Christ, in whom are mysterious compenetrations of other realities—the Adam of Genesis; the total Adam (all humanity); Christ as the second Adam (and in one sense the first Adam, since to his eternal image all things were made); and Christ, meaning all humanity to be saved. The basic parable weaves into other metaphors: for example, the sinful Adam fell in misery to the earth, but likewise the divine Adam falls on the earth—into human nature in Mary's womb—and makes the garden of the earth spring forth with food and drink for which the Father thirsts and longs, in his unending love for the treasure which was hidden in the earth.

The allegory of the Lord and the Servant, initially referred to in Julian's first revelation, [41] flows easily into the second great metaphor—that of the motherhood of Christ. For the Lord in the parable "rejoices to be our mother," and the deep Wisdom seen in the Trinity "is our mother." Julian then devotes four chapters to explaining how Christ is mother. He is mother because he gives birth to us in creation, in our again-making, and in our dying, a birth to eternal life. He carries out all the functions of motherhood: he nurtures, feeds, chides, rewards, and loves tenderly with more compassion and tenderness than any other mother could exercise.

This striking metaphor, rooted in Scripture, existed in an unbroken tradition from earliest Christian times and had antecedents in Judaism. It fell into disuse only under the impact of systematic theology in the thirteenth century. An ancient Hebrew teaching placed the feminine in the Godhead, [42] and Philo of Alexandria, a Hellenistic Jew who was a primary influence on early Christian exegesis, used maternal names for God. Among Christian exegetes who continued to use such images are Irenaeus, Justin Martyr, Clement of Alexandria, John Chrysostom, Hilary of Poitiers, Jerome, and Ambrose. St. Augustine assimilated what these Latin and Greek Fathers had said, and transmitted the concept through such expressions as "Our Mother, the Wisdom of God." In sermons and commentaries on the Psalms, on Isaiah, and other Old Testament texts, he repeated maternal imagery in several forms: for example, he says that Christ became incarnate because weak human beings could not eat the bread that is God, our Father, until it became milk at the breast of Christ, our Mother. The New Testament event in which Christ compared himself to a hen who desired to gather her chickens under her wings occasioned repeated analogies and was blended with the metaphor from the Song of Moses which portrayed God as the eagle sheltering the fledgeling people of God under her wings.

Echoes of Augustine's metaphors, together with some new variations, occur in an unbroken sequence to the time of Julian's *Showings.* Maternal imagery for God, and sometimes for Christ, occurs in such diverse writers as Cassiodorus, Remigius, Rabanus Maurus, Peter Lombard, Anselm, Bernard of Clairvaux, Albert the Great, and Bonaventure. The image also appears in Thomas Aquinas' gathering of texts from the Fathers, the *Catena Aurea.*[43]

Though there are these many suggestions in earlier writings giving a basis for applying the motherhood image to Christ and the Trinity, Julian worked out the appropriation more fully than any of her predecessors and with some original nuances. For her, Christ is our mother in the order of creation: "We have our being of him, there, where the ground of motherhood beginneth."[44] We are grounded in the Trinity through this motherhood: "And the deep Wisdom of the Trinity is our Mother, in whom we are enclosed."[45] In this same motherhood our sensual being is united to God, redeemed, and restored to harmony with our substance: ". . . I saw that the second Person, who is our Mother substantially—the same very dear Person is now become our Mother sensually. . . . He is our Mother of mercy in taking our sensuality . . . in our Mother Christ, we have profit and increase; and in mercy he re-formeth and restoreth us; and by the power of his passion, his death and uprising, oned us to our substance."[46]

Christ's motherhood in the work of grace has its roots in his experience of being formed by a mother—that is, of being a child in the womb and subject to a human mother:

> But now I must say a little more about this "overflowing" as I understand its meaning: how we have been brought back again by the motherhood of mercy and grace to that natural condition which was ours originally when we were made through the motherhood of natural love (kind love)—which love, indeed, has never left us.

Our Mother by nature and grace—for he would become our Mother in everything—laid the foundation of his work in the Virgin's womb with great and gentle condescension. (This was shown in the first revelation when I received a mental picture of the Virgin's genuine simplicity at the time she conceived.) In other words, it was in this lowly place that God most high, the supreme wisdom of all, adorned and arrayed himself with our poor flesh, ready to function and serve as Mother in all things.[47]

Thus Christ, whom the Scriptures say "learned through suffering," although he was God (Hebrews 5:8), learned motherhood through Mary. He exercised his own motherhood as a service—a word which suggests both the official liturgical service and the lowly service of the mother; and as an office, which is the same word used to designate the functions to which members of the Church are called and for which they are publicly ordained. What is only implied in these words is made explicit when Julian says, with reference to the Mass and the Eucharist, ongoing workings of grace:

He might die no more, but that does not stop him working, for he needs to feed us . . . it is an obligation of his dear, motherly love. The human mother will suckle her child with her own milk, but our beloved Mother, Jesus, feeds us with himself, and, with the most tender courtesy, does it by means of the Blessed Sacrament, the precious good of true life. And he keeps us going through his mercy and grace by all the sacraments.[48]

John Clark summarizes what is apparently new and more fully developed in Julian than in any of her known predecessors with reference to this motherhood metaphor:

It is now recognized that the image of God as "Mother" can claim a continuous tradition, with roots in the Bible and the Fathers; in particular the appropriation of *Sapientia* to Christ opens the way to applying to him some of those texts in the Sapiential books of the Bible which speak of Wisdom, God's agent in the creation and ordering of the world, as a female figure. At the same time, no full antecedent has yet been found for Julian's bold appropriation to Christ of Motherhood in the order of creation as well as of redemption, nor of her explicit development of a fully Trinitarian theology in which Motherhood is consistently appropriated to Christ as Wisdom.[49]

Thus, the metaphor becomes the most comprehensive, integrative, and significant one within Julian's *Showings*.

IS JULIAN A MYSTIC?

Those who study Julian's *Showings*, aided by recent research, should be able to grant that she is a writer of the first rank, and that she transmits an appealing message of love, expressed in skilled language, with consistent rhetorical strategies, and effective metaphors. It is also clear, from a survey of the meaning of her visionary experiences, that her book is not merely devotional but profoundly theological. But in what sense, if at all, is Julian a mystic? Are the attributes of mysticism, as commonly described, present in her experience? It seems that they are indeed present, despite the surface simplicity of her treatise.

The core of mysticism in the orthodox Christian tradition is a way of life. The authentic mystic is purified, illuminated, and transformed as the God of love reveals himself in such a manner that the mystic is explicitly conscious of the way of life demanded by God's own self-communication. The goal of the mystic is conscious union with God. The fully matured contemplative is ultimately united with the source of Love in a profound union, in which, nonetheless, God remains God, and the creature remains a creature. Transformed by God's love and wisdom, the Christian mystic discerns more than ever before how the Christ-life affects every dimension of human activity—not only of the individual but of the people of God.[50]

In general terms this view of mysticism applies to Julian. Yet, paradoxically, the very persistence with which she stresses that her way of life is for all who will be saved may distract us from her own path of purification, illumination, and transformation. Likewise, because what was revealed to Julian was not prophecy in the narrow sense but a deeper insight into the truths of faith already proposed for her belief, we may fail to attend adequately to the depth and breadth of God's self-revelation to her. It is useful, then, to review how Julian becomes one with the mystery of divine love, a growth experience comparable to what she invites her co-Christians to seek.

As the record of the two versions of the *Showings* witness, Julian persevered in her search of God from her youth, through the trials recorded in the revelations, and into some twenty years of reflection and prayer after the showings. Hers was a lifetime of purgation and enlightenment. However, unlike many other writers, she did not regard her spiritual journey as a series of progressive steps culminating in perfection. Rather, she saw human life as more like the teeth of a saw, a series of risings and fallings.[51] She reduced meditations, asceticism, and reflections to a single turning of attention to God, with the eye of faith, or with the beholding of confident love:

> If, because of our weakness, we fall back again into our old inertia and spiritual blindness, and experience suffering both spiritual and physical, God's will is for us to know that he has not forgotten us.[52]

Mystics often speak of experiences which they call the dark night, when they seem abandoned and on the verge of extinction. We may look in vain for an explicit example of this experience in the *Showings*, partially because Julian was of a strong, positive disposition, and experiences of the dark night are in some degree linked to the personality of the individual. Nonetheless, Julian explains that she shared in some way in the deepest desolation of Christ himself, in a mystical death which is followed by joy:

> I understood that in this life (as our Lord sees it)
> We are on his cross
>   dying with him in our pains and passion.
> Then suddenly his countenance shall be changed upon us
>   and we shall be with him in heaven.
> Between this disposition and the other there will be no
>   break in time and then—
> We shall all be brought into joy.[53]

Some awareness of divine transcendence is also part of the mystic's experience and testimony. Julian witnesses to such an awareness repeatedly:

> I had in some measure both touch, sight, and feeling of these three of God's attributes . . . the attributes are these three: Life, love, and light. . . . These three exist in one goodness.[54]

Her awareness of God extended but was not limited to his presence in the human soul:

> Our good Lord showed himself to me in various ways both in heaven and on earth. But the only *place* I saw him occupy was in man's soul. He showed himself on earth in his precious incarnation and his blessed passion. In another way he showed himself—on earth still—when I said, "I saw the whole Godhead as it were in a single point." [55]

It is in the twelfth revelation, an experience to which she refers again and again, that Julian felt the most overwhelming sense of the presence of God, with the resulting joy which flooded her whole being:

> After this our Lord showed himself, in glory even greater than I had seen before—so it seemed to me. By this was I taught that our soul can never rest until it comes to him, and knows him to be the fullness of joy, friendly and considerate, blessed and life indeed. And he said again and again "It is I; it is I; it is I who am most exalted; it is I whom you love; it is I whom you delight in; it is I whom you serve; it is I whom you long for, whom you desire; it is I whom you mean; it is I who am all. It is I whom Holy Church preaches and teaches; it is I who showed myself to you here." . . . . the joy I saw in that revelation surpasses all the heart could wish for or desire.[56]

True, mysticism is not only the hunger of the heart of God, nor is it just an intellectual activity. Rather, it begets an energy that organizes the whole life in an arduous search which transforms the person. Julian speaks of this transformation, applying it not only to the individual, but to corporate humanity:

> This blessed love works in us in two ways. In our lower part there are pains and passions, sympathy, pity, mercy and forgiveness, and so on . . . ; in the higher part are none of these, but altogether the most tremendous love and marvellous joy. And in this joy all our sufferings are set right . . . he also showed the honor and nobility to which he will bring us through the work of grace in the lower part of our nature, transforming our blameworthiness into eternal worthiness.[57]

Julian's *Showings* thus manifest characteristics found in other figures and writers whom we are ready to call "mystics." [58]

JULIAN'S INFLUENCE TODAY

Though, as stated at the beginning, Julian has not been given her rightful place in English letters, nonetheless traces of her influence exist. T. S. Eliot in *Little Gidding* has familiarized readers with a notable phrase from Julian—"All shall be well"—and has associated this saying with mystical symbolism:

> And all shall be well and
>   All manner of thing shall be well
>   When the tongues of flame are enfolded
>   Into the crowned knot of fire

And the fire and the rose are one.[59]

Likewise, Aldous Huxley ended the meditative chapter of *Eyeless in Gaza* with an echo of the same saying from Julian: ". . . he thought of what was in store for him. Whatever it might be, he knew that all would be well." [60]

Closer to our own days such popular writers as Annie Dillard and Mary Gordon make Julian known in prose works. Annie Dillard in *Holy the Firm*[61] has a Julie Norwich as a major character, in a prose-poem which presents some images and teachings from the *Showings*. And Mary Gordon in *Final Payments* has her narrator in the midst of a religious crisis discover a prayer card with words from Julian, printed in "the slant, liturgical script that had made its truth seem inevitable":

He said not thou shalt not be tempted
He said not thou shalt not be troubled
He said thou shalt not be overcome.[62]

Among well-known writers on the contemplative life, Thomas Merton has called Julian one of the great theologians of all time—equal to John Henry Newman, superior to John of the Cross and even to Teresa of Avila.[63]

Admittedly, these are small, scattered signs of recognition, and even the scholarship devoted to the *Showings* is recent and in need of supplements. But given these advances in scholarship and a growing interest in mysticism, Julian may soon attain the place she deserves in English letters.

BIBLIOGRAPHICAL NOTES

Editions and Translations

Julian of Norwich wrote *Revelations of Divine Love*, or *Showings*, which exists in both a long and a short version. The critical edition, which includes both versions, is by Edmund Colledge and James Walsh, *A Book of Showings to the Anchoress Julian of Norwich*, 2 vols. (Toronto, 1978). These two editors also issued a one-volume translation of both texts: *Showings* (New York, 1978). This translation, which includes a lengthy introduction, draws largely on the critical edition. An excellent student text in Middle English by Marion Glasscoe is available from Exeter University Press (Exeter Medieval Texts, 1978). Glasscoe's edition also has an introduction, notes, tables correlating the revelations with the chapters, and a selective glossary. The best translation of the short text is *A Showing of God's Love: The Shorter Version of Sixteen Revelations of Divine Love* (London, 1974), by Sister Anna Maria Reynolds. Her volume also includes the chapters on the motherhood of God from the long text. The entire long text is easily accessible in James Walsh's translation,

The Revelations of Divine Love of Julian of Norwich (St. Meinrad, IN, 1974), and in Clifton Wolters' version (Baltimore, 1973). Both are accurate. Wolters' translation makes use of a freer prose style than Walsh's.

Commentaries

It is difficult to select from the many distinguished studies devoted to Julian. However, a useful overview is by A. M. Allchin and the Sisters of the Love of God, in *Julian of Norwich: Four Studies to Commemorate the Sixth Centenary of the Revelations of Divine Love* (Fairacres, Oxford, 1975). In *Julian of Norwich: the Teaching of a Fourteenth-Century English Mystic* (London, 1958), Father Paul Molinari has laid to rest doubts about Julian's orthodoxy within Catholicism and also demonstrated that her experiences proceeded from a sound, intelligent mind. Lingering uncertainty about her teaching on sin has been dealt with appropriately by Deryck Hanshell, "A Crux in the Interpretation of Dame Julian," *Downside Review*, 92 (1974), 77–91. The *Downside Review* has carried a series of important studies by John P.H. Clark; among these are "Predestination in Christ According to Julian of Norwich," 100 (1982), 79–91, and "Nature, Grace and the Trinity of Julian of Norwich," 101 (1982), 203–20. Charles Brant Pelphrey in a lengthy theological study shows Julian's theological depths and the affinity of her teaching to Byzantine mystical theology and Greek Orthodox theology as a whole. Originally a 1976 dissertation at the University of Edinburgh, this book is now available under the title *Love Was His Meaning: The Theology and Mysticism of Julian of Norwich*, Salzburg Studies in English Literature, 92:4, by James Hogg (Salzburg, 1982). Robert Llewelyn, *With Pity Not With Blame* (London, 1982), has provided a guide to prayer and life in Christ according to Julian's teachings. *The 14th-Century English Mystics Newsletter* in 1979–81 published the major addresses of the Norwich observance of the 1973 Julian sexcentenary. Lastly, though the work is not yet fully available in English translation, there is a dissertation completed in 1978 at the Sorbonne University, Paris: Roland Maisonneuve, "L'Univers visionnaire de Julian de Norwich." Soon to be issued in book form in French, this study not only considers Julian as a visionary, but also supplies the most inclusive information about her to date in a single work—a review of the critical literature, analysis of the ideas and times of Julian's world, and useful tables, such as categories of metaphors in the *Showings*. Maisonneuve is beginning to publish articles in English from his research. See Publications and Reviews, *14th-Century English Mystics Newsletter*, continuing.

IX

Margery Kempe

MAUREEN FRIES

The most controversial of English mystics, Margery Kempe, was born about 1373, to John Brunham, a prominent citizen of Bishop's Lynn (now known as King's Lynn) in Norfolk; her mother's name does not appear in the records. Her father was Mayor of her natal city five times, as both Margery and its *Register* attest,[1] and held numerous other civic offices. The only sibling of hers to appear in the records is her (apparent) brother John, who was his father's heir. About 1393, she married John Kempe, apparently a brewer and probably son to a father of the same name, also active in the civic affairs of Lynn. At some indeterminate date after 1438, when she became a member of the Trinity Guild of Lynn, she died. So much of her life can we gather from official civic accounts.

A few more dates and events can be garnered from Margery's own account of her life, called *The Book of Margery Kempe*.[2] Of the fourteen children she bore to John Kempe, only one, John, is mentioned by name. From 23 June, 1413, to his death she and her husband lived chastely, and mostly apart in separate dwellings. He accompanied her on her earlier domestic pilgrimages; she undertook alone her foreign pilgrimages to the Holy Land and Italy, in 1413–15, and to Compostella in 1417, and (with her son's widow) to Germany and elsewhere in 1433–34, as well as further domestic journeys between the latter two voyages. After visiting the Brigittine monastery, Syon, on her return from her final foreign excursion, she revised the first part of her *Book* with a new scribe who also took down the much shorter second part, from 1436–38 (we do not know when the original version was written, but it was probably finished before 1432).

217

For many years (over 430), this *Book* was meagerly represented by few and, in the opinion of the majority of critics, misleading abstracts. The series of short selections printed first in 1501 by Wynkyn de Worde, and later reprinted in 1521, with verbal and spelling variants, by Henry Pepwell (who added the misleading designation that it was by "a devout anchoress" [3]) led to the identification of Margery Kempe as a "mystic of the type of Julian of Norwich." [4] The pious and greatly shortened redaction was not only unrepresentative of but gravely distorted its original. That original emerged in one of those surprising literary discoveries that have marked our era (the finding of Traherne's *Centuries* upon an old books' cart, and the emergence of a MS of Malory's *Morte Darthur* in a mutilated copy in the Winchester College library are other instances). Colonel Butler-Bowdon, of an old Catholic Yorkshire family, sent the manuscript for an evaluation to the Victoria and Albert Museum, where it was identified by Hope Emily Allen, from the Wynkyn de Worde fragments, as a copy of *The Book of Margery Kempe*, in 1934.[5] An edition co-edited by Miss Allen and Sanford Meech followed, under the auspices of the Early English Text Society, as did a popularized and sometimes inaccurate translation into modern English by Butler-Bowdon himself.[6] Now the full *Book* was available to be judged as part of the great resurgence of English mystical writing that marked the end of the Middle Ages.

That *Book* has been accused of lacking form—indeed, either Margery or her amanuensis or both were the first to note its lack of chronological consistency.[7] But whether consciously or not, Margery introduced a pattern, sometimes chronological, despite her disclaimer, sometimes associational, that can be discerned once the book is carefully outlined in a structural rather than a chronological fashion. In both Book I and Book II, the key event is a conversion—in the first instance, Margery's, and in the second, her son's. This is followed by alternation of periods at home and periods of journey/pilgrimage, either domestic or foreign, with certain returns home punctuated by sickness. Schematically this might be represented thus: Book One, home/conversion—domestic journeys—home—foreign journeys—home/sickness—foreign/domestic journeys—sickness/home; Book Two, home/son's conversion—son's foreign/domestic journeys—son's homecoming/sickness and death—Margery's foreign/domestic journeys—Margery's final homecoming. Movement from comparative stasis at home to the dynamism of journey is impelled by personal trouble, usually with Margery's clerical or lay enemies but, in Book II, by her son's death. Divine intervention, usually in talks with Christ and/or (less often) his mother often mediates between home and travel. But travel always brings further trouble: ostracism and even expulsion by fellow voyagers, domestic and foreign, lay and clerical; accusations of Lollardry and other heresy, of hypocrisy and vainglory; losses and gains of necessary male guides, since she usually must travel at least part of the time alone. The road again brings divine aid, as any of various sorts of direct message (visual, auditory or mental) and as Christ-appointed human helpers (even Saracens). Thus the physical and the spiritual aspects of Margery's life are ordered by the predominant medieval metaphor of both secular and spiritual literature, the quest; and a book meant for religious edification parallels the romance structures of Chrétien de Troyes and the *Gawain*-poet. Even the homecoming/illness motif is present in the Tristan stories.

But a great difference between Margery's quest(s) and those of romance, hagiography, and mystical treatises by others lies in her initial call to a new life. In none of the latter is that call a product of a painful and lengthy postpartum depression (apparently at its unipolar manic phase) [8] following upon a first childbirth. By her own testimony, she raved against herself, her husband and their friends; tore her skin and bit herself; and was finally bound and guarded day and night. Although the onset of this mania coincided with her inability to confess a secret sin of her youth, because of her confessor's harsh words, and her resultant fear of damnation, the brief appearance of Christ as a beautiful young man quieted her. Asking why she forsook him when he had never forsaken her, he slowly disappeared into the air. This evanescent vision restored Margery to her senses, but did not yet reveal to her the true "draught" (or drawing up to him) of our Lord.[9]

So little did she feel this "draught" that she indulged herself in pride and vainglory in her clothes and in her failed occupations as brewer and miller, as well as in her rebuking her husband with the worth of her kindred. Both she and her neighbors saw her business failures as God's curse, and Margery turned penitent. Hearing, one night, a paradisal melody, she embraced a life of austerity and prayer for two years. Although her husband refused her desire they live chaste, she fasted, wore a hairshirt and began the "plenteous tears" and "many boisterous sobbings" that were to cause her so much trouble for the rest of her life.[10] Unfortunately the constantly-worn hairshirt did not prevent her husband's conceiving children upon her, and the community reacted to her showy devotions with slander about her hypocrisy.

Such slander might have seemed appropriate had Lynn known of the three years' fall from grace that followed. Lechery, that very "delectation" of the opposite sex Margery had urged her husband to foreswear, was chief of the temptations that beset her.[10] Physically attracted to and propositioned by another man, she yields in the space of an (unheeded) evensong—only to be rejected. Her continuing fleshly temptation abates for two hours a day by grace of the Divinity. Margery mortifies herself and undergoes frequent shriving and penance, but falls into a despair from which only the return of the figure of Christ saves her. This return, after a five-year absence and a period of Purgation (first step on the threefold mystic way), marks the beginning of a personal relationship with Jesus, his saints, and eventually the Holy Spirit and the Godhead itself, which is to sustain Margery throughout her life.

This initial period of Illumination (second step on the mystic way) brought many, often to be repeated, promises from Christ. Margery is to be saved, at once, when she dies, in spite of her sins; their relationship is to be (as with many another mystic) that of lover and beloved—she is bidden to "boldly call me Jesus, your love"—or, as the Friar Preacher whom Christ commends to her as confessor puts it, "Daughter, you suck even at Christ's breast"; she follows, as handmaiden and precursor of the Annunciation, the life of the Blessed Virgin and participates in the Nativity; she is appointed as savior of hundreds of thousands of souls, her confessor included.[11] During this time, but related later in the book, Jesus significantly (in view of later events) assures her he loves her as well as any maiden although (by his will) she is again with child.[12]

Also during this time, Margery made what must have been her first religious journey, although she does not report it until much later, to Norwich—significantly after, newly delivered of a child, she had been assured by Christ that she should bear no more children; like most of the domestic and foreign journeys she was to undertake, its destination was divinely directed.[13] After satisfactorily answering the question of the Vicar of St. Stephen's as to how a woman could occupy an hour or two in the Lord's love with a list of her heavenly confidantes (all three persons of the Trinity, the Virgin, and Sts. Peter, Paul, Katharine or whichever saint she had devotion to) and winning over the Carmelite, William Southfield (both men were to be her lifelong supporters), Margery visited with the renowned anchoress and mystic who resided at St. Julian's. From her account, she valued Julian's advice (as to the discernment of spirits, the efficacy of tears and the bearing with one's enemies) which went on for "many days." [14]

Enemies multiplied during her other early domestic journeys as quickly as they had at home (in spite of the miracle by which, hit by falling stone and wood in her own parish church, she sustains no injuries, and the pain ceases through prayer). These forays she undertook with her husband, seemingly for the double purpose of achieving a chaste marriage and publicizing and ratifying her sanctity. A journey to and from York is important only because of her spouse's final agreement that they live chastely—*if* she will pay his debts and cease her Friday fast (undertaken to secure the marital chastity).[15] After revealing the sins of an immediately-converted monk, she visits Canterbury. Here for the first time, for weeping, she is called a Lollard and threatened with burning by priests and laity alike. Adding insult to this injury, her frightened husband forsakes her and she must be rescued by two strange young men. At Lincoln, the Bishop approves the Kempes' vow of marital chastity but refuses Margery the mantle and the ring (the widow's signs of perpetual chastity),[16] as well as permission to wear white clothes.[17] To obtain other favors husband and wife seek out the Archbishop of Canterbury at his London residence, Lambeth Palace; he gives Margery the right to choose her confessor and be houseled (receive the Eucharist) every Sunday.

On an earthly level, then, this first extended domestic sojourn was only a partial success. But spiritually it was greatly satisfying, as were events at Lynn which followed. After her serious problems at Canterbury, the Divinity assured her how grateful he was for her bearing of rebukes on his account. He also explained her multiple familial relationship to him—daughter, mother, sister, wife and spouse—and authorized her pilgrimages to Jerusalem, Rome, and Santiago de Compostella. Apparently his opinion was antiepiscopal, for he ordered her to wear white clothes.[18] But she had "so many enemies and so much slander that it seemed she might not bear it without great grace and a mighty faith." [19] One of her two confessors, the Dominican, showed great trust in her, the other had none; she had petty quarrels with two widows. But to counter this ill-will, God gave her great gifts, especially prophecy: she advised a vicar to keep his cure, knew the condition of dead and live souls and who should live and who die, correctly foretold that two men trusted by the priest who wrote her book were con men (this is obviously a future reference),[20] and predicted a Benedictine Chapel's failure to receive the right to baptize and purify.[21] No wonder she could see the host "flicker" like a dove, especially with Christ's assurance that St. Bridget "saw me never in this wise." [22]

Like St. Bridget, Margery now embarked upon the greatest of her foreign journeys—the great trek for all medievals—the voyage to Jerusalem. The pattern for her later foreign journeys, the late one to "Dutchland" [23] and (presumably) the earlier one to Compostella was here set. Throughout her passage to the Holy Land, her stay there, her homeward stops at Venice, Assisi and Rome, and her journey back to England, she was constantly rebuked by and often expelled

from whatever traveling companionship she had chosen for her usual
eccentricities: loud weeping, constant talk of heaven, and abstention
from meat—the same qualities that had often proved her domestic
undoing. As domestically, priests could be either her best friends or
her worst enemies—an uncharitable English priest on this journey
caused her much trouble. Yet God sent friends: in Constance, the
Papal Legate and a Devonshire guide; in Jerusalem, the Grey Friars
and even the Saracens (more "Christian" than the Christians); in
Venice, going home, a prophesied "crookbacked man"; in Assisi,
Margaret Florentine; from Italy to England, a good priest.

Such good "even-Christians" were accompanied by signs of increased sanctity such as had always surrounded Margery in periods
of abuse. Answering her prayers, God allowed her to see the Heavenly
Jerusalem at the same moment she saw the earthly one; on Calvary,
she was driven to loud cries such as she had not previously experienced and which were to further trouble most of her future life;
in Jerusalem she multiplied her weeping. Christ appeared on the
Cross for her, he and the Virgin spoke to her, and she dutifully
visited all the holy places. But her fellow-travelers would not even
eat with her, so much fuss she made. Only from the Grey Friars
who were conducting the tour and the Saracens who guarded it (one
of whom took her up Mt. Quarantine) did she get any charity.

On the way home, at Venice, charity failed so much as to cause
her countrymen to forsake her, but God assures her she will travel
home safely if only she puts on white clothes. Led by a brokenbacked
man, Richard, whom her confessor had prophesied to her, Margery
stops at an inn between Venice and Assisi, where she temporarily
loses and then recovers what she describes to "the good wife of the
house" as "my good married ring to Jesus Christ." [24] This fore-
shadows the major event of the stay in Rome, her marriage to the
Godhead, as distinguished from an earlier espousal of his Son for
which the ring was made.[25] She had previously donned white as
commanded, then put it off for her usual black clothes at the behest
of her German confessor, who also ordered her to serve a poor
woman. But at Christ's command, she doffed the black, put on the
white again, and left the woman's service. A suitable number of
miracles—her German confessor's understanding her though he knew
no English, heavenly smells and music, the sight of angels, the "heat
of the Holy Ghost" and St. John the Evangelist as confessor—mark
these events.[26] So do the usual persecutions from her countrymen,
especially the English priest, whose slander causes her removal from
the Hospital of Thomas à Becket; even the women of Rome ask her
if her white clothes have been stolen during the change to black.
But when, at God's command, she gives away her goods (and those

lent her by Richard, who is none too pleased), she is invited back into the Hospital and shown other favors, including the appearance of St. Jerome.

Favor was mixed when she arrived at Norwich. The Vicar of St. Stephen's, one of her first supporters, still believed in her goodness, but a former adherent, a foreign anchorite, "asked what she had done with her child . . . begotten and born while she was abroad." [27] He refused to believe her denials, and forbade her to wear white clothes. But, supplied by a good man of Norwich, these appeared, and Margery wore them, although they caused her trouble and shame in many places thereafter. Her husband came to fetch her home, where she suffered so severe an illness she was anointed and thought she would die. God, however, promised her that her time was not yet, so that she should see Santiago.

The pilgrimage to Santiago de Compostella is described very sketchily by Margery, and the details preceding it seem more important to her. She was without funds and in debt when two residents of Lynn supplied her with money, which God warned her she was not to worry about. At Bristol, she was able to repay Richard, her former guide, all of his money she had given away in Rome. During the six long weeks she waited for a ship, her tears, sobbings and newly-acquired cries while being houseled so scandalized the people of Bristol and other pilgrims waiting with her, that the usual antagonism arose. But as usual our Lord provided friends: Thomas Marshall of Newcastle, who paid her way to Santiago, and the Bishop of Worcester, who entertained her in his house. In spite of the rich man of Bristol who attempts to keep her from the ship, Margery embarks for Santiago and the most satisfying voyage and pilgrimage she must ever have had. Although only described in a few sentences, it had the attractions of now-friendly fellow-pilgrims and fourteen days of "great cheer" in Spain; she does not record any objections to her cries or tears at this time—undoubtedly because she had prayed Christ to "spare me until I come home to England." [28]

But England held unfriendliness and danger enough. After a friendly reception at the Shrine of the Blood of Hales (as after the Holy Land pilgrimage, Margery seems in no hurry to get home to Lynn), she is imprisoned by the Mayor of Leicester as a Lollard, and approached with lecherous intent by the Steward of Leicester. Thomas Marshall and another fellow-pilgrim are also arrested, but freed when (at Margery's prayer) God sends bad weather; and Margery too proves herself orthodox before a mixed (clerical and lay) court, and is freed providing she gets a letter from the Bishop of Lincoln. This she accomplishes; but a series of further arrests follows, at York (twice), at the Humber by the Duke of Bedford, over the Humber at Beverley,

with various accusers making charges ranging from heresy to alien-
ating husband and wife. Margery shows great resourcefulness during
this, her most trying period of public prosecution. The Archbishop
of York commends her scatalogical tale of the priest, the bear, and
the palmer; at Beverley, locked into an upper room, her "many good
tales" move the female passersby not only to tears but to fetching
a pot of wine for the thirsty prisoner.

Freed and close to home, she sets out with her husband to get
from Canterbury the letter and seal York has required of her before
she may re-enter Bishop's Lynn proper. Her long stay in London
is, unfortunately, summed up in a sentence. Return to Lynn brings—
besides continuing scorn and slander, and even a bowl of water
dumped on her head—much sickness to Margery, for eight years.
A new outbreak of sobs, cries, and exclamations leads to her expulsion
from the Prior's Chapel she had frequented, and only through the
friendship of her confessor, Master Springhold, is she allowed to
commune at St. Margaret's.[29] For ten years the loud crying continues,
especially on Good Friday, only occasionally alternating with "soft
and still" weeping.[30]

Such grief was alleviated somewhat by her "listerer" or reader, a
good priest who apparently came to Lynn in 1413 (before her trip
to the Holy Land) and had been reading to her ever since, at least
between pilgrimages.[31] But for doubting our Lord's revelations as to
who should be saved or damned Margery was tormented by lecherous
thoughts, centering upon men's "members," and particularly upon
those of men of religion: "she saw as she thought truly many men
of religion, priests, and many others, both heathen and Christian
coming before her sight . . . and therewith the Devil bade her in
her mind choose whom she would have first of them all and she
must be common to them all."[32] Only after twelve days and her
vow to believe his Revelations was Margery relieved of this phallic
burden.

Another sort of religious burden came with a Grey Friar who,
from the time he came to Lynn and for many years thereafter, refused
her entry into his church because of her cries, allied to her refusal
to agree with him that they were a physical disease. This implacable
man turned many against her, including initially the priest who
afterward wrote her book; but the latter returned to her side once
he had read the life of Mary of Oignes, also addicted to tears.[33]
Others, and the inimical friar, are more hostile, and friends suggest
she get out of town. At this juncture her cries are taken from her
by divine wish, so that she looks like a hypocrite; but our Lord
promises that she shall be vindicated and her friar-enemy thrown

down. She must, however, eat meat again, and cease fasting once a week.

Margery's obedience results in another local miracle: her prayers bring snow to save from destruction by fire her parish church, St. Margaret's.[34] A Doctor of Divinity wishes he might have her sorrow, a parson calls her crying (before she loses it) a gift, a famous Dominican approves of her soon after and persuades a friend to do likewise; an Austin friar warns the people to let her be, the Prior of St. Margaret's suffers her grief, and even the Bishop of Norwich is meek and patient toward her. But his provincial forbids her good friend Master Aleyn, the White Friar, to speak to her. At her prayer God not only sends her another confessor but, after the Friar's illness, provides that she has leave to speak to him again. By revelation she also knows the transfers and fate of two priors of Lynn.

Now begins a series of works of mercy. Many people desire her presence at their dying, to pray for them, "for, though they loved not her weeping nor her crying in their lifetime, they desired that she should both weep and cry when they should die."[35] For God's love, her confessor allows her to kiss (female) lepers whom she had formerly dreaded; she also leads one away from tempting thoughts. This experience echoes her own previous torment of the male "members"; so does her aid to a man, whose newly-delivered wife is out of her mind, echo Margery's earliest spiritual crisis, although Margery does not make either connection herself.[36] Climaxing these corporal and spiritual mercies is her care of her aged husband who, in his separate dwelling, had fallen barefoot down his stairs and suffered a grievous head wound. Margery is blamed, and found worthy to be hanged for not keeping her husband with her. At God's command, she takes him to her house and keeps him as long as he lives ("years after"), even though "in his last days he turned childish again and lacked reason that he could not . . . go to a privy . . . but as a childe voydyd his natural digestyon," which Margery of course had to clean up.[37] A punishment, she thought, for her young lust.

Her "wonderful cries" acquired in Jerusalem trouble her, and she begs the Lord to remove them; but he says she must keep them for the edification of others. Additionally, she suffers the Passion repeatedly, from Palm Sunday through Holy Week.[38] Tears evoked thus also appear on Candlemas (Purification) Day and at weddings even though she is glad. Her tears withdrawn by God, she feels barren. Testing her, two priests took her to a church in the fields, where she cried with no one around; and there were nuns who desired to witness her. Except when she denied his revelations God was always with her, and her name (as she saw) was written in the Book of Life just after the Trinity. Margery ends her first book with

a long vision/colloquy with Christ, promises of reward for her
confessors, and the statement that she had been having visitations
and contemplations twenty-five years when it was written.

The second book, very short and written by the same priest who
copied the first book, begins on the Feast of St. Vitalis, 1438. As
with the first, a conversion is the initial impetus, but in this case
not Margery's but her son's. Although she tried to save him from
worldliness, he went overseas, fell into lechery, and became physically
like a leper. He rebuked his mother, but she prayed for him: he
repented; was healed; lived and married and had a child in Prussia.
Coming home, he and his wife visited holy places, and also his
mother. But he fell sick the day after his arrival, and died a month
later, as did his father soon after. His widow, after eighteen months
with Margery, desired to return to Germany. Intending to accompany
her only to the sea, and escorted by a young hermit, Margery found
herself commanded to accompany her daughter-in-law. The ship
sailed on the Thursday of Passion Week and, encountering strong
winds and driven onto the Norwegian Coast, was delayed from Good
Friday until Easter Monday. A fair wind took it to Danzig, where
Margery stayed five or six weeks—until our Lord told her to depart.
On pilgrimage to Wilsnak with a man, by ship and on foot, she was
almost forsaken because he tired of her cries and tears; finally she
had to be carried to the shrine, only to be forsaken anyway as they
went toward Aachen, left alone at night because of her persistent
tears, and insulted and made lewd fun of by some priests. After a
"good wife's" pity gave her shelter, she joined a company of the
verminous poor, and in ten or more days at Aachen saw our Lady's
smock and other treasures. Rebuffed twice by a widow of London
with whom she wished to travel, she paid a proor friar's way to
accompany her to Calais; scorned by the same widow and others,
she switched ships and the scorners followed; preserved from sea-
sickness, she had the satisfaction of seeing her shipmates, "especially
the woman of London," seized by that infirmity.[38]

The instant they land those shipmates forsake her, and only through
the grace of a good poor man is she led to Canterbury. Going to
London poorly clad, she tries to hide her face with a kerchief; but
the Londoners recognize and reprove her with an old story she
denies.[39] When she spoke against these sinners, and then came to
church, she wept boisterously to the slander of all "especially the
curates and priests."[40] The tears continued at Shene (Syon Abbey),
where a young man wanted to know why she mourned; she explained
her unworthiness before the Redeemer, his charity, his revelations
to her. On Lammas Day, meeting the young hermit who had accompanied her to the sea, she greeted him, but he answered her

bitterly: " 'I was blamed for your default when I led you last; I will no more.' " [41] But he nevertheless brought her to London and then home to Lynn, where she managed to reconcile her confessor and others. Margery's second book concludes with a description of her prayers.

Margery's press has been almost as bad in the twentieth century as in her own. Many have detracted her as not a "true" mystic, and even to the few of her critics who found worth in her she is but a "minor" one. [42] Her reputation as a pious "anchoress" in the early fragments of de Worde and Pepwell vanished in the reaction to her entire work; David Knowles sums up the critical reaction well as positing both "a godsend and . . . a disillusionment": she is "not the equal of earlier English mystics," in spite of her "basic sincerity," and her revelations are "due to her subconscious imagination" with "nothing of the true mystical experience." [43] T.W. Coleman agrees that her "heavenly communications" have no "great illuminative value" like Julian's. [44] R.W. Chambers employs the most insulting metaphor: "poor Margery is to be classed with those hotels which Baedeker describes as 'variously judged' ": she is a "difficult and morbid religious enthusiast," whose *Book* takes its value chiefly from its worth as social history. [45] Even Louise Collis, in her fascinating adaptation of Margery's book with added background detail about her times and particularly her pilgrimages, makes constant snide remarks about her subject. [46]

This minimization of Margery's mysticism appears even in the arrangement of the Butler-Bowdon modernized edition, where the "mystical matters" are in small type, the rest in regular; in the English printing, they are even relegated to an appendix. Such distortion of her *Book* turns her into a mere memoirist of the fifteenth century rather than a religious aspirant in touch with God, as her text portrays her. Instead of being considered in conjunction with her revelations, her prose then becomes important for itself alone. Thus, R. K. Stone's *Middle English Prose Style*, while concluding that she is like Julian of Norwich in more ways than previously perceived, cites as her particular distinction her "direct view of the life of the times . . . rarely found in devotional literature," but ultimately deplores her style as possessing "a lively monotony, like that of the gossip." [47] R. M. Wilson also finds her style inferior, particularly her lack of construction, her digression, her tautology, although he praises her verve as a storyteller. [48] But John C. Hirsh has recently suggested that Margery does not even deserve the few accolades her prose has received; her book, he asserts, is effective only because of the influence of the second scribe, whom he regards as co-author of it. [49] Part of the prejudice against Margery has arisen because she is usually compared, both in mystical experience and in prose style, with Julian of Norwich, a far different person and writer, with whom she has in common little other than their being women and knowing each other for a few days. In a recent book, Wolfgang Riehle, making a comparative and stylistic analysis of the metaphorical aspect of mystical language, indicates that "Margery Kempe, inspired by Julian as her model, tried to adopt her language without, however, being able to attain to Julian's high stylistic level and spirituality." [50] That is, at this point, impossible to prove, and unlikely.

But a few critics have recognized Margery's virtues, though without any full agreement as to what they are. The most enthusiastic claim for her talent and sanctity is Katherine Cholmeley's; her book's title, *Margery Kempe: Genius and Mystic*, tells its story. [51] Eric Colledge, while noting that many will question the sincerity and genuine mysticism of the *Book*, and devoting less space to Margery than to the other medieval English mystics (a common practice of her critics) in his anthology, nevertheless credits her as providing "incomparable evidence of the literary and devotional sources of mysticism, of the exercises and preoccupations of those affected." [52] For an anonymous Benedictine of Stanbrook, she is important as showing the centrality of eucharistic devotion for herself and the fifteenth century. [53] In his small book on Margery, Martin Thornton—asserting that there has been too much emphasis on mystical and too little upon ascetic and pastoral tradition—stresses her value for the latter. [54]

The assessments of Thornton, the Stanbrook Benedictine and Colledge, while characteristic of friendly criticism of Margery, move the reader away from her mysticism and into peripheral areas of judgment. Like favorable judgments on her prose—for instance, that of one of the first reviewers of her work, John R. O'Connell, that the worth of her book lies in its being the first conscious autobiography in English and not in its mysticism [55]—they beg the question. In the few students of mysticism who have had a kind word for what Margery, at least, and (most of) her confessors and those she helped through prayer thought was her direct relationship with God, caution is the presiding tone. E. I. Watkin's spirited defense of Margery, after affirming her sincerity, spirituality, and strong personal qualities, faults her for lack of the intellectual and spiritual depths of greater mystics such as (inevitably) Julian. [56] From the scholar who knew the most about Margery's book, Hope Emily Allen, we have similar hesitation: the work is not "as I first thought . . . merely the naive outburst of an illiterate woman"; but "many factors forbid her idea of herself as a great mystic. . . . I would call her a minor mystic." [57] Even a recent, very sympathetic article by Roberta Bux Bosse, ending with a long overdue plea for charity ("She trusts too much in our faith in God and in the sincerity of our fellow *creatures*. For this we snigger at her"), Margery is seen as flawed.[58]

Such "flawing" in Margery results from the concatenation of a number of circumstances, mostly circumstances of her "being" rather than of her "mysticism" *per se*—or, if of her mysticism, of its "how" rather than of its "what." Her femaleness was a crucial circumstance. Women in the Middle Ages had almost overwhelmingly to conform to what Carolly Erickson has called the "enduring [patristic] formula: they loved virgins but hated women," [59] that is, initiated women, whose tarnished virtue (whether they had willed their deflowering or not) could only be redeemed by martyrdom. Margery was a married woman when her mystic experience began, and this state of life was not only inferior to virginity but also to widowhood (no wonder she had so much trouble with widows); her state of life precluded the claims she made to direct revelation from God. A further deterrent was the beginning of her holy revelations in the midst of a full-fledged postpartum depression, for its "hysteria" was an ancient reminder (for men perhaps more than women) of its origin as God's curse upon Eve, who had of course by this time become almost the sole actor in the drama of the loss of Paradise. The very number of her children, fourteen, might have reminded her more learned hearers of St. Paul's injunction against fertility as a necessary preparation for the *parousia*. And this especially in England, where mystics were by tradition enclaustrated as well as celibate, as opposed to the continental tradition of female mystics.

That tradition of enclosure, a very old one in Christianity indeed, was followed by Margery's predecessors and contemporaries who desired holy lives and transcended sex boundaries. Hilton and Rolle as well as the recluses for whom they largely wrote lived isolated if not completely cut-off lives. But, like the enjoining of virginity, the idea that communion with God was only fully possible in retreat from the world applied especially to women. The openness of the early Church toward females with religious impulses had given way to the dictum that, to be holy, women must be shut up away from temptation; the fate of the double monasteries is a paradigm of this attitude, and the doomed movement of Beguines a manifestation of its ubiquity.[60] The late medieval English ideal seems to have been epitomized in Julian of Norwich, who as an anchoress (albeit with her maid as companion) embodied the prime condition for female sanctity. Margery's acquaintance is her opposite in style of living; the two resemble constant motion opposed to complete stasis. It is further probably no accident that the former adherent, who asks Margery what she has done with her supposed bastard born during her pilgrimage to Jerusalem and Rome, is a (male) anchorite.

Margery's constant journeying, whether on pilgrimage or more
minor errand, must have struck him and many others as incompatible
with her claims to sanctity. Christ's injunction that Mary had the
better part over Martha had long ago sealed the superiority of the
contemplative over the active life. Yet for Margery the active is an
imperative; there is no hint in her book that she ever considered
becoming a contemplative, and one cannot imagine her contained
by a community—much less a cell. The pattern of her quest as I
have shown it structured in her life (significantly, the quest is originally a secular form and only late adapted to hagiography) shows
indeed an ever wider scope of ambitious journeying: from Norwich
as goal, to York and Canterbury, to Jerusalem, Rome and Compostella.
And always accompanied (except apparently on the trip to Compostella) by that boisterous weeping, those cries and sobs, which
ceased not even in her age, on the voyage to Dutchland.

A great advantage of structured religious life, whether communal
or cellular, is its containment of the more private and showy manifestations of divine communion. In Margery's case, besides the
intermittent distress, the ten years of loud crying (especially on Good
Friday) which succeed the active midlife series of journeys, bring
slander and expulsion from her favorite chapel and persecution. The
ecstatic religious exposed to the world has no protection from its
judgments, and this principle holds especially for the female ecstatic.
Echoing the contemporary voice, R. W. Chambers says: "Things
might have been better for Margery if she had been a recluse. . . .
But that she should wander about, rehearsing tales of scripture, was
felt to be irregular." [61] This behavior also explains the accusations
of Lollardry.

The Lollard feminism of Margery's day, approving even of female
priests (at least in theory), was eminently suited to Margery's own
idea of her vocation. Its teachings of personal faith and divine election
accorded with the tenor of Margery's visions, in which she was
singled out above all other humans, to be saved at once when she
dies without pains of Purgatory, to have her name written first after
the Trinity in God's book, even (it seems) to have her virginity
restored. Like the Lollards, she (implicitly) rejected what they (explicitly) denied, for instance, distinctive Church doctrines (in her case,
the way station of Purgatory for sinners) and the established hierarchy
(for her, disobedience of priestly and even episcopal authority, as in
her wearing of white clothes). Since she lived in an age when
Lollardry had moved from its academic origins to popularity among
the poor and lower middle classes, its teachings and especially its
championship of female ministry were available to her as justification
for her own unorthodox behavior. That she consistently denied and

does not record any connection with the Lollard movement may mean that she did not wish to be branded a heretic (an obvious conclusion from her compulsive search for clerical approval whether or not she gets it) or that she really did not have any conscious desire to be united with the followers of Wyclif. But her emotional and deviant behavior from the very first must have reminded her religious critics of others like her who, within not so many miles of Bishop's Lynn, ended at the stake.

Margery's behavior violated not only religious standards, but also social ones. Margery's having chosen marriage, borne fourteen children, and then rejected its obligations must have profoundly shocked her contemporaries. Her wish to separate from her husband in order to live chaste, her actual physical absence from him until his illness called her back to her vows, her very frequent absences from home once the children (apparently) were grown, all betokened as much of a revolt in the social sphere as her mystical mode did in the religious. The marital separation(s) especially, designed to increase her sanctity, deprived her of the most important prop to her conventionality and even to her physical safety. Two critics at least, Coleman and Stone, have claimed that her distrust of men and her fear of rape are due to a "sex aberration" (Coleman's phrase) and others have implied it; it has taken a sane and perceptive, and also male, critic to suggest of such commentators that they "must have led a sheltered life" to think Margery's fears of rape, at age sixty, groundless.[62] Rape, as any number of fictions, nonfictions, and sociological studies have proven, is a crime of politics rather than lust, and Margery's unorthodoxy made her a prime candidate for attack.[63]

If her sex role was judged harshly when it became unorthodox, it was praised when she returned to "proper femaleness" as defined by men. Conforming to societal expectations in her taking in and caring for her ill husband—a function of ancient importance for men if we are to judge by Hesiod, who cites nursing by a wife in old age as one of the few reasons for marrying, she earns the praise of her contemporaries. Indeed Knowles, Stone, and Coleman see in her decision to "nurse and serve" her spouse "in his declining years a splendid act of self-sacrifice."[64] One wonders whether they would expect such an act from a male mystic who had similarly abandoned his spouse for God. It is perhaps no accident that some of Margery's most perceptive readers, such as Hope Emily Allen and Roberta Bux Bosse, are female rather than male.

What must have puzzled her contemporaries most, and obviously leaves her male (and some female) critics still puzzled, is the mixture in Margery of male- and female-linked sex characteristics. On the one hand are the feminine manifestations of copious tears, shrieks, and lamentations, which may be permissible in public for a woman (though not, of course, if they are as extravagant, frequent, and loud as Margery's) but are certainly not permissible for a man. On the other, is the male prerogative of dominance in the marriage. We see a number of such incidents in the *Book*, but it is the prolonged struggle to live chaste (significantly reaching its climax on a journey) which is only settled by Margery's using her own money to buy her way out. This tone of male dominance also appears frequently in her conversations with clergy and civic officials. From her initial postpartum "hysteria" (female) to her spirited persuasion of her amanuenses (male) she must have been enigmatic to those who knew her. Her "weak" womanly behavior confirmed the ancient fears of men about the feminine, and her overstrong "masculine" actions increased them. As Phyllis Chesler has pointed out, society punishes both kinds of behavior in women—the overfeminine and the masculine—as extremes which move the female away from the desirable limited resourcefulness (male) and controlled weakness (female) which are the ideals of a male-dominated society.[65]

But not only Margery's personal life reflects the societally-imposed inadequacy and dichotomy she feels: her mysticism, as she records it, bears witness to the interpenetration of her psyche by these imposed conditions as well. God must reassure her both as to the necessity that she bear children and, later, as to her equality, in his Love, with any virgin. Only through celibacy, of which she is finally able to assume a somewhat tarnished simulacrum, can she at least partially overcome the stigma of being a married female—and a disobedient one at that. Margery's failure to fit into her society made her hungry, and she turned for nurture to God, and especially to Christ, for she found it nowhere else. One may trace the "busyness" of Margery's husband and father in the records of Lynn; of her mother we know, and she says, nothing. That her husband gave her what he could she records, but it could not have been enough. Significantly, the years which go unrecorded in the *Book*, the years of religious quiescence, were precisely those in which she raised and/or lost her children, with how little help we can only guess. As Sheila Delaney has suggested, Christ was the only "authority figure" not too "busy [or] ambitious . . . to love," and able to be father and husband both (and, significantly, mother as well).[66] In the Middle Ages as now, unless one had unlimited help like the rich and well-born St. Bridget, motherhood was undoubtedly a burden to mystic creativity, as it is to all creativity save its own.

There was no place, no acceptance, in English medieval mysticism for a woman like Margery. Although she knew some of them by name, Margery was removed in space and influence from the only

European sisterhood in which she might have found community, if only in the knowledge that they existed. The copiously-shed tears, which she considered a divine gift even as she found them distressing, she shared with the continental women mystics, not with the Julian to whom she is constantly compared. Her peers are Dorothea of Prussia and St. Bridget of Sweden and other *Frauenmystik*, as Hope Emily Allen long ago and Wolfgang Riehle only recently have suggested.[67] Like a sizable number of these and other holy women, Margery was married; she had children, and indeed her total of fourteen may be a record. Like them, she begged for and eventually received from her husband (with however limited clerical approval) permission to live chaste. Like them, she went on pilgrimage rather than staying home shut up in a cell or a community; like them, she expected sainthood. Seen against the background of this tradition, Margery's vanished virginity, her children, her travels, her separation from her husband, all seem more acceptable than they do against the background of the usual English mystical example.

There is more: one can find in the mystical experiences and lifestyles of these and other, earlier females from the twelfth to the fourteenth centuries, profound sex differences from their male counterparts. E. Ann Matter has demonstrated the differences, which parallel Margery's and allow the discovery of a tradition or style of medieval women's mysticism.[68] Among the characteristics of these female visions are a focus upon the Passion of Christ (with concomitantly little interest in the Virgin Mary), the exchange of hearts with the Savior, visions of him as a beautiful young man, the androgyneity of Jesus (Jesus as Mother)—in short a feminized version of God, whose tradition stretches from Anselm of Canterbury through Bernard of Clairvaux, and is therefore not peculiar to women's tradition. Matter suggests that what is different is that "the point of spiritual attention" is focused not beyond "the exemplum of suffering [in Christ] to find a mystical unity" as it is for male mystics but upon "the *object* of the Passion of Christ," so that "the ubiquitous vision of the crucified Jesus" creates a female tradition of "masochistic . . . experiences." Men were free to cultivate the Virgin as bride and spouse: "The women instead rallied around an all-purpose figure of Jesus: the lover, the spouse, the teacher, the mother, but especially the sufferer." Margery's sufferings in her life as in her vision, then, were merely an extreme form of a sex-linked and "self-fulfilling prophecy about the role of women" in the Christian tradition. As the more perceptive of them must always have known, women mystics were second-rate in religious experience as in everything else. The more conformist (i.e. to the required states of virginity and quiescence, since the mystic in Catholicism is always to some extent a nonconformist), however, often drew praise in their lifetimes, and have since, as newly-discovered "teachers" for our times which require "feminine models," even, very belatedly, earned the title of Doctor of the Church.[69]

Not for Margery this grudging recognition, this role modelhood. Although her *Book* records her treading of the threefold mystic way, her path was always too public, her voice too strident, her tears too copious for imitation. A Catherine of Siena or a Joan of Arc could become a virago because she remained virgin; her sacrifice of sexuality freed her from the constraints of "feminine" behavior, if not completely from male criticism. But Margery's marriage and many children were witness to a concupiscence demonstrated in her early lust at evensong as much as in her later visions of male "members"; unlike the temptations of St. Anthony and other celibates, these could be adduced, from her life, as wish-fulfillments. Neither in her own time nor in ours has Margery found appreciation of her mystical struggle, sincere as it was—who would go through all that unless it was inevitable?—and witnessed as genuine by the less biased of the clerics she met, some important churchmen. The fitting of her *Book* into a Procrustean bed has confused and negated the values she represents. Let us instead be grateful to her for a different view of feminine spirituality in the Middle Ages, for showing us an alternate if generally untaken route to God.

BIBLIOGRAPHICAL NOTES

The following bibliography, though not exhaustive, will introduce the reader to Margery:

Anon. "Margery Kempe and the Holy Eucharist." *Downside Review*, 56 (1938), 468–82.

Book of Margery Kempe, The. Ed. Sanford Brown Meech and Hope Emily Allen. EETS, OS 212 (London, 1940).

Book of Margery Kempe, The. Tr. W. Butler-Bowdon (New York, 1944).

Cholmeley, Katharine. *Margery Kempe: Genius and Mystic* (London, 1947).

Coleman, T. W. *English Mystics of the Fourteenth Century* (Westport, CT, 1938).

Colledge, Eric. "Margery Kempe." *Month*, 28 (1962), 16–29.

Collis, Louise. *Memoirs of a Medieval Woman: The Life and Times of Margery Kempe* (New York, 1964).

Delaney, Sheila. "Sexual Economics, Chaucer's Wife of Bath, and *The Book of Margery Kempe.*" *Minnesota Review*, N.S. 5 (1975), 104–15.

Hirsh, John C. "Author and Scribe in *The Book of Margery Kempe.*" *Medium Aevum*, 44 (1975), 145–50.

Knowles, David. *The English Mystical Tradition* (New York, 1961).

Medieval Mystics of England, The. Ed. Eric Colledge (New York, 1961).

O'Connell, John R. "Mistress Margery Kempe of Lynn." *Downside Review*, 55 (1937), 174–82.

Riehle, Wolfgang. *Studien zur englischen Mystik des Mittelalters unter besonderer Berücksichtigung ihrer Metaphorik* (Heidelberg, 1977). The new English version is *The Middle English Mystics*, tr. Bernard Stanring (London, Boston, and Henley, 1981).

Sawyer, Michael E., comp. *A Bibliographical Index of Five English Mystics* Bibliographia Tripotampolitana 10 (Pittsburgh, 1978).

Stone, Robert Karl. *Middle English Prose Style: Margery Kempe and Julian of Norwich* (The Hague, 1970).

Thornton, Martin. *Margery Kempe: An Example in the English Pastoral Tradition* (London, 1960).

Thurston, H., S. J. "Margery the Astonishing." *The Month*, 2 (1936), 446–56.

Watkin, E. I. "In Defence of Margery Kempe." *Downside Review*, 59 (1941), 243–63, rpt. *On Julian of Norwich and In Defence of Margery Kempe* (Exeter, 1979).

Wilson, R. M. "Three Middle English Mystics." *Essays and Studies*. n.s. 9 (1956), 85–112.

X
Meister Eckhart:
An Introduction

BERNARD McGINN

"This is Meister Eckhart from whom God hid nothing"—the title from one of the many sermons pseudonymously ascribed to Eckhart in the fourteenth century.[1] This title suggests some of the paradoxes involved in studying a thinker who has been judged one of the foremost mystics in the history of Christianity. The text purports to be by Meister Eckhart, but actually is not; the title ascribes to him knowledge of all divine mysteries, while the real Eckhart insisted on the absolute hiddenness of God; and while the sermon shows the continued reverence in which Eckhart's name was held, the very exaggeration of the title hints at knowledge that he ended his life under a cloud of suspicion and had been posthumously condemned by papal decree. Meister Eckhart's style is poetical and paradoxical; his thought deeply speculative and subtle. Like the works of many great mystics, his writings have a life of their own and can be read with some profit even by those who have no knowledge of the era in which he wrote and the issues with which he was concerned; but even moderate acquaintance with the life and times of an author brings a whole new dimension of insight into the meaning of his works. This is especially true in Eckhart's case. This essay is intended to serve as a general introduction to Eckhart's life and times and some major themes of his mysticism. It will conclude with a few remarks about his subsequent influence.

I. THE HISTORICAL CONTEXT

Eckhart's life (c. 1260-c. 1328) spans an age of transition from what has been called the High Middle Ages to the Late Middle Ages. Crude as such general periodizations always are, they hint at significant differences—economic, institutional, emotional, intellectual, and religious—between the world in which Eckhart was born and that in which he died. Though the fourteenth century was far from an age of unrelieved decline and loss of nerve, one cannot deny that this century witnessed severe and widespread crises, wrenching shifts in the political balance of power, and radical challenges to many traditional institutions and values. Meister Eckhart's thought has sometimes been seen if not as a cause, at least as an exemplification, of one element in these critical reactions. The mysticism he and some of his followers fostered has been interpreted as a threat to the medieval religious establishment. We shall evaluate this view later in this essay.

The Germany that Eckhart was born into and where he spent most of his life was politically fragmented, but in general economically flourishing, especially in the major cities like Cologne and Strassburg where he spent many years. France, where Eckhart lived for several periods at the University of Paris, was the wealthiest and most powerful state in Europe, not yet threatened by the debilitating series of struggles known as the Hundred Year's War. Eckhart's writings, however, show no interest in the politics of the day, and surprisingly little in directly social or economic concerns. He was far from being an advocate of social revolution. In one of his very few references to the social order, he supports the proper ordering of the soul's powers with an analogy from the established hierarchy of feudal society.[2] The Meister's teaching regarding inner transformation has no direct relation to one's social or economic status.

The intellectual, ecclesiastical, and religious context within which Eckhart lived is far more directly relevant to his thought than the contemporary political situation. Intellectually, Eckhart was a product of the medieval university system and the world of scholastic thought which reached an acme in the second half of the thirteenth century.[3] Much of his life, as student and then as teacher, was spent in the demanding regimen of the classroom with its lengthy lectures and public disputations. His surviving Latin works are fragments of an imposing plan as ambitious in scope as that of any of the other great medieval Masters of theology. Eckhart's Latin writings display their professional "scholastic" character on every page, and even his vernacular works presuppose the world of Scholasticism in countless ways. While it would be foolish to deny that Eckhart's preaching and writing in Middle High German constituted a new departure in the history of the communication of speculative theology, it is significant that it was one of the foremost professional scholastics of the day who achieved this breakthrough.

The university background of Meister Eckhart's thought is everywhere present; far less immediately evident, but absolutely essential for the understanding of the later reception of Eckhart's thought, is the role of the papacy. Meister Eckhart was neither indifferent nor hostile to the papacy. Everything in his life supports the sense of loyalty and obligation to the Holy See that he expressed when he told his Cologne inquisitors: "I am not held to respond to you or to anyone, except the pope and the University of Paris." [4] Eckhart's unswerving adherence to papal teaching authority was not shared by all his contemporaries, as the case of William of Ockham shows. The Meister's loyalty was put to a severe test at the end of his life during the year he spent at Avignon under investigation. The papal condemnation of propositions drawn from his works in the Bull "In agro dominico" of March 27, 1329 (the first condemnation of a Dominican for heresy) was a critical moment in the history of Christian mysticism and a perennial stumbling-block in the later reputation of the Meister. In order to understand the situation which made this condemnation possible, we must briefly note some important changes that the papacy was undergoing during Eckhart's lifetime.

In the 1260's Rome had recently emerged triumphant in her struggle against the Emperor Frederick II. By offering the throne of Sicily to Charles of Anjou, the King of France's brother, the papacy had begun an involvement with French interests that was to be crucial in her history for more than a century-and-a-half. Many of the popes of the later thirteenth century used all the spiritual authority of their office, including the invocation of crusade, in support of Angevin dynastic interests; others attempted to keep the French at arms' length. Involvement in narrow partisan politics brought the popes of the time under increased criticism,[5] especially when such involvement distracted them from pursuing the much-needed cause of Church reform. Despite the great efforts of Innocent III and the Fourth Lateran Council of 1215, the thirteenth-century Church continued to stand in need of reformation in head and members. The Second Council of Lyons (1274), which had promised much in the way of reform, achieved little, and the situation grew worse as the century neared its end.

The popes of this age, drawn from the ranks of the canon lawyers, diplomats and politicians, seemed less and less to be spiritual men; hopes were voiced for a coming holy pope who would set all things right with the Church. What Christendom got instead was Boniface VIII (1294–1303), an intransigent canon lawyer with a highly inflated view of papal power. Boniface challenged the powerful King Philip the Fair of France and was soundly defeated. In 1305 the deeply divided Cardinals elected the Archbishop of Bordeaux as Pope Clement V and the long sojourn of the papacy at Avignon soon began. Clement's successor, John XXII (1316–34), the archetypal Avignon pope, brought all his considerable talents and forceful personality to bear on three issues: a fruitless quarrel with the Emperor Lewis of Bavaria over papal claims in imperial elections; a policy of increased taxation of the Church designed to secure the financial independence of the papacy now cut off from its traditional revenues; and finally, a rigid insistence on uniformity in the life of the Church. Upon this basis, John moved rapidly and ruthlessly to restore canonical order wherever he saw something amiss. Where his predecessors had temporized, as in the case of the long dispute over poverty in the Franciscan order, John acted decisively without thought of consequences, crushing the Spiritual Franciscans first, and then deeply dividing the majority Conventual party by his condemnation of the traditional Franciscan doctrine of the absolute poverty of Christ and the apostles.[6] What all these trends point to is clear. By the end of the first quarter of the fourteenth century the papacy in the eyes of many had come to be seen as the opponent rather than the proponent of reform.

The papacy, however, was only one part of the religious world of the late thirteenth and early fourteenth centuries. Two other major components of this world exerted influence on Meister Eckhart's life and thought: the Mendicant movement and the lay piety centered on the Beguines and Beghards.

Meister Eckhart was a Dominican, a member of one of the two great Mendicant orders whose rapid spread was one of the most astonishing events of the thirteenth century. Like almost all the new religious movements of the High and Late Middle Ages, the Mendicants expressed the search for the *vita apostolica*, the perfect form of imitating the life of the apostles, the closest followers of Jesus.[7] Debates about the true meaning of the apostolic life and its relation to action and contemplation were many. In distinction from monastic understandings, the Mendicant interpretation of the *vita apostolica* centered on poverty and preaching in an urban setting. Their poverty was corporate as well as individual, their mode of life itinerant rather than monastically stable, their organization constitutionally flexible and international in scope. But it was their preaching and administration of the sacrament of penance which gave them such an immense influence on the urban faithful. In an era when the ordinary secular clergy were frequently ignorant and ill-prepared for their task, and when the established religious, such as the monks and canons, tended to be conservative toward new ideas and religious practices, the Mendicants opened their arms to both. From the outset of his reform, St. Dominic (1170–1221) stressed the need for the best theological education for his wandering poor preachers; for St. Francis (1182–1226) the preaching of the central message of poverty was more by way of example than by learned argument, but during his own lifetime his followers had already begun to move into the world of the universities and has begun relaxations of the strict rule of poverty in part necessitated by this shift. Within two decades of the deaths of the founders, the new Mendicant orders had come to dominate the intellectual life of Europe. The theological squabbling between Franciscans and Dominicans—a clear case of sibling rivalry in which Eckhart played his part—should not blind us to the fundamental similarity with which each group met the challenge of the new intellectual world of the thirteenth century.

The same picture obtains when we glance at the Mendicant attitude toward new forms of piety. Always allowing for the significant differences between the two orders, both the Franciscans and the Dominicans did much to encourage new religious devotions. Among these were devotions to the Passion of Christ, the stress on the Real Presence in the Eucharist with its host of attendant practices, the concern for working out a practical theology of private property and the just price, and the fostering of lay confraternities and third orders.[8] Finally, we must note something that set both the major Mendicant orders off from many contemporary attempts to pursue the *vita apostolica*—the intense loyalty of both founders to the Holy See. This loyalty did not go unrewarded. From the very beginning, the papacy encouraged the new orders, frequently supporting them against attacks made by the secular clergy. The alliance between the papacy and the Mendicants was crucial to the religious history of the thirteenth century.

Papal encouragement of reform in the case of the Mendicant orders also extended to the Beguine movement, at least in its earlier phases.[9] From the latter part of the twelfth century, women began to take a new interest in the religious life. Women's houses soon became part of the established reform orders of the Premonstratensians and Cistercians. In the thirteenth century, with Rome's support, houses of devout women also came to play a large part in the Mendicant orders, despite considerable male opposition for a half-century.[10] Women's houses were especially prevalent among the German Dominicans—we know of seventy-four by the year 1300.[11] The most remarkable chapter of the "women's movement" *(Frauenbewegung),*

however, was the spread of the Beguines, women who elected to
live a common life of poverty, chastity and devotion without taking
vows or following an established rule. Their witness to the most
popular religious ideal of the day, that of poverty, was well brought
out by an early supporter, James of Vitry (d. 1254):

> You have seen (and you have rejoiced) in the gardens of the
> Lord great crowds of holy women in diverse places who,
> despising fleshy charms for Christ and likewise scorning the
> riches of this world for the love of the heavenly kingdom,
> cleaving in poverty and humility to their divine husband, are
> seeking by the labor of their hands their meager nourishment
> although their relatives abound in great wealth.[12]

Like the Mendicants, the Beguines preferred an urban environment.
They frequently lived on alms (also like the Mendicants), or else
worked for their own support. The Beguines originated in the Low-
lands, and spread rapidly down the Rhine valley and into a number
of other parts of Europe. The causes for their rapid growth as well
as the social status of their members have both been the subject of
much discussion, mostly inconclusive due to the nature of our sources.

The problem of the ecclesiastical status of the Beguines and the
closely allied, though less numerous, groups of men known as Beghards became increasingly troublesome during the thirteenth century.
Herbert Grundmann has stressed the fundamental dialectic underlying
the history of all religious movements in the Middle Ages—groups
either gained approbation by incorporation into the Church's institutional structure as religious orders, or, failing such approval, they
were pushed to the periphery and came to be rejected as dangerous
and heretical.[13] The Beguines received considerable encouragement
from local ecclesiastics and from several popes in the first half of
the thirteenth century; but the suspicions that had been voiced from
the beginning grew markedly in the second half of the century, a
change due as much to the increasing rigidity of the ecclesiastical
establishment as to the difficulties of institutionalizing the amorphous
Beguines and Beghards. These troubles culminated in the condemnations of the Beguines and Beghards as proponents of the heresy
of the "Free Spirit" at the Council of Vienne (1311–12) by John
XXII's predecessor, Clement V.[14] It was Pope John who actually
promulgated the decree, and he was only too happy to do everything
to enforce it.

The *Frauenbewegung* of the thirteenth-century Germany developed
a form of piety, evident most prominently in the Beguines but also
found in the houses of the established orders. The spiritual interests
of the pious women of the era are closely allied to those we have

already seen in the Mendicants; hence it is not surprising how hard women fought to be incorporated into these orders or how zealously they sought out Mendicant confessors. Allowing for individual differences, we can describe this piety as centered on devotion to the Eucharist, the practice of poverty and ecstatic mysticism. Mary of Oignies early in the century fostered new forms of Eucharistic piety, and this was typical of many Beguines. On the second point, Grundmann has argued that Beguine poverty was the historical foundation for the development of the distinctive "German Mysticism" of which Eckhart was the most famous proponent.[15] As he put it: "Only in the movement of female piety in Germany did the idea of poverty expand in the direction of its original religious meaning, not into the organizational or the dogmatic and not into the polemical, but rather into the mystical—the striving after inward, spiritual poverty." [16] For him external poverty as a part of a life of mystical prayer was dialectically lifted up or synthesized *(aufgehoben)* into a higher state of interior stripping of the spirit, and this was the historical source for Eckhart's distinctive teaching regarding detachment *(abegescheidenheit)* as the way to God.[17]

The ecstatic mysticism cultivated by the Beguines is evident in all their literature. Many Beguines experienced visions, or were rapt out of their senses; others received the stigmata; still others practiced the *iubilus*, a form of charismatic prayer.[18] As suspicions against the Beguines mounted, doubts about the orthodoxy of their beliefs concerning mystical union with God became more prevalent. Two traditional accusations levelled at mystics in many cultures and times, those of pantheism (total identification with God) and antinomianism (feeling free of the moral law because of one's divine status), were soon directed at them. In 1310 such accusations resulted in the death by fire of Marguerite Porete, a well-known French Beguine,[19] and they also appear in condemnatory Bull "Ad nostrum" of the Council of Vienne referred to above.[20]

We must also note the role of the Beguines in the use of the vernacular for preaching and theological writing.[21] A number of earlier Beguines, such as Beatrice of Nazareth (later a Cistercian) and Hadewijch were noted vernacular authors; later in the century we have Mechthilde of Magdeburg (d. 1280) and her famous work *The Flowing Light of Godhead.* But the Beguines, Beghards, nuns, as well as the pious laity (many accounts tend to forget them) constituted both a new source of literary production, and a new kind of audience as well. Beguine circles and subsequently Dominican nunneries appear to have been the earliest centers of the writing down of devout letters, poems, treatises, and sermons in the vernacular. Initially, much of this material was in the form of translations from the Latin,

but even prior to Eckhart we have examples of sermons taken down
from the preached vernacular—the beginnings of German as a theological language. The last years of Eckhart's life were intensely
occupied with vernacular preaching to audiences among whom religious women, both Beguines and nuns, played a large part. The
characteristic themes and modes of expression of these sermons can
hardly have been unaffected by this setting.

II. ECKHART'S LIFE

Eckhart was born at Hochheim in Thuringia about 1260. As a
young man he entered the Dominican order at nearby Erfurt and
was then sent to Paris, where he appears to have studied in the
Arts faculty about 1277, that is, following hard upon the second
Paris period of Thomas Aquinas (1268–72) whom Eckhart, as a good
Dominican, took as his model and theological guide. If Eckhart did
not know Aquinas personally, there seems to be reason to believe
that he studied with Thomas' teacher, Albert the Great (c. 1200–1280),
probably at the Dominican house of theology (studium generale) in
Cologne where the great scholastic spent his last years. Albert's many
interests included a concern for the classics of Neoplatonism, such
as the Pseudo-Dionysius on whom he had written commentaries.
Acquaintance with at least some Neoplatonic texts was widespread
among the scholastics, but Eckhart's mixing of Neoplatonism and a
profound knowledge of Aristotle appears to be in part due to the
heritage that Albert had bequeathed to the Rhineland Dominicans.[23]
A crucial element in this particular revival of Neoplatonism was the
influence of Proclus, known both through the Book of Causes, an
Arabic reworking of the Elements of Theology translated into Latin in
the twelfth century, and through new translations from the Greek
made by the Dominican scholar William of Moerbeke.

Eckhart returned to Paris in 1293–94 to lecture on the Sentences
of Peter Lombard, a standard practice in academic advancement
toward the position of Master of Sacred Theology.[24] From 1294 to
about 1300 he was prior of the Dominican house at Erfurt and vicar
of Thuringia. Here he appears to have composed his first surviving
vernacular work, the Counsels on Discernment, a book of advice to
his Dominican charges.[25] Eckhart was back in Paris 1302–03, teaching
now as a full Master in one of the two Dominican chairs, and
engaging in public disputation with the Franciscan Master, Gonsalvo
of Spain.[26] In late 1303 he was named provincial of the newly-
created north German province of Saxony, an office he held down
to 1311, when he was again sent to Paris. Both positions indicate
the high favor he was held in by the order both as a scholar and

an administrator. It was probably during this period as provincial that Eckhart wrote the most famous of his vernacular treatises, the *Book "Benedictus"* in two parts.[27] The first section, the *Book of Divine Consolation*, is a speculative summary of his thought that he sent to Queen Agnes of Hungary to provide her solace in a time of personal crisis. It is accompanied by a long vernacular sermon, *On the Nobleman*, on the theme of the return of the just soul to God. The mature style and content of Eckhart's other surviving vernacular treatise, *On Detachment*, suggest that it comes from late in his career.[28]

It was probably during his second magisterial period in Paris (1311–13) that Eckhart conceived the plan for his theological masterpiece, the *Opus tripartitum*, or *Three-Part Work*. The few remaining sections show the originality and genius of the Meister. The first part, or *Work of Propositions*, was designed to lay out the systematic bases of his thought through the analysis of key axioms or propositions, a method based on Proclus. Only the general prologue and the prologue to the first proposition "Existence is God" remains.[29] *The Work of Questions* forming the second part does not survive. It was to be a series of disputed questions, roughly following the order of Thomas' *Summa theologiae*. The bulk of Meister Eckhart's surviving Latin writings comes from the third part, the *Work of Commentaries*, and consists of six interpretations of scripture (two on Genesis, one each on Exodus, Wisdom, Sirach, and a lengthy *Commentary on John*), as well as fifty-six Latin sermons illustrating ways of preaching on select biblical texts.[30] These remains of the Latin writings, while stylistically less striking than the vernacular works, are of equal importance for understanding Eckhart's thought.

The final years of Eckhart's life were devoted primarily to vernacular preaching. Ironically, the immense popularity of this preaching was to bring him under suspicion. For about nine years, from 1314 to 1323, Eckhart lived at Strassburg, then a center for Dominican nunneries and Beguine houses. He appears to have had some official function in relation to these houses, and a good number of the eighty-six vernacular sermons accepted as authentic by Josef Quint, the major editor of *Deutsche Werke*, were preached in such contexts.[31] About 1323 Eckhart was called back to Cologne to act as master of studies in the Dominican theologate. His popular vernacular preaching continued unabated, and within a few years this brought him to the attention of Henry of Virneburg, the aristocratic Archbishop of Cologne, a noted opponent of heresy and of the suspect Beguines.

The story of Eckhart's two trials and subsequent condemnation is complex; the evaluation of this tragic ending to his distinguished career is fraught with difficulties. This is not the forum to attempt more than a needed outline and a summary of an interpretation advanced in greater detail elsewhere.[32]

Early in 1326 the Archbishop instituted proceedings against Eckhart, setting up a commission under two inquisitors to peruse all his works and extract passages which seemed dangerous or unsound. The articles extracted were arranged into lists called "rolls" (rotuli), two of which survive, though originally there must have been four or five. On September 26, Eckhart responded in writing to a list of forty-nine articles drawn from a variety of his Latin and German works, and not long after he answered a list of fifty-nine excerpts from his vernacular sermons.[33] In early 1327 Eckhart and his superior, Nicholas of Strassburg, who had been cited for obstructing the process, denounced the investigation and appealed to the pope. Eckhart made a public profession of faith in the Dominican church on February 13, and sometime in the Spring set off for Avignon.[34] Pope John XXII set up a second commission composed of cardinals and theologians of the curia to study the rotuli sent from Cologne. This group reduced the mass of articles to a manageable set of twenty-eight, and then had Eckhart respond again, as an important surviving document shows.[35] Sometime early in 1328 the pope also submitted the articles to the famed inquisitor, now cardinal, James Fournier.

The aged Meister did not live to see the outcome. On April 30, 1328, Pope John wrote to Archbishop Henry that the investigation was proceeding despite Eckhart's death. Throughout the process, Eckhart had proclaimed his loyalty to the teaching of the Church and had denounced any proceedings against him as a heretic. "I am able to be in error, but I cannot be a heretic, for the first belongs to the intellect, the second to the will." [36] Eckhart did admit that some articles from the vernacular sermons were badly expressed, and even erronea vel falsa (never heretica). He was consistent in his willingness to retract or reject anything that had led anyone into error. The papal Bull of 1329 informs us that before he died Eckhart "revoked and deplored" the twenty-six articles he admitted preaching and teaching. This was not a change of heart or deathbed collapse, because, as Edmund Colledge has pointed out,[37] the Bull notes that the revocation was not of the articles as such, but only of the articles insofar as they might generate error or heresy in the minds of some hearers. Eckhart remained true to his principles to the end. He never ceased to maintain that everything he had said or written proceeded from a good intention, and, properly understood, was consonant with faith and morals, but because many of his teachings were rara . . . et subtilia,[38] they could be misunderstood by the ignorant or perverted by the envious.

Eckhart's line of defense did not avail. The Bull "In agro dominico" condemned the twenty-eight propositions singled out at Avignon, but in two groups, some as openly heretical (articles 1–15 and two appended articles which Eckhart did not admit were his own), and others as suspect of heresy but capable of a Catholic understanding (articles 16–26). The Bull was promulgated only in the Archdiocese of Cologne, but its repercussions were felt in the Dominican order and elsewhere.[39]

III. ECKHART'S MYSTICISM

Many descriptions of Eckhart's mysticism begin from or conclude with an attempt to fit him into some category or type of mysticism. Indeed, the creation of typologies of mysticism and laundry lists of their characteristics has been a widespread practice in modern studies.[40] This investigation will proceed according to different premises. Unfortunately, I do not have the space here to argue the validity of these premises, but it seems fair to the reader at least to state them.

I believe that at the present stage of the study of mysticism we should try to use the word in a qualified sense, that is, not to speak of "mysticism" as such, but of "Christian mysticism" or "Buddhist mysticism," or better yet, of varieties of Christian and Buddhist mysticism. The elusive search after a common core experience of all mysticism has thus not been convincing or even especially illuminating. Analyses designed to reveal such a core have rather tended to uncover the biases of the investigators.[41] The mystic as a human subject never perceives experience "raw," but always within a situation mediated by a host of personal, cultural, and religious elements. Whatever theological and/or philosophical arguments one might wish to make for the existence of a transcultural element in all mystical experiences, it is difficult to see how this can be recaptured from the culturally-mediated accounts of the mystics themselves.[42] This position complicates, but by no means renders impossible the comparative study of mysticism, nor does it prevent the pursuit of another important element in the investigation of mysticism, the testing of the value of mystical claims to knowledge. The assertion that some special form of knowledge is made available through mystical experience is in no way prejudiced by the admission of the mediated condition in which this knowledge is appropriated and expressed. In the account that follows, then, rather than trying to identify a type of mysticism into which Eckhart falls, I will isolate and present the essential themes of his message about the relation of God and man as a contribution to the study of the varieties of Christian mysticism.

Let us begin with the negative rather than the positive—some features that set Meister Eckhart off from other classic Christian mystics, especially in the Middle Ages. The Beguines and the nuns to whom Eckhart preached were frequently gifted with a wide range of special mystical experiences—visions, locutions, experiences of timelessness, rapture, or being taken out of the body, and union (sometimes marital) with God. The hallmark of their descriptions of these states is their "special" character—something out-of-the-ordinary is seen, heard or felt. Even the more sober representatives of Cuthbert Butler's "Western Mysticism," such as Augustine, Gregory, and Bernard, weave descriptions of special mystical experiences into their writings.[43] Eckhart does not deny that ecstasy or *raptus*, that is, literally "standing outside" common experience, exists, and that Paul, Augustine, and other privileged souls had tasted it, but he shows no real interest in rapture, let alone in the lower stages of unusual mystical experiences, such as visions.[44] Within the context of the intense preoccupation of the nuns and Beguines with these manifestations and with rapture, it is difficult not to think that if Eckhart was incorporating aspects of the new piety of the *Frauenbewegung*, such as the stress on interior poverty, into his thought, he was also criticizing others. For Meister Eckhart, it is a new awareness of the "depth dimension" of everyday human experience that is the important thing.[45]

A second major discrimination between Eckhart and many other Christian mystics concerns the role of the *imitatio Christi* and the sacraments as the sources by which Christ's life comes to us. For most of the great schools of Christian mysticism, the Cistercian as represented by Bernard, the Franciscan as found in Bonaventure, and later the Ignatian as re-expressed in our own day by Teilhard de Chardin, the *imitatio Christi*, founded upon, guided by, and lived through participation in the sacramental life of the Church, especially the Eucharist, is at the heart of the mystical ascent to God.[46] This is not the case with Meister Eckhart. We must, however, proceed with considerable caution at this point. Eckhart's attitude toward the sacraments and toward all external works of asceticism and piety is neither one of disdain nor of indifference—he would have been horrified at such a suggestion, and it is worthwhile to note that his opponents never accused him of anti-sacramentalism. The cosmic Christ plays a central role in the Meister's thought, as is especially evident in his commentary on the prologue of John's Gospel;[47] but there is not a large role for consideration of the historical Jesus and for the imitation of the mysteries of his life.[48] Similarly, some attention is given to the sacraments in the early *Counsels on Discernment*,[49] and there are a few sermons devoted to the Eucharist,[50] but these do not bulk large in the mass of Eckhart's mystical writings. What are we to make of this?

Some scholars have read this fact as the expression of a radical tendency present in mysticism as such, i.e., the creation, or at least the suggestion, of an alternate way to salvation that could easily come into conflict with established sacramental and institutional religion.[51] It is in this sense that Eckhart's thought has been viewed as one of the major critical elements of the fourteenth century. Such interpretations of the potential dangers of mysticism, of course, should not be extended to cover forms of mysticism that make a sacramental *imitatio Christi* crucial to the soul's progress. It is more difficult to determine whether or not they are a legitimate reading of the outcome, if not the original intent, of the thought of a mystic like Eckhart who gives relatively little attention to the ordinary channels of grace and who concentrates on the soul's direct interior contact with God. It is true that for Eckhart the internal attitude of the soul is so central that all external expressions begin to seem relatively indifferent and unimportant. This view led him to incautious statements on the efficacy of prayer and on the relation between intention and action, among other things. Such statements also encourage the anti-institutional reading of the possibilities of the Meister's thought. It would be as foolish to deny these possibilities as it would be to point out that he himself never drew them and at least in some sense guarded against them by other elements in his thought and life, especially by his unswerving loyalty to the teaching authority of the Church. The crucial judgment is how far an author can be held responsible for the development of implications of his or her thought which pervert the original intention of the whole. Radically anti-institutional and even pantheistic positions can be drawn from a selective reading of Eckhart, and the Meister's own followers were aware of this possibility, as Suso's condemnation of the "Nameless Wild One" who cited Eckhart in support of his pantheism shows.[52] We may well answer our question by asking whether Suso or his opponent was the more legitimate disciple of Meister Eckhart.

Eckhart sets forth the content of his preaching in several ways.[53] This is not the place to try to give even an introductory notice of the theological basis for his mystical message.[54] Rather, I intend to give a brief sketch of three broad themes that may serve as an entry into the reading of his works: the ground of union with God, the dynamics of the soul's reformation, and the mode of life that follows from union.

The theological anthropology at the basis of most of the major mystical theologies of the Patristic and Early Medieval periods centered on the notion of man as the *imago Dei*. According to the Genesis account, man, made in God's image and likeness, damaged this image and/or lost the accompanying likeness in the Fall. The purpose of Christ's coming and the Christian economy of sacramental grace is the restoration and perfection of man as image. Eckhart by no means breaks with this tradition—he not only makes considerable use of it in his Genesis commentaries,[55] but he has some profound considerations of the nature of man as *imago* and *similitudo* in his sermons.[56] Still, it must be admitted that the Meister understands this traditional teaching in an original and distinctive way best presented in his saying ". . . God's ground and the soul's ground are one ground." [57]

For Meister Eckhart the fundamental reality found in any particular existing thing is not its individual existence, its particularity as "this or that existence" *(esse hoc et hoc)*, but its existence "in the principle" *(in principio)*, the virtual reality it has in God, the universal formal cause of all things.[58] This is true of man in a deeper and more wonderful way, because man is an intellectual being who possesses *intelligere* and shares with God the dialectical relation between the ground and the manifestation or procession from the ground that is the theological foundation of Eckhart's mysticism. Just as in the one total divine reality there is both an unmanifested utterly undifferentiated ground or Godhead (" . . . the darkness or unknownness of the hidden Godhead") [59] and the three co-equal divine Persons, Father, Son, and Holy Spirit, identical with this ground, but "boiling" *(bullire)* from it by way of simple formal emanation,[60] so too in the soul there is the "ground," "spark," "little castle," or "uncreated light" that forms the deep source and reality behind the powers of understanding, memory, and will. On this deep level God and man are one, that is, "not-to-be-distinguished," [61] but we must remember that the full picture demands a recognition of the dialectical relation of this Absolute Unity *(unum*, or *esse indistinctum)* to the manifested levels where distinction is to be found. Globally viewed, Eckhart's thought always allows for an expression of identity-in-difference, however satisfactory we may judge his formulations. When challenged during his trial regarding the many ways in which he asserted the identity of God and man, the Meister had a consistent reply, viz., that he was always speaking of the pious person (or "noble man," or "just man") insofar as *(inquantum)* he was just, that is, that he was not speaking of the total concrete existential subject as identical with God in all respects.[62]

The dynamics of the soul's reformation, the way by which ". . . man shall be formed anew in the simple goodness that is God," [63] are designed to make the unity-identity of God's ground and the soul's ground both fully conscious and fully effective. This oneness of ground can never really be lost; otherwise man would cease to exist. But sin has caused us to loss sight of it and prevents us from living "out of the ground," that is, from expressing in our lives our true oneness with God. To bring us to this new awareness of the " . . . dearest freshness deep down things," as Gerard Manley Hopkins once put it, Eckhart counsels a fundamental way of life, that of absolute detachment *(abegescheidenheit)*, that is meant to result in two inter-related processes, the Birth of the Word or Son in the soul, and the "Breaking-Through" *(durchbrechen)* to the Hidden Godhead.

The short treatise *On Detachment* provides us with a summary of Eckhart's thought on this simple but subtle notion. The Meister defines it thus:

> . . . true detachment is nothing else than for the spirit to stand as immovable against whatever may chance to it of joy and sorrow, honor, shame and disgrace as a mountain of lead stands before a little breath of wind. This immovable detachment brings a man into the greatest equality with God, because God has it from his immovable detachment that he is God, and it is from his detachment that he has his purity and his simplicity and his unchangeability.[64]

True to the basic metaphysical principle that a receptive power cannot accept a form unless it is empty of other forms, the soul cannot receive God unless it becomes detached, that is, unless it has emptied itself of all created things. The detached soul is utterly poor and stripped, naked of all in its pursuit of the naked Godhead. It desires no reward, prays for no reward, but only for God himself. Further, the truly detached soul compels *(twinget)* God to come and fill it with himself.[65] Detachment becomes the transfigured summation of all the virtues. Eckhart praises it as superior to humility and charity, but subsequently asserts that perfect humility is a necessary component of perfect detachment. He also seems to identify the height of detachment with a form of pure disinterested love. We must leave aside until later the question as to whether or not Eckhart's notion of detachment is to be seen as encouraging withdrawal from and total indifference to the everyday world.

True detachment brings about two effects in the soul, two "processes" by which the soul comes to true unity-identity with God—the Birth of the Word and the "Breaking-Through" to the Godhead.

The Birth of the Word or Son in the soul is an ancient theme in Christian spirituality, as Hugo Rahner has shown.[66] As in so many other cases, however, Eckhart's appropriation of the tradition has a distinctive character. The Father does not give birth to the Son once and for all in some past time; but since he is totally independent of the temporal process, he must always be bearing the Son in the now of eternity. If God's ground and the soul's ground are one ground, then the eternal procession of the Son must be taking place in the depths of the soul; yet more, the soul as "principially" (in principio) identical with the divine ground must in a sense itself be the source of the three divine Persons. Hence we find such statements as " . . . he gives me birth, me, his Son and the same Son";[67] and " . . . he everlastingly bore me, his only-born Son, into the same image of his essential Fatherhood, that I may be Father and give birth to him of whom I am born."[68] Further, the soul not only shares in the inner processions of the Persons of the Trinity (bullitio), but also in the divine creation (ebullitio), and hence Eckhart also affirms " . . . in the same being of God where God is above being and distinction, there I myself was, there I willed myself and committed myself to create this man."[69] Daring and paradoxical statements, some of which were included in the Bull of condemnation.

Yet when challenged on them during his trials, Eckhart always made the same response. He pointed to the scriptural and traditional bases of his teaching and noted that in other texts he had stressed the needed distinctions between our adoptive sonship and the natural Sonship of Christ which is its source.[70] Some modern interpreters have seen Eckhart's teaching on the Birth of the Word as fundamentally in conformity with traditional Catholic theology of grace and of the Mystical Body of Christ.[71]

Eckhart's doctrine on the Birth of the Word in the soul and the consequences of this for our lives is found throughout his vernacular works and at times in the Latin writings too. Less frequent, but by no means less important, is a second way to understand the soul's return to where, in its deepest reality, it has always been (or better "is"), the "Breaking-Through" to the Godhead or simple ground. Sermon Forty-Eight says that the soul is not content with the Trinitarian Persons, or even with " . . . the simple divine essence in its repose, as it neither gives nor receives; but it wants to know the source of this essence, it wants to go into the simple ground, into the quiet desert, into which distinction never gazed, not the Father, nor the Son, nor the Holy Spirit."[72] This penetration into the divine ground appears to be the ultimate stage in the realization of man's unity-identity with God. As befits its highly apophatic character, Eckhart presents it most often by way of metaphors, such as those of the desert and of silence, and even of the bridal chamber.[73] It is the conscious appropriation of union without a medium, the unity-identity in which the soul wins its way back to its own true ground.

Given the importance of this stage, we may well ask what the relation between the Birth of the Word and the "Breaking-Through" to the ground is. In order to answer this question, we must turn to the final theme under which we are presenting Eckhart's mysticism— the manner of life that flows from his message.

Just as in God the divine ground is in a sense prior to, but dialectically the same as the Trinity of Persons, so too in the just or noble soul the "Breaking-Through" is more ultimate than the Birth of the Word in one way, but is completed by it in another. It is completed by it in the same way that in a famous sermon Eckhart says that the perfect soul must be not only a virgin, that is, stripped of all things in total detachment, but also a mother, one fruitful in all things, bringing forth works of love.[74] As John Caputo puts it: " . . . the birth of the Son *crowns* and *perfects* the unity with the Godhead as fruitfulness perfects virginity." [75]

The active fruitful character of this union with God is brought out in the remarkable way Eckhart transposes the traditional Mary-Martha theme. Rather than express a preference for Mary, the symbol of the contemplative life, over Martha, the active life, Eckhart says that as long as we are in this world we should strive to be like Martha, the soul who is inseparably joined with God but at the same time fully active in the world,[76] or, in the words of the earlier sermon, both virgin and mother. This we may say is Eckhart's own special contribution to the speculation on the *vita apostolica* which played such a large role in the religious debates of his era. Like many other great mystics of the medieval period,[77] Eckhart's thought is fundamentally opposed to any solipsistic view of contemplation that would remove the human person from the world of moral and social involvement.

What Eckhart does counsel throughout his writings is a new way of living in this world—a mode of totally spontaneous being and acting that he describes as "living without a why" *(sunder warumbe)*. God has no cause outside himself; he exists and acts solely from the effortless joy and spontaneity of his own being. The soul who has attained the consciousness of its inner identity with the divine ground demonstrates this awareness by also "living without a why." "He who lives in the goodness of his nature, lives in God's love; and love has no why." [78] Analyzing what it means to live without a why highlights some of the essential themes of Eckhart's mystical ethics.

First of all, the soul that lives without a why is able to find God in all things. Without denying the higher status of pious works, such as prayer and alms-giving, the Meister insists that " . . . it is not what we do which makes us holy, but we ought to make holy what we do." [79] The just soul lives its union with God as easily by the fireside or in the stable as it does in church or in private contemplation. In the second place, the soul that lives without a why is immune to the shocks and misfortunes which assail and trouble those who have not yet attained this state. The brunt of Eckhart's *Book of Divine Consolation* is an extended presentation of this message. Third, living without a why is the ground for Eckhart's insistence, already noted above, that the true "noble man" or "just man" must be, as St. Ignatius would later put it, *in contemplatione activus*, or "active in contemplation." For Meister Eckhart, the truly detached person who has learned to live out of the ground in joyful acceptance of all is paradoxically the most fruitfully active in loving all things with pure and indistinct *caritas*.

The final feature of living without a why returns us to what we may justly call the *leitmotif* of Eckhart's thought, its stress on interiority. For Meister Eckhart it is not so much what we do as the spirit in which we do it that is important, a position analogous to the lack of interest he always showed to special mystical experiences as compared with the new mode of awareness into the depth or "ground" dimension of all experience. In harmony with this tendency, Eckhart also taught that exterior acts add nothing to the goodness of interior acts, a teaching for which he was condemned at Avignon.[80] The Meister certainly believed that the interior and exterior act should be in harmony, but he insisted that God's command was always properly directed to the inner work alone. This emphasis must be counted among the more ambiguous elements in his teaching.

IV. ECKHART'S HERITAGE

Several detailed studies of Eckhart's reputation and influence exist,[81] but many chapters of the story still have not been fully investigated. It may be helpful to distinguish three broad periods in Eckhart's posthumous fame: the era down to the Reformation when his influence was broad and deep, though always controversial due to the papal condemnation; the period from the Reformation to the early nineteenth century when Eckhart's writings gradually fell from view and he became a legendary figure; and finally, the modern revival which has seen a continually growing interest in the great Dominican mystic.

The most striking evidence for the profound influence that Eckhart had upon the religious world of early fourteenth-century Germany is to be found not only in the large number of manuscripts (over 200) in which his vernacular works survive, but also in the proliferation of the Middle High German treatises and sermons pseudonymously ascribed to him.[82] Eckhart was the first great theological author in the German language, and he found an audience ready and waiting for him. Subsequent preachers both in Latin, like the Augustinian Jordan of Quedlinburg (died c. 1380), and in the vernacular, like the anonymous Dominican author of the *Paradisus anime intelligentis*, drew heavily on his work. Despite repeated papal condemnations and the sporadic attacks of inquisitors, the Beguines and Beghards remained a powerful force in the religious life of the times, and houses of women Cistercians and Dominicans were still centers of devotion and mystical contemplation. The pseudo-Eckhart literature appears to go beyond the Meister's own positions at times, as when in the famous treatise *Schwester Katrei* the Beguine declares, "Sir, rejoice with me, I have become God"; [83] but the surviving pseudonymous works do not give evidence for widespread pantheistic and antinomian tendencies among an underground movement of amoral "Free Spirit" mystics, as the fearful ecclesiastic authorities of the time, and, following them, many modern historians have believed.[84] Of course, it is possible to exaggerate in the opposite direction, too. Mysticism was a problem in the fourteenth century in a sense that it had not previously been in the Latin West. There were aspects of Eckhart's thought which, as we have seen, could be used to support indifference to the Church and its institutions, and the Meister's language regarding the soul's unity-identity with God is still a subject for debate.

Eckhart's two greatest disciples, both of whom appear to have known him in life, were aware of these difficulties. Both made conscious efforts to combat what they viewed as erroneous interpretations of his thought. Henry Suso (c. 1296–1366) and John Tauler (c. 1300–61) were major mystics in their own right. Though each made considerable use of Eckhart's thought, they did so for their own purposes and within the confines of their own systems. On many significant issues, among them the role of special mystical experiences, they differ significantly from their fellow Dominican. The third great Continental male mystic of the fourteenth century, the Dutch Jan van Ruysbroeck (1293–1381), seems to have included Eckhart's influence among the dangerous trends of his time.

In the fifteenth century Meister Eckhart's ambivalent reputation became an issue in the controversy between the Platonic scholar and mystic Nicholas of Cusa (1401–64) and Johannes Wenck. Cusa had been considerably influenced by Eckhart and gathered a notable collection of his Latin works.[85] His covert use of the Meister in *On Learned Ignorance* (1440) was one of the major handles used by Wenck, a Heidelberg theologian, in the attack he penned on Cusa, a treatise entitled *On Unknown Writing*. Cusa's response, his *Apology for Learned Ignorance*, praised the useful and subtle points to be found in Eckhart, but did allow that his books should be removed from public places " . . . because the public was not ready" for what was found in them.[86]

During the religious crisis of the sixteenth century, Eckhart's name was still known and cited, but direct contact with his works began to slacken. Nevertheless, the treatise on prayer known as the *Temple of Souls* (1543) was a potent source of knowledge of Eckhart for post-Tridentine Catholicism.[87] Despite the efforts of scholars such as Daniel Sudermann (d. 1631), who collected Eckhart manuscripts, and the mystical post Angelus Silesius (d. 1677), who was deeply influenced by the Meister, if mostly at second-hand, Eckhart began to fade from view. Knowledge of his name and ambiguous reputation never totally died out, but during the centuries from 1500 to 1800 it played a smaller role than it had in the pre-Reformation period.

The rediscovery of Meister Eckhart in the modern era began in Germany in the early nineteenth century and has grown steadily since. German Idealism and Romanticism were instrumental in this revival of interest, but it would require a lengthy account to mention all the currents at work, let alone the various stages in the evolution of Eckhart scholarship over the past century-and-a-half (Carl Schmidt's monograph of 1839 was the first modern study).[88] The complexity of Eckhart's mysticism has invited a wide variety of interpretations, not only from within traditions of Western thought, but also on the comparative level where both European and Asian scholars have found Eckhart a favored partner for dialogue with non-European forms of mysticism.[89] Disagreements about the proper interpretation of the elusive Eckhart are as strong today as ever; one thing that all serious students can share is an admiration for the masterful edition of Eckhart's works published under the auspices of the Deutsche Forschungsgemeinschaft since 1936 and now nearing its completion.

"This is Meister Eckhart from whom God hid nothing." Eckhart himself would have undoubtedly rejected the claim, and it would be foolish to take this title too seriously. Eckhart's proponents have often done him as much disservice as his detractors by their exaggerated claims. Meister Eckhart is frequently obscure and repetitious; he is often paradoxical and daring; at times he is one-sided and incomplete. Nevertheless, the pungency of his style, and the profundity and power of his thought mark him as one of the greatest mystics of any age and any religious tradition. Anyone who has read him with attention will find him difficult to forget.

BIBLIOGRAPHICAL NOTES

Some Basic Works on Meister Eckhart in English

I. Background.

Ancelet-Hustache, Jeanne. *Master Eckhart and the Rhineland Mystics* (New York, 1957).
Butler, Cuthbert. *Western Mysticism* (New York, 1923).
Clark, James M. *The Great German Mystics: Eckhart, Tauler and Suso* (Oxford, 1949).
Knowles, David. *The English Mystical Tradition* (London, 1961), Chaps. I–II.
Lerner, Robert. *The Heresy of the Free Spirit in the Late Middle Ages* (Berkeley, 1972).
Otto, Rudolf. *Mysticism East and West. A Comparative Analysis of the Nature of Mysticism* (New York, 1932).
Southern, Richard W. *Western Society and the Church in the Middle Ages* (Baltimore, 1970).
Zaehner, R.C. *Mysticism Sacred and Profane* (New York, 1961).

II. Meister Eckhart.

Translations

Colledge, Edmund, and McGinn, Bernard. *Meister Eckhart. The Essential Sermons, Commentaries, Treatises, and Defense* (New York, 1981).
Maurer, Armand. *Meister Eckhart. Parisian Questions and Prologues* (Toronto, 1974).
Schürmann, Reiner. *Meister Eckhart. Mystic and Philosopher* (Bloomington, 1978).

Studies

Caputo, John. *The Mystical Element in Heidegger's Thought* (Athens, OH, 1978).
Kelley, C.F. *Meister Eckhart on Divine Knowledge* (New Haven, 1977).
Kertz, Karl G. "Meister Eckhart's Teaching on the Birth of the Divine Word in the Soul." *Traditio,* 15 (1959), 327–63.
Kieckhefer, Richard. "Meister Eckhart's Conception of Union with God." *Harvard Theological Review,* 71 (1978), 203–25.
McGinn, Bernard. "Eckhart's Condemnation Reconsidered." *The Thomist,* 44 (1980), 390–414.
McGinn, Bernard. "The God beyond God. Theology and Mysticism in the Thought of Meister Eckhart." *Journal of Religion,* 61 (1981), 1–19.
The Thomist. Vol. 42, no. 2 (April, 1978). Meister Eckhart of Hochheim. (Articles and Bibliography.)

XI

John Tauler

RICHARD KIECKHEFER

There is, no doubt, no such thing as a "typical" mystic; each one has his or her distinctive emphases and formulations, if not wholly original insights. If one were seeking a mystic who did not display marked idiosyncrasies, however, Tauler would be a natural choice. By contrast with his older contemporary Meister Eckhart, he seems less bold, less provocative, more obviously balanced. He avoided the daring formulations of Eckhart, and thus spared himself the accusation of heresy, though some might argue that his being less adventuresome made him also less interesting. In comparison with Henry Suso, he appears less emotional; he showed no leanings toward the highly distinctive asceticism or richly poetic imagination of Suso. If he was thus more prosaic, he was again more clearly practical and balanced. While he had neither the speculative depth of Eckhart nor the poetic power of Suso, his practical bent may well have made him a more effective spiritual guide and a more lucid pastoral theologian. His sermons are not devoid of philosophical interest, but for the most part he devoted himself to questions of practical morality and spirituality. He was capable of dealing in a straightforward way with problems of sin and temptation, and with the antagonisms and other personal problems that arose in the religious houses of late medieval Germany. Presumably he was appreciated for his pastoral insight and not disdained for being less inspired than other preachers.

While refined and capable of great sophistication, he could be direct and earthy in his mode of expression—a trait that he shared with Eckhart and with Luther, who was fond of him on other grounds. At one juncture he told his congregation that God is capable of making noble use of even their defects: the manure that a horse makes in a stable is unclean and foul-smelling, but if spread over a field it produces fine grain and sweet wine; so also, one's defects, carried out to the field of God's loving will, can produce good and delightful fruit.[1] His affection for humanity shows in a sermon in which he called to the attention of the assembled nuns the the merits of laypeople. There are many housewives and cobblers out in the world, he said, who support themselves with hard labor, and many poor villagers who carry manure and earn a bit of bread with backbreaking effort, who may possibly be a hundred times as successful in the spiritual life as those seated in the congregation.[2] Though he was able to appreciate the accomplishments of theologians and the dignity of churchmen, he had high regard for simplicity.

Little is known of his life. He was born around 1300, spent most of his life in the Rhineland, and died in 1361. He knew both Eckhart and Suso, and apparently studied under the former. Twice in his sermons he makes reference to his mentor,[3] but the influence of Eckhart's thought can be seen in virtually every one of Tauler's sermons: common motifs, such as detachment (*Abgeschiedenheit*), the birth of God in the soul, and the "ground" of the soul, abound throughout his corpus. Whereas Eckhart's thought found expression in Latin as well as German, and in treatises as well as sermons, all we have from Tauler are approximately eighty-four vernacular sermons (if one accepts the judgment of a recent editor as to which texts are authentic).[4] He presents himself to us, therefore, as even less of a systematic theologian than Eckhart, since everything we have from his pen was composed for a specific occasion. The sermons are arranged according to the liturgical calendar, each one being designated for a particular Sunday or feast day, and each one being based on scriptural reading for that day.

Like many of the spiritual writers who have been dubbed "mystics," Tauler was at least as much concerned with everyday morality, in the sense of norms for orienting oneself throughout life toward God and creation, as he was with distinctively mystical experience. Indeed, he seems to have seen mystical states as a kind of special outgrowth of a moral life developed to its fullest. They were good, even desirable, but it was everyday morality that claimed primary attention and furnished the necessary background to any special experiences.

Tauler's moral norms may be summarized under three basic principles. First, he insists that his listeners free themselves from undue attachment to worldly objects, thus preparing themselves for spiritual progress. Secondly, he says that they must submit "passively" to God's will, especially in times of suffering; in doing so they will be following the example of Christ. And thirdly, they must not content

themselves with a life of spiritual idleness, but must dedicate themselves to devotional and charitable works. None of these principles
was peculiar to Tauler; they are all thoroughly traditional. Yet for
an understanding of his sermons one must note the ways in which
he develops these moral commonplaces and relates them to mystical
themes.

The requirement of detachment from worldly objects is a motif
that Tauler might have adopted from Eckhart, though in its essence
it is original to neither of them. From the fourth century, at least,
it was routine for spiritual writers to advocate an ascetic turning
away from worldly objects so that one could be free to devote oneself
fully to spiritual matters.[5] While Tauler stresses this point repeatedly,
he seldom does so at length, and in that sense the theme remains
undeveloped. Still, one can discern the basic outlines of his thought.
His essential principle is simple: one must practice detachment by
turning away from everything that is not purely God, and since
God's gifts are not God himself, one should not take pleasure in
them, but only in God himself.[6] Strictly speaking, this detachment
is only the first of four ways one must prepare oneself for the entry
of the Spirit into one's soul: after detachment one must exercise
renunciation, inwardness, and solitariness. Yet it is detachment that
is the most radical demand, since it involves a turning of one's mind
and soul away from creaturely reality, and the following steps are
essentially unfoldings of what one has already accomplished in
detachment.[7] Two natures or forms cannot exist beside each other;
if warmth is to enter into an object, cold must leave. So likewise,
if God is to enter into the soul, creatures must make way, and one
must abandon all that is distinctively one's own.[8] Posing the question
what makes for a pure heart, Tauler says it is a heart entirely free
from all creatures, so that when God comes to enter into it he may
find it unhindered.[9] If one is thus purged of all "images," or attachment to worldly notions, God must necessarily enter into one's
soul, for he cannot withhold himself.[10] If one is inwardly detached
from creatures, however, the external possession of them need not
be harmful. Given the proper freedom from dependence on worldly
things, one may own whatever one needs, indeed one may even
possess a kingdom, without endangering one's soul.[11]

Tauler cites an extreme example of such indifference to creatures.
There was once an "old father," or an early Christian ascetic, who
was so devoid of worldly attachments that he could not even retain
the memory of them. Once someone knocked on his door and asked
him for something, and he said he would fetch it, but when he got
into his house he forgot about the request. The visitor knocked again,
and the ascetic asked what he wanted. Again he promised to get

the object, but again he forgot. When this happened a third time, the ascetic said in desperation, "Come and take it yourself. I cannot retain this image long enough, for my spirit is so devoid of all earthly images." [12] What a modern observer might take as a sign of senility becomes here a signal of high virtue. Worldly objects can only distract from God, and ideally one should become oblivious to them.

Two further passages not only develop the motif of detachment but demonstrate how Tauler used his scriptural texts. In one sermon he cites the story of Abraham, in which God commanded the patriarch to go out from his own land and leave his family behind, because he wanted to show him everything that was good. Tauler interprets all this allegorically. The reference to "everything good" means the birth of God within us, since that experience contains all that is truly good. The land that Abraham left behind stands for the body, with all its pleasures and disorders; the relatives he abandoned are the inclinations of the senses which lead to states of passion. All these things, he concludes, must be set aside if one is to enjoy the divine birth within oneself.[13] In another sermon, for Epiphany, he says that all creaturely things must become as bitter and repugnant as myrrh. To be sure, one must continue to satisfy the requirements of nature— one must eat, drink, and sleep—but one must not allow these satisfactions to become inward, or to exercise influence on one's innermost state of soul. Rather, one should get them over with quickly, perhaps even perfunctorily, and not become devoted to or dependent upon such pleasures. What Tauler here advocates is more than a spirit of moderation: he insists that the satisfaction of bodily needs should actually become repugnant.[14] He is writing from the perspective of a dualistic world-view which perceives the demands and pleasures of nature essentially as distractions from one's higher calling, and which recognizes nature's demands only grudgingly.

The second moral imperative that can be gleaned from Tauler's sermons, the demand for "passivity," is related to the first. The notion here is that one should become so thoroughly detached from all creaturely objects and activities that one does not even assert oneself in one's striving for spiritual perfection; one does not exercise one's own creaturely will, but surrenders oneself to God. Just as one has abandoned material possessions, or at least become detached from them, and turned instead toward God, so also one must surrender one's own moral striving and let God accomplish what is necessary. As Tauler says in one sermon, all the works that a person performs amount to nothing whatsoever, no matter how great they are, in contrast to the smallest work that God performs in that person. To the same degree that God is better than all his creatures, so his work surpasses any work that a person may contemplate.[15] The contrast that he frequently draws is between *wirken* and *leiden:* the former term means "working" or "acting," while the latter, like the Latin *pati,* can mean either "suffering" or "being passive" (which is to say, suffering or allowing someone else to act upon one). Thus, he states that *leiden* is better than *wirken,*[16] and that while it is God's nature as pure act to *wirken* it is man's nature to *leiden.*[17] Rather than presuming to work oneself, one should let God do the work and become God's instrument.[18] Commenting on the parable of the woman who lost a drachma, he says that there are two ways to go about seeking the lost coin. The first way, in which one works, is actually subdivided: one may work in an external manner, with pious deeds and exercises of virtue, or one may turn within oneself and ransack one's inner house, ridding it of all sense impressions, fantasies, and concepts. The latter is far preferable to the former, but even so it is only preparatory to the "suffering" mode of quest, in which God himself takes over and the person becomes the object of God's seeking.[19] At this point the correspondence between the parable and the interpretation becomes weak, since the woman in the parable is not invited to become the object of the quest. The unexpected twist, however, has the impact of a surprise, and calls to the listeners' attention that however noble one's agenda there are higher goals to be attained by abandoning one's intent and submitting to God's.

In some contexts Tauler makes the same point by distinguishing between speech and silence. "If God is to speak," he says, "all creatures must be silent."[20] Elsewhere he expresses the identical point in reverse: "If you wish to speak, God must be silent."[21] Better than the distinction between *leiden* and *wirken,* this contrast of speech and silence conveys the sense that there is in fact something for the individual to do rather than merely sit by idle: there is if nothing else the task of waiting attentively for God to address oneself.[22] Indeed, Tauler tries to make it clear that the demand for "passivity" does not mean that one should jettison all good intentions and habits of pious spiritual exercise. Rather, one should not depend on such things, but while maintaining them should wait patiently for God to reveal his will through his deeds.[23]

In a sermon for Pentecost, Tauler distinguishes two phases in the Spirit's entry into the soul. First there is an emptying (or detachment), and then there is a filling (with the Spirit through grace). From an external viewpoint it may appear that the first stage is one for human effort, and the second for divine—but in fact it is the Spirit which accomplishes both phases, and any human attempt to intervene can only spoil the Spirit's operation. One who does so is like a fool who tries to improve on the painting of a master. Indeed, even if one is so presumptuous as to ascribe the Spirit's work to oneself, one ruins the effect. One must be conscious that at every stage one is acting with divine aid, and that the norm for action is God's will rather than one's own.[24]

It is in particular when God sends us suffering that our submission to his will is tested—or, to use the double meaning of the German term, it is only when God causes us to *leiden* (suffer) that our ability to *leiden* (submit passively or patiently) is tested.[25] Whatever afflictions we feel, inwardly or outwardly, we should receive them with love, because God sends them to us out of the same love from which he brings forth the highest and best gifts. From all eternity, God foresaw and intended even the smallest imaginable of our pains, such as the loss of a single hair. Whenever we lose our friends, our possessions, our honor, or whatever, the experience will help to form our character and lead us to genuine peace if we can accept it properly. We should not concern ourselves with the question whether the suffering is or is not deserved; rather, we should resign ourselves gratefully to God's will.[26] If we do so, no suffering will be unbearable, since God himself will bear it for us, which is to say that he will give us the strength necessary to endure.[27]

Such patient acceptance of suffering is the primary way in which we imitate Christ. While Tauler repeatedly sets Christ forth as a moral example, and sometimes refers to Christ's life as well as his death as a source of guidance, he does not refer explicitly to Jesus' compassion, forgiveness, humility, poverty, or other virtues manifested throughout Christ's years of ministry.[28] Instead, he focuses on the submission to suffering that Christ displayed in his Passion. Imitation of Christ is accomplished especially by taking up one's own cross.[29] One must bow oneself under the cross, whether it takes the form of inward or of outward suffering; one must bend one's proud mind under the crown of thorns, and one must follow the "crucified God" with downcast spirit, in utter self-abasement, just as Christ allowed himself to be destroyed, condemned, and crucified by his creatures. "In this manner you should suffer patiently, and in all humility you should imitate his suffering and submit to him." [30] One should even be grateful to share in the sufferings of Christ.[31] If a person wishes to imitate the suffering and crucified savior, God will send him the most fearsome darkness and the deepest misery of that total abandonment which Christ felt on the cross.[32] Yet it was throughout his life, and not just on the cross, that Jesus gave example of suffering: "Take before your eyes the precious model of Jesus Christ, and consider the working of his love. It brought him suffering, more than all the saints and others have ever experienced. In all his life, he found less comfort than anyone. He ended his life in the most bitter death that any person has died—yet in his higher powers he was no less blessed than he is now."[33]

A life of detachment from creatures and submission to God would not be complete, however without the third principle, that of action. One must be cautious in reading Tauler's texts, since in speaking of "works" he often means such devotional works as fasts, vigils, or pilgrimages, while a modern reader might assume that he is referring to charitable works. Both forms of exertion, though, had their place in Tauler's scheme of the spiritual life. To be sure, his typical attitude toward works is one of great caution, since he is keenly aware of the temptation to become dependent on a meaningless regimen of prayers, fasting, vigils, and other devotions. He maintains that inward practices such as contemplation are better than outward ones in which one observes prescribed forms of behavior. Outward practices derive all their power, he says, from inward dispositions. It is as if a single drop of wine were able to transform a vat of water into noble wine: so a proper inward disposition has marvelous power to transform outward works.[34] If one can become properly disposed inwardly even for the duration of a mass, all of one's work and all of one's life will become peaceful, calm, virtuous, gentle, and composed.[35] Tauler is open to the possibility that external works may hinder one's inward spiritual life, and in that case he recommends that they be set aside, presumably temporarily.[36] More typically, however, he says that one should perform outer works but not rely on them and not allow oneself to become disordered or to lack composure in their performance.[37] His practical approach to such matters can be seen also in his comments about ascetic rigors: he says that fasts and vigils can be splendid aids to the spiritual life, but should be set aside if they begin to undermine one's health, and indeed even a prescribed fast day can be dispensed with for the sake of health, since the Church never intended to destroy anyone's constitution. Provided that one maintains due moderation and does not become obsessively dependent upon one's devotions, though, they are integral to the life of the spirit. Indeed, Tauler says that up to age forty they should be the mainstay of one's spiritual life, and only after then is it safe to become more fully absorbed in inward piety.[38]

What Tauler is trying to do in such texts is steer a middle path between the notion (traditionally called Pelagianism) that one may attain holiness and salvation by one's own effort, without God's aid, and the opposite extreme (known as Quietism) which maintains that since God will accomplish everything there is no reason for human beings to exert themselves. On the one hand, he condemns the presumptuous claim that we can bring ourselves to sanctity or even contribute anything genuinely our own. On the other, he ruled out that "false inactivity" and "inner idleness" which refuses any mode of human effort. He may appear to contradict himself, but there is an underlying consistency. What he argues essentially is that human beings do need to prepare themselves for God's work, but that there is a deeper level at which the preparation which appears to be ours is in fact God's work: when we pick up a devotional book, or go to a sermon, or perform any other devout task, we are submitting to God's work within us. Indeed, it is difficult for Tauler to distinguish strictly between God's work and ours because in the last analysis he does not recognize a full distinction between God's *being* and ours—but this is a point that must be raised later.[39]

One sermon in particular praises the value of outer works—a sermon based on the text, "There are diverse works, but one spirit" (I Cor. 12:6).[40] Tauler asks why it is that people complain about having to immerse themselves in work, as if it were a hindrance to their spiritual progress. Work is, after all, given by God, and if it poses a hindrance that is only because one is not properly composed in its execution. One should do one's work with God alone in mind, neither loving the favor nor fearing the disfavor one may incur, and seeking neither use nor pleasure but only God's honor. When Christ rebuked Martha (the Christian prototype of the active life, in contrast to her contemplative sister Mary), he did so not because she was doing work, which was good and holy, but because she was too anxious or obsessive about it. A person should live according to his or her lot, performing good and useful work, proceeding carefully and quietly, and leaving all care about the outcome to God. Outward works are opportunities to exercise oneself in virtue—and one should not expect that God will enter into a person who does not exercise himself thus. Tauler cites the example of a man who was thrashing grain when he fell suddenly into a rapture, and would have hit himself with his flail if an angel had not held it. This interruption, sent by God, was good but extraordinary, and to desire such release from work would be a sign of mere laziness. To be sure, the extent to which one engages in work will depend on one's calling. At this point Tauler draws on the Pauline analogy of the Church as a body, and assigns to the contemplatives the noble role of eyes, with the warning that not all should expect to fulfill this role. The implication, then, is that some form of outer work—manual labor, charitable service, or at least outward rituals—is incumbent on all, even if there are some who are released from such duty more than others, presumably after many years of preparation through active works.

None of these general principles for living, however, would qualify Tauler as a mystic. In what sense, then, is it meaningful to apply this term to him? Since the very word is one applied to Tauler and other such figures by modern scholars rather than by contemporaries, the question is not one with an obvious or ready-made answer. If one equates the term "mystic" with "contemplative," surely Tauler may be included. He described, fostered, and presumably practiced the non-discursive or contemplative form of prayer, in which one dispenses with images and concepts and gives oneself over to the infused grace of spontaneous consciousness of God. More broadly stated, he qualifies as a mystic because he emphasizes in his spirituality an intuitive sense of God's immanence. Thus, the mystical elements in his thought are essentially twofold: he encouraged an ongoing sense of God's presence within human personality, and he cultivated that special contemplative prayer to which relatively few Christians have felt themselves called. To be sure, he has relatively little to say about the techniques of contemplation, or the ways one opens oneself to this infused grace—but he has a great deal to say about those ecstatic states that characterize contemplation in its highest form.

To begin with, he expresses in several sermons a consciousness of God's presence in human life. God is not always revealed openly,[41] yet he is present through grace, and consciousness of him is a central goal of Tauler's spiritual thought. He exhorts his hearers not to be lazy or to persist in devotion to things that are not divine, but to search diligently within themselves with the light of their reason and attend to themselves and to God within themselves with loving desire.[42] Just as the Holy Spirit filled the disciples on Pentecost, so likewise he does so today, every hour, without ceasing. He fills all souls to overflowing, wherever he finds room, filling them with riches, graces, love, and indescribable gifts. Out of his inexhaustible bounty he fills the valleys and depths that are open to him. His presence is ordinarily not discerned: just as the soul mediates life to the body in a hidden way, so also the Spirit works within the soul in an unperceived manner.[43] These and other passages indicate a fascination with God's inward presence that characterizes all the mystics. Purely rational, non-mystical theologians may share this conviction, but it is the mystics who advise that one attend to God's indwelling with "loving desire" and strive for an intuitive apprehension of God's presence.

Like Meister Eckhart and many of his predecessors, Tauler speaks of God's entry into the soul as a "birth." [44] Again like Eckhart, he devotes a Christmas sermon to this topic, in which he says that the three Christmas masses celebrate the three births: "the eternal begetting of the Son by the Father, the birth of Jesus from the Virgin, and the birth of God every day and every hour, in a true and spiritual manner, through grace and out of love, in a good soul." To become aware of this process, a person must turn all his or her powers of perception inward.[45] Elsewhere he says it is an event always preceded by adversity;[46] while he is not clear in spelling out what this means, what he seems to have in mind is that submission to God's will, particularly in adversity, is a condition for the occurrence of the birth. The infusion of God into the soul may be hindered by various alien births—by the birth of temporal, transitory desires within one's soul, however insignificant they may seem.[47] By practicing detachment from such objects, however, we may free ourselves for the birth of God through grace within us. The consequence of this process is that a person is transformed, indeed made godlike or clothed in divine form.[48] Just as humankind was weighed down by the norms of the Old Testament before the birth of Jesus, so also each individual is burdened by an "Old Testament" existence of misery and reliance on external works until the liberating influence of the spiritual birth brings a new kind of joy and release.[49]

Thus, there are passages in which Tauler speaks of the birth as an ongoing, constant process within the soul that has been spiritually purged. Such texts are in keeping with the statement cited above, that God cannot withhold himself from the soul that has emptied itself of distracting influences. But there are other sermons in which he speaks of God's birth in the soul as a special event with presumably limited duration. Thus, he says at one point that God's birth in the soul brings unspeakable joy, and that one should not disrupt a person in such a state, or draw him out into the worldly multiplicity of outer affairs, but should let God perfect his work in him. This person's joy is so great that it gushes forth within him, like new wine rising in a flask. Indeed, his exhilaration may break out in external manifestations, lest it become pent up and cause blood to spurt from the mouth and nose. Still, Tauler adds that exuberance of this kind is an inferior kind of spiritual experience, far removed from the higher stages.[50] What is clear from this passage is that Tauler envisions the birth in two ways: as an ongoing process and as a specific experience. The latter meaning is suggested again by a passage in which he says that the union of the soul with God that occurs through the eucharist brings about a fulfillment of the birth of God in the soul, in which the spirit becomes no longer just similar to God but united with him, immersed in the divine unity.[51]

Tauler provides a convenient summary of his teaching on mystical states in a sermon for the fifth Sunday after Trinity.[52] He says that there are three stages in the spiritual life. The first and lowest is that in which one turns entirely to the wonderful works and revelations of God's gifts and to the outpouring of his goodness, in such a way that one bursts forth in jubilation. This state occurs when one diligently considers how God has lavished wondrous signs of love in his celestial and terrestrial wonders, bringing benefits to all creatures, which flourish and blossom and are full of God. In particular, God devotes himself patiently to human welfare and calls each person to come near to himself. Overwhelmed by consideration of these things, a person breaks out in some form of outward manifestation—possibly singing, spontaneous oral prayer, or bodily motions. Otherwise, as already pointed out, blood might gush from his or her mouth; Tauler claims that this fate has often been observed to happen. All these experiences are good, but the person undergoing them remains a spiritual child. Upon maturation, the soul embarks on a wild, dark, lonely path, on which God takes away all that was ever bestowed, even knowledge of himself. Greatly distraught, the individual is unsure whether he has ever been on the right path, whether there is a God for him or not, whether he himself is alive. It is as if he were suspended between two walls, with a sword threatening him in back and a spear in front. All he can do is sit down and say, "God bless thee, bitterness most bitter, full of all grace!" The stronger his previous consciousness of God, the greater his present sorrow. To be sure, the Lord is nearby, and the soul thus downcast should maintain faith in his imminent relief, yet he cannot imagine the removal of such insufferable darkness. Only after this period of tribulation does the Lord raise the soul to the third stage, where he removes the cloak from its eyes and lets it see the truth. Feeling as if he has been raised from the dead, the person is now so divinized that God within him is and does all that he is and does, and he becomes by grace what God is by nature. He knows nothing of sense data, but is totally lost in the experience of union with God.

One might readily find parallels for this schema in the writings of other mystics: the categories of illumination, the Dark Night of the Soul, and the unitive state are perhaps the most obvious, and no doubt Tauler would recognize much of what other mystics have said about such phenomena as corresponding to his notions. The sense of this passage—and of those numerous briefer passages in which Tauler expresses similar ideas—is altogether orthodox and traditional. When he speaks of the individual as divinized, or as becoming by grace that which God is by nature, he does not mean to suggest that there is literally no distinction between the soul and God. Rather, he is using a traditional formulation to express the radical transformation that grace works in the soul—though the additional factor here is that in ecstatic union with God the soul is presumably no longer conscious of its distinction from God, because its attention is riveted entirely on the divine unity in which it is immersed. He says elsewhere that when united with God the human spirit is so much penetrated by the divine that it loses itself and all sense of differentiation—and that to be in this state for a single hour or even a moment is a thousand times more useful than to live forty years according to our own intentions.[53] Again, he says that just as an insignificant small coin is paltry in comparison with 100,000 gold marks, so also all exterior prayer is meager in contrast to the true union with God, or the "sinking of created spirit into the uncreated spirit of God."[54] Repeatedly he speaks of union with God as a foretaste of the afterlife—a tantalizing preview of what the saints will enjoy in eternity.[55]

The mystical themes in Tauler are summarized nicely in a sermon for the eighth Sunday after Trinity, where he says that the Holy Spirit works two ways in a human being. First, a person is led about and moved at all times by the Spirit, who constantly exhorts, drives, and entices him to lead an ordered life. The Spirit does this with all those who prepare for his work. Secondly, however, the Spirit at times will bring a person to the highest spiritual goal quite suddenly, taking him or her beyond the natural capacities of human beings. Those to whom the Spirit does this are God's dearest children.[56] In other words, the ordinary work of God in the soul, his working or presence through grace, is adequate to attain that for which human beings strive. For those he has singled out for special favors, though, God works marvelous spiritual progress beyond their expectations. He breaks the ordinary rules of the game for their sake. While he does not say so explicitly, it is clear enough that Tauler has in mind here those whose contemplative prayer has brought them to ecstatic states in which they have experienced union with God.

Throughout his sermons, Tauler refers to the *Grund* of the soul— the "ground," or (to use a less common but more poetic translation) the "depth." This is the noblest element of the soul, where the true image of the Trinity lies hidden.[57] It is the Temple, of unspeakable dignity and value, to which one should turn in prayer.[58] God works and dwells in it, and enjoys himself there; one can no more sever God from it than one can sever him from himself.[59] It is a kind of root element in the soul, the soul's substance, from which all the faculties emerge. It is there that union with God occurs.[60] The reason for this is that the ground of the human soul and the ground of God intersect, so to speak, so that the way to reach God's ground is by entering into one's own.[61] Indeed, the human ground proceeds from God—meaning, presumably, that it existed as an archetype within the divine mind even before the human individual was created—and has a natural tendency to return to the source from which it emerged.[62] This return is a marvelous process: "In hiddenness the created Spirit is brought back to its uncreatedness, where it existed from all eternity in the ground of God, before it was created. It recognizes itself as God in God, and yet as in itself a creature and created. Yet in God all things in which this ground finds itself are God."[63] To turn within one's own ground, focusing all one's powers of perception on that juncture between oneself and God, brings great results even if it is only brief; if one spent an entire year in which one accomplished nothing more than a fleeting glimpse of one's ground, that would be a well spent year.[64] Furthermore, it is through one's ground that one returns to God those gifts that he has given—by which Tauler seems to mean that whatever God has bestowed upon us, if we use it to further the development of the grounds within our souls we can thus return the gift to God.[65]

Yet Tauler maintains throughout his sermons a sense of the overbrimming goodness and generosity of God, which is so strong that ultimately one cannot repay him. It is, he says, as if a man went to donate a gulden to the pope, and each time the man did so the pope gave him 100,000 pounds of gold. So likewise, when a person turns in gratitude toward God, praising him for his gifts and consolations, each time God hastens to give him more of these favors.[66] There is a sense of exuberance here that Tauler cannot and would not restrain: his image of God is one of unbounded beneficence, and his reaction to that insight is to submit himself totally to God's work within him, both in suffering and in enjoyment of spiritual delights.

BIBLIOGRAPHICAL NOTES

The standard editions of Tauler's original texts are *Die Predigten Taulers*, ed. Ferdinand Vetter (Berlin, 1910), and *Sermons de J. Tauler*, ed. Adolphe Léon Corin (Liège, 1929). There is an excellent translation into modern German: Johannes Tauler, *Predigten*, tr. Georg Hofmann (Freiburg, 1961), recently reissued with an introduction by Alois Haas, 2 vols. (Einsiedeln, 1979). No corresponding English translation exists, but some of the sermons are available in Susanna Winkworth, *The History of the Life of the Reverend Doctor John Tauler* (London, 1905), and John Tauler, *Spiritual Conferences*, ed. and tr. Eric Colledge and Sister M. Jane (Rockford, IL, 1978).

Ephrem Filthaut, ed., *Johannes Tauler, ein deutscher Mystiker* (Essen, 1961), contains an extensive bibliography as well as a useful series of essays. The most important German addition to this bibliography is Gösta Wrede, *Unio Mystica: Probleme der Erfahrung bei Johannes Tauler* (Uppsala, 1974).

English literature on Tauler has been sparse. James M. Clark has a chapter on him in *The Great German Mystics* (Oxford, 1949), and more recently there is Steven E. Ozment, *Homo Spiritualis: A Comparative Study of the Anthropology of Johannes Tauler, Jean Gerson and Martin Luther (1509–16)* (Leiden, 1969).

See also Richard Kieckhefer, "The Role of Christ in Tauler's Spirituality," *Downside Review*, 96 (1978), 176–91; "Mysticism and Social Consciousness in the Fourteenth Century," *University of Ottawa Quarterly*, 48 (1978), 179–86; and "The Notion of Passivity in the Sermons of John Tauler," *Recherches de théologie ancienne et médiévale*, forthcoming.

XII
The Cloud of Unknowing

JOHN P. H. CLARK

The Carthusian James Greenhalgh (d. 1529/30), who annotated many manuscripts of the works of Richard Rolle and Walter Hilton, believed that it was Hilton who wrote the *Cloud of Unknowing*. This theory is now discounted, though there was almost certainly a link, direct or indirect, between Hilton and the *Cloud*'s author. The linguistic and manuscript evidence seems to indicate that the *Cloud* (and its attendant treatises) were written in the North-East Midlands of England in the later part of the fourteenth century, at the time when Hilton was active. One of Hilton's correspondents, Adam Horsley, became a Carthusian of Beauvale, in Leicestershire, and Hilton himself died at Thurgarton, outside Nottingham, as an Augustinian Canon in 1396. The similarities of literary expression between the *Cloud* corpus and Hilton, together with the manner in which similar expressions are often used to express apparently similar but in fact quite distinct theological concepts as between the two bodies of works, become explicable if we suppose that the *Cloud* was in part a response to Hilton's *Ladder of Perfection*, Book One, while the second part of Hilton's diptych was in turn influenced by the language and theology of the *Cloud*, without fully assimilating it.[1]

As to the identity of the *Cloud*'s author, the internal evidence of his writings indicates that he was a priest, dedicated to the contemplative life, and recognized as a spiritual director. He was a competent theologian, with a good knowledge of patristic and monastic literature, who knew at any rate some elements of the teaching of St. Thomas Aquinas. Beyond this, all would seem to be speculation.[2]

273

The *Cloud* is associated in the manuscript tradition with six other English treatises: the *Book of Privy Counselling*, the *Epistle of Prayer*, *Denis' Hid Divinity*, the *Epistle of Discretion in Stirrings*, the *Study of Wisdom*, and *Of Discerning of Spirits*. Of these, the first three are explicitly said to be the work of the *Cloud*'s author, while the fourth is so closely related in subject-matter, thought, and expression to these that it is almost certainly his. The *Study of Wisdom* is very probably, though not certainly his; the authorship of *Discerning of Spirits* is more problematic. The *Book of Privy Counselling* takes up some of the points made in the *Cloud*, and elaborates them so as to avoid confusion or suspicion of unorthodoxy, apparently in response to criticisms that had been made. *Hid Divinity* is an English version of the *De Mystica Theologia* which for many centuries passed under the name of St. Paul's disciple Dionysius the Areopagite, but is now known to have been written by a fifth-century Syrian monk, and embodies elements derived from Gregory of Nyssa's *Life of Moses*. The translation is made, of course, from the available Latin versions, and contains important modifications of the Pseudo-Areopagite's thought, characteristic of Latin but not of Byzantine theology. The *Study of Wisdom* is a rendering of the famous *Benjamin Minor* of Richard of St. Victor, a standard medieval text-book of psychology and spiritual theology. *Discerning of Spirits* is built around Bernard's twenty-third and twenty-fourth *Sermons on Various Subjects*.[3]

The Prologue of the *Cloud* declares that the book is not intended for the intellectually curious or for chatterers and gossips; nor, the author says, is it even intended for those whose form of life is "active"—who do good Christian works, but whose life is in the world and who are neither by state nor disposition called to be "contemplative." Nevertheless, it is recognized that men outside the cloister as well as within may benefit from its teaching; God may grant contemplation where he will, though it is not to be expected that those living in the world will have the constant habit of contemplation that is properly to be sought by religious.[4] In fact, the *Epistle of Discretion in Stirrings* (assuming common authorship) deals with disposition to the same work of contemplation that the *Cloud* describes, and is apparently addressed to one who was not a vowed religious: "Thou askest me counsel of silence and of speaking, of common dieting and of singular fasting, of dwelling in company and of dwelling alone by thyself. . . ."[5] The author takes it that his reader may indeed receive just such a direct and God-given contemplation as described at length in the *Cloud* and the *Book of Privy Counselling* and may have this not merely as an occasional gift, but as a settled habit—"if thou mayest by grace keep it in custom and in continual working. . . ."[6] The *Cloud* repeats the traditional contrast (deriving from Augustine and Gregory the Great) between the two lives of action and contemplation considered both as states or callings and as function or interior reality, and exemplified in the persons of the sisters Martha and Mary (Luke 10:38–42). Following the saying of Christ, the life of Mary, the contemplative life of waiting directly on God, is taken to be the higher, and the active life, the practical life of the works of mercy, is a preparation for it, and subordinate to it. The active life, in this sense, begins and ends in this world, because in Heaven there will be no need for the works of mercy as such. What is further implied here, though not stated in so many words, is that the Christian life in the end is a matter of "being" more than of "doing"; it is charity, love of God for himself, and of our neighbor in and for God, which gives value to our actions (cf. 1 Corinthians 13:1ff.). It is a charity that is nourished within the framework of contemplation, i.e., waiting directly on God. In fact, for all his predilection for the properly contemplative life, to which he sees involvement in activity as an impediment, our author is realistic enough to affirm that everyone has in some measure to lead something of both lives—what is commonly termed the "mixed life." Following traditional patterns, he sees three levels in the spiritual life. The first is the lower part of the active life, the basic, practical works of mercy; the second is at once the higher part of the active life and the lower part of contemplative life, meditation on one's own sins, the Passion of Christ, and "compassion" towards God's creatures arising from this; the third is the higher part of the contemplative life, attending upon the "darkness" and the "cloud of unknowing" in which God is hidden, "with a loving stirring and a blind beholding to the naked being of God himself only." [7] The successive phases of the active and contemplative lives are a process of growth in recollection, in which recollection issues in a reaching out towards union with God:

> In the lower part of active life a man is without himself and beneath himself. In the higher part of active life and the lower part of contemplative life, a man is within himself and even [i.e. equal] with himself. But in the higher part of contemplative life, a man is above himself and under his God.[8]

In contrast to Walter Hilton, who encourages the anchoress (to whom the first book of the *Ladder of Perfection* is addressed and in her all those who are called to contemplative life) to respect those who have active and pastoral responsibilities, and who, indeed, has a lively concern for those who are called to serve God in the world,[9] the author of the *Cloud* is much more of a specialist. He emphasizes the misunderstanding that contemplatives receive from actives, rather than the obverse.[10] Whereas Hilton at various points touches on the whole range of the moral and spiritual life, the author of the *Cloud* concentrates his attention on a single phase of the life of prayer. In the *Book of Privy Counselling* he describes the signs of the call to such a simplified, contemplative prayer. The first sign is that meditation on one's own sinfulness, or on the Passion of Christ, leads directly into the "blind desire" for God; the second, following on the former, is that the "blind desire" becomes a settled habit at all times, rather than a passing sensation that vanishes when spiritual reading (or listening to a spiritual discourse) is over. In conjunction with this second sign—and here the writer obviously has in mind the contemplative religious to whom the *Cloud* and the *Book of Privy Counselling* are specifically addressed—one becomes sought out for counsel, and one's words, though few, are full of wisdom.[11]

It is the "cloud of unknowing" that hides God from us. The author takes it for granted that this is not a physical cloud,[12] just as later on he will point out that a lifting up of the mind to God, or a movement of introversion, is not of course to be taken in a physical sense;[13] in line with the words of Augustine and Bernard, a chapter-heading points out that "the high and the nearest way to heaven is run by desires and not by paces of feet." [14] To avoid the possibility of misunderstanding in a crudely spatial sense, the author even rejects the language of recollection and introversion, which was a commonplace repeated by such as Hilton:

> Where another man would bid thee gather thy mights [i.e., faculties] and thy wits wholly within thy-self, and worship God there—although he saith full well and truly, yea! and no man trulier if he be well conceived—yet for fear of deceit and of bodily conceiving of his words, I care not to bid thee do so . . . . Nowhere bodily is everywhere ghostly [i.e., spiritually]. Look then busily that thy ghostly work be nowhere bodily. . . .[15]

So we are to work in the "blind nought" of unknowing. To enter the cloud of unknowing that surrounds the being of God, we have to put a "cloud of forgetting" between us and all created things.[16] The "forgetting" of creatures suggests the words of St. Paul (Phillippians 3:14): "Forgetting those things which are behind . . ., I press towards the mark for the prize of the high calling of God in Christ Jesus." This implies no denigration of God's good creation, but it presupposes that, in consequence of Adam's fall, our love of human beings and our use of created things has become "disordered," and that, paradoxically, we only begin to love and use them freely as we begin, through the grace of Christ, to have God at the center of our thoughts and actions, and to see creatures in relation to him rather than as ends in themselves or means to our own enjoyment. The image of the "cloud of unknowing" derives from the *Mystical Theology* of Pseudo-Dionysius and refers to the hidden presence of God in the darkness of Sinai. In the new Exodus, the Christian follows the pattern of Moses' and Israel's journey, passing through the waters of baptism and the pilgrimage that follows from this.

Pseudo-Dionysius bids his reader leave behind both the senses and the operations of the intellect and follow Moses in his ascent of the mountain and entry into "the truly mystical darkness of unknowing," where he is united *(henoumenos)* with God at a supra-intellectual level—"by knowing nothing he knows at a level above that of the intellect." [17] He goes on to speak of two ways of conceiving God, viz. the way of affirmation and the way of denial. Of these, the second, commonly called the apophatic way, is the less imperfect; yet in fact, God, who is "beyond being," is beyond both all that may be affirmed of him and all that may be denied of him.[18] The author of the *Cloud* refers to a famous saying of Pseudo-Dionysius in his book *On the Divine Names:* "The most godly knowing of God is that which is known by unknowing," [19] and affirms boldly, "Whosoever will look at Denis' books shall find that his words will clearly affirm all that I have said or shall say, from the beginning of this treatise to the end. . . ." [20]

It must be remembered here that the claim to sub-apostolic authorship gave the Dionysian writings an enormous vogue in the Middle Ages. In fact, Pseudo-Dionysius is only one component element in the *Cloud*'s theology, which owes a great deal to Augustine, Gregory, Bernard, and the practical monastic tradition of spirituality, as well as to the scholastics from Richard of St. Victor to Thomas Aquinas. Although Latin theologians, including Bonaventure and Thomas Aquinas, refer to Pseudo-Dionysius, they do not follow his teaching strictly, but often subtly transform it as they incorporate elements from it within a framework that derives from Augustine. Whereas in Byzantine theology, for example, the unknowability of God is not excluded even in Pseudo-Dionysius' account of the vision of God enjoyed by the blessed,[21] the Latin tradition approaches this mystery by a different route. When Augustine and Gregory the Great, and their successors, speak of the "darkness" that impedes our awareness of God, they have in mind not so much the ontological "unknowability" of God as the condition of sin within man himself which hinders our vision.[22] Thomas Aquinas takes it (following Augustine) that it is man's rational nature that constitutes the "image of God" in him (cf. Genesis 1:26); in his view, the goal of the created intellect is, at least in some sense, to "see" God in his essence, even though the realization of this lies beyond this life, and in the beatific vision itself one can never "comprehend" God fully.[23] There are passages in the *Cloud* that imply that the "unknowability" of God is the consequence of the darkness of sin in the human soul in this life rather than, at any rate in the first instance, of the absolute unknowability of God in himself. So Mary Magdalene

> . . . hung up her love and her longing desire in this cloud of unknowing, and learned to love a thing the which she might not see clearly *in this life* by light of understanding in her reason [italics mine], nor yet verily feel in sweetness of love in her affection. . . .[24]

Likewise a passage which reflects the moral understanding of darkness in the Latin tradition indicates that, although, as Pseudo-Dionysius says of the "luminous darkness" that hides the presence of God, "a soul is more blinded in feeling of it for abundance of ghostly [i.e., spiritual] light, than for any darkness or wanting of bodily light," [25] it is not only the transcendence of God's light that dazzles us. In the light that comes from God we begin to see the horror of our sins:

> At the first time that a soul looketh thereupon, it shall find all the special deeds of sin that ever he did since he was born . . . painted thereupon. . . . Sometimes in this travail he thinketh that to look thereupon is to look as on hell. . . .[26]

John of the Cross likewise, in whom the tradition of Pseudo-Dionysius combines with the perspective of (among others) Augustine and Gregory the Great, will write:

> There are two reasons why this divine wisdom is not only night and darkness for the soul, but also affliction and torment. First, because of the height of the divine wisdom which exceeds the capacity of the soul. Second, because of the soul's baseness and impurity. . . .[27]

For Pseudo-Dionysius, God is "beyond being," and while admitting the inadequacy of any human name for God, he says that the (Platonic) name of "Good" is the most appropriate.[28] For Augustine, on the contrary, the most appropriate name for God is the biblical name, He-Who-Is (cf. Exodus 3:13), and in common with Augustine, Thomas (and John of Damascus!) the *Cloud's* author prefers the name of He-Who-Is for God:

There is no name . . . so much according unto everlastingness (the which is God), as is that the which may be had . . . in the blind and the lovely beholding of this word Is. For if thou say "Good" or "Fair Lord," or "Sweet," "Merciful" or "Righteous," "Wise," or . . . "Mighty" . . ., it is all hid and enstored in this little word "Is." [29]

There is one further significant modification which the *Cloud's* author makes to the Dionysian teaching. Here too he is no innovator, but follows the tradition already found in Hugh of St. Victor in his *Commentary on the Celestial Hierarchies* and in the translators John Sarracenus and Thomas Gallus. Pseudo-Dionysius had emphasized the silencing of the senses and of intellectual apprehensions in the approach to union with God, but in the *Mystical Theology* at any rate there is no explicit reference to this union as a union of love; when he does refer to ecstatic union with God as involving "love," in his book *On the Divine Names*, he uses the word *eros*.[30] It is left to the Latin translators and expositors of the *Mystical Theology* to introduce such terms as "affection" and "contrition" in speaking of the movement of the soul towards union with God—terms which are repeated, and even reinforced, in our author's English version of the *Mystical Theology*.[31] So in the *Cloud* we are bidden to strike the cloud of unknowing with a "sharp dart of longing love," [32] a "little blind love," [33] and so on, repeatedly.

It is theological commonplace—repeated by Thomas Aquinas— that we may be directly united to God by love while we are as yet unable to apprehend him in this life by the intellect.[34] The *Cloud* repeats, and even sharpens, this commonplace:

Our soul, by virtue of this reforming grace, is made sufficient to the full to comprehend all of him by love, the which is incomprehensible to all created knowing powers.[35]

Thomas Aquinas, as a follower of Augustine, had held that love implies some knowledge, however inadequate, of the object of love. The *Cloud* opposes love to knowledge in a way that goes beyond Thomas, and stands closer to the view of William of St. Thierry that love itself provides its own kind of knowledge of God.[36] The antithesis of love to knowledge is reaffirmed:

[God] may well be loved, but not thought. By love he may be gotten and holden, but by thought neither.[37]

In the same way, in the *Epistle of Discretion in Stirrings*, the author takes up a familiar verse from the Song of Songs (4:9), "Thou hast wounded my heart with one of thine eyes," to contrast reason's knowledge of God from his effects, which remains a deductive and indirect knowledge, with love's direct knowledge:

> Eyes of the soul are two, reason and love. By reason we may trace how mighty, how wise and how good [God] is in his creatures, but not in himself. . . . By love we may find him, feel him and strike him even in himself.[38]

Thomas Gallus, one of the Dionysian translators and expositors whose work was used by the author of the *Cloud*, speaks of a supra-intellectual faculty, by which he may be united to God, which he terms the "point of highest affection" *(apex affectionis principalis)*;[39] something of this is suggested when the *Book of Privy Counselling* speaks of a union with God "in the sovereign point of thy spirit." [40] But in fact Thomas Gallus is only a subordinate source for our author's teaching even in this passage; far more central to the general thought of the *Cloud* corpus is the idea of unit of spirit with God expressed by Paul in 1 Corinthians 6:17: "He that is joined to the Lord is one spirit," a text that has deep significance for Bernard and the early Cistercians,[41] and that, especially through their influence, became pervasive; this test is indeed drawn by Thomas Gallus into his exposition of Pseudo-Dionysius, *On the Divine Names.*[42] In conjunction with this text there is a firm distinction between Creator and creature, nature and grace, that forestalls any possibility that "union" may be understood as absorption of the soul into God in a pantheistic sense—perhaps a necessary precaution, since pantheism had been one of the features of the heresy of the "free spirit" associated with the Beghards especially in Germany and the Low Countries. There are some indications that English theologians towards the end of the fourteenth century were on their guard against errors of this kind, as well as against the incipient Lollard movement: [43]

> He purposeth to win thither by grace, whither he may not come by kind [i.e., nature]. That is to say, to be knit to God in spirit, and in onehead and accordance of will.[44]

Pseudo-Dionysius speaks of God as simple and without "quality." [45] The *Cloud*'s author says that we have to grow in simplicity in our apprehension of God, and that this means that we stop reflecting deliberately on his distinct and particular qualities, just as we are to grow in self-forgetfulness by ceasing to reflect deliberately on our own qualities: "In this work thou shalt have no more beholding of the qualities of the being of God than of the qualities of thine own being." [46] The *Cloud* speaks of a "naked intent unto God." [47] "Nakedness" in this context in fact means far more than simply the rejection of mental images. In keeping with that affective note which Augustinian theologians introduced into the apophaticism of Pseudo-Dionysius, the "naked intent" is synonymous with "a devout and a meek [humble] blind stirring of love." [48] In Book One of the *Ladder of Perfection* Walter Hilton sees the whole of the Christian moral life as implied in the "inclusive" virtues of humility and charity, and so does the author of the *Cloud*. Humility means that recognition of our creaturely and contingent status, dependent on God both for our existence and for every gift of grace, without which we stop the way by which God's grace may come to us. Charity, love of God and of our neighbor, is for the Christian the summary of the law. The author makes his own that definition of charity in Augustine's *Christian Doctrine*, familiar to all medieval theologians: "love of God for himself above all creatures, and of man for God even [i.e., equal] with thyself." [49] More precisely, charity is seen as the "chaste love" of which Bernard speaks, still on the basis of Augustine's teaching: the love of God for himself rather than for the benefits or rewards which he may give: [50]

> Although it be good to think upon the kindness of God, and to love him and praise him for it, yet it is far better to think upon the naked being of him, and to love him and praise him for himself.[51]

Similarly:

> A naked intent I call it. Because in this work a perfect prentice asketh neither releasing of pain, nor increasing of meed [i.e., reward], nor . . . nought but [God] himself. In so much that he neither recheth [i.e., cares] nor regardeth whether he be in pain or in bliss, but only that his will be fulfilled whom he loveth.[52]

The theme of "chaste," disinterested love of God for himself, occurs again in the little *Epistle of Prayer*,[53] as well as in the passage already referred to in the *Book of Privy Counselling*.[54]

It is sin that holds us back from the union with God for which we are made. The *Cloud*'s author, like Hilton, is against extremes of bodily austerity; he sees the interior disposition as far more effective in destroying the roots of sin than exaggerated outward penance:

> Beat evermore on this cloud of unknowing that is between thee and thy God with a sharp dart of longing love. . . . This only, by itself, is that work that destroyeth the ground and the root of sin. Fast thou never so much, watch thou never so

long, rise thou never so early . . . , all this would help thee
right nought. . . .[55]

Temptations to old habits of sin are to be put under the "cloud
of forgetting."[56] Since the author is no mere theoretician, but an
experienced and practical guide, he offers two suggestions as to how
pressing temptations to sin may be overcome. First, "try to look as
it were over their shoulders, seeking another thing, the which thing
is God. . . ." A second device, appealing to humility and to the
sense of the need of grace, matches the insight given to Paul (2
Corinthians 12:9) that God's strength is made perfect in weakness:

> When thou feelest that thou mayest in no wise put them [i.e.,
> temptations] down, cower them down under them as a caitiff
> and a coward overcome in battle, and think that it is but folly
> to strive any longer with them; and therefore thou yieldest
> thyself to God in the hands of thine enemies. . . . This
> meekness meriteth to have God himself mightily descending,
> to venge thee of thine enemies. . . .[57]

In keeping with this emphasis on the movement of love towards
God as an interior disposition, and as a detachment from all that
can appeal to the senses, the Cloud's author also shares with Hilton
a mistrust of the "enthusiasm" associated with followers of Richard
Rolle, if not with Rolle himself. Granted that it is a little unfair to
Rolle that he should be judged too much on the basis of some of
his more emotional writing in the Fire of Love, which for modern
English readers is the only one of his works that is readily available,
Rolle's Mending of Life, equally popular in the Middle Ages, to say
nothing of some of his other writings, does contain much wise and
balanced teaching on prayer and the Christian moral life. In the Fire
of Love Rolle lays great emphasis on sensible feelings of heat and
sweetness in the breast, in conjunction with devotion to the Holy
Name of Jesus, and to conscious and sensible participation in the
angels' praise of God. Other features of the book suggest a certain
emotional and spiritual immaturity, or at any rate a lack of the
peaceful wisdom which we find in Hilton and the Cloud: there is a
fear and awkwardness where women are concerned, and a bitterness
towards those whom Rolle holds to be materialistic (he sees cov-
etousness as the root sin), or who, in his opinion, have let him
down. Rolle has insisted in the Fire that anyone who is a genuine
lover of Jesus will never lose the sensible awareness of "heat, sweetness, and song." The Cloud, which is probably following Hilton at
this point, emphasizes that since the life of the spirit is supernatural,
and therefore not at any rate in the first instance something that

can fall under the cognizance of the senses, we should not attach too much importance to such sensible feelings as Rolle describes: the Yorkshire hermit is not actually named by either writer, but the implied reference is clear. The *Cloud* allows that there may be a certain "spiritual gladness" within the soul, which is bound up with true devotion, but anything that impinges on us from without—anything that theologians would call a corporeal or imaginary vision—should be treated with suspicion. Such visions are taken to be of angelic origin, but may be good or bad. Even if they are sent by a good angel, they are not to be treated as if they were ends in themselves or to be enjoyed for their own sake. Rather, since God is pure spirit, it is the "devout stirring of love," beyond all particular or distinct images, which alone unites us to him. This stirring of love is indeed not our work, or the work of any creature, including an angel; it is the work of God himself "without means," and therein lies our security from delusion.[58] There is indeed a place for sensible "sweetness" in religious experience; God deals with every soul according to its capacity and disposition, and so such "sweetness" may be given to weaker souls—or to those incapable of bodily penance due to their physical frailty—in order to help them on their way. Souls that are stronger in spirit do not need these consolations in order to offer their wills to God. But the writer leaves judgement to God: "Which of these be holier or more dear with God . . . God knoweth and I not." [59]

The writer warns against other distortions that militate against the growth of the inner life and conformity of the will to God. There is a lively chapter on disordered and unseemly gestures.[60] Indeed, the Devil has his own contemplatives, and he inflames their imagination with the fire of hell (in contrast to the fire of charity) so that in a spirit of pride they take it on themselves to condemn the sins of others without that discretion which springs from humility, charity, and proper insight.[61] Again, there are some who leave the "common doctrine and counsel" of the Church, and, lacking in the "meek blind feeling and virtuous living," they blaspheme all the saints, sacraments, statutes, and ordinances of the Church; this heresy, the author says, appeals to worldly men who think the Church's laws too hard.[62] He may well be thinking here of the Lollards; the reference to "blasphemy" against the saints and sacraments accords more closely with their outlook than with that of the heretics of the "free spirit," who would not "blaspheme" the sacraments so much as simply look on them as superfluous.

Conformity to the will of God is attained through humility and openness to the leading of the Spirit and to grace. The *Cloud* distinguishes between two kinds of humility, one imperfect, the other perfect. The first is in a sense self-centered, since it arises from the sense of our own sinfulness; the second looks beyond ourselves to the greatness and the love of God. The author is standing close to the traditional distinction between servile fear and filial fear of God. The first is based on fear of punishment for our sins, the second is based on fear of offending God's love. He is careful to say that in fact we can never out-grow the need to know that we are sinners; although the first kind of humility may be "imperfect," yet it remains indispensible.[63] Taking Mary Magdalene as the type of the penitent and the contemplative, he says that she knew well that she was the greatest of sinners, and yet the awareness that she had received a forgiveness which she could never possibly deserve was itself the most powerful incentive to look beyond herself to God in Christ, "in so much that she had often little special mind [i.e., awareness] whether she had ever been a sinner or not."[64] This loving self-abandonment to God is far from a spirit of moral indifference such as we associate with the Beghards; rather, it is a most efficacious means of conformity to God's will. Hilton, perhaps building on the Cloud's teaching, develops this in the second book of the Ladder of Perfection, and obviates even more emphatically than the Cloud any possibility that this might be interpreted in a quietist or antinomian direction.[65]

Thomas Aquinas had distinguished between two manners in the operation of grace: between "co-operant" grace, and "operant" grace.[66] While all grace is the unmerited gift of God, there is a progressive spontaneity in our response to grace as the obstacles in our will to its free operation are removed. Those who are led by the Spirit of God are the sons of God (Romans 8:14). "Co-operant" grace represents the deliberate conjunction of our will with grace; "operant" grace represents the free and spontaneous working of our will under grace, led by the Spirit, where all is experienced as God's work and we are not conscious of any distinct working of our own apart from grace. If the goal of the Christian life is conformity to the will of God, then Thomas' "operant grace" accurately describes this fulfillment. The Cloud's author, like Tauler and Ruysbroeck, distinguishes on the basis of Thomas' teaching between the movement of our will towards God "with means" (by "co-operant grace") and "without means" (by "operant grace"). The first entails the formation of distinct, mental concepts, through the exercise of meditation or through images impressed upon the mind by God; in the second, meditation as a deliberate exercise has given place to a simpler and more direct receptiveness to God's inspiration. We are made humble by God, as we are shown that though we may by grace dispose ourselves to receive the gift of the "work" that the Cloud describes—the "work" which opens our wills to God's service—yet it remains an utterly unmerited gift:

And if thou ask me by what means thou shalt come to this work, I beseech Almighty God of his great grace and his great courtesy to teach thee himself. . . . It is the work of only God, specially wrought in whatever soul he liketh, without any merit of the same soul. . . .

And yet he giveth not this grace, nor worketh this work, in a soul that is unable thereto. And yet there is no soul without this grace, which is able to have this grace: none, whether it be a sinner soul or an innocent soul. For it is neither given for innocence, nor withholden for sin. . . .

Wert thou verily meek thou shouldst feel about this work as I say: that God giveth it freely without any desert. . . . Forasmuch as thou willest it and desirest it, so much hast thou of it. . . . And yet is it no will, nor desire, but a thing thou knowest never what, that stirreth thee to will and desire thou knowest never what. . . .

Let it be the worker [i.e., active], and thou but the sufferer [i.e., passive]. . . . Meddle thee not therewith as though thou wouldst help it, for dread lest thou spill all. . . . Be blind in this time, and shear away desire of knowing, for it will more hinder thee than help thee. It sufficeth enough unto thee that thou feelest thyself stirred sweetly with a thing thou knowest never what, except that in thy stirring thou hast no special thought of anything under God, and that thine intent be nakedly directed unto God.

And if it be thus, trust then steadfastly that it is only God that stirreth thy will and thy desire, plainly by himself, without means either on his part or on thine. . . .[67]

In the approach to contemplation, we have to put aside deliberate reflection on particular attributes of God: "In this work it profiteth little or nought to think of the kindness or the worthiness of God . . . with a special beholding to them. . . ."[68] Meditation on human sin and on the Passion of Christ is indeed the essential way to come to contemplation; whoever thinks to come to contemplation without these, the writer says, will certainly be deceived and fail of his purpose. Yet even these have to be put behind under the "cloud of forgetting" after we have been long practiced in them. We are to fall back on the essentials of our experience of God as the Blessed Trinity: "Mean God that made thee, and bought thee, and that graciously hath called thee to this work. . . ." Yet even here there is a growth in simplicity: "And yet not all these, except you desire it; for a naked intent directed to God, without any other cause than himself, sufficeth wholly"—and the writer goes on to urge the use of a single short syllable in prayer, such as "God" or "Love." [69]

Does this mean that "contemplation" opens the way to some higher awareness of God, in which belief in the Incarnation and the Trinity can be superseded—that the distinctively Christian element in prayer can be lost in a sort of generalized mysticism? This is not at all the mind of the *Cloud's* author, any more than it was the mind of John of the Cross, with whose teaching his own has so many points of resemblance. He takes for granted the repetition of the Holy Name of Jesus, e.g. ". . . in the love of Jesus there shall be thine help." [70] Indeed, for all his emphasis on the rejection of particular images of God, when the *Cloud's* author speaks of "God" he always has in mind the God who is revealed in the incarnate Jesus. So Mary Magdalene, the typical contemplative ". . . regarded the sovereignest wisdom of his Godhead lapped in the dark words of his Manhood." [71]

In the *Book of Privy Counselling* he makes explicit what is taken for granted in the *Cloud*, that, as Augustine and Bernard had pointed out, there is a transition from attachment to our Lord's humanity—and love of the sensible consolations that this brings—to love of his divinity. We cannot come to Christ except by the way in which he chose to come to us, in his humanity; yet just as he said to his disciples (John 16:7) that his departure in the flesh was expedient for them, so it is necessary that we should not rest in attachment to him simply as man.[72] In the same way the writer appeals to the words of Christ in John 10:9, viz., that he is the door of the sheep-fold. In fact, he says, Christ is both the porter of the door, and the door: the porter by his divinity, the door by his humanity; and he points to John 10:1, that anyone who enters the sheep-fold except by the door is a thief and a robber. Just so, there is no way to Christian perfection and to contemplation but by the common way of the Church, through conformity to Christ in his humanity, Passion, and virtues.[73]

What the author describes, then, is no by-passing of the Christian and Trinitarian way, but a growth in simplicity within that way—a simplicity which is not superficial but costly—yet the work of grace. The deliberate exercise of the imagination and intellect is to be reduced as the habit of recollection enables us to come to God in Christ in a single movement of heart and will. Indeed, since intellect and will are bound up with each other, the "stripping" of the one from attachment to anything that is less than God implies the stripping of the other; the purification of the heart entails the stripping away of images that are less than God from the intellect, thus, the "chaste" love of God for himself and not for his consolations. Short, imageless prayer follows the teaching of Christ, viz. that whoever wants to follow him should deny himself, take up his cross and follow him (Matthew 16:24):

> This it is that setteth thee in silence, as well from thoughts as from words. This maketh thy prayer full short. In this thou art learned to forsake the world and to despise it. And—that more is—in this thou art learned to forsake and despise thine own self, according to the teaching of Christ . . . , *Si quis vult venire post me, abneget semetipsum.* . . .[74]

In keeping with the emphasis in Pseudo-Dionysius, the *Cloud* emphasizes the "active" element in our self-stripping; it is we who, through grace, put down all created things, including deliberate cerebral reflection on the distinct mysteries of our Lord's human life, under the cloud of forgetting. A chapter-heading shows how, on the basis of Pseudo-Dionysius, the author recognizes that neither sense nor intellectual operation can give us knowledge of God in himself: "That right as by the failing of our bodily wits we begin most readily to come to the knowing of ghostly things, so by the falling of our ghostly wits we begin most readily to come to the knowledge of God. . . ."[75] The logical consequences of this point are not, however, worked out with the rigor shown in John of the Cross.

But it is commonly recognized that in the way of purification there is, complementary to the "active" element, the more severe and painful "passive" element, in which God purifies us even apart from anything that we may will or do. In the pattern worked out by John of the Cross, which owes something to (among others) Pseudo-Dionysius as well as to empirical observation, there is the further division of the "passive" element into the purification or "night" of sense and of spirit. His "passive night of sense" represents the inability to meditate (discursively). We should note that for St. John of the Cross "meditation" was a more cerebral and analytical exercise than it was for the mediaevals; for the latter it was simply the fruit of prayerful Bible-reading or reflection on the mysteries of the Faith. Because for John of the Cross "meditation" is a deliberate mental exercise, it is to be expected that the change to a simpler approach— to a more directly God-given, "infused" prayer—will come as a more violent shock than it will to a less analytical soul. For John of the Cross, the "passive night of sense" coincides with the entry into the way of proficients, the illuminative way. The purpose is now no longer in the first instance to "mortify" the senses by stripping them of attachment to created things in order that we may feed more readily on God and things pertaining directly to his service; although the active mortification of the senses can never be left behind, sufficient progress has now been made in this for an advance to the next stage, which is to mortify the spiritual sources of sin—pride and the like: to cut down sin at the root. Moreover, if the inability to meditate has been a time of desolation and trial, in which we have been held to God through the infused virtues of faith, hope, and charity, this is not the last such trial that we may be called upon to endure; for souls advancing further towards union with God there will be far more terrifying trials, including, perhaps, the sense of forsakenness and divine hostility, in which God's light is experienced as darkness. In John of the Cross' teaching this trial is called the passive night of the spirit.[76] (John Tauler recognized such a second, more severe phase of trial, well on in the illuminative way, though he does not distinguish between a passive night of sense and of spirit as the Spanish saint does.[77]

It is natural, too, to make a comparison between the *Cloud* (and its related treatises) with Walter Hilton, who in Book Two of his *Ladder of Perfection*, though not in his earlier works, uses the Dionysian phrase "lightsome darkness." In fact, Hilton is not at all Dionysian in his theology; his "darkness" refers, as in Augustine and Gregory the Great, in most cases to the darkness of sin within man himself, and not to the darkness that surrounds the being of God by virtue of his transcendence. In the case of the "lightsome darkness" of *Ladder*, Book Two, the reference is to the pain within man caused by the process of doing to death habits of sin which in our lower nature we still find attractive, while man is not yet of sufficient purity of heart to receive God's illumination. Hilton may well have adopted the phrase under the influence of the *Cloud's* author, but in any case he radically changes its meaning; if one can say that the *Cloud's* doctrine has a modified Dionysian outlook, colored by the Latin tradition, not even this degree of Dionysian influence can be discerned in Hilton.[78] If the Augustinian and Thomist theology of grace is important in the *Cloud*, it is equally obvious in Hilton. Moreover, in distinction from the *Cloud's* author, Hilton shows familiarity with the *Remedies against Temptations* of the Augustinian friar William Flete. Flete writes on how God may allow us to experience a sense of desolation and trial in order that we may hold to him in faith, and how through this "passive" purification, brought on us by God for our own profit, we may be brought to greater conformity to God's will. Hilton's *Ladder of Perfection*, in both its parts, holds together the active and passive elements in our purification in a more even balance than the *Cloud*—with its more specialized and restricted scope—attempts to achieve.[79]

But in the *Book of Privy Counselling* the "passive" aspect also emerges as a necessary prelude to that docility to the will of God, which is the goal of the Christian life, and which the contemplative is expressly committed to seeking. No more than Hilton does the author explicitly distinguish even here between a passive night of sense and of spirit; it would be wrong to seek to impose too strictly the terminology of the sixteenth-century Carmelite John of the Cross upon the earlier English writers, for all the coincidence of experience and interpretation.[80] The writer describes how the signs of a call to simpler, contemplative prayer may be withdrawn, so that one is left in aridity, yet remains united to God through the supernatural virtues of faith and love, which remain despite the loss of conscious devotion. One notices too, in the description below an echo of that *vicissitudo*, or fluctuation, pictured by Bernard in his *Sermons on the Song of Songs*. There the soul is the bride of Christ, and in their wooing the apparent absences of the Bridegroom alternate with an ever deeper awareness of union: [81]

If . . . thou be left as though thou wert barren, thou thinkest, as well from the feeling of this new fervour as from thine old wonted work, so that thou thinkest thee fallen down betwixt the two . . . yet be not over heavy for this; but suffer meekly and bide patiently the will of our Lord. For now art thou in the ghostly sea . . . crossing over from bodilyness into ghostlyness. Many great storms and temptations, peradventure, shall rise in this time, and thou knowest never whither to run for sorrow. All is away from thy feeling, common grace and special. Be not overmuch afraid, then, although thou have matter, as thou thinkest; but have a lovely trust [MS reads: loue-trist] in our Lord, so little as thou mayest get for the time, for he is not far. He shall look up, peradventure, right soon and touch thee again with a more fervent stirring of that same grace than ever thou feltest any before. . . . Suddenly, or ever thou knowest, all is away and thou left barren in the boat, blown with blundering blasts now hither and now thither, thou knowest never where nor wither. Yet be not abashed; for he shall come, I promise thee, full soon, when he liketh, . . . far more worthily than ever he did before. Yes! and if he after go, after will he come again; and each time, if thou wilt bear thee by meek suffering, will he come more worthlier and merrylier than other. And all this he doth because he will have thee made as pliant to this will ghostly as a roan glove to thine hand bodily.[82]

I have referred at a number of points to similarity of doctrine between the *Cloud* (and Walter Hilton), the German and Flemish fourteenth-century mystics, and John of the Cross. Despite speculation to the contrary, no firm evidence has yet been adduced that John of the Cross knew the *Cloud* (or related works), or the works of Hilton. The suggestion that something of the English contemplative tradition may have permeated to Spain through the oral teaching of the Carmelite novitiate can be neither proved nor disproved. Again, no evidence has been found that the teaching of either Eckhart or Tauler was known in fourteenth-century England. Suso's *Horologium Sapientiae*—the Latin version of his *Book of Eternal Wisdom*—was known in England towards the end of the fourteenth century, and some of Ruysbroeck's work soon after. However, it was not the specifically mystical elements in these writers so much as the devotional commonplaces that appealed to the English authors who translated and borrowed from them, and this continental source is not the source of the *Cloud*'s doctrine. The traditional and orthodox (and partly Thomist) teaching on contemplation and the life of grace, which we find in the *Cloud* (and in Hilton), confirms the existence of circles in England where the monastic wisdom held firm, and where in the area of scholastic theology the understanding of grace as an intrinsic principle of supernatural life in the soul had not been affected by nominalist speculations; these speculations tended to see grace as a relationship towards God (or perhaps one should say, acceptance by God) without necessarily implying a new principle of life in the soul. John of the Cross certainly knew some of the teaching of Eckhart (which he received from Latin works passing under the name of Tauler), and for that matter some of the teaching of Tauler and Ruysbroeck, through Latin versions and compilations. The coincidences of doctrine between the English contemplatives and their Rhineland precursors on the one hand or the Carmelite Mystical Doctor on the other remain best understood as arising from a comparable experience interpreted in the light of a common tradition that includes elements from Augustine, Gregory the Great, Bernard, Thomas Aquinas, and (in the case of *Cloud* and John of the Cross) Pseudo-Dionysius as interpreted and modified in the Latin tradition.[83]

BIBLIOGRAPHICAL NOTES

Readers beginning a study of the *Cloud of Unknowing* and its tradition will find the following helpful:

Texts

Hodgson, Phyllis, ed. *The Cloud of Unknowing and the Book of Privy Counselling*, EETS OS 218 (London, 1944) (=*Cloud*); *Deonise Hid Diuinite* and *Other Treatises on Contemplative Prayer*, EETS OS 231 (London, 1955) (=*D.H.D.*); Prof. Hodgson has issued an abridgment and part-revision of the EETS editions as: *The Cloud of Unknowing and related Treatises*, Analecta Cartusiana 3 (Salzburg, 1982).

Modernized Editions

McCann, Dom Justin. *The Cloud of Unknowing and Other Treatises* (London, 1952).
Walsh, James, ed. *The Cloud of Unknowing* (Ramsey, NJ, and London, 1981).
Wolters, Clifton C. *The Cloud of Unknowing and Other Works* (London, 1973).
———. *A Study of Wisdom* (Oxford, 1980).
NOTE: In this article I have cited Abbot McCann's version, having checked it against Prof. Hodgson's text. In the footnotes I have given references to both Hodgson (=H) and, where appropriate, McCann (=M). For works not in McCann's edition I have produced my own lightly modernized version of Hodgson's text.

Studies

Clark, John P.H. "The *Cloud of Unknowing*, Walter Hilton and St. John of the Cross: a Comparison." *Downside Review*, 96 (1978), 281–98.
———. "Sources and Theology in the *Cloud of Unknowing*." *Downside Review*, 98 (1980), 83–109.
Hodgson, Phyllis. "Walter Hilton and the *Cloud of Unknowing*." *Modern Language Review*, 50 (1955), 396–406.
Johnston, William. *The Mysticism of the Cloud of Unknowing*. New York, 1967.
Knowles, Dom David. *The English Mystical Tradition*. London, 1961

XIII

Nicholas of Cusa's
The Vision of God

CLYDE LEE MILLER

Nicholas of Cusa (1401–64) has been one of the least well-known and appreciated thinkers of the early Renaissance, at least among English-language readers. Born in the town of Cues on the Moselle River, he was educated at Heidelberg and Padua and Cologne. As a canon lawyer he attended the council of Basel where he began a public career of struggle for Church reform and unity among feuding ecclesiastical factions. He traveled to Constantinople in 1437 to prepare for the council of Ferrara. During the following ten years he traveled as papal legate to Germany to work for reform. Pope Nicholas V made him a cardinal in 1448. In 1450 he was appointed bishop of Brixen (Bressanone) in South Tyrol, where he clashed with Archduke Sigismond over local church reforms. Called back to Italy and the papal curia by Pius II in 1458, Nicholas remained there until his death at Todi.

Cusanus' career involved much more than his work as ecclesiastical statesman and reformer. His varied writings show that he was abreast of all the learning and intellectual ferment of his times. A true Renaissance man, Nicholas was acquainted with the humanists and the revival of classical letters, but made his own contributions in mathematics, astronomy, and cosmology. His major writings are theological and philosophical in character. Paradoxically, the center of his original speculation was traditionally medieval, the relation of God and creatures. Nicholas drew especially from Neoplatonic sources—thinkers such as Proclus, Pseudo-Dionysius, Scotus Eri-

293

ugena, and Augustine. He transformed what he inherited from these predecessors, as well as from Thierry of Chartres, Raymond Lull, and Meister Eckhart, employing even borrowed terminology and hallowed formulae for his own theoretical purposes. His theoretical treatises and dialogues should be read as so many speculatively imaginative variations on the theme of God's inconceivable infinite oneness and its "contracted" manifestation in created things.

Given the breadth of his learning, intellectual interests, and commitment to religion, it is hardly surprising that Nicholas was also familiar with the tradition of Christian contemplation and mystical theology. In 1453 he sent his short treatise, *The Vision of God, or The Icon*, to the Benedictine monks at Tegernsee in Austria after repeated requests from their abbot. That Nicholas himself was a mystic is open to question, though he recounts the decisive insight about "learned ignorance" *(docta ignorantia)* in language akin to that used in accounts of mystical experience.[1] And while his other works often touch on mystical knowledge and its divine object, Nicholas states explicitly that the purpose of *The Vision of God* is to "open an easy path unto mystical theology" (1E, 94L).[2] This essay will concentrate on *The Vision of God* in order to bring out the main points of Cusanus' doctrine on mystical theology.

The Vision of God does not recount Nicholas' own mystical experiences in an autobiographical way. In the book he propounds no practical or theoretical treatise about the stages of growth in prayer or the exercises required for reaching mystical experience. Nicholas does speak of mystical knowledge or vision as a human phenomenon and offers some advice (mostly warnings) to those who desire to see God. But his constant and most important focus throughout is the infinite God as the object of mystical vision and the sort of not-seeing that alone can "see" such a God. After his introductory pages Nicholas writes the whole in the mode of personal prayer reminiscent of Augustine's *Confessions*. Because this is teaching, cast in prayer form, we may come to share in a more intimate way both Cusanus' inquiry into mystical theology and his own yearning to see the God beyond. Just the prayer form itself lets us realize that to teach in and through praying is to acknowledge the priority of God's reality and graciousness to human creatures, whether we are exploring the nature of what the mystic seeks, or taking up the human response to the loving God.

As so often in his writings, Nicholas' treatise uses a striking object lesson with a painting to symbolize and make palpably concrete what he has to say about God's relationship to those who seek him. From this exercise in visual thinking Nicholas draws a series of prayerful reflections about the God who attracts humans and the extraordinary knowledge humans who respond may receive. God's reality and human vision are framed in peculiarly Cusan terms—a metaphysics of God's unlimited or "absolute" oneness and creatures' limited or "contracted" otherness, a corresponding restriction of human knowledge to "ignorance" regarding God, and an interpretation of Christ Jesus as mediator. Nicholas' own order of exposition in *The Vision of God* should provide a helpful introduction to his distinctive ideas about mystical theology.

Cusanus uses the preface and first three chapters of his book to explain how the painting is a symbol or icon of the relation between God and the soul. He elaborates both sides of this relationship through chapters four to nine, each time turning to the painting for some aspect of seeing or being seen. Chapters ten through thirteen turn to more abstract considerations of this God who is beyond normal religious experience and typical theological discourse. Nicholas wants his readers to understand and even reach that "learned ignorance" required to "see" the divine reality placed by Nicholas beyond "the coincidence of opposites." In chapters fourteen through eighteen he speaks of God's infinity, unity, and trinity in moving terms and explains Jesus' place as mediator of vision and union with God in the final chapters of the book.

FIRST LESSONS FROM THE ICON

Nicholas sent a painted portrait with *The Vision of God*, directing the monks to use the painting as an icon of the vision of God. "Vision of God" is a deliberately ambiguous title phrase. It stands for both God's all-seeing gaze upon, or vision of, human creatures, and for our human vision or mystical sighting of God. The painting he sent to Tegernsee modeled both meanings. The portrait was painted in such a way that its eyes seemed to look directly into each viewer's eyes, no matter how many people looked at the painting at a given time and no matter where each stood to view it. And when one walked past it, the painting's stationary eyes never left the moving viewer's gaze. For Nicholas, these features of the omnivoyant painting symbolize aspects of the mutual relation of God and the soul. In the Platonic tradition images are used in conscious awareness that they are images. We are to "see through" them to the original or exemplar they reflect and manifest. Nicholas was surely intrigued that the painting he wanted to image God's vision already was a portrait or image of another reality, a human face.

But there are qualifications and adjustments to be made if we are to understand looking at the painting (looking at us) as an icon of God's vision and our response. The painted face does not see at all;

its apparent gaze into onlookers' eyes is an illusion. But God's vision *is* omnivoyant: every person and, indeed, all created things, are objects of his infinite knowledge at one and the same time. We may imagine the painting's eyes as looking at us before we notice them, but in fact God's gaze encompasses all persons whether they advert to God or not. While the portrait's vision seems capable of more than ordinary human eyesight, we have to discard even the limits of these painted eyes to understand God's vision. God's gaze is no more like human visual perception than the portrait's seems to be.

The painting's gaze appears to vary while staying unchanged, to move while being fixed, to look simultaneously on every viewer as if each were its sole object. So it is with God's vision of created things, yet the divine vision so far surpasses this icon that Nicholas terms it "absolute." He gives this word its etymological sense of the Latin *ab-solvere*, to "loosen or free from." God's vision is "freed from" every restriction or limitation in even the most perfect vision or knowledge we might imagine or conceive. Human visual perception is limited (Nicholas' word is *contractus*, "restricted, contracted") to the particularities of time, place, viewpoint, object or focus, plus other standard conditions of light, color, contrast, distance, visual acuity and health, and so on. God is omnivoyant in a way that includes but surpasses all the knowledge we term vision—from sense perception to intellectual insight—in a way already utterly perfect and "absolute."

And all created ways of seeing have reality only because of God's absolute vision. Just viewing the painting is an activity dependent on God's sustaining reality. Human perception of the icon itself exists in God as nothing else than God, whose causal activity as creator sets the limits we find in all the varied modes of created seeing. This ontological reminder underscores the deepest connection Nicholas sees between mystical vision and the rest of reality—in both, God's action comes first, preceding all created beings, their activity, and, *a fortiori*, all created response to God. This priority is not simply historical or temporal but ontological; without God there can be no other reality at all.

These initial considerations circumscribe Nicholas' subsequent discussion. He has a normative view of God's nature, partly inherited from earlier thinkers, partly the outcome of his own speculation. So he is anxious that it be this God, not some lesser putative deity, to whom human seekers direct their efforts. In fact, the Cusan God is perfect simpleness, even though our talk about God may suggest he is complex or manifold. In God those aspects we distinguish as we think and talk are not really diverse. Therefore,

. . . any one of His attributes is affirmed of another, and to have is with God to be, and to move is to stand, and to run is to rest, and so with the other attributes. . . . Yet because He is Himself the Absolute Ground, in which all otherness is unity, and all diversity is identity, that diversity which is not identity proper, to wit, diversity as we understand it, cannot exist in God. (12–13E, 102L)

What we say, therefore, about God's vision as we reflect on the icon is simply not true of God in the ways we are likely to imagine as possible. The illusion created by the painter whereby the depicted eyes appear omnivoyant may well parallel the illusions normal human thought fashions for itself in attempting to conceptualize and understand God's own "vision." In each case the illusions point up the limitations of painted eyesight and natural human insight. The Cusan God, the God of authentic mystical theology, resides beyond all such illusions and every limitation.[3]

TURNING TOWARD GOD'S LOVING GAZE

Chapters four through nine of *The Vision of God* spell out both sides of the human person's relationship to God as this leads to mystical vision. God's attracting love precedes, the human soul turns toward God, seeks and is helped to find the transcendent God beyond the ordinary realm of thought and language. Chapters four through six lead up to the kind of "not-knowing" involved in mystical vision; the next three chapters culminate in a mysterious God beyond the "coincidence of opposites." All six chapters provide an introduction to the complementary Cusan themes of "learned ignorance" and "the coincidence of opposites" as these bear on mystical vision.

Nicholas throughout acknowledges the priority of God's seeing for nature and for grace, but he here underscores human freedom to turn toward or away from God as well. "And this power, which I have of Thee, wherein I possess a living image of Thine almighty power, is free will" (16E, 106L). Just as the icon's eyes follow the onlooker's only if the latter looks at the painting, so God's loving care for each individual is fully effective only when the soul attends to God, "when all my endeavor is turned toward Thee because all Thy endeavor is turned toward me" (17E, 106L). No less than the icon are we human beings God's images. However, persons are not depictions but living images; that is, human beings can grow and develop by choosing or not to become more receptive of God's grace and goodness.

The human situation is thus one where each man and woman is already anticipated by a God whose loving concern constantly invites and elicits human response. "Thou art present before I turn unto Thee" (22E, 110L), writes Nicholas, "If, therefore, I have rendered myself by all possible means like unto Thy goodness, then according to the degree of that likeness, I shall be capable of the truth" (16E, 104L). In chapter seven he attributes to God words which urge us to choose the likeness and therein the divine truth:

> Nay more, how wilt Thou give me Thyself if Thou has not given me mine own self also? . . . Thou, Lord, makest reply within my heart, saying: Be thou thine and I too will be thine. —O Lord, Thou Sweetness most delectable, Thou hast left me free to be mine own self, if I desire. Hence, if I be not mine own self, Thou art not mine, for Thou dost make freewill needful, since Thou canst not be mine if I be not mine own. Since Thou hast thus left me free, Thou dost not constrain me, but Thou awaitest that I should choose to be mine own. (31–32E, 120L)

To turn and seek God in mystical and beatific vision is thus a matter of human choice; what is remarkable in the above passage is that to choose and love God is at once to choose and love oneself. Consent to and acceptance of oneself as God's image is required ("according to the degree of that likeness") to move toward the divine original, "the truth" of oneself and of all other things.

THE DARKNESS BEYOND

In chapter six, Cusanus proposes that the painting's face, no less than its eyes, may symbolize God's vision of created thing: "Thy glance, Lord, is Thy face" (24E, 112L). God's face and its radiant beauty thus stand as the absolute measure and paradigm for all created faces and their beauty. When I look upon God's face, I see myself in the original after which my face is patterned. But if I stop there, I constrict divinity to what I find of myself in God and I thus conceptualize God in too human a way, understanding the divine original after the fashion of its limited human image.

But how is a person to move beyond such limits to see God, "beyond all faces, and all likenesses and figures of all faces, and all concepts which can be formed of a face, and all color, adornment, and beauty of all faces" (26E, 114L) ? Cusanus' answer provides both warning and rule: "Wherefore he that goes forward to behold Thy face, *so long as he formeth any concept thereof, is far from Thy face*" (26E, 114L; emphasis added). To believe that mystical vision will produce some conceptual realization of *what* God is would be a blunder. Rather, a person has to enter "a certain secret and hidden silence," a "mist, cloud, darkness or ignorance." God's face remains hidden before this point, but this dark obscurity ironically "reveals Thy face to be there, beyond all veils" (26–27E, 115–16L).

To see the divine face unveiled we have to come to that dark place of the spirit where we can no longer see reflections or images of God, even our own ideas of God. Nothing else than the brilliance and beauty of God's face causes the experience of obscure not-knowing in which God is truly near. Cusanus recalls the ancient Platonic analogy of the blinding face of the sun to drive home his point.

> A man seeking to see a light beyond his seeing knoweth that, so long as he seeth aught, it is not that which he seeketh. Wherefore it behoveth him to go beyond all visible light. For him, then, who must go beyond all light, the place he entereth must needs lack visible light, and is thus, so to speak, darkness to the eye. And while he is in that darkness which is a mist, if he then knows himself to be in a mist, he knoweth that he hath drawn nigh the face of the sun; for that mist in his eyes proceedeth from the exceeding bright shining of the sun. . . . 'Tis thus and not otherwise, Lord, that the light inaccessible, the beauty and radiance of Thy face, may, unveiled, be approached. (27E, 116L)

This vivid imagery is a concrete explanation of what Nicholas means by "learned ignorance." Such ignorance comes from realizing or learning that one does not see or understand in the usual ways (where there is "visible light") what God is. Such ignorance includes the awareness that "in that darkness" one blindly sees what surpasses the objects of typical human seeing and knowledge. Cusanus has moved in a series of dramatic steps from God's vision and God's face to our seeing ourselves in God's face to our "seeing" in darkness that we do not see because of the "radiance" of God's face—a face revealed only beyond verbal and conceptual "seeing."

In chapter nine Nicholas begins by again paralleling the icon and God's gaze. God's vision is one with his essence and the divine essence "pervades" *(penetrat)* every finite being, just as his glance encompasses them all. Seeing God as "the essential being of beings" is "seeing . . . the Absolute in the limited, like the cause in the effect, and the truth and exemplar in the image" (41E, 130L). God is the original source from whom come all finite images of the divine; that is, God is their sustaining efficient cause and exemplary formal cause. But God is not to be identified with any finite being's nature or activity, and not with its seeing, movement, or rest as we know them.

> For if both motion and rest be individuated at the same time in divers beings, and if naught can exist apart from Thee, and no motion be apart from Thee, nor any rest; then Thou, Lord, art wholly present to all these things, and to each, at one and the same time. And yet Thou dost not move nor rest, since Thou art exalted above all, and freed from all that can be conceived or named. Wherefore, Thou standest and proceedest, and yet at the same time dost not stand or proceed. . . . [Thy face] is above all standing or motion, in simplest and absolute infinity; and 'tis on the hither side of this infinity that are found motion, and rest, and their opposition, and whatever may be uttered or conceived. (42E, 130L)

Several crucial points should be noted about this passage. First, Nicholas points both to God's immanence ("wholly present to all") and to the divine transcendence ("exalted above all, and freed"). In other words, God's causal efficacy regarding created things does not mean that God is just one more thing or being as are the beings he creates and sustains in existence. Second, Nicholas explains that this divine freedom "from all that can be conceived or named" implies that God is not subject to the limitations we recognize when we contrast motion and rest in discussing created things which move. Paradoxically, it is true to say God moves and God does not move *and* it is false to say God moves and does not move! ("Thou standest and proceedest, and yet at the same time dost not stand or proceed.") Simultaneous contradictory judgments about God's connection with created things moving or not moving are valid.[4]

Third, we are to learn that this is what happens to our language and thought when we attempt to deal with God. The underlying reason for the anomaly, paradox, and contradiction is God's "simplest and absolute infinity." But absolute simpleness and infinity hardly explain or allow for some positive grasp of what God is; they become alternate verbal pointers that lead the mind toward God, just as do paradox and contradiction. Fourth, in spite of the cognitive frustration we must feel, Nicholas remains convinced that mystical vision is not beyond human competence (with God's help); rather it is beyond normal human reason as the typical source and comfortable home of distinctions, contrasts, and oppositions ("the hither side of infinity"). Such reasoning is required for making our way in the natural and human world. Here the principle of contradiction is the basic law for literal thought and discourse ("whatever may be conceived and uttered"). But seeing God in darkness requires moving toward the realm of the infinite and thus learning how not to think of God as one among other beings.

In this vein Nicholas continues:

> Hence I observe how needful it is for me to enter into the darkness, and to admit the coincidence of opposites, beyond all grasp of reason, and there to seek the truth where impossibility meeteth me. And beyond that, beyond even the highest ascent of intellect, when I shall have attained unto that which is unknown to every intellect, and which every intellect judgeth to be most far removed from truth, there, my God, art Thou, who art Absolute Necessity. And the more that dark impossibility is recognised as dark and impossible, the more truly doth His Necessity shine forth, and is more unveiledly present, and draweth nigh. (43E, 132L)

Here Cusanus joins learned ignorance and the coincidence of opposites. The special ignorance results from a learning process here described as culminating in human acceptance of what seems impossible: contradictory statements ("that dark impossibility") signal the truth and presence of God. What cannot be valid in the ordinary thought of human beings must be valid "beyond all grasp of reason." What reason finds impossible is exactly what is necessary in God since the infinite simpleness encompasses as nothing else than God all that human reason classifies as impossible and as necessary.

PARADISE WALLED

At the end of chapter nine, Nicholas introduces a way to map an imaginary region on which to locate his discussion of mystical knowledge and its divine object. Using a motif that recalls the story of Eden after Adam's expulsion (Genesis 3:23–24), Cusanus speaks of God as dwelling in paradise, walled round by the coincidence of opposites!

> Thou hast inspired me, Lord, who art the Food of the strong, to do violence to myself, because impossibility coincideth with necessity, and I have learnt that the place wherein Thou art found unveiled is girt round with the coincidence of contradictories, and this is the wall of Paradise wherein Thou dost abide. The door whereof is guarded by the most proud spirit of Reason, and, unless he be vanquished, the way in will not lie open. Thus 'tis beyond the coincidence of contradictories that Thou mayest be seen, and nowhere this side thereof. If, then, in Thy sight, Lord, impossibility be

necessity, there is naught that Thy sight seeth not. (43–44E, 132L)

What is impossible for human reason is thus imaged concretely as a wall defended by reason itself in angelic guise. For reason's pride—the principle of contradiction—must be overcome, the wall must be crossed so that the mystical quest achieve its goal of seeing God, of reaching paradise. The next several chapters of *The Vision of God* (chapters 10–13) make constant reference to this image of paradise walled, as Nicholas proposes various ways of attempting to "think through" the coincidence of opposites and move to the God within.[5]

Chapter ten imagines a door or entryway in the wall where the angel of reason stands guard. Nicholas locates some first examples of opposites coinciding at this entrance. Turning again to the icon, he points out that from our viewpoint God's seeing is different from his being seen, but that in God they are identical in the divine gaze that creates and supports our seeing. In fact, the oppositions we make and the distinctions we draw between sensing and being sensed are matters of discursive human thought; in God's simpleness there are no such contrasts or oppositions, just utter oneness.

> For Thou art there where speech, sight, hearing, taste, touch, reason, knowledge, and understanding are the same, and where seeing is one with being seen, and hearing with being heard, and tasting with being tasted, and touching with being touched, and speaking with hearing, and creating with speaking. (46–47E, 134L)

Nicholas is next reminded how God's creating and speaking coincide with his power or concept (conceiving) in eternal identity. He wonders rhetorically how created things come into being in temporal succession when God conceives them but once from all eternity. In answer Cusanus imagines himself approaching the doorway of the coincidence of opposites: "Thou dost enlighten me while I am on the threshold of the door, showing me that Thy concept is pure and simple eternity itself" (48E, 136L). His explanation is traditional: earlier and later are temporal characterizations of the things created, not of God's creative conceiving. God's concept encompasses in strict identity all things that occur in historical succession. "Thus, because Thou art God Almighty, Thou dwellest within the wall of Paradise, and this wall is that coincidence where later is one with earlier, where the end is one with the beginning, where Alpha and Omega are the same" (49E, 136L).

In chapter eleven, Cusanus combines the analogy of a clock and his own technical terms for interpreting creation, "unfolding" (*ex-*

plicatio) and "enfolding" *(complicatio)*. The clock's single mechanism "enfolds" all its successive movements, and those regular movements "unfold" all that the clock is capable of as a timepiece. God's eternity similarly enfolds all temporal succession in one eternal now; the moments of historical time are the unfolding of the divine eternity. So created beings in their multiplicity and finite otherness unfold God's creative oneness on which they depend. That same creative power enfolds them all in God's simpleness as identical with God.

Nicholas next locates enfolding and unfolding in relation to the wall of the coincidence of opposites. "I return again to find Thee beyond the wall of the coincidence of enfolding and unfolding, and as I go in and go out by this door of Thy word and Thy concept, I find sweetest nourishment" (53E, 140L). Unfolding, or going out, is moving from divine cause to created effect; going in, or enfolding, is returning from effects to cause. For Nicholas, these opposite movements coincide, since unfolding and enfolding are inseparable. Thus each creature is an unfolding of God's oneness; its being is not God's being yet it is not separable from God in the way it is distinct from other creatures. As God's image it reflects God's enfolding oneness and depends on God's sustaining power to be what it is. If we turn to the creator, there all created things are enfolded in utter oneness— in God they are nothing but God. But Nicholas presses beyond this coincidence to within the wall.[6]

To follow Cusanus here involves three stages of seeing how enfolding and unfolding apply to God and creatures. These stages correspond to the soul's movement from ordinary light into the darkness where mystical vision occurs. First, to take unfolding as distinct from enfolding is to distinguish creatures from their ontological source or creator. Second, to identify unfolding and enfolding is to understand that opposites coincide in God's oneness while thinking God and creature together. This is the wall where opposites coincide and unfolding is not separate from enfolding, where any limited thing that unfolds God's oneness is only fully understood and seen for all it is in relation to that enfolding oneness. Third, to place God beyond unfolding and enfolding as understood in the first two stages is to assert God's transcendence beyond the coincidence of opposites, to point beyond the wall toward the God who is incomprehensible, "set free from all that can be spoken or thought" (ibid.).

Chapter twelve's title announces two paradoxes that Nicholas pursues along similar lines: how God is invisibly visible and uncreated creator. In their straightforward sense these expressions may mean that God is "visible" in what he creates but remains invisible in himself; God is creator of other things but is himself uncaused.

Nicholas presses further. God is both seer and seen in his absolute vision: identically the one who sees, the visible object, and the seeing all at the same time. In the divine transcendent power, God is both created and uncreated: identically the one who creates, the "creatable," and the creating. All that is possible is thus actual in God. That we cannot think such distinctions as identical points again toward where God is to be found—beyond human comprehension. And Nicholas also underscores God's ontological priority and causal presence in regard to created things while denying that God is limited as they are. "And creating and being created alike are naught else than the sharing of Thy Being among all, that Thou mayest be All in all, and yet mayest abide free from all" (56E, 144L).

Nicholas ends chapter twelve by returning to the analogy of the wall. To say God creates is to stand outside the wall; to see God as both creating and creatable is to arrive at the wall of contradiction but not yet to have entered Paradise.

> But when I behold Thee as Absolute Infinity, to whom is befitting neither the name of creating Creator nor of creatable Creator—then indeed I begin to behold Thee unveiled, and to enter in to the garden of delights! . . . albeit without Thee naught is made or can be made, Thou art not a Creator, but infinitely more than Creator; unto Thee be praise and glory through endless ages. Amen. (57E, 144L)

INSIDE THE WALL

The center chapter of the twenty-five in *The Vision of God* is chapter thirteen; here the movement of the first half of the treatise culminates in what lies beyond the wall of the coincidence of opposites: God's absolute infinity. In this domain the soul does not know what it sees; it merely realizes that God is not visible or knowable in any human way familiar outside the wall. This divine presence cannot be named or conceived or grasped in any analogy. For Nicholas, all names and concepts end at the wall surrounding Paradise; that is, their sense cannot apply in a domain of thought where the principle of contradiction is no longer valid, where the object of thought is inconceivable. This is precisely to place God beyond human grasp, for only there can we contact God. Cusanus sums the human side of the situation as follows:

> But how shall he attain unto Thee who art the End toward whom he striveth, if he must ascend above the end? He who ascendeth above the end, doth he not enter into what is undefined and confused, and thus, in regard to the intellect,

into ignorance and obscurity, which pertain to intellectual confusion? It behoveth, then, the intellect to become ignorant and to abide in darkness if it would fain see Thee. But what, O my God, is this intellectual ignorance? Is it not an instructed ignorance *(docta ignorantia)*? Thou, God, who art infinity, canst only be approached by him whose intellect is in ignorance, to wit, by him who knows himself to be ignorant of Thee. (59–60E, 146L)

This ignorance or darkness is the human side of mystical encounter; what it sees or encounters is the incomprehensible divine infinity. Here human reason *(ratio)* is blind and mute, ignorant because confronted with what is beyond conceptual understanding. Nicholas teaches that at this point mental "vision" or intuition *(intellectus)* may come into play. As he puts this later in chapter seventeen, "The wall is a barrier to the power of every intellect, albeit the eye penetrate beyond it into Paradise. But what it there seeth it cannot tell nor understand . . ." (84E, 172L). In his earlier dialogue entitled *The Layman: About Mind*, Cusanus described this special ability of the human mind as a direct intuition of "absolute entity itself beyond all participation and variety." [7] In *The Vision of God* Nicholas refers to it as the vision or seeing that occurs beyond the wall of the coincidence of opposites, a vision whose object and content remain unavailable for later speech or conceptualization.

Chapter thirteen exhibits the paradoxical expressions that remain Cusanus' favored way of pointing toward absolute infinity. Nicholas plays with the Latin root of "infinite"—*finis. Finis* means "end" in the twofold sense of limit and of goal. God may be described as "infinite end" *(finis infinitus)* or as its equivalent, "end without end" *(finis sine fine)*. God is without limit or restriction of any sort and he has no goal outside divinity. Nothing limits God, yet as creative source and final goal he sets the limits for all other things: "without end" himself, God is "end" for all other beings.

In God's infinity not only can there be an end without end, but a contradiction without contradiction and an opposition without opposition. Nicholas writes, "therein [in God] the opposition of opposites is an opposition without opposition, just as the end of things finite is an end without an end" (61–62E, 148L). These riddling phrases are attempts to let us think God and creatures together without distorting either side of the relationship. God is opposed to creatures in that he is not one of them and he is the cause of all the differences or oppositions among creatures (thus God is the "opposition of oppositions"). At the same time in God's infinite oneness all such oppositions are reconciled or "coincide" in God's oneness. So God is also "an opposition without opposition." [8]

Nicholas stresses this latter point, "Infinity, accordingly, existeth, and enfoldeth all things, and naught can exist outside it, hence naught is alien to it or differing from it. Thus infinity is alike all things and no one of them all" (62E, 150L). In all Neoplatonic Christian thinkers, no limited or derived reality can be understood for what it is without accounting for its relation to the first or ultimate principle from which it derives. For Cusanus finite beings and the infinite God cannot be separated and dealt with adequately; neither can they be identified or amalgamated without distorting both sides. Whichever we begin with, God's unfolding and enfolding must finally be thought together. But as absolute infinity, God is all things as nothing else but himself in the divine enfolding. It is this that human discursive reason cannot comprehend, that infinite oneness available only in vision.

At this point the Cusan doctrine of the coincidence of opposites should not be misinterpreted. Whether Nicholas says that in God opposites coincide or that God is beyond the coincidence of opposites, the ontological import of either expression is the same: the absolute infinity of God remains utterly one and simple.[9] In God there is no diversity or multiplicity or otherness at all. All the created things and their characteristics with which human reason deals by distinction, contrast, and contradiction are in God eternally and identically one with God's simpleness. In this way Nicholas' imaginative schema of outside the wall, in the wall or at its entrance, and inside the wall of the coincidence of opposites points rather to the human side of approaching God. In this way the wall stands for what is beyond the grasp of human reason and attempting to think through paradoxes and contradictions as these apply to God at least sets us in the correct direction and lets us acknowledge that here we are ignorant. God is incomprehensible and beyond any proportion we might propose to understand him in human fashion. Placing God beyond the wall in imagination is a way of recognizing the darkness and unknowing state of reason (ratio) in the face of contradiction. Only when discursive reason is set aside can God's gift of the vision occur.

TRINITARIAN AND INCARNATE LOVE

In a way Nicholas' exploration of mystical vision may seem complete at the middle of his treatise. Chapters fourteen and fifteen work through God's simpleness and oneness as corollaries to his infinity. But in fifteen there is a sudden change from the rather abstruse discussion of the previous six or seven chapters as Nicholas begins to stress the affective side of both God's attracting and human responding. Nicholas turns to the revelation of the Trinity and the Incarnation as manifesting God's love and goodness in drawing us to himself. Heartfelt warmth and affection pervade Nicholas' prayerful teaching as he reflects on the mysteries of faith.

But this is more than pious orthodoxy, however authentic. By the middle of *The Vision of God* Nicholas has shown the impotence of reason for encountering God. No human words or concepts or analogies enable us to touch or grasp or understand even partially what God is. Reason is at an impasse, for God abides beyond. But God himself offers help in our cognitive frustration by revealing the Trinity of loving persons and manifesting what is beyond our ken in the human nature of Jesus. Here is a mediator to help us see and be united with the God we desire but cannot fathom. Little wonder that Nicholas seems to let go of the straining paradoxes and respond with wonder, gratitude, and praise.

This shift begins in chapter fifteen where Nicholas returns to the portrait and then recalls how God's gaze can seem a mirror in which the soul sees just itself, as if its divine original were no different from any mirror's reflection of its viewer. In fact the human viewer is looking on his or her "true type" or exemplar in the divine gaze and is but the image or semblance of the divine face. In a similar way God's gaze follows his creature just as its own shadow does, but it is creatures who are shadows and God light. Or rather, since God is light and truth, he sustains both his creaturely shadows and mirror images without suffering their limitations.

Nicholas sees this also as manifesting God's attitudes to those who turn toward his gaze. Out of goodness and kindness God adapts himself to us so that we can love more easily what seems familiar— our own selves in their original—and come to love the truth of ourselves that is God.

> In Thee, God, being created is one with creating, since the image which seemeth to be created by me is the Truth which createth me. So that thus I may at least comprehend how closely I ought to be knit unto Thee, since in Thee being loved is one with loving. For if I ought to love myself in Thee who art my likeness, I am most especially constrained thereto when I see that Thou lovest me as Thy creature and Thine image. How can a father not love a son who is alike father and son? (75E, 160–62L)

Cusanus again turns to love when he takes up the Trinity. Borrowing from Augustine's *On the Trinity*, he points out that the reality of love includes lover, beloved, and their connection or, again, the one loving, the loveable one, and their union.[10] No less is true in the case of God where all limits fall away and lover, loveable, and their union are one and the same divine essence in the triune divinity. Nicholas entitles chapter seventeen "How God, Unless He Were One and Three, Could Not Be Perfectly Seen." In explanation he turns again to the parallel with love of oneself.

> Thou, Lord, grantest me to see in Thee love, because I see myself as lover. And seeing that I love myself I see myself as loveable, and myself to be the most natural bond between the twain: I am lover, I am loveable, I am bond. . . . Suppose, then, that my love were my essence, as 'tis in my God—then in the unity of my essence there would exist the unity of all three constituents aforesaid, and in their trinity, the unity of my essence: all would exist in limitation in my essence, after the manner in which I perceive them to exist truly and absolutely in Thee. (84–85E, 172L)

In the human image Nicholas thus discovers something of the divine original. Human love reveals distinction without loss of oneness as a faint reflection of love within the Trinity.

Nicholas puts this analysis of the Trinity as love between two chapters on human desire and human happiness. In the first human desire and longing are analyzed as without limits and hence only to be satisfied by a God who is unlimited. In the second, God is our happiness (felicitas) just because he draws us to himself as triune love. Vision and love of God are borne on intellectual desire which nothing finite can satisfy. Only in the infinite triune love who has first loved us will we discover happiness.

Nicholas again praises this divine love which in its generosity awaits human response. "But Thou art so magnanimous, my God, that Thou willest reasoning souls to be free to love Thee or not" (89E, 176L). And the soul who responds in love will find that the Trinity guarantees its fulfillment.

> 'Tis because Thou art an intellect that understandeth and an intellect that is understood and again the bond between them, that the created intellect can attain in Thee, its intelligible God, union and bliss. In like manner, 'tis because Thou art loveable love, that the created will, by loving, can attain in Thee, its loveable God, union and bliss. For he that receiveth Thee, O God, Thou light that may be received by the reason, might attain unto so close a union with Thee as that of a son with his father. (89–90E, 178L)

Without denying vision Nicholas has moved to union with God achieved by knowing and loving response to the Trinity's self-giving. By calling the human side of this union sonship Nicholas takes up the New Testament theme which parallels Jesus' sonship and our own. And it is to the place of Christ Jesus as mediator of mystical vision and union that the closing chapters of *The Vision of God* turn.

Much of what Nicholas says about Christ repeats teaching he had expounded earlier in Book Three of *On Learned Ignorance.*[11] Nicholas works within the orthodox Christology of the Council of Chalcedon, but the prayer form of these chapters breathes with Nicholas' own religious response to the wonder of the person who is God and man. And Nicholas' teaching about God's incomprehensibility and about human ignorance keeps mystical vision and union beyond our grasp. Jesus' position as mediator is necessary so that our passion for the infinite will not be in vain and God remain utterly transcendent.

There are two ways in which God the Son is mediator. As word or concept of the Father, the Son mediates between the Trinity and all other created things. In assuming human nature in Jesus, the Son unites humanity to the Trinity. Jesus is teacher and light for all rational spirits and through him "they attain unto absolute truth, as by their mediator" (101E, 188L). As Son of God and Son of Man, Christ unites all consenting persons to the God beyond their comprehension. Thus Jesus is within the wall of paradise where human reason could not enter.

> I see Thee, good Jesu, within the wall of Paradise, since Thine intelligence is alike truth and image, and Thou art alike God and creature, alike infinite and finite. And 'tis not possible that Thou shouldst be seen this side of the wall, for Thou art the bond between the divine nature that createth and the human nature that is created. (100E, 188L)

Chapter twenty-one underscores the importance of Jesus' mediation for mystical vision and union with God. If we share Jesus' spirit as we share the same human nature, we are enabled to approach the transcendent Father: "the humanity of every man soever is united unto Thee, Jesu, as unto the one and only means whereby the Father draweth all men" (104E, 192L). That Jesus is the revelation of the invisible Father comes directly from the New Testament writings, but in the context of mystical vision prepared for by the recognition that reason is ignorant of God its meaning becomes even more compelling. God becomes visible even for mystical intuition only through union with Jesus Christ. Without him even the learned cannot attain happiness.

Every blissful spirit beholdeth the invisible God and is united
in Thee, Jesu, unto God the unapproachable and immortal.
And thus in Thee the finite is united unto the infinite, and
unto that which is beyond union, and the incomprehensible is
possessed in an eternal fruition which is bliss most joyous and
inexhaustible. (105E, 192L)

Christ is thereby not merely the mediator for the ordinary religious
life of believers, but standing at the entryway to Paradise he mediates
as well that vision of the incomprehensible that is a foretaste of the
final eternal vision.

ASSESSMENT AND REPRISE

A cursory reading of *The Vision of God* may hardly distinguish it
from other traditional works of late medieval piety. Its scope and
tone, apart from the novel use of the portrait and the fondness for
paradoxical expressions, fall well within the central tradition of Christian spirituality. So much of Nicholas' language echoes that of the
New Testament, Augustine and Bonaventura, so many of the ideas
occur in related forms in his Neoplatonic and Christian predecessors.
Again following Augustine, Nicholas refuses to give more emphasis
to either cognitive or affective dimensions of human response to
God. Nor is the vision which humans seek discontinuous with
ordinary religious response to the Christian mysteries. Even as we
recognize the sincerity of Nicholas' prayerful teaching, we may wonder what about it keeps its author numbered among the important
Christian teachers of mysticism.

Perhaps the key to assessing the significance of Nicholas' teaching
is to view it in terms of his purpose—to provide a way to "mystical
theology." Here he clearly has in mind Pseudo–Dionysius' treatise
of the same name and so is not concerned with describing mystical
experience as a merely human phenomenon or proposing a regimen
of "mystical techniques" for achieving status as a mystic. Rather he
wants to combine his own unique metaphysics of God with his
Christian belief that God draws human beings to himself as their
destiny. What he does is therefore a work of interpreting how God's
inaccessible and absolute face or vision may come to be "seen" in
a kind of not-seeing when humans respond in freedom. What remains
original when Nicholas interprets "mystical" vision is precisely the
original interpretative framework spelled out in his other works for
relating the absolute God and the limited creation.

At this point a concluding summary of Nicholas' teaching in *The
Vision of God* is in order.

1. The *object* of "mystical" vision. From beginning to end of his writings about God Cusanus stresses that human knowers possess no cognitive means for understanding God's nature. All our analogies, conceptions, and names for God are but probes or conjectures which may be true as far as they go, but never grasp what divinity comes to—that continues to elude discursive reason *(ratio)*. In God all that God can do is actual, but enfolded in the oneness of the divine simpleness and infinity. It is this oneness without limit that enables Nicholas to say that in God opposites coincide or that God is beyond the coincidence of opposites. This is the God of whom we receive a glimpse in darkness through vision.

2. *Preparation* for vision—the use of concrete analogies. In the use of the portrait or icon and in the extended image of the wall girding paradise and the quest to enter, Nicholas provides clues for understanding the human situation *vis-a-vis* God and for coming to appreciate God's caring gaze. Both concrete analogies put together God's love and God's inaccessibility, the need for free human response and effort, and the work to overcome reason by recognizing one's knowledge as ignorance where God is concerned. One has to acknowledge *that* contradictories coincide in God's oneness, even if one cannot conceptualize of what sort of being this would be true. Nicholas proceeds here by advancing paradoxes that reason tries to understand but finally must use as pointers for the God beyond comprehension. No less than faith in the God revealed in Christ, the human effort to understand the coincidence of opposites is a prerequisite for attaining that learned ignorance to which vision of God is granted.

3. The *vision* itself. Given the impotence of discursive reason *(ratio)* where God is concerned and given human acknowledgement of reason's inadequacy, one is prepared to receive some vision of God, a sighting in darkness that is more like not-seeing. Yet Nicholas teaches that we have the cognitive capacity *(intellectus)* to intuit, with God's help, the absolute divinity itself. Continuous with the rest of our cognitive experience this "seeing" is mediated for believers by Christ in and through whom we may be united to the Trinity.

So Nicholas of Cusa's *The Vision of God* extends his speculative doctrines about the relation of God and creation and our knowledge of God to the domain of seeing God. Yet it is the object lessons with the portrait and the effort to enter the wall of paradise that keep us imaginatively and emotionally in touch with the core of Nicholas' teaching about seeking and seeing God. His own words, finally, can summarize the outcome:

> O Lord my God, the Helper of them that seek Thee, I behold
> Thee in the entrance of Paradise, and I know not what I see,

for I see naught visible. This alone I know, that I know not
what I see, and never can know. (58E, 146L)

BIBLIOGRAPHICAL NOTES

Emma Gurney Salter's 1928 translation of *The Vision of God* with a brief
introduction by Evelyn Underhill has been reissued by Frederick Ungar (New
York, 1960). Elisabeth Bohnenstädt's German translation, *Von Gottes Sehen*
(Leipzig, 1942), and Edmond Vansteenberghe's French translation, *La Vision
de Dieu* (Louvain, 1925), both have lengthy introductions placing the treatise
within Nicholas' own life and within the spirituality of the times. H. Lawrence
Bond's contemporary English version of *The Vision of God* is to appear shortly
in the Paulist Press Series, *The Classics of Western Spirituality*, under the title
Nicholas of Cusa; the same volume will contain translations of Nicholas'
other works that bear on spirituality, including *On Learned Ignorance*, *The
Summit of Contemplation*, *Seeking God*, *The Hidden God*, *The Gift of the Father
of Lights*, *On Divine Sonship*.

The critical Latin edition of *De Visione Dei* has yet to appear in the
Heidelberg Academy Series of Nicholas' *Opera omnia* (Leipzig/Hamburg,
1932 etc.). Until its appearance, the best Latin text will remain that of the
1514 Paris edition reprinted in three volumes (Frankfurt, 1962). This is
available with a facing German translation in Nikolaus von Kues, *Philosophisch-theologische Schriften* III, tr. D. and W. Dupré (Wien, 1967), pp. 93–219.
(These three volumes also contain the most available Latin texts of the other
works of Cusanus that relate his teaching in *The Vision of God*.)

There are few studies of Nicholas' mystical and spiritual teaching apart
from the introductions to the translations of *The Vision of God* already
mentioned. Brief comments may be found in Thomas Katsaros and Nathaniel
Kaplan, *The Western Mystical Tradition* (New Haven, 1969), pp. 294–97, and
in Jean Leclercq, François VandenBroucke, Louis Bouyer, *The Spirituality of
the Middle Ages* (New York, 1968), pp. 444–46; Lewis White Beck, *Early
German Philosophy* (Cambridge, MA, 1969), pp. 57–71; *Late Medieval Mysticism*, ed. Ray C. Petry (Philadelphia, 1957), pp. 352–91—includes two of
Nicholas' sermons; Friederich-Wilhelm Wentzlaff-Eggebert, *Deutsche Mystik
Zwischen Mittelalter und Neuzeit* (Tübingen, 1947), pp. 150–60.

XIV
Jewish Mysticism in the Sixteenth Century

DAVID BIALE

The expulsion of the Jews from Spain in 1492 inaugurated a period of intellectual and social ferment in Jewish history which left its mark for centuries to come. The sixteenth century witnessed the wholesale movement of Jews from the Iberian peninsula to the eastern Mediterranean, northern Europe and even the New World. Accompanying the profound social turmoil of the period was a variety of intellectual movements which altered the face of medieval Judaism. On the one hand, the tragic fate of the Marranos or crypto-Jews produced various heterodox personalities such as Uriel Acosta.[1] For the first time, a type of secular Judaism came into being, exemplified best by the heretic philosopher Baruch Spinoza in the seventeenth century. As a result of these first glimmerings of secularism, some historians date the Spanish expulsion as the real beginning of modern Jewish history. On the other hand, the sixteenth century was a time of religious creativity in mainstream Judaism.[2] Joseph Karo's *Shulḥan Arukh* ("The Set Table"), written in the middle of the century, became the standard code of Jewish law and laid the basis for what would later be called "orthodox" Judaism. At the same time, the Jewish world was swept by messianic and mystical ideas which very much set the tone for the following centuries. The emergence of new forms of Jewish mysticism in the sixteenth century must therefore be understood on the background of the many other changes of that time.

313

Medieval Jewish mysticism had its first period of creativity in the late twelfth and thirteenth centuries in Provence (southern France) and Spain.[3] Here, small groups of mystics developed a new mystical doctrine which would come to be called the *Kabbalah* (literally meaning "tradition"). As opposed to the earlier *Hekhalot* mysticism of the Talmudic period (ca. 100–500 CE), which devoted itself to descriptions of the soul's wanderings in the heavenly palaces *(hekhalot)*, the new Kabbalah gave on account of the divine anatomy itself. Its theory of the *sefirot* (sing. *sefirah*) was perhaps its most distinctive contribution. The *sefirot* (generally ten in number) were the emanations or inner structure of the hidden God (termed by these mystics the *Eyn Sof* or Infinite). Much of the thirteenth-century Kabbalah concerned itself with a discussion of the development and interrelationships of these divine emanations.

The kabbalistic movement of the thirteenth century developed in circumstances not totally unfavorable to Jewish life in Christian Spain (contrary to the opinion of those who see mysticism solely as a product of persecution).[4] Despite the gathering clouds of persecution which were to burst at the end of the fourteenth century, the mystics could work in relative isolation from the currents of history. Thus, with few exceptions, these Kabbalists generally did not try to relate their mystical doctrines to the contemporary scene. Far from it: the focus of their speculations was the progressive unfolding of the divine emanations that led to the creation of the world. Nothing could be more remote from contemporary concerns than the mysteries of creation! Moreover, the Kabbalists had little interest in propagating their ideas among the general Jewish public. They worked in small circles, exchanging manuscripts and passing on their esoteric teachings to a few initiates.

Another characteristic of the early Kabbalah, as pointed out by Gershom Scholem, was its theoretical nature. Again, with a few notable exceptions, most of the Kabbalists were very reticent to discuss personal mystical experiences. Instead, their writings dealt primarily with mystical theories about God (Scholem believes that the Kabbalah should therefore more properly be called *theosophy* rather than mysticism). Rather than writing about their own contemplations, the Kabbalists wrote theoretical treatises and commentaries on the Bible and earlier mystical tracts. Whether genuine mystical encounters stood behind their speculations remains largely a mystery.

In the sixteenth century, a radical change overcame Jewish mysticism and sparked a second creative period in its development.[5] Although the mystics continued to devote great attention to problems of creation, the emphasis shifted to interest in the *end* of history: the messianic redemption. This shift was a clear consequence of the expulsion of the Jews from Spain, perhaps the most important and traumatic event in medieval Jewish history. The expulsion devastated the most populous and culturally active community in the Jewish world. As a result of the Jewish love affair with Spain, the exiles carried with them a distinct identity and culture. They could not help but compare their own situation with the general condition of the Jews since the destruction of the Second Temple in 70 CE: the exile they had experienced personally sharpened the feeling of historical exile from the land of Israel. Consequently, the Spanish expulsion heightened the desire for redemption to fever pitch.

Many of the mystics we shall encounter in this essay traced their origins to Spain, and the memory of the exile was fresh in their minds. Already within a decade of the expulsion, mystical texts began to take up messianic speculations with a new urgency. Around 1500, a commentary was written on the Book of Psalms (called *Kaf Ha-Ketoreth*) which gave the Psalms a thoroughly apocalyptic interpretation. At about the same time, another text, *Sefer Ha-Meshiv*, argued, following the old formula that the Torah has seventy faces, that the face revealed to this generation (the generation of the exile) was that of exile and redemption.

In connection with this heightened interest in redemption came a desire to turn the Kabbalah from an esoteric into a public teaching. The acceptance of kabbalistic doctrines by the general Jewish public was thought to be a factor in bringing the Messiah. As an anonymous text from the middle of the sixteenth century put it:

> The decree from above that one should not discuss Kabbalistic teaching in public was meant to last only for a limited time— until 1490. We then entered a period called 'the last generation' and then the decree was rescinded and permission given. . . . And from 1540 onward, the most important commandment will be for all to study it in public, both old and young since this will bring about the coming of the Messiah.[6]

To be sure, it was only really in the seventeenth century that the Kabbalah began to achieve wide currency throughout Jewish intellectual circles, but the groundwork was laid in the sixteenth century. As Gershom Scholem has argued, the Kabbalah of the sixteenth century—and particularly the teachings of Isaac Luria—was to become *the* theology of Judaism in the late Middle Ages.[7] There can be no doubt that the sensitivity with which Jewish mysticism—much more than Jewish philosophy or law—responded to the psychological trauma of the Spanish expulsion accounts in large measure for its later popularity. As we shall presently see, the great myth of divine exile and redemption propounded by Luria and his disciples was to give a mystical explanation for the exile so many Jews had experienced personally.

At the same time that the Kabbalah was gradually becoming a "public" teaching, the Kabbalists were also pushing their investigations in an ever more esoteric direction: toward the mysteries of the hidden *Eyn Sof*. The thirteenth-century Kabbalists and their successors had generally refrained from speculating about the Infinite and had even defined this aspect of God as beyond investigation. Their theories dwelt instead on the revealed aspects of God, the *sefirot*. But it may well be intrinisic to all mystics that no mystery can be left unfathomed. That aspect of God declared off-limits by the earlier Kabbalah attracted increasing attention in the sixteenth century. We shall see that both Moses Cordovero and Isaac Luria, the most important Jewish mystics of the century, entered into realms of the divine about which earlier writers had, at best, only hinted.

A final innovation of the sixteenth-century Kabbalists was the combination of theoretical speculations about the nature of God with personal experience (sometimes also called "practical" Kabbalah). Where the personal or experiential element played a muted role earlier, it became an integral part of mysticism in the sixteenth century, particularly in Safed. Mystics went out in groups to the fields to greet the Sabbath as part of a mystical ritual. Perhaps the most striking instance of such mystical wanderings is Moses Cordovero's *Sefer Gerushin* (Book of Self-Imposed Exiles). In this work, Cordovero, the greatest systematizer of the theoretical Kabbalah, prescribes that "one should wander, as if exiled . . . and thereby make oneself a vessel for the *shekhinah* in exile."[8] According to kabbalistic doctrine, the feminine aspect of God, *shekhinah* (which also corresponds to the tenth *sefirah, malkhut*) is in a state of exile from the other aspects of God. By the physical act of wandering, the mystic duplicates the condition of the *shekhinah* and thereby becomes a "vessel" for her. Mystical *praxis* is here an indispensable complement to mystical theory. Another instance of this new emphasis on mystical practice is Issac Luria's *kavvanot* or prayer rituals which have a virtually magical function. Given this intertwining of theoretical Kabbalah with the personal experience and practice of the mystic, it is no surprise that the writings of many of the Safed mystics contain a new awareness of nature, for the natural world is considered a precise parallel to the divine and therefore action within this world is held to have a direct influence on God.

An important indicator of this new interest in the mystic's own experience is the phenomenon of *maggidism*, described in great detail by R.J. Zvi Werblowsky in his book on Joseph Karo.[9] In the sixteenth century, many mystics either claimed or were considered to have received personal communications from spiritual voices or *maggidim* (sing. *maggid*). Among those reported to have a *maggid* were Karo (of whom more later), Joseph Taytazak, Menachem Azaryah, Moses Cordovero, and Isaac Luria. Karo left a whole book reporting the messages of his *maggid*, which was a personification of the *Mishnah* (the great law compendium of about 200 CE). A related phenomenon was revelation through dreams, best exemplified by Haim Vital's *Sefer Ḥezyonot*. Vital developed a whole theory of magical *devekut* or communion with God in which the mystic is illuminated with a prophetic revelation. All of these phenomena point to something quite new in Jewish mysticism and, indeed, in medieval Judaism in general: a yearning for the kind of direct communication with God that most Jews believed ended with the biblical prophets. Perhaps as a result of the expulsion from Spain, there emerged for the first time in the Middle Ages a widespread desire for divine revelation.

The major characteristics of sixteenth-century Jewish mysticism were therefore a new focus on redemption, a desire to turn the Kabbalah into a public teaching, ever bolder speculations about the inner mysteries of God, and, finally, the combining of theoretical mysticism with personal mystical experience and practice. The historical events which many of the mystics personally experienced prompted them to see mysticism no longer as an ivory-tower pursuit, but rather as the vital key to Jewish history itself. We shall see how these ideas developed in the teachings of a number of the central figures of the period, but first we must mention briefly *where* Jewish mysticism flourished in the sixteenth century.

THE MYSTICAL CITY OF SAFED

The Spanish city of Gerona is the place most commonly associated with the rise of the thirteenth-century Kabbalah. Sixteenth-century Kabbalah is perhaps even more closely tied to a specific place: the small town of Safed in the north of Palestine.[10] To be sure, in the years following the expulsion from Spain, important Kabbalistic centers developed in Italy, North Africa, and especially in Salonika. But these were all quickly overshadowed by Safed, especially from the end of the 1530's.

It remains something of a puzzle why Safed should have enjoyed such a distinguished position, for unlike Jerusalem or Hebron, it has no holy status in the Jewish religion nor any biblical associations. It appears that Safed's intellectual prominence may have owed more to pure economics. Following the Spanish expulsion, many Sefardic Jews poured into the Ottoman empire, which was by far the most religiously tolerant area in the Mediterranean. For those choosing to settle in the land of Israel, the established Jewish communities such as Jerusalem were burdened by heavy local taxes. The situation in Safed, a relatively new Jewish community, was much better and opportunities existed in the textile trade and other crafts. One of the outstanding features of the Safed community was the extent to which its resident scholars supported themselves economically. As the town flourished and attracted newcomers, its spiritual life boomed. By 1603, after it had already passed its peak, the Safed community had eighteen *yeshivot* (seminaries) and twenty-one synagogues. Economic and spiritual prosperity went hand in hand.

Although Safed is known primarily as a center of Jewish mysticism, it must be emphasized that it was equally a center for Talmudic, that is, legal studies. One of the most famous of Safed's residents in the sixteenth century was Joseph Karo (1488–1575) whose *Shulḥan Arukh* became the universally recognized code of Jewish law. Yet, Karo is the best example of how Jewish mysticism had become well-integrated in the mainstream of Jewish intellectual life.[11] In addition to his legal writings, Karo was a student of mysticism, although his contributions to the discipline were less important than to Jewish law. His *Megillat Mesharim* ("Book of the Righteous"), which is a diary of the communications he received from his *maggid*, is composed mainly of kabbalistic speculations (even though the *maggid* was the *Mishnah*, a book of Jewish law). The early seventeenth-century Kabbalist Solomon Shlomel Dresnitz described the revelations of Karo's *maggid* in his collection of legends about Isaac Luria:

> every time he recited the *Mishnah* by heart, the *maggid* appeared to him and people would hear his voice through the door at the back of the house saying: "Peace upon thee, Rabbi Joseph Karo. I am the *Mishnah* which thou hast studied. I came forth to teach thee understanding. . . ." And all the revelations of the *maggid* he collected in a book entitled *The Book of the Maggid.*[12]

That Karo could be at once a sober legal scholar of the first rank and also a fervent mystic says a great deal about the place of mysticism in Jewish history, especially in the sixteenth century.

Karo, who arrived in Safed in 1537, was also involved in an important episode that reflects the messianic atmosphere of Safed at the time. In 1538, Jacob Berav, the leading rabbi in Safed, attempted to renew the ordination of rabbis which had lapsed during the Talmudic period. If the ordination could be renewed, a rabbinical Sanhedrin (high court) might be constituted, which had clear messianic connotations. Berav ordained a number of rabbis, including

Karo. Although this messianic experiment failed (as a result of the opposition of rabbis from Jerusalem), it set the tone for years to come. One can hardly imagine Safed mysticism without its strong messianic flavor. It is also interesting that Karo himself took part in this bold enterprise at exactly the time he was working on his great legal compendium. Here is striking evidence that law is not always associated with the most conservative elements in society! Indeed, one might even speculate that the hidden impetus behind Karo's codification was the expectation of the imminent coming of the Messiah.

The Safed of Karo's time was therefore an extraordinarily vital city. Although never very large numerically, it had quickly become an intellectual center, with legal studies flourishing side by side with mystical. *Yeshivot* and synagogues sprang up everywhere. And most important were the kabbalistic *havurot* or mystical societies whose members studied and practiced together. There is perhaps no example before the Hasidic movement of the eighteenth century of mystical fellowships such as those which emerged in Safed. Here, mysticism was not only the study of esoteric texts; it was even more a way of life.

MOSES CORDOVERO

The mystical schools in Safed developed around certain teachers and we shall briefly discuss two of them, Moses Cordovero and Issac Luria. Cordovero (1522–70) was one of the first mystics to work in Safed.[13] As his name attests, his family was of Spanish origin (from the city of Cordova). We know very little about his life, but we do know that he became the most respected Kabbalist in Safed at a very early age. By twenty-six he had finished his *magnum opus*, the *Pardes Rimonim* (Pomegranate Orchard). This work remains today one of the best systematic treatments of the main themes of the Kabbalah. Where earlier kabbalistic works generally have an asso-ciative structure, Cordovero systematically takes the major bones of contention in earlier literature, gathers the various opinions, and renders his own judgment. Even without his innovations—which are significant and interesting in their own right—his *Pardes* would have won him a central place in the history of the Kabbalah as a kind of *Summa Kabbalistica*. But if Cordovero has been considered a Thomas Aquinas of the Kabbalah, an equally apt Jewish analogy might be his colleague in Safed, Joseph Karo. What Karo succeeded in doing in his *Shulḥan Arukh* to the *Halakhah* (Jewish law), Cordovero did to the Kabbalah. One has a sense of Safed as a place in which a great impetus was felt for the summary and synthesis of various Jewish disciplines.

Cordovero has occasionally been considered a "philosopher" of the Kabbalah, and it is indeed true that his *Pardes* has a certain philosophical style and that he acknowledges his debt to the philosophers (particularly Moses Maimonides) for certain fundamental theological principles. But Cordovero was no philosopher. Although he tried to answer questions which had perplexed philosophers, his work owes a tremendous amount to the mythological symbols of the classic thirteenth-century text, the Zohar. It is perhaps fair to say that Cordovero, like his predecessors, started where the philosophers left off: where they denied the possibility of describing God, the Kabbalists give us the most intimate descriptions of his inner workings.

Cordovero concentrates on questions which had received at most passing attention from earlier Kabbalists. He is chiefly interested in the subtle relationship between the hidden God *(Eyn Sof)* and the *sefirot*. In a daring formula, which has led some to regard him as a pantheist or panentheist, he says: " (God's) substance is present in his *sefirot* and He himself is everything and nothing exists outside Him." [14] Elsewhere, he asserts that "God is all reality, but not all reality is God." [15] The *sefirot* are God's instruments, but they also appear to contain God's substance. Since the lower worlds are created directly and without interruption as emanations of the *sefirot*, Cordovero seems to be suggesting that God's substance is to be found in the lower worlds as well.

Even before the hidden God emanated the *sefirot*, he "knew" them in the form of *tzahtzahot* (which might be translated as "inner lights"). The *tzahtzahot* can be understood as points within the Infinite which were the *sefirot in potentia* before their emanation. Hence, according to this theory, the whole world existed in a potential state within God before the process of emanation and creation began. However, the *tzahtzahot* could not have come into existence without the *Eyn Sof willing* them to do so. Yet, even this "will" could not have existed without a prior will willing it. Cordovero therefore postulates an infinite regression of divine wills which approach asymptotically the "will of all wills," the *Eyn Sof* itself. Throughout this difficult argument, what concerns Cordovero is the old Neoplatonic question of how the infinite One could become the Many. He pushes the question as far as one can and, long before the discovery of the infinitesimal calculus, suggests an almost mathematical solution to an ancient theological problem. We have here an example of one of the general characteristics of sixteenth-century Kabbalah: the tendency to search ever deeper within those areas of God that the earlier Kabbalah had considered impenetrable mysteries.

Cordovero follows the old Kabbalah in emphasizing the problems of creation, namely the first acts of differentiation within God. It is possible to say that with Cordovero, the Kabbalah of the thirteenth century reached its theoretical limits. In the Kabbalah of Isaac Luria, a whole new approach to the old questions emerged and with it, a shift in emphasis to the redemption of the world.

ISAAC LURIA

Isaac Luria (1534–72) was born to a family of Ashkenazic (northern European) origin which had settled in Jerusalem.[16] He spent most of his youth in Egypt where he received his kabbalistic training. Luria only came to Safed in 1569 at the earliest and died in 1572 at the age of 38. His Safed period was therefore no longer than two to three years, yet in this time he made an enormous impact on the kabbalistic circles in the city. We actually possess very few authentic writings of Luria, which is rather unusual in the history of Jewish mysticism; if nothing else, the Kabbalists were incorrigible writers and were rarely content to pass on their teachings orally. In Luria's case, however, most of the doctrines have come down to us in the sometimes conflicting versions of his disciples, chiefly Haim Vital and Joseph ibn Tabul. Immediately after Luria's death, various stories of his legendary deeds began to circulate and were collected in texts such as *Shivḥei Ha-Ari* (In Praise of the Ari, Ari being Luria's acronym which stands for "The divine, Rabbi Isaac") and *Toledot Ha-Ari* (Biography of the Ari). In the history of Jewish mysticism, there is perhaps no other figure up to the time of eighteenth-century Hasidism who had such a charismatic impact on his disciples.

Luria was only in Safed for a year or so before Moses Cordovero died. There is evidence that he studied with Cordovero, but the relationship between them still awaits a full investigation. Luria considered Cordovero his teacher, but the Lurianic school believed that Cordovero had only revealed the "exoteric" truths while the deeper mysteries awaited Luria. Whatever debt Luria may have owed to Cordovero—or, for that matter, to other predecessors—there can be no doubt as to the bold originality of his thought.[17]

Virtually all earlier Kabbalists, including Cordovero, held that the *sefirot* and the lower worlds emanated in an unbroken progression from *Eyn Sof*. There were many disputes about whether the divine substance was to be found in the lower worlds (as we saw in the above discussion of Cordovero), but none of the mystics postulated a clear break between God and his creation. As we have seen, the theory of continuous emanation led to the possibility of pantheism. Luria decisively solved the problem of pantheism with which Cordovero had struggled, and, as opposed to Cordovero, argued that a deep chasm existed between *Eyn Sof* and the *sefirot*. This chasm, which Luria called the *halal ha-panui* (empty space), was created by an act of divine contraction *(tzimtzum)*. The *Etz Haim* or "Tree of Life" (the great work attributed to Luria) begins with the following lines:

> Know that before all the emanations were emanated and the creations were created, the simple supernal light filled all existence and there was no empty space in the sense of vacant air or void, but everything was filled by this undifferentiated infinite light. [This light] had neither beginning nor end [technical terms for two of the *sefirot*] but was rather undifferentiated light that was entirely homogeneous and it was called the infinite light.

> And when it arose in His undifferentiated will to create the worlds . . . He contracted Himself at the center-most point that was within Him and the light was contracted and withdrew towards the sides surrounding the central point, thus leaving an empty space, a vacuum, an empty void (where) the central point (had been).[18]

The theory of *tzimtzum* was Luria's most original contribution to the Kabbalah. He took the idea from an anonymous early thirteenth-century text, but developed it into the cardinal principle of his teaching. According to an old midrash, God had contracted *(tzimtzem)* himself in order to dwell within the Holy Tabernacle of the Temple. Luria totally inverted the meaning of this legend. He argued that the world could not be created without God making room for it. It was therefore necessary for God to withdraw within himself in order to create an empty space in which his creations might exist. Hence, the contraction did not mean that God *condensed* himself into the Holy of Holies, but, on the contrary, *absented* himself. The first act of creation was not the *outflowing* of divine energy (as in the earlier Kabbalah) but a divine *withdrawal*. The idea of a divine withdrawal as a prerequisite for creation can be seen as an attempt to counter pantheism at the outset: since the world is fundamentally different from God, it could not be created within God, but instead required an empty space. It is a striking coincidence that Luria developed his idea of empty space at about the same time as philosophers of science began to accept the possibility of a vacuum, which had been considered logically impossible by Aristotelian science.

Why did God contract himself and create an empty space within himself? Lurianic Kabbalah gives several answers. One is that God willed the contraction in order to create the world as a result of his overflowing love. But another, much more radical answer is that the contraction was a cathartic act within God in order to rid him of certain elements which disturbed his inner harmony. These elements are called the *shorshei ha-dinim* (roots of judgment) which are understood as principles that limit God. Since the Infinite cannot, by definition, be limited, God had to expel these roots of limitation. In an even more radical formulation, the *shorshei ha-dinim* are the very roots of evil itself. Hence, the Lurianic Kabbalah—building on certain ideas in the Zohar—suggests that evil originates in God himself and is the root cause for the creation of the world. Creation is an act of divine expurgation. Moreover, this creation is not willed by God, but is instead determined by laws over which he seemingly has no control.[19]

Here, then, is a radical, dialectical theory of creation in which the traditional theological formula, *creatio ex nihilo* (creation out of nothingness) is given an entirely new meaning.[20] In the thirteenth century, the Kabbalists suggested that the *Eyn Sof* could be understood metaphorically as the divine nothingness *(ayin)*, an idea one finds in certain Christian mystics as well, such as Jacob Böhme. Creation out of nothingness meant creation out of God himself. Luria took this bold idea a step further. Not only does creation out of nothingness mean creation out of God, but God first creates the nothingness (the empty space) in which the lower worlds are built. We might note, parenthetically, that Luria's theory bears an interesting resemblance to the nineteenth-century philosopher Hegel's *Logik* in which Being passes through a moment of Nothing, turning into Becoming.

Later Kabbalists, including Luria's own disciples, were divided about the precise meaning of the *tzimtzum* and the term was at the center of many kabbalistic arguments in the centuries to come. Did Luria *literally* mean that God created a space totally empty of the divine presence? Such an interpretation would certainly be anti-pantheist, but it would also contradict the cherished principle that "God fills all worlds." It was virtually unthinkable to traditional Jewish thinkers that there could be a place totally void of God. On the other hand, if Luria meant the *tzimtzum* metaphorically, what was left in the "empty" space after the contraction? According to Joseph ibn Tabul, God left a thin film or *reshimu* in the ḥalal. Within this *reshimu* were trapped the *shorshei ha-dinim* mentioned earlier. The idea that God had expelled some "foreign" elements from within himself was surely as unsettling and problematic to traditional Jews as the literal interpretation of the *tzimtzum*.

The events following the *tzimtzum* in Luria's teachings are extremely complicated. The main event was the emanation of divine light into the empty space and the organization of the light into vessels *(kelim)*. According to some accounts, the light entered the *halal* in the form of the primordial man *(Adam Kadmon)*. At this point, a disaster occurs and the vessels break, scattering divine light throughout the empty space in the form of sparks *(nitzotzot)*. The breaking of the vessels *(shevirat ha-kelim)* was really the event that inaugurated the unfolding of the lower worlds.

The reason for the breaking of the vessels, like for the *tzimtzum*, was cloaked in controversy among Luria's disciples. However, the most prevalent explanation seems to be that the vessels were not strong enough to hold the divine light that filled them. In some accounts, the weakness of the vessels was due to the fact that they were composed of *shorshei ha-dinim* which were themselves the cause of the *tzimtzum*. These "principles of limitation" were elements of weakness in the original *Eyn Sof* and thus became the source of structural weakness in the vessels. In other, related accounts, the vessels contain the seeds of materiality—and thus evil—and this is the reason why they cannot hold the divine light. These "husks" of materiality are called the *klippot* and after the breaking of the vessels become the basis for the material world. The realm of the *klippot* is known in the Lurianic Kabbalah as the realm of evil. Thus, the origin of the material world and evil itself was the catastrophic breaking of the vessels.

It is immediately evident that there are great similarities between the first contraction and the breaking of the vessels, especially in the more radical interpretations of Luria's teaching. Both were caused by a disturbance of the divine harmony due to small foreign particles that limit or explode God's homeostasis, and both attempt to purge God of the disturbing matter. In both cases, there is a strong undercurrent of determinism: God does not will either development, but is instead a captive of an inevitable process. Finally, both have elements of tragedy or catastrophe since God ends up in a state of lesser perfection or greater disorder following the event. We may therefore see the *tzimtzum* and the *shevirat ha-kelim* as two stages in the same process where God is shattered and parts of him are exiled from the rest.

The contraction and scattering of the divine sparks are essentially myths of divine exile. The idea that God has gone into exile with his people is an old one that can be traced back to rabbinic legends and plays an important role in Jewish folklore. But Luria's theory takes this old theme much further. Here, the very creation of the world is tied up with the concept of exile; creation is implicitly a divine catastrophe. Luria therefore provided a theological and mystical dimension to the powerful feelings of exile experienced by so many Jews of the sixteenth century. Moreover, he made the Jewish condition of exile an historical symbol for a much more profound and seminal exile which has characterized the whole cosmos since its creation. The tremendous popularity of the Lurianic Kabbalah must have owed a great deal to this novel combination of the mystical and historical realms.

Once the divine sparks and the husks of materiality have been scattered, God's emanations reorganize themselves for the task of restoring the primordial harmony. In place of the *Adam Kadmon* (primordial man) out of which emanated the original *sefirot*, a series of "faces" *(partzufim)* constitute the divine realm. Luria suggests that the *sefirot* system described in the earlier Kabbalah does not exist in its ideal form after the *shevirat ha-kelim*. In general, the whole order of creation is demoted to a lower level as a result of the breaking of the vessels. Thus, the four worlds mentioned already in the Zohar (the worlds of "emanation," "creation," "forming" and "making") are each lowered to the level of the world below and the "world of making" becomes the material world as it mixes with the *klippot*. The creation of our world is therefore a result of what might be called "divine degeneration."

The whole function and task of this creation is to restore God's original state before the divine Fall. God succeeds in restoring most of the fallen sparks, but not all of them. Here is where man plays the crucial role. God requires man as his helper. By effecting the redemption of his own soul—itself a divine spark trapped in the *klippah* of his body—man contributes to the reconstruction of God. Only by redeeming the divine spark can the husks of materiality be defeated and banished. This process of redemption is called *tikkun* (meaning literally "fixing" or "restoration") in the Lurianic Kabbalah. The term gives us a sense of the almost mechanical nature of Luria's cosmos: man must literally "fix" God by redeeming his world.[21]

Luria seems to have emphasized that the *tikkun* of the outer world is not man's task; man must redeem only that which is in the inward, spiritual realm. Such a position would avoid the temptation toward heresy which became so prevalent in the later Sabbatian movement. In radical Sabbatianism, a belief developed that the Messiah—and even his followers—had to enter into the realm of *klippot* in order to redeem sparks trapped there. This concept of "holiness through sin" was entirely foreign to Luria who insisted that the *tikkun* required correct performance of the commandments *(mitzvot)* incumbent on every Jew. His Kabbalah is a mystical justification of the commandments and is therefore entirely orthodox in spirit.

The correct performance of the commandments requires the proper intention, and Luria composed special prayers toward this end called *kavvanot*. These *kavvanot* were considered an integral part of the process of *tikkun* and give us a hint of the dimension of *praxis* that accompanied Lurianic theory. The role of man in redeeming the sparks has a certain magical quality about it, and this is particularly evident in the doctrines of Luria's disciple Haim Vital: by action within this world, man can affect God. Although earlier Jewish mysticism had posited a distinct relationship between man's actions and God (man was seen as a microcosm of God), Luria gave this notion a central position in his Kabbalah. If Jewish mysticism was never purely contemplative, it became downright *active* with Luria. Once one has read Luria, it becomes impossible to hold that mysticism must necessarily lead to passivity.

An interesting element in the *tikkun* is the doctrine of *gilgul* (transmigration or reincarnation of souls).[22] Luria did not invent the theory of *gilgul*; it was already present in the earlier Kabbalah and was highly developed by other sixteenth-century Kabbalists, such as Cordovero's brother-in-law, Solomon Alkabets. But it played an especially important role in the process of *tikkun*. According to the theory, a soul might be returned to earth after its death for a variety of reasons:

> [God] in His mercy upon His creatures devised devices so that none should be cast out, and instituted the *gilgul* which is return to this world. This dispensation is divided into three parts. . . . Those who return (a) not on account of their having omitted a religious duty, let alone for having committed a trespass, but solely out of compassion with their contemporaries; such was the case with our master Moses . . . (b) to receive punishment . . . and this is the mystery of infants and sucklings that die in their youth. But this applies only to souls that did not repent with perfect repentance. Those who thus transmigrate and yet do not turn to good after three times will henceforth be incarnated in pure and impure animals . . . (c) in order to complete certain religious acts.[23]

According to the theory of *tikkun*, each soul has a "quota" of divine sparks to redeem and failure to do so led to *gilgul*. A man's soul was thought to belong to a family of souls and one might redeem the souls of one's "soul family" by *gilgul*. The doctrine of *gilgul* therefore implied a strange kind of moral calculus (as Scholem calls it) in which a person might suffer for sins of a previous life or be burdened with obligations not ostensibly his own. Such a moral system was quite foreign to the mainstream of Jewish ethics.[24]

The emphasis on *tikkun* and man's role in it are central to Lurianic Kabbalah and suggest again the great concern with redemption in the sixteenth century. For Luria, the process of *tikkun* began immediately after the *shevirat ha-kelim*. The world has been striving for redemption ever since its creation. Here, then, was a new messianic theory: instead of a sudden act of redemption in which the Messiah would overturn the world of evil and exile in one swift act, redemption would come gradually, with each generation contributing its "quota" of redeemed sparks. Where most earlier messianic theories had imagined that this world would end with a "bang," Luria's catastrophe took place at the *beginning* of history; after the *tzimtzum* and *shevirat ha-kelim*, history was to be a gradual, non-catastrophic process of redemption, reminiscent in a sense of the nineteenth-century's idea of progress. Earlier theories believed that messianic times would come in a generation that was either "totally good or totally sinful." Luria seems to have held that redemption might come in any generation and his messianic teaching actually devotes little attention to the person of the Messiah himself.

It seems that Luria's disciples considered him a messianic figure, perhaps the Messiah son of Joseph who was to precede the Messiah son of David. Whether Luria encouraged such ideas is hard to determine. We do know that Haim Vital had messianic pretensions and there were strong redemptive expectations in his circle. In any case, Lurianic messianism had a tremendous impact on subsequent Jewish history. In his classic biography of Sabbatai Ṣevi, the leader of the mass messianic movement of the seventeenth century, Gershom Scholem has shown how the Lurianic Kabbalah laid the groundwork for this most important of messianic outbreaks in medieval Jewish history. The language of the Sabbatian propagandists was thoroughly Lurianic and their justifications for the movement based on Lurianic arguments, if taken to an heretical extreme never anticipated by Luria. Whether or not Lurianic Kabbalah was actually the *cause* of this messianic movement—as Scholem believes—it is clear that Luria provided the symbols and ideas without which the Sabbatian movement would have been very different.

THE SPREAD OF THE LURIANIC KABBALAH

One of Scholem's main arguments for the importance of the Lurianic Kabbalah as a cause of seventeenth-century Sabbatianism is that it became a virtually universal theology of the Jews in the years following Luria's death.[25] It is interesting that Luria's main

disciples did not play a direct role in the diffusion of his teaching
and may have even tried to keep it hidden. One of the main figures
responsible for the spread of the Lurianic Kabbalah was Israel Sarug
who, at the end of the sixteenth century, traveled through Italy and
Poland and circulated manuscripts with Lurianic teachings. Where
he got these manuscripts remains something of a mystery since his
claim to have been a student of Luria has been shown to have been
false. In fact, many of Sarug's writings are permeated with his own
ideas. Another important figure in the diffusion of the Lurianic
Kabbalah was the German Kabbalist, Naphtali Bacharach whose main
work was *Emek ha-Melekh* ("The Valley of The King") (1648).

Another important factor in the widespread acceptance of Lurianic
Kabbalah and the Safed Kabbalah in general was the sudden explosion
of kabbalistic homiletic or moralistic literature.[26] This venerable genre
goes back to the early Middle Ages, but no attempt was made to
incorporate kabbalistic doctrines in the moralistic literature before
the sixteenth century. One of the earliest such works was Cordovero's
Tomer Devorah ("The Palm of Deborah"), but much more important
in terms of their influence were the works of two other Safed
Kabbalists, Eliezer Azikri's *Sefer Haredim* ("Book of The Pious") and
Elijah de Vidas' *Reshith Hokhmah* ("Beginning of Wisdom"). Perhaps
the most popular and influential kabbalistic *musar* work was Isaiah
Horowitz's *Shnei Luhot ha-Berit* ("The Tablets of the Covenant"),
written in Poland in the seventeenth century. There can be no
question that the introduction of Kabbalah into the homiletic literature
played a very important role in the spread of kabbalistic ideas, for
this was a literature widely circulated among the general population.

We have mentioned the importance of Lurianic Kabbalah in the
outbreak of messianism in the seventeenth century. But Luria's teachings were equally important in another mass movement, Hasidism.[27]
When, in the eighteenth century, this pietistic movement spread
throughout large areas of Eastern Europe, it was accompanied by a
popular version of the Lurianic Kabbalah. Although by no means
merely a kabbalistic movement, Hasidism's main ideas, such as the
role of the *Zaddik* (Hasidic sect leader) and the emphasis on redeeming
the everyday world, owe much to Luria's doctrines.

Sixteenth-century Kabbalah, and particularly its Safed incarnation,
therefore has an importance far beyond the history of Jewish mysticism. With the development and dissemination of Luria's teachings,
the Kabbalah broke out of its narrow scholastic bonds and played
a powerful role in subsequent popular movements in Jewish history.
As perhaps one of the most profound intellectual responses to the
tragedy of the Spanish expulsion, sixteenth-century Kabbalah voiced
in highly abstruse language the longings of the Jewish people as a

whole. Yet, its message is of interest to all students of religion, for its novel ideas are answers to theological questions by no means limited to Jewish thought alone.

BIBLIOGRAPHICAL NOTES

Ben Shlomo, Joseph. *Torat ha-Elohut shel Rabbi Moses Cordovero* (Jerusalem, 1965).

Dan, Joseph. *Sifrut ha-Musar ve-ha-Derush* (Jerusalem, 1975).

Schechter, Solomon. "Safed in the Sixteenth Century," *Studies in Judaism*, 2nd ser. (Philadelphia, 1908), 203–306.

Scholem, Gershom. *Kabbalah* (Jerusalem, 1975); *Major Trends in Jewish Mysticism*, 3rd ed., (New York, 1961), chapter 7; *Sabbatai Sevi. The Mystical Messiah, 1626–1676*, revised English ed., tr. R.J.Z. Werblowsky (Princeton, 1973), esp. introductory chapter.

Tishby, Isaiah. *Torat ha-Ra ve-ha-Kelippah* (Jerusalem, 1942).

Werblowsky, R.J. Zvi. *Joseph Karo, Lawyer and Mystic* (London, 1962).

Notes

I. AUGUSTINE

1. W. R. Inge, *Christian Mysticism* (London, 1899), pp. 6–7, 22.

2. See especially *Ennead I*, treatise 6, "On Beauty," and *Ennead V*, treatise 1, "On the Three Divine Hypostases," which Augustine certainly read.

3. This typical sequence—knowledge first of the self, then of God—is found in Augustine's early writings, especially *Soliloquies*, II, 1, 1 and 6, 9. It is based on *Enneads I*, 6, 9 and V, 1, 1.

4. For a general discussion of this pattern of ascent, see Suzanne Poque, "L'Expression de l'anabase plotinienne dans la prédication de saint Augustin et ses sources," *Recherches Augustiniennes*, 10 (1975), 187–215. Note, for example, *Enarrationes in Psalmos* 41, 8, according to which even the soul which has already "understood" through the things that are made still strives to "see" the invisible things of God, and this is achieved when the soul reaches out above itself.

5. *Confessions*, VII, 10, 16 (all translations mine).

6. *Conf.*, VII, 17, 23.

7. *Conf.*, VII, 17, 23.

8. *Conf.*, VII, 20, 26.

9. *Contra Academicos*, I, 8, 22; II, 2, 5; *De beata vita*, IV, 35; *De ordine*, I, 10, 29; *Soliloquiae*, I, 6, 12; I, 14, 25.

10. For the problems of interpretation see Pierre Courcelle, *Recherches sur les Confessions de saint Augustin* (Paris, 1950), pp. 157–67, and especially André Mandouze, "Où en est la question de la mystique augustinienne?" *Augustinus Magister*, III, pp. 103–63.

11. *Enn. I*, 6, 6–8.

12. *Soliloquiae*, I, 6, 12; *De libero arbitrio*, II, 16, 42.

13. *Epistola* 147, 13, 31; *De Genesi ad litteram*, XII, 5, 14; 12, 25; 26, 53; 27, 55; 34, 67; 36, 69.

14. *Conf.*, VII, 9, 12–15; 20, 26.

15. It is possible that he refers to Platonists as well as Christians when he speaks (*De quantitate animae*, 33, 76) of "certain great and incomparable souls whom we believe to have seen, and to see, these things." In his later writings he continues to affirm the Platonists' apprehension of God; cf. esp. *De Trinitate*, IV, 15, 20 and *De civitate Dei*, X, 2.

16. In the later writings, see esp. *De Trinitate*, IV, 13, 18; 15, 20; 17, 23.

17. *Conf.*, IX, 10, 23–25.

18. It is not clear what meaning the word *ictus* (used in *Conf.*, VII, 17, 23, quoted above, as well as here) has in Augustine's mystical passages. It means a "stroke" or "beat," but whether it is to be understood as a "reach" or "lunge" or "leap" on the part of the human mind, or a "blow" or "shock" received by it, cannot be proved conclusively. There are several terms used by Plotinus that might stand behind Augustine's language, but of course he was reading a Latin translation, and in any case he may have understood or used the term in his own way (for various possibilities see Mandouze, "La première expérience augustinienne de l'extase," *Augustinus Magister*, I, 73, n. 3). The term could also simply mean a "beat" to measure time, and thus an "instant"; this is clearly the meaning in another passage (*De Trin.*, VIII, 2, 3) in which Augustine speaks of the "first moment"—which is also the last and only moment—in which one is touched by the light, as by a flash (*in ipso primo ictu qua uelut coruscatione perstringeris*). In view of the difficulties I have translated the term differently in each passage, according to the context.

19. *Conf.*, IX, 10, 25.

20. For a discussion of some of the issues see Courcelle, *Recherches*, pp. 222–26; Mandouze, "La première expérience augustinienne de l'extase," *AM*, I, 67–84; and the prefatory discussion by Aimé de Solignac in the edition of the *Confessions* in the Bibliothèque Augustinienne, XIII, pp. 191–97.

21. *Western Mysticism: The Teaching of Augustine, Gregory and Bernard on Contemplation and the Contemplative Life*. Third edition, with "Afterthoughts" (from the second edition of 1927) and a new Foreword by David Knowles (London, 1967).

22. See esp. Joseph Maréchal, "La vision de Dieu au sommet de la contemplation d'après saint Augustin," and Endre von Ivánka, "Die unmittelbare Gotteserkenntnis als Grundlage des Erkennens und als Ziel des übernatürlichen Strebens bei Augustin," and also the survey by Mandouze, "Où en est la question de la mystique augustinienne," *Augustinus Magister*, III, 103–63.

23. Ephraem Hendrikx, *Augustins Verhältnis zur Mystik. Eine patristische Untersuchung* (1936) and more recently "Augustins Verhältnis zur Mystik. Ein Rückblick" (1975). See Bibliographical Notes above.

24. In Sermon 52, 6, 16, he says, "I have seen I know not what in ecstasy, which I was unable to bear for long (*diu*)," and this is paralleled by *Enarrationes in Psalmos* 134, 6, where he asserts that contact with the supreme Good is

possible, and that there are those, stronger than he, who are able to fix their gaze on it "at length" *(diu)*.

25. See the short "book on the vision of God," printed as Epistle 147 in the editions, and especially book XII of his Literal Commentary on Genesis. They were probably written in that order, for in the former he seems to be feeling his way, with the help of a sermon of Ambrose, while in the latter he launches directly into his own discussion of visions and ecstasies. The influence of this Augustinian theory of threefold vision can be seen not only in the medieval tradition of theology and biblical interpretation, but also in literary practice, as shown, for example, by F. X. Newman, "The Structure of Vision in 'Apocalypsis Goliae,' " *Mediaeval Studies*, 29 (1967), 113–23.

26. *Ep.* 147, 13, 31.

27. *De Genesi ad litteram*, XII, 27, 55. There were also other medieval traditions concerning Paul's rapture, influenced especially by the *Visio Pauli* (really an apocalypse in its genre), a work allegedly "rediscovered" in 388 at the house of Paul in Tarsus—and rejected as inauthentic by Augustine, who read it a few years later *(In Joannis evangelium*, tr. 98, 8). This writing relies entirely upon the first and second modes of vision, giving detailed accounts of the geography of heaven and hell in a manner which anticipates Dante. For a translation and critical introduction see *New Testament Apocrypha*, ed. Edgar Hennecke and Wilhelm Schneemelcher, tr. R. McL. Wilson (Philadelphia, 1965), II, 755–98; for a fuller discussion of the text and its tradition, see Theodore Silverstein, *Visio sancti Pauli: The History of the Apocalypse in Latin, Together with Nine Texts*, Studies and Documents, IV (London, 1935). There is an even earlier work (possibly from the second century), which had no influence on the one just mentioned; a Gnostic *Apocalypse of Paul*, recently discovered at Nag Hammadi in a Coptic translation, which describes Paul's journeys through successive heavens, up to the tenth, using the language of sense and imagination but conveying spiritual meanings for those who "understand." See *The Coptic Gnostic Library. Nag Hammadi Codices V, 2–5 and VI with Papyrus Berolinensis 8502, 1 and 4*, edited by Douglas M. Parrott (Leiden, 1979), pp. 47–63.

28. *Enarr. in Ps.* 41, 10.

29. *Conf.,* XI, 29, 39–30, 40.

30. *The Mystic Way*, p. 301, paraphrasing *Conf.* VII, 20, 26, " [patriam] non tantum cernendam sed et habitandam."

31. For this see especially John Burnaby, *Amor Dei: A Study of the Religion of St. Augustine* (London,1938), and also Rudolph Lorenz, "Fruitio Dei bei Augustin," *Zeitschrift für Kirchengeschichte*, 63 (1950–51), 51–132.

32. *Enn.* I, 6, 8.

33. *De moribus*, I, 11, 18; *De musica*, VI, 13, 40; *Conf.,* VIII, 8, 19; *Ennar. in Ps.* 94, 2; *Ep.* 155, 5.

34. *Conf.,* X, 40, 65.

35. *Conf.,* XIII, 9, 10.

36. See *De Trin.,* VIII, 8, 12 and his *Homilies on the First Epistle of John*, 5, 7; 7, 6; and 9, 10.

37. *In Ioannis epistolam*, tr. 8, 12.

38. *Ibid.,* 8, 14.

39. *De Trin.*, VIII, 8, 12.

40. Ibid., 9, 13.

41. *Conf.*, IX, 19, 25; *Ep.* 147, 19, 47; *De Gen. ad litt.*, XII, 27, 55.

42. *Enn.* VI, 5, 10. Cf. *De beata vita*, IV, 33; *De ord.*, I, 8, 24; *C. Acad.*, II, 9, 22; *Solil.*, I, 13, 22; *De lib. arb.*, II, 14, 37. The theme of spiritual marriage receives its classic expression in Origen; see especially *The Song of Songs: Commentary and Homilies*, translated and annotated by R. P. Lawson, Ancient Christian Writers, vol. 26 (Westminster, MD, 1957). For a general survey of the motif, see Pierre Adnès, "Mariage spirituel," *Dictionnaire de spiritualité ascétique et mystique*, fascicles 64–65, 388–408.

43. *Enn.* V, 1, 3 and 6; cf. *Solil.*, I, 13, 22; *De Trin.*, XI, 5, 8.

44. *Conf.*, III, 6, 11: "interior intimo meo, superior summo meo."

45. Maréchal, "La vision de Dieu," pp. 191–96, seems to emphasize the former; Ivánka, "Die urmittelbare Gotteserkenntnis," 533–38, the latter. (See my Bibliographical Notes to the present essay.)

46. *De lib. arb.*, II, 11, 32.

47. The later career of Platonism (which had its magical as well as mystical aspects) is traced in D.P. Walker, *The Ancient Theology: Studies in Christian Platonism from the Fifteenth to the Eighteenth Century* (Ithaca, 1972). Mystical theologies of a more orthodox Christian sort are expressed in John Smith, "A Discourse Concerning the True Way or Method of Attaining to Divine Knowledge," *The Cambridge Platonists*, ed. Gerald R. Cragg (New York, 1968), pp. 76–90, and Jonathan Edwards, "A Divine and Supernatural Light immediately imparted to the Soul by the Spirit of God, shown to be both a Scriptural and Rational Doctrine," *Works* (London, 1817, rpt. New York, 1968), VIII, 3–20. Theories verging on pantheism—but interesting precisely because they see a mystical potentiality in all of human experience—can be seen in Benedict Spinoza, *Ethics*, with Introduction by George Santayana (London, 1910), Part V, propositions 14ff., esp. 30 and 36, and in G.W.F. Hegel, *The Christian Religion*, Lectures on the Philosophy of Religion, Part III, ed. and tr. Peter C. Hodgson; American Academy of Religion, Texts and Translations Series, No. 2 (Missoula, MT, 1979), pp. 1–10, 26–34, 169–83.

An immediate intuition of the divine is asserted, although cautiously, by two twentieth-century philosopher-theologians: John Baillie, *Our Knowledge of God* (second edition New York: Charles Scribner's Sons, 1959), pp. 178–98, 240–58, and Paul Tillich, "Two Types of Philosophy of Religion," *Theology of Culture* (New York, 1959), pp. 10–29, and, more briefly, *Systematic Theology* (Chicago, 1951), I, 204–10.

48. Cuthbert Butler, *Western Mysticism: The Teaching of Augustine, Gregory and Bernard on Contemplation and the Contemplative Life* (London, 1967), p. lxviii, referring specifically to Numbers 12:8.

49. See especially Robert J. O'Connell, *Art and the Christian Intelligence in St. Augustine* (Cambridge, MA, 1978), and Margaret Miles, *Augustine on the Body*, American Academy of Religion, Dissertation Series, No. 31 (Missoula, MT, 1979).

II. SMARAGDUS

1. What has been said here about the life and works of Smaragdus comes from Eberhard, as cited in the bibliographical notes, and from a distillation of the works he himself cites.

2. For an introduction to the doctrines of these works see my *Témoins de la Spiritualité Occidentale* (Paris, 1965), pp. 58–83.

3. *Patrologia Latina* 102, 596.

4. PL 102, 784, 699.

5. PL 102, 594.

6. PL 102, 594.

7. PL 102, 924–25.

8. PL 102, 630.

9. PL 102, 772–73.

10. PL 102, 756.

11. PL 102, 772.

12. Ibid.

13. PL 102, 784.

14. Ibid.

15. PL 102, 596–97.

16. PL 102, 686.

17. PL 102, 595.

18. Ibid.

19. PL 102, 686.

20. PL 102, 888.

21. PL 102, 613–14.

22. PL 102, 607–08.

23. PL 102, 679.

24. PL 102, 687.

25. PL 102, 596.

26. PL 102, 783.

27. PL 102, 711.

28. PL 102, 677.

29. PL 102, 616.

30. PL 102, 811.

31. PL 102, 594.

32. PL 102, 673.

33. PL 102, 840.

34. PL 102, 699.

35. PL 102, 679–80.

III. NEOPLATONISM AND THE MYSTICISM OF WILLIAM OF ST.-THIERRY

1. See E. R. Dodds, *Pagan and Christian in an Age of Anxiety* (Cambridge, 1965), and A. H. Armstrong, ed., *The Cambridge History of Later Greek and Early Medieval Philosophy* (Cambridge, 1970). Also helpful are several articles in R. Baine Harris, ed., *The Significance of Neoplatonism* (Albany, NY, 1976).

2. For translations of the *Enneads*, see A. H. Armstrong, Vol. I: *Ennead I*, 1–9 (1966); Vol. II: *Ennead II*, 1–9 (1966); Vol. III: *Ennead III*, 1–9 (1967), published in the Loeb Classical Library (Cambridge, MA). An excellent selection of texts can be found in Elmer O'Brien, S.J. ed. and tr., *The Essential Plotinus* (Indianapolis, 1975). Also, now out of print, Joseph Katz, *The Philosophy of Plotinus* (New York, 1950).

3. *Ennead* IV. 3. 17, O'Brien, p.145.

4. *Ennead* V. 1. 10, Katz, p. 21: "Now it must be held that as these three realities exist in nature, they also exist in us. (I do not mean that these three realities exist in the sense part of the self. For the intelligible exists apart from sense, that is, exists outside the sense part of our nature in the same way in which we say that it exists outside the celestial spheres.) Thus is constituted what Plato calls 'the inner man.' Our soul, too, then is something divine."

5. See note 43 below. See Anderson, *Enigma*, nos. 25–35.

6. *Ennead* IV. 3. 18, O'Brien, pp.145–46; and pp. 20–23, 157–51.

7. In a homey expression, William begins his *On Contemplating God* with the image of climbing the mountain of mystical ascent, and having to return to care for practical matters and for others. All his works are descriptive of applied moral theology derived from his mystical theology.

8. Cf. Stephen Gersh, *From Iamblichus to Eriugena* (Leiden, 1978), pp. 267–73.

9. Ibid., pp. 274–75.

10. John Scottus Eriugena, *Periphyseon*, ed. I. P. Sheldon-Williams (Dublin, 1968), I, pp. 81–83; and especially, p. 217: "And this is the prudent and catholic and salutary profession that is to be predicated of God: that first by the Cataphatic, that is, by affirmation, we predicate all things of Him, whether by nouns or by verbs, though not properly but in a metaphorical sense; then we deny by the Apophatic, that is, by negation that He is any of the things which by the Cataphatic are predicated of Him, only (this time) not metaphorically but properly—for there is more truth in saying that God is not any of the things that are predicated of Him than in saying that He is; then, above everything that is predicated of Him, His superessential Nature which creates all things and is not created must be superessentially More-than-praised."

I have preferred to use the word "kataphatic" which more closely approximates the Greek spelling; Sheldon-Williams prefers the Latinized form.

For further references for the metaphorical status of positive statements about God, see Ibid., pp. 89, 97, and 197.

11. *Ennead* VI. 9. 4, O'Brien, pp. 78–79; VI. 9. 7, pp. 82–83; VI. 9. 11, pp. 87–88; V. 1. 6, pp. 97–98; and finally the marvellous treatise on Contemplation, III. 8. 1–11, pp. 162–75.

Also, see the Pseudo-Dionysius, *The Mystical Theology*, in Elmer O'Brien, ed., *The Varieties of Mystic Experience* (New York, 1965), pp. 69–73.

12. The Pseudo-Dionysius, *On the Divine Names*, in C. E. Rolt, tr. *Dionysius the Areopagite: On the Divine Names and The Mystical Theology* (New York, 1957), pp. 95–96.

See Ronald F. Hathaway, *Hierarchy and the Definition of Order in the Letters of Pseudo-Dionysius* (The Hague, 1969), pp. 37–60.

13. William, *Epistola ad fratres de Monte Dei*, ed. Robert Thomas (Chambarand, 1968), pp. 70–72: "The cell is holy ground, a holy place, where the Lord and His servant often speak together, as one does with a friend. There the faithful soul is frequently joined to the Word of God, the *sponsa* is united to the *Sponsus*, the heavenly is made one with the earthly and the divine with the human. Just as the church is the holy place of God, so the cell is the holy place of God's servant. Divine affairs are conducted in the church and in the cell, yet more frequently in the cell than in the church. For in the church the sacraments are dispensed visibly and figuratively only at certain times; but in the cell, as in heaven, it is the essence of all the symbols and signs of our faith that is made known, in its very truth and nature, although not yet in its absolute splendor nor in the security of eternity." Translations of William are mine, unless otherwise noted. Cf. Theodore Berkeley, O.C.S.O., tr., *The Golden Epistle* (Spencer, MA, 1971), p. 22.

14. Cf. *Ennead* VI. 9. 11, O'Brien, pp. 87–88. Concerning metaphors of "mixture," and union see Gersh, *From Iamblichus*, pp. 192–203. Stephen Gersh provides a rather incisive comment on analogy in late Neoplatonism, specifically Proclus, in his *Kinesis Akinetos: A Study of Spiritual Motion in the Philosophy of Proclus* (Leiden, 1973), pp. 83–94.

The relation of the soul and mathematicals is actually the foundational notion on which the Neoplatonic doctrine of analogy depends. For a treatment of the soul and mathematicals, see Philip Merlan, *From Platonism to Neoplatonism*, 2nd ed., rev. (The Hague, 1960), pp. 11–33.

15. Cf. my article, "William of Saint-Thierry Against Peter Abelard: A Dispute on the Meaning of Being a Person," *Analecta Cisterciensia*, 28 (1972), 3–76. The article, unfortunately, has untold printing errors.

16. Words used to designate the "Fall," properly understood as the transgression or sin of Adam, or actual sin in general, are: *paraptoma*, *paraptosis*, and *ptoma*. For references to some works of the Church Fathers where these terms appear see G. W. H. Lampe, ed., *A Patristic Greek Lexicon* (Oxford, 1976). Plotinus uses the word *ptoma* in *Ennead* I. 8. 14, 25 and 44 in relation to the soul, and in *Ennead* III. 6. 6, 61 in relation to bodies.

Kathodos, referring to the descent of the soul, appears in Plotinus, *Ennead* IV. 3. 12, 18 and 21, and IV. 8. 3, 6; Clement of Alexandria, *Stromata*, 5. 14; Origen, *Contra Celsum*, IV. 40, 25, *Commentary on the Gospel of St. John* 12. 43, *On First Principles (Peri archon)*, IV. 16; Proclus, *The Elements of Theology*, ed., tr. E. R. Dodds, 2nd. ed. (Oxford, 1971), 180, 26 and 182, 21, where we read: "The vehicle of every particular soul descends by the addition of vestures increasingly material; and ascends in company with the soul through divestment of all that is material and recovery of its proper form, after the analogy of the soul which makes use of it: for the soul descends by the acquisition of irrational principles of life; and ascends by putting off all those faculties tending to temporal process with which it was invested in its descent, and becoming clear and bare of all such faculties as serve the uses of the process"; Damascius, *Commentary on Plato's Phaedo*,ed., L. G. Westerink (New York, 1977), Vol. II, I. 134, 3; I. 168, 2; I. 204, 2.

17. Philo of Alexandria, *In legum allegoria* II. 19, refers to two parts of the soul, man *(noûs)* and woman *(aísthesis)*, and states that it was fitting that the creation of the mind should be followed by that of sense-perception, which is to be an ally to the mind. The moral of the story is that it is the woman's nature to be deceived by what is exterior. The male part of the soul adheres to God, the female part turns to what comes about and passes away, and stretches out its hand to catch blindly what comes by. In *De specialibus legibus* III. 178 he points out that the man is to leave behind the feminine and to move toward that which is spiritual, manly (virtue). See Richard A. Baer, Jr., *Philo's Use of the Categories Male and Female* (Leiden, 1970), pp. 16–44.

Plotinus, *Ennead* VI. 9. 9, O'Brien, pp. 85–86: "Every soul is an Aphrodite, as is suggested in the myth of Aphrodite's birth at the same time as that of Eros. As long as the soul stays true to itself, it loves the divinity and desires to be at one with it, as a daughter loves with a noble love a noble father. When, however, the soul has come down to human birth, it exchanges (as if deceived by the false promises of an adulterous lover) its divine love for one that is mortal."

The notion of an interior hermaphroditism also appears in the gnostic gospels. In the *Gospel of Philip*, logion 71, one reads: "When Eve was in Adam, there was no death; but when she was separated from him death came into being"; and at logion 28: "If the woman had not separated from the man, she would not die with the man. His separation became the beginning of death."

Reflecting the similar notion found in Philo, William says, *Epistola*, Thomas, pp. 22–24: "*Anima*, the soul, is incorporeal, capable of reason, adapted to enliven the body. Such an adaptation makes men animals, whereby they cling to the senses of the body. When, however, the soul begins to be not only capable of, but actually participates in, perfect reason, then this *anima* progressively sheds its feminity and becomes *animus*, the *spiritus* participating in reason, suitable to rule the body and to contain itself interior to itself. In effect, while it is still *anima*, it easily becomes effeminate in the presence of that which is carnal. But *animus* or *spiritus* has thought only for that which is manly and spiritual."

18. Eriugena remarks, *Periphyseon* IV. 7, that even had man not sinned he would have been an animal; being animal is not due to sin but to nature, for no one holds that the transgressing angels became animals, and that would follow if animality were the result of sin. William reiterates the same notion in his *Physica animae*, PL 180, 710B-C. Plotinus remarks that the soul's inclination to inform the body, which is properly in its care, is not wrong, at *Ennead* I. 1. 12.

19. *Meditativa oratio* IV, in Robert Thomas, ed. and tr., *Prière, Contemplation de Dieu, Nature et dignité de l'amour* (Chambarand, 1965), pp. 72–74. Déchanet, "Guillaume et Plotin," *Revue du moyen-âge latin*, 2 (1946), 242 indicates this passage as stemming from Plotinus, *Ennead* I. 8. 13.

20. Thomas, p. 70. A similar notion is found in Macrobius, *Commentary on the Dream of Scipio*, ed., William Harris Stahl (New York, 1952), XI, 11: "According to this sect [the Neoplatonists], which is more devoted to reason, the blessed souls, free from all bodily contamination, possess the sky; but the soul that from its lofty pinnacle of perpetual radiance disdains to grasp after a body and this thing that we on earth call life, but yet allows a secret yearning for it to creep into its thoughts, gradually slips down to the lower realms because of the very weight of its earthly thoughts."

The notion of the seduction of the soul goes back to the Eleusinian mysteries, the myth of Persephone, who was raped by Hades and dragged down to the lower regions (region of unlikeness) while she was in a field picking the flower called Narcissus. The myth reiterates that of Narcissus who, mistaking an image for a reality in the mirror of Dionysus, proves his mortality. Plotinus reflects this in *Ennead* IV. 3. 12, O'Brien, p. 140: "And the souls of men? They see their images as if in the mirror of Dionysus and come down to their level with a leap from above." See also *Ennead* IV. 3. 15; III. 2. 4; I. 8. 4. Perhaps one can recognize here an early version of "Alice-through-the-looking-glass." For a note on Plotinus's notion of the soul being bewitched by bodily natures, see *Ennead* IV. 3. 17.

The moral is provided by Plotinus, *Ennead* V. 1. 10, O'Brien, pp. 91–92: "This evil that has befallen them [souls] has its source in self-will, in being born, in becoming different, in desiring to be independent. Once having tested the pleasure of independence, they use their freedom to go in a direction that leads away from their origin. And when they have gone a great distance, they even forget that they came from it. Like children separated from their family since birth and educated away from home, they are ignorant now of their parentage and therefore of their identity.

"Our souls know neither who nor whence they are, because they hold themselves cheap and accord their admiration and honor to everything except themselves. They bestow esteem, love, and sympathy on anything rather than on themselves. They cut themselves off, as much as may be, from the things above. They forget their worth. Ignorance of origin is caused by excessive evaluation of sense objects and disdain of self, for to pursue something and hold it dear implies acknowledgment of inferiority to what is pursued. As soon as the soul thinks it is worth less than things subject to birth and death, considers itself least honorable and enduring of all, it can no longer grasp the nature and power of the divinity.

"A soul in such condition can be turned about and led back to the world above and the supreme existent, the One and first, by a twofold discipline: by showing it the low value of the things it esteems at present, and by informing—reminding!—it of its nature and worth." The second discipline Plotinus develops at II. 4. 12; III. 4. 15; VI. 4. 22; and III. 6. 26.

21. This is the underlying theme of St. Gregory of Nyssa's treatise on virginity, PG 46, 317–416, the notion of which is the female becoming male in the ascetical sense, the *anima* wedding herself and conforming herself to her *animus*; thus virginity becomes the witness of immortality. St. Gregory is indebted for this notion to Alexandrian Neoplatonism, perhaps even to

Philo. See Baer, *Philo's Use of the Categories*, pp. 44–64 for Philo's treatment of making the female male.

22. William, *Epistola*, Thomas, pp. 30–34. The same idea occurs in Plotinus, *Ennead* VI. 9. 9, O'Brien, pp. 84–85.

23. Heraclitus, in G. S. Kirk and J. E. Raven, *The Presocratic Philosophers* (Cambridge, 1966), p. 189, Fragment 60 taken from Hyppolytus of Rome, *Refutation of all Heresies* IX. 10. 4.

Plotinus, *Ennead* I. 1. 3, O'Brien, pp. 93–94: "So divine and precious is The Soul, be confident that, by its power, you can attain to divinity. Start your ascent. You will not need to search long. Few are the steps that separate you from your goal. Take as your guide the most divine part of The Soul, that which 'borders' upon the superior realm from which it came.

"Indeed, in spite of the qualities that we have shown it to have, The Soul is no more than an image of The Intelligence. Just as the spoken word is the image of the word in the soul, The Soul itself is the image of the word in The Intelligence and is the act of The Intelligence by which a further level of existence is produced. . . . The Soul does not become completely separated from The Intelligence."

On the ascent, and the structure of the soul which permits ascent, see my article, "The Three Theological Virtues as Modes of Intersubjectivity in the Thought of William of Saint-Thierry," *Recherches de Théologie ancienne et médiévale*, 38 (1971), 89–120.

24. *Ennead* VI. 9. 8.

25. *Meditativa oratio* XI, Thomas 62–64. This text is also reminiscent of that of the Pseudo-Dionysius, *On the Divine Names* II. 5. An interesting drawing, the diagram of the mystical compass, of this very notion by the Elizabethan Neoplatonist, Robert Fludd, is reproduced in Frances A. Yates, *Giordano Bruno and the Hermetic Tradition* (Chicago, 1964), opposite p. 339.

26. (Pseudo-) Gregory of Nyssa, *De eo, quid sit, ad imaginem Dei et ad similitudinem*, PG 44, 1331B: "If you wish to know God, first know yourself. You can recognize God from your nature, your structure, from all that is interior to you. Enter more deeply into yourself, look back into your soul as you would in a mirror, discern her structure, and you will be able to see that you are made to the image and likeness of God."

William employs the same theme, depicting the relation of the soul *(sponsa)* and God *(Sponsus)*, in his *Exposition on the Song of Songs*, tr. Hart, p. 50: "Next comes this: 'If you know not yourself, O fairest among women, go forth and depart, after the steps of the flocks.' As if to say: What you ask me to show you, this you know; but you know not yourself. For you suppose you know me not, because you know not yourself. And you know not yourself because you have gone forth from yourself."

And again, p. 51: " 'If you know not yourself, O fairest among women, go forth!' This reminder of her fairness may be viewed as a reproach for her neglect of it. . . . 'If you know not yourself, go forth!' would therefore mean: If you go forth from yourself, it is because you know not yourself. Know yourself, then, to be my image; thus you can know me, whose image you are, and you will find me within you."

This is the same notion at the base of the Delphic injunction, "Know thyself." See J.-M. Déchanet, *Aux sources de la spiritualité de Guillaume de Saint-Thierry* (Bruges, 1940), p. 26.

Plato explains the Delphic command by a simile drawn between the soul and a reflecting, mirroring eye *(kore)*—an indirect reference to Persephone. Just as an eye must look at another eye to see itself, so the soul must look at a soul to comprehend herself. *Alcibiades* I, 132D-133C.

27. Plotinus, *Ennead* VI. 9. 9. William, *On the Nature and Dignity of Love*, Webb and Walker, p. 11: "The art of all arts is the art of loving, and the teaching of this art belongs exclusively to God. But since God has rooted love in our very nature, it is equally true to say that nature is our teacher. And when love, which is of free and noble birth, preserves its liberty in the face of deceiving passions, we may count love itself as the third professor of this art. . . .

"Love is a power which carries the soul along by a natural tendency toward its destination. Every creature, whether spiritual or physical, has a place which God has designed for it, and a tendency which moves it in the right direction. Philosophy tells us that this tendency is not always a weight in the strict sense, dragging a thing downwards. Water goes down, it is true, but fire goes up. Man for his part has a natural bent by which his spirit tends toward higher things and his body to the things of the earth; but in both cases the direction is toward a natural destination or goal."

See my article, "William of Saint-Thierry on the Myth of the Fall," *Recherches de Théologie ancienne et médiévale*, 46 (1979), 45–52.

28. John D. Anderson, tr., *The Enigma of Faith* (Kalamazoo, 1974), pp. 38–39, 51; Mother Columba Hart, O.S.B., tr., *Exposition on the Song of Songs* (Spencer, MA, 1970), pp. 72–74; *The Golden Epistle*, Berkeley, pp. 78–105; *In Epistolam ad Romanos*, PL 180, 567D–569A.

29. Geoffrey Webb and Brian Walker, tr., *The Mirror of Faith* (London, 1959), pp. 21–24. This is the concept at the heart of the *Nature and Dignity of Love*.

30. *Expositio super Cantica*, Déchanet, p. 312: ". . . there, in the secret of her little room, in the solitude of the heart, in the inner place of conscience, she [the soul] loves to sit, applying herself to cleansing her heart, anxious to purify her face in the mirror, in the enigma, so that one day she may see face to face."

31. *Speculum fidei*, in M.-M. Davy, text and tr. *Deux traités sur la foi: Le Miroir de la foi; L'énigme de la foi* (Paris, 1959), p. 24. See *Mirror*, p. 13ff.

32. Ibid., p. 28.

33. See "William of Saint-Thierry Against Peter Abelard," 8–14; and also my article, "William of Saint-Thierry on the Phenomenon of Christ: The Paradigm of Human Possibilities," *Analecta Cisterciensia*, 31 (1975), 213–20.

34. "William of Saint-Thierry on the Phenomenon of Christ," 220–33.

35. *Aenigma fidei*, Davy, pp. 102–04; see *Exposition on the Song of Songs*, Hart, p. 69.

36. *Speculum fidei*, Davy, pp. 60; 64–66.

37. *Aenigma fidei*, Davy, p. 174. See *Mirror of Faith*, Webb and Walker, pp. 49–53.

38. *On the Nature and Dignity of Love,* Webb and Walker, pp. 42–57.

39. *Speculum fidei,* Davy, p. 88; see Sister Penelope, C.S.M.V., tr., *On Contemplating God, Prayer, Meditations,* Cistercian Fathers Series 3 (Spencer, MA, 1971), pp. 59–60; and *Meditation VI,* Penelope, pp. 126–27.

40. *Meditativa oratio VI,* Davy, pp. 142–44; cf. Penelope, p. 128.

41. *Aenigma fidei,* Davy, pp. 122–24.

42. Rejecting the Boethian definition of the person as "an individual substance of a rational nature," William supplies the definition, "cujus pro sui forma, certa sit agnitio" (the sure recognition of which is established in accordance with the distinctive appearance of oneself), *Enigma of Faith,* Anderson, pp. 65–67. Dom Odo Brooks has commented on this definition proposed by William, "The Speculative Development of the Trinitarian Theology of William of Saint-Thierry in the 'Aenigma fidei,' " *Recherches de Théologie ancienne et médiévale,* 28 (1961), 37 note 148.

43. *Aenigma fidei,* Davy, p. 94: "John the Evangelist says, 'No one has ever seen God'; at least, certainly, not in the same way that one sees things commonly called perceptibles. And for this reason he immediately appended the following statement: 'it is the only Son, who is nearest to the Father's heart *[qui est in sinu Patris],* who has made Him known.' In effect, no one has ever seen God with these bodily eyes; but since the only Son is the very insinuation of the Father *[in sinu Patris],* and thereby uncovers the Father in an unspeakable telling *[narratione ineffabili],* the purified and holy rational creature is permeated with this inexpressible vision. The creature is able to understand the Speaker narrating because He is *logos*—not the kind of word that strikes the ear as sound, but rather something like an *imago* disclosed to the spirit. By an interior and manifest light this telling clarifies the words of the Lord: 'Philip, whoever see Me sees the Father too.' "

The same insinuating structure of the person is attributed to the *animus-anima,* the *sponsa,* Déchanet, *Super Cantica,* p. 214: ". . . clarified from above herself, the *sponsa* begins to show herself and to find within herself the one she seeks. They mutually insinuate one another; they are delighted with each other, they witness each other in their mutual love and in their familiar conversation, tasting in advance the joy of mutual union."

By reason of this mutual insinuation, God and the inner man become mutual paradigms. Eriugena, *S. Maximi scholia in Gregorium Theologum* (Oxonii, 1681), ch. 8: "Dicunt enim inter se invicem esse paradigmata Deum & hominem."

44. *Speculum fidei,* Davy, pp. 80–82.

45. See *Meditation VI,* Penelope, pp. 126–27. Also, "William of Saint-Thierry on the Phenomenon of Christ," 234–45.

46. *Super Cantica,* Déchanet, pp. 220–22. See *Mirror of Faith,* Webb and Walker, pp. 62–67.

IV. St. Bernard, the Canticle of Canticles, and Mystical Poetry

1. Kilian Walsh and Irene Edmunds, tr., *Bernard of Clairvaux: On the Song of Songs,* 4 vols. (Kalamazoo, 1971–80).

2. R. P. Lawson, tr., *Origen: The Song of Songs* (London, 1957), p. 21; W. B. Baerens, ed. *Origenes Werke*, VIII (Leipzig, 1925), p. 61.

3. Friedrich Ohly, *Hohelied-Studien* (Wiesbaden, 1958), pp. 145–46.

4. Two manuscript texts edited by Frederick J. Furnivall as "Quia Amore Langueo," EETS OS 15 (London, 1866), pp. 180–89. I adapt and normalize these.

5. Etienne Gilson, *The Mystical Theology of Saint Bernard*, tr. A. H. C. Downes (London, 1940).

6. Lawson, p. 239; Baerens, p. 223.

7. André Wilmart, ed., *Le "Jubilus" Dit de Saint Bernard* (Rome, 1944).

8. Gilson, "Sur le *Iesu Dulcis Memoria*," p. 325.

9. Carleton Brown, ed., *Religious Lyrics of the XIVth Century*, 2nd ed., rev. George Smithers (Oxford, 1952), p. 111.

10. See her *Das Fliessende Licht der Gottheit*, tr. Lucy Menzies as *The Revelations of Mechthild of Magdeburg* (London, 1933), esp. the first three Parts, pp. 1–92.

11. William Ralph Inge, *Christian Mysticism* (New York, 1933), p. 43.

12. One of several published translations into English of these poems is that of John Frederick Nims, *The Poems of St. John of the Cross* (New York, 1959), pp. 2–21 (with Spanish original on facing pages).

V. The Zohar: Jewish Mysticism in Medieval Spain

1. Nineteenth and early twentieth century scholarship treating the history of Judaism generally relegated Kabbalah to an obscure and somewhat shameful corner. Such treatment was motivated by apologetics, by a set of theological presuppositions about Judaism rendered difficult by the presence of Kabbalah, and by a genuine distaste for the material. This attitude was epitomized by the treatment of Kabbalah in the works of the great Jewish historian Heinrich Graetz. The study of Kabbalah has been revolutionized by the career of Gershom Scholem, the leading historian of Judaism in this century, who has devoted his full energies to a study of Jewish mysticism and its restoration to its rightful place in the history of Judaism.

2. See the extended discussion by Scholem in *Ursprung und Anfänge der Kabbala* (Berlin, 1962) also appearing as *Les origines de la Kabbale* (Paris, 1966). An English translation of this volume is planned, but its publication has not yet been announced. Summaries of Scholem's views on the earliest Kabbalah can be found in his articles *Kabbalah* and *Bahir* in the *Encyclopedia Judaica*, re-issued in the volume *Kabbalah* (Jerusalem, 1974). See also the article by Shulamit Shahar in *Tarbiz*, 40 (1971), 483–507.

3. The Bahir was translated into German by Scholem, published in Berlin, 1923. An English translation by Aryeh Kaplan was published in New York, 1974. It is generally reliable as a translation, through the introduction that accompanies it is not historically grounded.

4. Bahir 78. References to the Bahir follow the standard edition of R. Margulies (Jerusalem, 1951).

5. Bahir 156. See Scholem, *Ursprung*, p. 155.

6. Bahir 141–45. See Scholem, *Ursprung*, pp. 111–14.

7. On the nature of myth and symbol in the Kabbalah see Scholem, "Kabbalah and Myth" in his collection *On the Kabbalah and Its Symbolism* (New York, 1965). A further study of kabbalistic symbols is that by Tishby in his *Netivey Emunah u-Minut* (Israel, 1964), pp. 11–22.

8. The seeming contradiction between claims of antiquity and assertions of new revelation was not a problem for the Kabbalists or the intended audience for such claims. Ancient secrets, hidden in documents unknown or whispered through the ages by an esoteric elite, have the same flavor as heavenly secrets, preserved above through the ages, and now freshly given by the angels or through a visit of Elijah.

9. On the Gerona period in Jewish mysticism see Scholem, *Ursprung*, pp. 324–420. For those who read Hebrew but not French or German, Scholem's lecture notes from courses at the Hebrew University have been printed and are available from the university's Akademon Press. Among these is an entire volume of lectures on Kabbalah in Gerona. The English reader must meanwhile remain satisfied with the summaries to which we have referred in n. 2.

10. Scholem, *Encyclopedia Judaica* 10:607.

11. Rather little research has been done on this so-called "gnostic" school. Their basic texts have been edited and studied by Scholem in *Mada'ey ha-Yahadut* 2 (1927) and *Tarbiz* 2–5 (1931–35). Two new studies by Joseph Dan also treat of this circle: "Samuel, Lilith, and the Concept of Evil in the Early Kabbalah," *AJS Review* 5, (1982) and "The Beginning of the Messianic Myth in Thirteenth Century Kabbalah" (Hebrew), Hebrew University Institute of Jewish Studies (Jerusalem, 1981).

12. Quoted by Scholem in *Major Trends in Jewish Mysticism* (New York, 1954), p. 156ff.

13. The complicated tale of the search Isaac of Acre conducted for this manuscript, culminating in De Leon's widow's assertion that it never had existed at all, is told in full by Scholem in *Major Trends*, pp. 190–92. *Major Trends* contains two chapters devoted to the Zohar. These constitute the best summation of current scholarship regarding this work.

14. A number of these terms are discussed in the footnotes to *Major Trends*. The "dictionary" which Scholem promises in n.7, p. 385, is partially available now in the dissertation of his student Yehuda Liebes, *Sections of the Zohar Lexicon* (Jerusalem, 1976). This lexicon, concentrating on the most interesting and unusual of the Zohar's vocabulary, has become an indispensible aid to an understanding of the Zohar.

15. Zohar II 11a–12.

16. In the immediately preceding narrative Rabbi Eleazar himself is discoursing on Ezekiel 37:9.

17. Zohar II 13a–b.

18. Zohar I 232a–b. Color symbolism is quite extensive in the Zohar. Scholem has discussed this matter in *Eranos Jahrbuch*, 41 (1972), 1–49, now translated into English in *Diogenes* 108–09 (1979–80).

19. *Major Trends*, lecture five.

20. Quoted from ibid., p. 201ff. Scholem's translation.

21. This matter is discussed fully by Tishby in *Mishnat ha-Zohar*, v.1 (Jerusalem, 1957), pp. 107–11.

22. Zohar I 15a.

23. Zohar II 68b.

24. *Major Trends*, p. 15ff.

25. The four letters of *binah* in Hebrew, *bet, yod, nun, heh*, are thus accounted for: the two "parents" and their "son."

26. Zohar III 290a, Idra Zuta. The Zohar has a penchant for daring sorts of religious imagery that sound nearly christological. These certainly reflect not a christianizing tendency (as many a latter-day Christian Kabbalist has dreamed), but rather a search for a new anthropomorphism appropriate to kabbalistic thinking. "Son" goes with "daughter"; this same pair are "bridegroom" and "bride." Still, the extra measure of cautionary language surrounding this paragraph is easy to understand.

27. Here the author seems to have taken an earlier conventional phrase, *bet 'olam*, usually thought of as "eternal home," and allowed his imagination to give it pictorial content. Many examples of this intentional over-literalism can be found in the Zohar.

28. Zohar I 172a. Compare Bahir 156, quoted above. This passage may be better understood with a glance at the sefirotic chart printed below. We have intentionally avoided placing such a chart at the outset of our discussion of the *sefirot*, and here too we offer it with hesitancy. When the kabbalistic symbols are overly conventionalized, either in terms of name or position with respect to the others, they tend to lose their freshness and richness of meaning. Charts are especially susceptible to this danger, and none is included in the Zohar itself. But here the spatial relations will be helpful. The bottommost *sefirah, malkhut*, is the house, again in feminine symbol. She is at the center of all, being the lowest link in the sefirotic chain but the uppermost in the worlds below, as we shall see presently. The tree that rises within her is *yesod;* the "male" principle that links her with the worlds above fructifies her so that abundance for all will be provided. *Yesod* reaches upward to the three great mountains (or patriarchs), *ḥesed, din*, and *tiferet*, is hidden behind them, and then rises on still higher, though now his ascent is hidden in clouds of obscurity. The entire sefirotic world, from *keter* to *malkhut*, is connected by a single "central pillar," though its upper reaches cannot be seen. The male principle *(yesod, or tiferet)* rules during the day, while *malkhut*, moon, she who has no light of her own, rules at night.

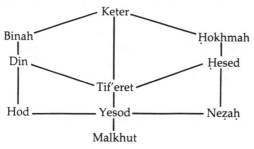

29. On the *shekhinah* see Scholem, *Von der mystischen Gestalt der Gottheit* (Zürich, 1962), pp. 135–91; Hebrew version in *Pirqey Yesod be-Havanat ha-Qabbalah u-Semaleha* (Jerusalem, 1976), pp. 269–307.

30. The relationship between the Song of Songs, as midrashically understood, and the literature called *shi'ur qomah*, comprising mainly gigantic measurements of the limbs of a divine body, has yet to be fully clarified. There is a large literature on the *shi'ur qomah* in recent scholarship. Its relationship to the Song of Songs was first suggested by Saul Lieberman in an addendum (in Hebrew) to Scholem's *Jewish Gnosticism, Merkabah Mysticism, and Talmudic Tradition* (New York, 1960).

31. Zohar II 245a.

32. Zohar I 17a. See Tishby, *Mishnat ha-Zohar*, v. 1, p. 296ff. and the further sources quoted there.

33. The reader is referred to the chart in n. 28.

34. Zohar II 89a–b.

35. Zohar III 152a. Translation from Scholem's *Zohar* (New York, 1949), p. 121ff. On the Torah in Kabbalah see also his *On the Kabbalah and its Symbolism*, pp. 32–86.

36. Zohar II 213b.

VI. MYSTIC ON CAMPUS: FRIAR THOMAS

1. St. Thomas, *Sum. theol.* I, q. 1, a. 8 ad 2; q. 2, a.2 ad 1.

2. See J. A. Weisheipl, O. P., "The Meaning of *Sacra Doctrina* in *Summa Theologiae* I, q. 1," *The Thomist*, 38 (1974), 49–80.

3. On the intimate relation between theology, sanctity, and Christian faith, see Jean-Pierre Torrell, O. P., *Revue Thomiste*, 71 (1971), 205–21; M.-D. Chenu, O. P., *Nature, Man, and Society in the Twelfth Century*, tr. J. Taylor and L.K. Little (Chicago, 1968).

4. "Gratia nihil aliud est, quam quaedam inchoatio gloriae in nobis" (*Sum. theol.* II-II, q. 24, a. 3 ad 2); this is because by grace we participate in the intimate nature of the Godhead: "Gratia est participatio divinae naturae." *Sum. theol.* I-II, q. 110, a. 3, a. 4; q. 112, a. 1; q. 113, a. 9; q. 114, a. 3; II-II, q. 19, a. 7; III, q. 2, a. 10 ad 1; q. 3, a. 4 ad 3; q. 62, a. 1; *De verit.* q.27, a.7; *De virt. in com.* q. 2, a. 2 ad 15.

5. "Lumen gratiae, intellectum dirigit et affectum movet" *In IV Sent.* dist.18, q. 1, a. 2, q1.1 ad 2. Note that St. Thomas discussed three kinds of life for man: "Vita cuius auctor est Deus, est triplex, scilicet naturae, gratiae et gloriae" (I-II, q. 112, a. 4 ad 3).

6. The fullest presentation of miracles, visions, levitations and the like in Thomas's life is to be found in William of Tocco's *Hystoria beati Thomae de Aquino*, ed. Angelico Ferrua in *S. Thomae Aquinatis Vitae Fontes Praecipuae* (Alba, 1968), pp. 29–123. This first presentation of his life was written to promote the cause of Thomas' canonization (1323). The *Legenda*, written around the same time by Bernard Gui, was chosen for translation by Kenelm Foster, O. P. (*The Life of Saint Thomas Aquinas* [London, 1959]) "because he allows less place to pious comment and rhetorical decoration," p. 9. The

true and necessary effects of charity (II-II, qq. 28–33) are clearly distinguished from *gratiae gratis datae*, which may or may not be associated with charity (II-II, qq. 171–78).

7. This is the foundation of St. Thomas' whole discussion of virtues, grace, and merit in the second part of the *Summa theologiae*, but see especially I-II, q. 114 and III *Sent. dist.* 30, and *De verit.* q. 26, a. 6.

8. "Nullius virtutis actus est meritorius nisi sit informatus charitate" (I-II, q. 114, a. 4 ad 3 *et multoties*).

9. Details of Thomas' life and context may be found in my *Friar Thomas d'Aquino: His Life, Thought and Works* (Garden City, 1974), also available in England (1975) and in translation into German (1980), Spanish (1982), and Italian (1982).

10. Bernard Gui, *Legenda*, c. 5, in Foster, p. 27.

11. Tolomeo of Lucca, *Historia Ecclesiastica*, lib. 22, c. 20, in Foster, p. 129.

12. William of Tocco, *Hystoria*, c. 11, ed. Ferrua, p. 41.

13. Ibid., pp. 41–43.

14. Bernard Gui, *Legenda*, c.8, in Foster, pp. 30–31.

15. Thomas of Cantimpré, *Bonum universale de apibus* I, c. 20 (Douai: Baltazar Bellerus, 1627), p. 83.

16. William of Tocco, *Hystoria*, c. 12, ed. Ferrua, p. 44.

17. The list of suggestions is given in *Chartularium Universitatis Parisiensis*, ed. H. Denifle 1:385–86, n. 335.

18. These are the reasons Thomas gives for composing the *Summa*: "To remove impediments faced by novices, namely multiplicaiton of useless questions, articles, and arguments, scatlered discussions occasioned by the book being taught, and needless repetition generating both distaste and confusion" *(Prol.)*.

19. "Unumquodque dicitur bonum bonitate divina, sicut primo principio exemplari, effectivo et finali totius bonitatis" *Sum. theol.* I, q. 6, a.4. On the cause of evil, see *Sum. theol.* I, q. 49.

20. This is magnificently portrayed by G. K. Chesterton in his life of St. Thomas Aquinas, originally published in London, 1933.

21. See my *Friar Thomas d'Aquino*, p. 244.

22. R. A. Gauthier, "La date du Commentaire de saint Thomas sur l'Ethique à Nicomaque," *Recherches de théologie ancienne et médievale*, 18 (1951), 103, fn. 91.

23. O. Lottin, *Psychologie et morale*, I (Paris, 1942), pp. 252–62.

24. J. M. Ramírez, *De hominis beatitudine*, III (Madrid, 1947), p. 192.

25. E. Gilson, "Pourquoi saint Thomas a critiqué saint Augustin," *Archives d'histoire Doctrinale et Littéraire du Moyen Âge*, 1 (1926–27), 5–127; also "Les sources gréco-arabes de l'augustinisme avicennisant," ibid., 4 (1929), 5–149.

26. *De perfectione spiritualis vitae*, ed. Leonina, *Opera Omnia* 41 B (Rome, 1969), 69–111.

27. "Ratio autem diligendi proximum Deus est; hoc enim debemus in proximo diligere, ut in Deo sit. Unde manifestum est quod idem specie actus est quod diligitur Deus, et quo diligitur Deus et quo proximus" *(Sum. theol.*

II-II, q. 25, a.1). One of the dominant themes of St. Catherine of Siena's *Dialogue* is the identity of the virtue by which we love God and neighbor.

28. *De perfectione spiritualis vitae*, c.7, ed. Leon, 41:B 72.23–27.

29. Ibid. c. 30, ed. Leon, p. 111.49–54. The quotation is from Jerome, *Contra Vigil*, n.15 (PL 23, 351B) by way of the *Decretum* 16, q. 1, c. 4.

30. *Contra doctrinam retrahentium a religione*, c. 16, ed. Leon, 41:C 74, 164–71.

31. See especially *Sum. theol.* II-II, q. 188, a.6: "Sicut enim maius est illuminare quam lucere solum, ita manius est contemplata aliis tradere quamsolum contemplari." The whole discussion from q. 179 to q. 189 has to do with religious life and should be read against the background of the Parisian controversy.

32. "Istae perfectiones vocantur dona, non solum quia infunduntur a Deo; sed quia secundum ea homo disponitur ut efficiatur *prompte* mobilis ab inspiratione spiritus," *Sum. theol.* I-II, q. 68, a.1.

33. A number of these occasions are grouped by Bernard Gui in his *Legenda* (ed. Ferrua, pp. 161–62) under the heading "De abstractione mentis eius a sensibus," tr. Foster c. 28, p. 47.

34. These 13 propositions are listed in the *Chartularium Universitatis Parisiensis*, ed. cit. I:486–87, n. 432.

35. English translation of this letter is in Foster, pp. 153–55.

36. William of Tocco, *Hystoria*, c. 43, ed. Ferrua, c. 44, pp. 89–91.

37. Bernard Gui, *Legenda*, ed. Ferrua, c. 94, pp. 154–55; tr. in Foster, c. 25, p. 45.

38. This is fully discussed by St. Thomas in II-II, q. 45 where he "considers the gift of Wisdom which corresponds to charity."

39. "Et subiunxit sibi: 'Omnia que scripsi videntur michi palee respectu eorum que vidi et revelata sunt michi.' " Testimony of Bartholomew of Capua at the process of canonization in Naples, n. 79, ed. Ferrua, p. 319. Cf. William of Tocco, *Hystoria*, c. 53, ed. Ferrua, pp. 100–01.

40. Ibid., pp. 318–20.

41. Ibid., n. 78, ed. Ferrua, pp. 316–18.

42. For the details of Thomas' last days, see my *Friar Thomas d'Aquino*, pp. 320–31.

43. L. H. Petitot, O. P., *The Life and Spirit of Thomas Aquinas*, tr. Cyprian Burke, O. P. (Chicago, 1966), pp. 148–74.

44. See my *Friar Thomas d'Aquino*, p. 322.

45. Quoted by Jean Gerson, *Opera* (Antwerp, 1706), 2:712.

VII. THE MEDIEVAL CONTINENTAL WOMEN MYSTICS: AN INTRODUCTION

1. Evelyn Underhill, *Mysticism. A Study in the Nature and Development of Man's Spiritual Consciousness* (London, 1911; rpt. New York, 1961), pp. 453–54.

2. Ruth J. Dean, "Elizabeth, Abbess of Schönau, and Roger of Ford," *Modern Philology*, 41 (1944), 209.

3. Wendy Wright, "The Feminine Dimension and Consciousness," *Studia Mystica*, 3 (1980), 38.

4. Elizabeth Petroff, "Medieval Women Visionaries: Seven Stages to Power," *Frontiers*, 3 (1978), 34–45. This highly useful study of Italian women mystics in the thirteenth and fourteenth centuries is supplemented by her *Consolations of the Blessed* (New York, 1979).

5. Lucia of the Incarnation, "The Western Spiritual Tradition," *The Way*, Suppl. 16 (1972), 16.

6. Peter Dronke, *Poetic Individuality in the Middle Ages* (Oxford, 1970), p. 151.

7. I am indebted to Sr. Victorine Fenton, O.S.B. for her unpublished study of Hildegard's music and musicianship.

8. Hildegard of Bingen, *Scivias*, ed. Adelgundis Führkötter and Angela Carlevaris, *Corpus Christianorum Continuatio Medievalis* 43–43A (Turnholt, 1978). Hildegard's complete works are contained in *PL* 197.

9. Rufus Jones, *The Flowering of Mysticism: The Friends of God in the Fourteenth Century* (New York, 1939), p. 45.

10. Ed. Führkötter and Carlevaris, *CCCM* 43, pp. 3–4.

11. Ed. Führkötter and Carlevaris, *CCCM* 43, p. 124.

12. Barbara Grant, "Hildegard and Wisdom," *14th-Century English Mystics Newsletter*, 7 (1981), 8–19. For a further exploration of this approach to Hildegard, see Barbara Newman, "O Feminea Forma: God and Woman in the Works of St. Hildegard," diss. Yale University, 1981.

13. Marianna Schrader, *Dictionnaire de Spiritualité* 7, Pt. 1, 512.

14. Lucy Menzies, *Mirrors of the Holy: Ten Studies in Sanctity* (London and Milwaukee, 1928), p. 23.

15. A recent exemplary collection of critical essays is Anton Ph. Brück, ed. *Hildegard von Bingen, 1179-1979: Festschrift zum 800. Todestag der Heiligen* (Mainz, 1979).

16. Menzies, p. 21, taken from F. M. Steele, *Life and Vision of S. Hildegard* (London, 1915), p. 15.

17. Kurt Köster, "Elizabeth von Schönau: Werk und Wirkung im Spiegel der mittelalterlichen handschriftlichen Überlieferung," *Archiv für mittelrhein-siche Kirchengeschichte*, 3 (1951), 243–315; Dean, pp. 209–20; and also her "Manuscripts of St. Elizabeth of Schönau in England," *Modern Language Review*, 32 (1937), 62–71.

18. C. C. Martindale, "Shadow of the Living Light: Two Medieval Mystics," *Month*, 185 (1948), 82.

19. Mechthild of Hackeborn, *Liber Specialis Gratiae* in *Revelationes Gertrudianae et Mechthildianae* vol. 2, ed. Ludwig Paquelin (Poitiers—Paris, 1822), i–xvi, 1–442.

20. Mary Jeremy Finnegan, *Scholars and Mystics* (Chicago, 1962), p. 59.

21. Ibid., pp. 56–57.

22. Theresa A. Halligan, ed., *The Booke of Gostlye Grace of Mechthild of Hackeborn* (Toronto, 1979). Also see N. F. Blake, "*Revelations* of St. Matilda," *Notes & Queries*, 20 (1973), 323–25; and Halligan, "The *Revelations* of St. Matilda in English: *The Booke of Gostlye Grace*." *Notes and Queries*, 21 (1974), 443–46.

23. Mechthild of Magdeburg, *The Revelations of Mechthild of Magdeburg (1210–1297)* or *The Flowing Light of the Godhead*, tr. Lucy Menzies (London, New York, Toronto, 1953), Prologue, p. 3. All quotations are taken from this edition.

24. Mechthild of Magdeburg, *Sororis Mechtildis . . . Lux Divinitatis* in Paquelin, 2, 425–750. Also *Offenbarungen der Schwester Mechhild von Magdeburg oder Das Fliessende Licht der Gottheit*, ed. G. Morel (Regensburg, 1869; rpt. Darmstadt, 1963, 1976).

25. On this Latin rendering, see Odo Egres, "Mechthild von Magdeburg: The Flowing Light of God," in *Cistercians in the Late Middle Ages*, ed. E. Rozanne Elder (Kalamazoo, MI., 1981), pp. 29–31.

26. James C. Franklin, *Mystical Transformations: The Imagery of Liquids in the Work of Mechthild of Magdeburg* (London, 1978), pp. 17–31.

27. Alice Kemp-Welch, "Mechthild of Magdeburg. A Thirteenth-Century Mystic and Beguine," in *Of Six Medieval Women* (London, 1913), p. 77.

28. St. Gertrude, *Revelationes Gertrudianae et Mechthildianae*, 1, ed. Ludwig Paquelin (Paris, 1875).

29. *The Exercises of St. Gertrude*, ed. A Benedictine Nun of Regina Laudis (Westminster, MD, 1956).

30. Finnegan, p. 170.

31. Ibid., p. 134.

32. Ibid., p. 125.

33. Anna Groh Seeholtz, *Friends of God: Practical Mystics of the Fourteenth Century* (New York, 1934), pp. 123–26; Jones, pp. 163–69.

34. For a wide-ranging but thorough study, see Walter Blank, *Die Nonnenviten des 14. Jahrhunderts*, diss. Freiburg, 1962; also see Hope Emily Allen and Sanford B. Meech, ed., *The Book of Margery Kempe*, EETS OS 212 (London, 1940), pp. 376–78; and Simon Tugwell, ed., *Early Dominicans—Selected Writings* (New York, Ramsey, Toronto, 1982), pp. 412–24.

35. See Hester Reed Gehring, "The Language of Mysticism in South German Dominican Convent Chronicles of the Fourteenth Century," diss. University of Michigan, 1957.

36. Allen and Meech, pp. 378–80; also Ute Stargardt, "The Influence of Dorothea von Montau on the Mysticism of Margery Kempe," diss. University of Tennessee, 1980.

37. For an overview of the women's movement of the twelfth and thirteenth centuries, see Herbert Grundmann, *Religiöse Bewegungen im Mittelalter* (Berlin, 1935; rpt. Hildesheim, 1961; Darmstadt, 1970), pp. 319–54; Ernest McDonnell, *The Beguines and Beghards in Medieval Culture* (New Brunswick, NJ, 1954), pp. 81–119; Brenda M. Bolton, "Mulieres Sanctae" in *Women in Medieval Society*, ed. Susan M. Stuard (Philadelphia, 1976), pp. 141–59; and Michael Goodich, "The Contours of Female Piety in Later Medieval Hagiography," *Church History*, 50 (1981), 20–33.

38. E. Colledge, ed. and tr., *Mediaeval Netherlands Religious Literature* (Leyden and New York, 1965), p. 71.

39. R. W. Southern, *Western Society and the Church in the Middle Ages* (Grand Rapids, MI, 1970), pp. 300–01.

40. A welcome addition to the literature on these women will be *Monastic Women of the Medieval Period*, ed. Sr. M. Thomas Shank, to be published in 1984 by Cistercian Publications.

41. Carl Horstmann, "Prosalegenden. Die Legenden des MS. Douce 114," *Anglia*, 8 (1885), 102–84.

42. Beatrice of Nazareth, *The Seven Steps of the Ladder of Spiritual Love*, tr. F. Sherwood Taylor (Westminster, MD, 1943).

43. Stephen Axters, *The Spirituality of the Old Low Countries*, tr. Donald Attwater (London, 1954), p. 21.

44. Hadewijch, *The Complete Works*, tr. M. Columba Hart (New York, Ramsey, Toronto, 1981). All quotations are taken from this edition. Also see Hart's "Hadewijch of Brabant," *American Benedictine Review*, 13 (1962), 1–24; and Frances Gooday, "Mechthild of Magdeburg and Hadewijch of Antwerp: A Comparison," *Ons Geestelijk Erf*, 48 (1974), 305–62.

45. Suzanne F. Wemple, *Women in Frankish Society. Marriage and the Cloister, 500–900* (Philadelphia, 1981), p. 149.

46. Roland Maisonneuve, "L'Expérience Mystique et Visionnaire de Marguèrite d'Oingt (d. 1310), Carthusian Nun," in *Kartäusermystik und -Mystiker*, I, ed. James Hogg, *Analecta Cartusiana* 55 (Salzburg, 1981), 81–102. The best edition of her works, published under the aegis of the Centre National de la Recherche Scientifique, is *Les Oeuvres de Marguerite d'Oingt*, ed. Antonin Durafflour, Pierre Gardette, and Paulette Burdilly (Paris, 1965).

47. Angela of Foligno, *The Book of Divine Consolation of the Blessed Angela of Foligno*, tr. Mary G. Steegmann (London and New York, 1909; rpt. New York, 1966). All quotations are from this edition.

48. Johannes Jørgensen, *Saint Bridget of Sweden*, vol. 1, (1303–49); vol. 2, (1349–73) tr. Ingeborg Lund (London, New York, Toronto, 1954), 1, p. 171. See pp. 171–82 for a detailed account of the Rule of St. Savior.

49. Jørgensen, 2, 175.

50. St. Birgitta, *Revelations*, ed. William P. Cumming, EETS OS 178 (London, 1929 [for 1928]), 63–87.

51. See Jørgensen, 2, 247–70 for an excursus on these visions.

52. E. Colledge, "*Epistola Solitarii ad Reges:* Alphonse of Pecha as Organizer of Birgittine and Urbanist Propaganda," *Mediaeval Studies*, 17 (1956), 19–49.

53. Birgitta of Sweden, *Revelationes Sanctae Birgittae*, ed. Bartholomew Ghotan (Lübeck, 1492); ed. Gonzales Durante (Rome, 1606; 2d. ed. Antwerp, 1611; rpt. 1628, 1680). A critical edition of the Latin text is being done in *Series Samlingar utg. av Svenska fornskriftsällskapet (SFSS)*, Ser. II *(Latinska Skrifter)*.

54. Ernest Graf, tr., *Revelations and Prayers of St. Bridget of Sweden* (New York, 1928).

55. Roger Ellis, " 'Flores ad fabricandam . . . coronam': An Investigation into the Use of the *Revelations* of St. Bridget of Sweden in Fifteenth-Century England," scheduled to appear in *Medium Aevum*.

56. Cumming, pp. xxxi–viii.

57. John Rory Fletcher, *The Story of the English Bridgettines of Syon Abbey* (Syon Abbey, South Brent, Devon, 1933); F. R. Johnston, *Syon Abbey: A Short*

History of the English Bridgettines (Eccles and District History Society, in association with Syon Abbey, 1964).

58. Sebastian Bullough, "Catherine the Dominican," *Life of the Spirit*, 15 (1961), 447–52.

59. Vida D. Scudder, ed. and tr., *Selected Letters of Catherine Benincasa: Saint Catherine of Siena as Seen in Her Letters* (New York, 1927); Kenelm Foster and Mary John Ronayne, ed. and tr. *I, Catherine: Selected Writings of St. Catherine of Siena* (London, 1980). A translation of the *Prayers* by Suzanne Noffke is scheduled to appear in the Paulist Press Classics of Western Spirituality Series.

60. Catherine of Siena, *The Dialogue*, tr. Suzanne Noffke (New York, Ramsey, Toronto, 1980). All quotations are taken from this edition. For the critical edition of the Italian text, see *Il Dialogo della Divina Provvidenza ovvero Libro della Divina Dottrina*, ed. Giuliana Cavallini (Rome, 1968).

61. Lucia of the Incarnation, p. 20.

62. Raymond of Capua, *The Life of Catherine of Siena*, tr. Conleth Kearns (Wilmington, DE, 1980).

63. Phyllis Hodgson and Gabriel Liegey, ed., *The Orcherd of Syon*, I,EETS OS 285 (London, 1966); also see Hodgson, "*The Orcherd of Syon* and the English Mystical Tradition," *Proceedings of the British Academy*, 50 (1964), 229–49; and Mary Jeremy Finnegan, "Catherine in England: *The Orchard of Syon*," *Spirituality Today*, 32 (1980), 13–24.

VIII. Julian of Norwich: Writer and Mystic

1. For the records in wills see Edmund Colledge and James Walsh, critical edition, *A Book of Showings to the Anchoress Julian of Norwich*, 2 vols. (Toronto, 1978), 1, 33–34. See also, F. I. Dunn, "Hermits, Anchorites and Recluses: A Study with Reference to Medieval Norwich," in *Julian and Her Norwich*, ed. Frank Dale Sayer (Norwich, 1973), pp. 18–26; and Ann K. Warren, "The Anchorite in Medieval England 1100–1539," diss. Case Western Reserve, 1980 (available on microfilm).

2. Chap. 2, tr. Wolters (Baltimore, 1973), p. 64. Unless otherwise indicated, all references in this paper are to the Long Version.

3. Chap. 3 (tr. Wolters), p. 143.

4. Tr. M. B. Salu (London, 1955). This guide for anchoresses contains directives for their daily lives, devotions, work, and relations with others.

5. See B. A. Windeatt, "Julian and Her Audience," *Review of English Studies*, n.s. 28 (1977), 1–17.

6. William Butler-Bowdon, ed., *The Book of Margery Kempe* (London, 1954), p. 38.

7. Chap. 6, Short Text (tr. Colledge and Walsh, *Showings*), p. 135.

8. Chap. 9 (tr. Wolters), p. 75.

9. Chap. 6, Short Text (Colledge and Walsh, *Showings*), p. 135.

10. For a fuller history of the manuscripts see Chaps. I-V, Introduction, Part One of critical edition, Colledge and Walsh, pp. 1–33.

11. T. A. Birrell, "English Catholic Mystics in Non-Catholic Circles—I," *Downside Review,* 94 (1976), 60–81.

12. Sheila Upjohn, *Mind Out of Time* (Julian Shrine Publications, 1979), p. 6.

13. Introduction, Colledge and Walsh, Critical Edition, Part One, p. 13.

14. *A Critical Edition of the Revelations of Julian of Norwich* (1342-c. 1416), prepared from all the known manuscripts, presented as a thesis for the degree of Doctor of Philosophy in the School of English Language and Literature, Leeds Univ., May, 1956: Amherst, pp. 1–52; Westminster, Appendix B., 36 pp.

15. See Valerie Lagorio and Ritamary Bradley, *The 14th-Century English Mystics: A Comprehensive Annotated Bibliography* (New York, 1981), items 503, 505, 512, 517–19.

16. Chap. 7 (tr. Wolters), p. 72.

17. Maisonneuve, Vol. I, 74–75.

18. See Donald F. Homier, "The Function of Rhetoric in Suggesting Stages of Contemplation in the Vernacular Writings of the Fourteenth Century English Mystics," diss., Northern Illinois Univ., 1975.

19. The anonymous author of *The Cloud of Unknowing* is an experienced spiritual director whose works come from the latter part of the fourteenth century. A widely-circulated edition is that of Clifton Wolters (Baltimore, 1961) and subsequent re-printings. See the essay by John P. H. Clark below.

20. Richard Rolle, *The Fire of Love,* ed. Clifton Wolters (Baltimore, 1971), p. 136.

21. Roland Maisonneuve, "L'Univers Visionnaire de Julian de Norwich."

22. Chap. 73 (tr. Wolters), pp. 191–92.

23. Ritamary Bradley, "Christ, the Teacher, in Julian's *Showings:* The Biblical and Patristic Traditions," *The Medieval Mystical Tradition in England,* Papers Read at the Dartington Symposium, 1982 (Exeter, 1982), pp. 127–42.

24. Tr. Wolters, p. 66.

25. Brant Pelphrey, *Love Was His Meaning. The Theology and Mysticism of Julian of Norwich* (Salzburg, 1982), p. 105.

26. Ibid., p. 163.

27. Chap. 58 (tr. Wolters), p. 166.

28. Pelphrey, p. 193.

29. Chap. 36 (tr. Wolters), p. 115.

30. Chap. 36 (tr. Wolters), p. 106. This is the quotation contained in Colwich Abbey Ms. 18.

31. Chap. 72 (tr. Wolters), p. 190.

32. Chap. 86 (tr. Wolters), p. 211–12.

33. See Ritamary Bradley, "Cloth and Clothing Metaphors in the *Showings* of Julian of Norwich" (to be published in *Mediaevalia*).

34. Chap. 11 (author's translation from critical edition, Colledge and Walsh), p. 336.

35. Sr. Anna Maria Reynolds, "Some Literary Influences in the *Revelations* of Julian of Norwich," in *Leeds Studies in English and Kindred Languages,* 7–8 (1952), p. 24.

36. *Divine Comedy,* Paradiso, Canto 27.

37. William Johnston, *The Still Point. Reflections on Zen and Christian Mysticism* (New York, 1970), pp. 132–33.

38. Chap. 6.

39. Chap. 35 (tr. Wolters). The same idea is expressed again in Chap. 52, p. 152.

40. For a systematic explication of the teachings underlying this parable, see Thomas Merton, *The New Man* (New York, 1961), pp. 134–37. Merton does not refer in this book to Julian, however.

41. Chap. 7.

42. Maisonneuve, Part One, pp. 349–50. See also David Biale, "The God with Breasts: El Shaddai in the Bible," *History of Religions*, 21 (1982), 240–56.

43. Ritamary Bradley, "Patristic Background of the Motherhood Similitude in Julian of Norwich," *Christian Scholar's Review*, 8 (1978), 101–13. See also Carolyn Walker Bynum, *Jesus as Mother: Studies in the Spirituality of the High Middle Ages* (Berkeley, 1982).

44. Chap. 59 (tr. Walsh), p. 161.

45. Chap. 54 (tr. Walsh), p. 150.

46. Chap. 58 (tr. Walsh), pp. 159–60.

47. Chap. 60 (tr. Wolters), p. 169.

48. Chap. 60 (tr. Wolters), p. 170.

49. John P. H. Clark, "Nature, Grace and the Trinity in Julian of Norwich," *Downside Review*, 100 (1982), 211.

50. Harvey D. Egan, "Mystical Crosscurrents," *Communio*, 7 (1980), 4–23.

51. Maisonneuve, Part II, p. 417.

52. Chap. 64 (tr. Wolters), p. 178.

53. Chap. 21 (tr. Walsh), p. 82.

54. Chap. 83 (tr. Wolters), pp. 208–09.

55. Chap. 81 (tr. Wolters), p. 206.

56. Chap. 26 (tr. Wolters), pp. 102–03.

57. Chap. 71 (tr. Wolters), p. 188.

58. These criteria are based on a standard work on mysticism, Evelyn Underhill, *Mysticism* (New York, 1961), Chap. 4, "The Characteristics of Mysticism," pp. 70–94.

59. T. S. Eliot, *Collected Poems, 1909–1962* (London, 1970), p. 223.

60. Aldous Huxley, *Eyeless in Gaza* (New York, 1936), p. 473.

61. Annie Dillard, *Holy the Firm* (New York, 1977).

62. Mary Gordon, *Final Payments* (New York, 1978), p. 300.

63. Thomas Merton, *Conjectures of a Guilty Bystander* (Garden City, 1968), p. 211; and *14th-Century English Mystics Newsletter*, 4 (1978), 2.

IX. MARGERY KEMPE

1. Sanford Brown Meech, ed., *The Book of Margery Kempe*, EETS OS 212 (London, 1940; rpt. 1961), "Appendix III. Extracts from Documents," p. 360. Hereinafter referred to as *Book*.

2. The *Book* was edited not from the original MS but from the only extant MS copy. See Meech, *Book*, "Introduction," pp. xxxii–xxxiv.

3. See *Book*, "Appendix II. Printed Extracts from the Book of Margery Kempe," pp. 353–57. The quotation, from p. 357, n. 11, is modernized, as are all subsequent Middle English passages in the text.

4. David Knowles, *The English Mystical Tradition* (New York, 1961), p. 138.

5. For the account of the discovery and a description of the MS, see *Book*, "Introduction," "THE MANUSCRIPT," pp. xxxii–xlvi.

6. *The Book of Margery Kempe: Fourteen Hundred & Thirty-Six*, A Modern Version by W. Butler-Bowdon (New York, 1944).

7. "Thys boke is not wretyn in ordyr, euery thyng aftyr other as it were don, but lych as the mater came to the creatur in mend whan it schuld be wretyn, for it was so long er it was wretyn that sche had for-getyn the tyme & the ordyr whan thyngys befellyn," *Book*, p. 5. Translations of modernized passages appear, as here, in the notes. "Creatur" or "creature" is Margery's usual way of referring to herself, a created being, in opposition to the triune God, uncreated and all-creating.

8. H. Thurston, S. J., "Margery the Astonishing," *The Month*, 2 (1936), 446–56, diagnosed the postpartum illness as hysteria. The overwhelmingly sex-linked character of such a judgment is obvious—one doubts it would be applied to a male mystic with similar symptoms (postpartum aside). Manic-depressive illness is a much likelier diagnosis, and the mania which "covers" the unbearable depression a much likelier manifestation.

9. *Book*, p. 9.

10. *Book*, p. 13.

11. "Dowtyr, the sowkyn euyn on Crystys brest," *Book*, p. 18.

12. *Book*, pp. 48–53. The time period is identifiable by the key phrase, "reuelacyons," on p. 48. Ill health prevented Hope Emily Allen from completing her chronology of Margery's mysticism, nor can I attempt it here; but such a study is indeed a *desideratum*.

13. The trek to Norwich, *Book*, pp. 38–43, is similarly identifiable by the phrase, "whyl thys creatur was beryng chylder," p. 38.

14. The visit with Julian, *Book*, pp. 42–43, is our only contemporary witness to her reputation as a spiritual counselor.

15. John Kempe's words have been misinterpreted by a number of critics: his, "as fre mot yowr body ben to God as it hath ben to me," *Book*, p. 25, refers to the concept of the marital debt, and is not ironic.

16. Undoubtedly it would have been irregular for the Bishop to give a non-widow a widow's emblems (on which see *Book*, "Notes," p. 274, n. 34/ 10–12). Margery had a lifelong history of trouble with widows which may have originated here.

17. White clothes could stand either for chaste living or for salvation without time in Purgatory, as Margery reminds the Bishop, *Book*, 34/13.

18. Yet she does not obey Christ's order until her arrival at Rome, on her way home from Jerusalem.

19. "Sche had so many enmys & so mech slawndyr that hem semyd sche myte not beryn it wyth-owtyn gret grace & a mygty feyth," *Book*, p. 43.

20. I am assuming that this priest is he who copied over the First Book, and to whom the Second was dictated. The original amanuensis is referred

to as "a man dwellyng in Dewchlond whech was an Englyschman in hys byrth & sythen weddyd in Dewchland & had ther bothe a wyf & a chyld, hauyng good knowlach of this creatur & of hir desyr, meued I trost thorw the Holy Gost . . . dwellyd wyth the forseyd creatur tyl he had wretyn as mech as sche wold tellyn hym," who then died, *Book*, p. 4. I am inclined to agree with Joan Wake's suggestion that this first scribe was Margery's son, in spite of Sanford Meech's objections, *Book*, "Introduction," pp. vii–viii.

21. This added fuel to a family cause. See *Book*, "Appendix III," VII, pp. 372–74.

22. "Flekeryd to & fro"; "My dowtyr, Bryde, say me neuyr in this wyse," *Book*, p. 47. St. Bridget of Sweden, who died in 1373, the year of Margery's birth, bore a number of children to her husband, spent most of the years after his death (1344) in Rome, founded the Brigittine Order, and was canonized in 1391. Margery had had her *Revelations* read to her, *Book*, p. 39, and somewhat took her as model.

23. "Dewchlond," an indeterminate geographical territory basically Teutonic and comprising "various parts of what we now call Germany," *Book*, "Notes," p. 257, n. 4/4.

24. "The good wyfe of the hows," "my bone maryd ryng to Ihesu Crist," p. 78.

25. Yet her marriage to the manhood of Christ is not mentioned in the narrative until the episode of the lost ring, except in *Book*, p. 31, where the usual multiple-relationship of the mystic to God is invoked.

26. This "flawme of fyer" lasts sixteen years, the heavenly sounds twenty-five, *Book*, pp. 88, 90.

27. "Askyd where sche had don hir chylde . . . begotyn & born whil sche was owte," *Book*, p. 103.

28. "Spar me tyl I come a-geyn into Inglond," *Book*, p. 110.

29. Even there the priest withholds the Eucharist until she has ceased her cries, *Book*, p. 139.

30. "Sumtyme sche xulde wepyn ful softely & stilly," *Book*, p. 139.

31. Besides Bride's book (see n. 22 above), he read Bonaventure, Walter Hilton, and Richard Rolle to her.

32. "Sche sey as hir thowt veryly dyuers men of religyon, preystys, & many other, bothyn hethyn & Cristen comyn be-for hir syght that sche myth not enchewyn hem ne puttyn hem owt of hir syght, schewyng her bar membyrs vn-to hir. & therwyth the Deuyl bad hir in hir mende chesyn whom sche wolde han fyrst of hem alle & sche must be comown to hem alle," *Book*, p. 145.

33. This Belgian noblewoman's life may also have inspired Margery to her later practice of kissing lepers. See *Book*, p. 322, n. 153/1.

34. Bishop's Lynn Guild Hall was burned Jan. 23, 1420–21: *Book*, p. 327, n. 162/29–31.

35. "For, thow thei louyd not hir wepyng ne hir crying in her lyfe-tyme, thei de[si]ryd that sche xulde bothyn wepyn & cryin whan thei xulde deyin," *Book*, pp. 172–73.

36. The woman is violently manic, as Margery had been, and not at the unipolar depressive end of the spectrum as are most postpartum cases.

37. "In hys last days he turnyd childisch agen & lakkyd reson that he cows not . . . go to a sege . . . but as a childe voydyd his natural digestyon," *Book,* p. 181.

38. As the woman and other shipmates have previously tried to avoid her by switching ships, Margery may be pardoned for a certain self-righteous smugness here. Unlike, for instance, Richard Rolle, she is usually charitable to even her worst enemy.

39. For this rather witty anecdote about Margery's abstinence, see *Book,* pp. 243–44.

40. "Specyaly of the curatys & preistys," whose animosity forced her from one church to another, *Book,* p. 245. That the common people should "magnify" her instead is a common theme with Margery.

41. Margery had had leave from her confessor only to take her daughter-in-law to ship, therefore her escort's reply, " 'I was blamyd for yowr defawte whan I led yow last; I wil no mor,' " *Book,* p. 247.

42. The words "true" and "minor" are value judgments by outsiders: the mystic way of Purgation, Illumination, and Union is followed by the mystic alone, who then tries to express the ineffable in words.

43. David Knowles, *The English Mystical Tradition* (New York, 1961), pp. 139, 146, 148.

44. T. W. Coleman, *English Mystics of the Fourteenth Century* (Westport, CT, 1971), p. 175.

45. R. W. Chambers, "Introduction," *The Book of Margery Kempe: A Modern Version,* tr. W. Butler-Bowdon (New York, 1944), pp. xviii, xxii.

46. Louise Collis, *Memoirs of a Medieval Woman: The Life and Times of Margery Kempe* (New York, 1964).

47. Robert Karl Stone, *Middle English Prose Style: Margery Kempe and Julian of Norwich* (The Hague, 1970), pp. 155–56.

48. R. M. Wilson, "Three Middle English Mystics," *Essays and Studies,* n.s. 9 (1956), 99, 196.

49. John C. Hirsh, "Author and Scribe in *The Book of Margery Kempe,*" *Medium Aevum,* 44 (1975), 145–50.

50. Wolfgang Riehle, *Studien zur englischen Mystik des Mittelalters unter besonderer Berücksichtigung ihrer Metaphorik* (Heidelberg, 1977), as summarized by Professor Riehle, in English, in *14th-Century English Mystics Newsletter,* 3, 1 (March, 1977), 8.

51. Katharine Cholmeley, *Margery Kempe: Genius and Mystic* (London, 1947).

52. Eric Colledge, ed., *The Medieval Mystics of England* (New York 1961). See also the same author's "Margery Kempe," *The Month,* 28 (1962), 16–29.

53. Anon., "Margery Kempe and the Holy Eucharist," *Downside Review,* 56 (1938), 468–82.

54. Martin Thornton, *Margery Kempe: An Example in the English Pastoral Tradition* (London, 1960).

55. John R. O'Connell, "Mistress Margery Kempe of Lynn," *Downside Review,* 55 (1937), 174–82.

56. E. I. Watkin, "In Defence of Margery Kempe," *Downside Review,* 59 (1941), 243–63.

57. *Book,* "Prefatory Note," p. 1vii, 1xi.

58. Roberta Bux Boss, "Margery Kempe's Tarnished Reputation: A Reassessment," *14th-Century English Mystics Newsletter,* 5 (March, 1979), 9–19; quotation from p. 17.

59. *The Medieval Vision: Essays in History and Perception* (New York, 1976), p. 189.

60. For discussion, see Brenda M. Bolton, "Mulieres Sanctae," in *Women in Medieval Society,* ed. Susan Masher Stuard (Philadelphia, 1976), pp. 141–58.

61. Chambers, "Introduction," p. xxii.

62. P. J. C. Field, *Speculum,* 48 (1973), 184–85, reviewing Coleman, p. 158.

63. See, for instance, Jean Genet's *Our Lady of the Flowers* or, even more convincingly, Eldridge Cleaver's *Soul on Ice.* Among the sociology texts, *Rape: The First Sourcebook for Women,* ed. Noreen Connell and Cassandra Wilson (New York, 1974), is superior.

64. Knowles, p. 150 and Coleman, p. 158, respectively.

65. In *Women and Madness* (New York, 1972), passim.

66. In "Sexual Economics, Chaucer's Wife of Bath and *The Book of Margery Kempe,*" *Minnesota Review,* n.s. 5 (1975), 113–14.

67. Riehle has "no doubt at all that Julian and Margery must have received some kind of information about their continental predecessors," p. 8.

68. "A Panorama of Women Mystics in the High Middle Ages," unpublished paper read at the Southeastern Medieval Association, Richmond, VA, March, 1977, 11 pp. Quotations in the next few sentences are from pp. 9, 10, and 11.

69. Jean Leclercq, "Preface," *Julian of Norwich: Showings,* tr. Edmund Colledge and James Walsh (New York, 1978), p. 3.

X. Meister Eckhart: An Introduction

1. F. Pfeiffer, *Deutsche Mystiker des vierzehnten Jahrhunderts,* II, *Meister Eckhart* (Leipzig, 1857), Sermon 1, p. 3.

2. Sermon 31 in *Meister Eckhart. Die deutschen und lateinischen Werke. Deutsche Werke,* II, (Stuttgart, 1971), p. 122. Hereafter the volumes of the *Deutsche Werke* will be abbreviated as DW, those of the *Lateinischen Werke* as LW. Vernacular sermons will be cited with Arabic numbers; Latin sermons with Roman numbers.

3. For an introduction, see Gordon Leff, *Paris and Oxford Universities in the Thirteenth and Fourteenth Centuries* (New York, 1968).

4. From Eckhart's "Vindicatory Document," or *Rechtfertigungsschrift,* as edited by G. Théry, "Édition critique des pièces relatives au procès d'Eckhart contenues dans le manuscrit 33ᵇ de la Bibliothèque de Soest," *Archives d'histoire littéraire et doctrinale du moyen âge,* 1 (1926), 196.

5. R. W. Southern in his *Western Society and the Church in the Middle Ages* (Harmondsworth, 1970), p. 146 put the problem thus: "As a secular ruler, however, the pope was insignificant unless he could harness his spiritual authority to political ends. This was the papal dilemma. By deploying his

whole strength for political ends, he could win; but then he lost the unique position that made his victory possible. He was lost in the common world of political manoeuvre."

6. For an introduction, see M. Lambert, *Franciscan Poverty* (London, 1961).

7. See M.-D. Chenu, *Nature, Man and Society in the Twelfth Century* (Chicago, 1968), especially chapters 6 and 7.

8. L. K. Little, *Religious Poverty and the Profit Economy in Medieval Europe* (Ithaca, NY, 1978).

9. For the Beguine movement, see H. Grundmann, *Religiöse Bewegungen im Mittelalter* (Hildesheim, 1961); and E. W. McDonnell, *The Beguines and Beghards in Medieval Culture* (New Brunswick, NJ, 1954).

10. Grundmann, chap. V.

11. Grundmann, p. 313.

12. Quoted by J. B. Freed, *The Friars and German Society in the Thirteenth Century* (Cambridge, MA, 1977), p. 7.

13. Grundmann, p. 5.

14. On the relation between the Beguines and the "Free Spirit," see R. E. Lerner, *The Heresy of the Free Spirit in the Later Middle Ages* (Berkeley, 1972).

15. H. Grundmann, "Die geschichtliche Grundlagen der deutschen Mystik," in K. Ruh, ed., *Altdeutsche und Altniederländische Mystik* (Darmstadt, 1964), pp. 72–99.

16. Ibid., p. 85.

17. Ibid., pp. 86, 92–97.

18. Ibid., pp. 87–89.

19. See Lerner, pp. 68–78 and 200–08.

20. Lerner, pp. 78–84.

21. The best summary is in Grundmann, *Religiöse Bewegungen*, chap. VIII.

22. The fullest account of Eckhart's life remains J. Koch, "Kritische Studien zum Leben Meister Eckharts," *Archivum Fratrum Praedicatorum*, 29 (1959), 1–51, and 30 (1960), 1–52. More recently, see T. Beckmann, *Daten und Anmerkungen zur Biographie Meister Eckharts und zum Verlauf des gegen ihn angestrengten Inquisitionsprozesses* (Heidelberg, 1978).

23. This concern for Neoplatonism was shared by such fellow German Dominicans as Ulrich of Strassburg (d.1277), Dietrich of Vrieburg (d.1310), and Berthold of Mossburg (d.1365).

24. A fragment of this commentary survives and has been edited in LW V, pp. 17–26.

25. DW V, pp. 185–311.

26. The "Parisian Questions" edited in LW V, pp. 37–83, appear to come from this period, though Eckhart's second magisterial period cannot be excluded. Eckhart also delivered a University sermon as *Magister* that has been edited in LW V, pp. 89–99.

27. DW V, pp. 8–119.

28. DW V, pp. 400–37.

29. LW I, pp. 148–82. Over 1000 propositions divided into 14 books were planned.

30. The commentaries have been edited in LW I-III, and the sermons in LW IV.

31. DW I-III.

32. See B. McGinn, "Meister Eckhart's Condemnation Reconsidered," *The Thomist*, 41 (1980), 390–414.

33. The critical text of this and the other trial documents has not yet appeared in LW V. The *Rechtfertigungsschrift* has been edited previously by A. Daniels and G. Théry (see note 4).

34. Other trial documents, including the Bull "In agro dominico" have been edited by M.-H. Laurent, "Autour du procès de Maître Eckhart. Les documents des Archives Vaticanes," *Divus Thomas* (Piacenza), series III, 13 (1936), 331–48, 430–47.

35. The *Gutachten*, or *votum theologicum*, of the Avignon commission was edited by F. Pelster, "Ein Gutachten aus dem Eckehart-Prozess in Avignon," *Aus der Geisteswelt des Mittelalters. Festgabe M. Grabmann* (Münster, 1935: Beiträge Supplement III), pp. 1099–1124.

36. Théry, p. 186.

37. See "Introduction" to E. Colledge and B. McGinn, *Meister Eckhart: Selections from his Latin and German Works* (New York, 1981), p. 15.

38. Théry, p. 186.

39. The Dominican General Chapter of Toulouse of 1328 warned against preaching *subtilia* to the people.

40. Just to mention some classic examples: the subjective and objective mysticism of W. R. Inge, *Christian Mysticism* (London, 1899); the inward and outward ways of R. Otto, *Mysticism East and West* (New York, 1932); the nature, soul, and God mysticism of R. C. Zaehner, *Mysticism Sacred and Profane* (New York, 1957), and the extrovertive and introvertive mysticism of W. T. Stace, *Mysticism and Philosophy* (London, 1960).

41. A point emphasized by a number of the essays in the recent collection *Mysticism and Philosophical Analysis*, ed. S. T. Katz (New York, 1978).

42. On this point, see J. R. Price III, *The Reintegration of Theology and Mysticism* (unpublished Ph.D. Dissertation, University of Chicago, 1980), especially Appendix B.

43. C. Butler, *Western Mysticism* (New York, 1923).

44. Eckhart frequently warns against the sensible consolations of religion, e.g., Sermon 16b (DW I, p. 272).

45. On this point, see B. McGinn, "The God beyond God: Theology and Mysticism in the Thought of Meister Eckhart," *Journal of Religion*, 61 (1981), 16–19; and R. Kieckhefer, "Meister Eckhart's Conception of Union with God," *Harvard Theological Review*, 71 (1978), 203–25.

46. This is not to claim that Cistercian, Franciscan, and Ignatian mysticisms are to be confounded, or even to be reduced to a single type.

47. LW III, pp. 3–114.

48. The best example of the role of the *imitatio Christi* in Eckhart is found in his Sermon XLV (LW IV, pp. 374–87).

49. E.g., DW V, pp. 262–84.

50. Sermons V.1–3 (LW IV, pp. 33–49), and 20a and b (DW I, pp. 326–52).

51. E.g., S. Ozment, *Mysticism and Dissent* (New Haven and London, 1973); and "Mysticism, Nominalism and Dissent," in C. Trinkaus and H. A. Oberman, *The Pursuit of Holiness in Late Medieval and Renaissance Religion* (Leiden, 1974), pp. 67–92.

52. *The Little Book of Truth*, chap. 6.

53. E.g., the four themes set forth in Sermon 53 (DW II, pp. 528–29). On these four themes, see R. Schürmann, "Eckhart and Soto Zen on Releasement," *The Thomist*, 42 (1978), 285–312. This same volume of *The Thomist* dedicated to Eckhart contains a useful summary of the themes of Eckhart's mysticism by J. Caputo, "Fundamental Themes in Meister Eckhart's Mysticism," 197–225.

54. I have tried to do this in two other places, my article "The God beyond God," *Journal of Religion*, 61 (1978), 1–19; and the "Introduction: Theological Summary" of the volume referred to in n. 37 above.

55. E.g., the commentary on Gen. 1:26 (LW I, pp. 270–76) and on Gen. 3:1 (LW I, pp. 602–36).

56. E.g., Sermons XLIX.1–3 (LW IV, pp. 421–28), and Sermon 69 (DW III, pp. 159–80).

57. Sermon 15 (DW I, p. 253).

58. On this theme, see C. F. Kelley, *Meister Eckhart on Divine Knowledge* (New Haven and London, 1977).

59. Sermon 15 ibid.

60. On this point, see "The God beyond God," pp. 14–15.

61. The crucial text on Eckhart's dialectical understanding of *unum* as meaning "not-to-be-distinguished" is found in the commentary on Wisdom 7:27 (LW II, pp. 481–94). On this see V. Lossky, *Théologie négative et connaissance de Dieu chez Maître Eckhart* (Paris, 1960), pp. 261–65.

62. McGinn, "Meister Eckhart's Condemnation Reconsidered," pp. 406–09.

63. Sermon 53 (DW II, p. 528).

64. DW V, pp. 411–12. Translation of E. Colledge from *Meister Eckhart. Selections from his Latin and German Works*, p. 288.

65. Both the "quietistic" indifference of detachment and its power over God led Eckhart to some dangerous expressions and indeed articles seven through nine of the Bull condemn three extracts relating to the former theme as heretical. It is worth noting that parallels to both sorts of statements can be found in Christian mystics who have not been condemned.

66. H. Rahner, "Die Gottesgeburt. Die Lehr der Kirchenväter von der Geburt Christi im Herzen der Gläubigen," *Zeitschrift für katholische Theologie*, 59 (1933), 333–418.

67. Sermon 6 (DW I, pp. 109–10). This forms art. 22 of the condemnation.

68. Sermon 22 (DW I, pp. 382–83).

69. Sermon 52 (DW II, p. 502).

70. See McGinn, "Meister Eckhart's Condemnation Reconsidered," pp. 408–09.

71. E.g., K. Kertz, "Meister Eckhart's Teaching on the Birth of the Divine Word in the Soul," *Traditio*, 15 (1959), 327–63.

72. Sermon 48 (DW II, p. 420).

73. Sermon 22 (DW I, p. 388), where the breakthrough, however, is to the hidden Fatherhood.

74. Sermon 2 (DW I, pp. 24–45).

75. J. Caputo, "Fundamental Themes," p. 224.

76. Sermon 86 (DW III, pp. 481–92).

77. E.g., Bernard's stress on the superior obligations of active love over affective, contemplative love in his *Sermons on the Song of Songs* 50, 57, 85, etc. For a comparison of Bernard and Eckhart on this and other themes, see B. McGinn, "St. Bernard and Meister Eckhart," *Cîteaux*, 31 (1980), 373–86.

78. Sermon 28 (DW II, p. 5).

79. *Counsels on Discernment* 4 (DW V, p. 198).

80. "In agro dominico," arts. 16–19, drawn from the Latin works, and condemned as "suspect of heresy," but capable of an orthodox explanation.

81. Notably I. Degenhardt, *Studien zum Wandel des Eckhartbildes* (Leiden, 1967).

82. For a survey of Eckhart's early influence, see J. Koch, "Meister Eckharts Weiterwirken im Deutsch-Niederländischen Raum im 14. und 15. Jahrhundert," *La mystique rhénane* (Paris, 1963), pp. 133-56. See also M. A. Lücker, *Meister Eckhart und die Devotio moderna* (Leiden, 1950).

83. Pfeiffer, *Meister Eckhart*, Traktate VI, p. 465.

84. On this question, see R. Lerner, *The Heresy of the Free Spirit*.

85. For Eckhart's influence, see H. Wackerzapp, *Der Einfluss Meister Eckharts auf die ersten philosophischen Schriften des Nikolaus von Kues (1440–1450)*, *Münster Beiträge . . . 39.3, (1962)*.

86. *Apologiae doctae Ignorantiae*, ed. R. Klibansky (Leipzig, 1932), p. 25.

87. E. Colledge, "Introduction," *Meister Eckhart. Selections from his Latin and German Works*, pp. 21–23.

88. For more on the modern period, see T. Schaller, "Die Meister-Eckhart-Forschung von der Jahrhundertwende bis zur Gegenwart," *Freiburger Zeitschrift für Philosophie und Theologie*, 15 (1968), 262–316, and 403–26; and "Zur Eckhart-Deutung der letzten 30 Jahre," *Freiburger Zeitschrift*, 16 (1969), 22–39.

89. Besides R. Otto's noted *Mysticism East and West*, see the works of such Oriental scholars as D. Suzuki, *Mysticism: Christian and Buddhist* (New York, 1957); S. Ueda, *Die Gottesgeburt in der Seele und der Durchbruch zur Gottheit: Meister Eckhart und der Zen-Buddhismus* (Gütersloh, 1965); and M. Nambara, "Die Idee des absoluten Nichts in der deutschen Mystik und ihre Entsprechungen im Buddhismus," *Archiv für Begriffsgeschichte*, 6 (1960), 143–277.

XI. JOHN TAULER

1. Ferdinand Vetter, ed. *Die Predigten Taulers* (Berlin, 1910), no. 6; Georg Hofmann, tr. *Johannes Tauler, Predigten* (Freiburg, 1961; Einsiedeln, 1979), no. 6.

2. Vetter, No. 53; Hofmann, No. 65.

3. Vetter, No. 15, 64; Hofmann, No. 15a, 53.

4. Hofmann's collection has 84 sermons, some of them subdivided.

5. This question is, of course, highly complex. On the rise of Christian asceticism, see Bernhard Lohse, *Askese und Mönchtum in der Antike und in der alten Kirche* (Munich and Vienna, 1969).

6. Vetter, No. 23; Hofmann, No. 23.

7. Vetter, No. 23–24; Hofmann, No. 23–24.

8. Vetter, No. 60f, and cf. No. 55; Hofmann, No. 31, and cf. No. 64.

9. Hofmann, No. 71.

10. Vetter, No. 80; Hofmann, No. 79.

11. Vetter, No. 6, 8; Hofmann, No. 6, 8.

12. Vetter, No. 6; Hofmann, No. 6. Another sermon (Vetter, No. 80; Hofmann, No. 79) gives a similar anecdote, borrowed from Cassian.

13. Vetter, No. 1, and cf. No. 9; Hofmann, No. 1, and cf. No. 9.

14. Hofmann, No. 3–4.

15. Vetter, No. 43, and cf. No. 38; Hofmann, No. 45, and cf. No. 38.

16. Vetter, No. 60f; Hofmann, No. 31.

17. Hofmann, No. 71.

18. Vetter, No. 15; Hofmann, No. 15b.

19. Vetter, No. 37; Hofmann, No. 37.

20. Vetter, No. 43; Hofmann, No. 45.

21. Vetter, No. 1; Hofmann, No. 1.

22. I am grateful to James Poag for pointing out to me this application of Rainer Schürmann's terminology.

23. Vetter, No. 43; Hofmann, No. 45.

24. Vetter, No. 60e; Hofmann, No. 25. Cf. Kieckhefer, "Notion of Passivity."

25. On this general subject see Christine Pleuser, *Die Benennung und der Begriff des Leides bei Johannes Tauler* (Berlin, 1967).

26. Hofmann, No. 3–4.

27. Vetter, No. 73; Hofmann, No. 50.

28. One sermon (Vetter, No. 15; Hofmann, No. 15b) does cite such virtues, quite summarily.

29. Hofmann, No. 60.

30. Vetter, No. 45; Hofmann, No. 51.

31. Hofmann, No. 71.

32. Vetter, No. 50; Hofmann, No. 56.

33. Vetter, No. 66, and cf. No. 67; Hofmann, No. 62, and cf. No. 63.

34. Vetter, No. 62; Hofmann, No. 39.

35. Vetter, No. 63; Hofmann, No. 42.

36. Vetter, No. 15, 62, and cf. No. 7; Hofmann, No. 15a, 39, and cf. No. 7.

37. Vetter, No. 13, 60a, 60e; Hofmann, No. 13, 17, 25.

38. Vetter, No. 79; Hofmann, No. 84.

39. See Kieckhefer, "The Notion of Passivity in the Sermons of John Tauler," *Recherches de théologie ancienne et médiévale*, forthcoming.

40. Vetter, No. 42; Hofmann, No. 47.

41. Vetter, No. 12; Hofmann, No. 12.

42. Vetter, No. 24; Hofmann, No. 24.

43. Vetter, No. 60e; Hofmann, No. 25.

44. See Karl G. Kertz, "Meister Eckhart's Teaching on the Birth of the Divine Word in the Soul," *Traditio*, 15 (1959), 333–62.

45. Vetter, No. 1; Hofmann, No. 1.

46. Vetter, No. 41, 60f; Hofmann, No. 31, 41.

47. Vetter, No. 49; Hofmann, No. 55.

48. Vetter, No. 63; Hofmann, No. 42.

49. Vetter, No. 73; Hofmann, No. 50.

50. Vetter, No. 40; Hofmann, No. 43.

51. Vetter, No. 32; Hofmann, No. 32.

52. Vetter, No. 39; Hofmann, No. 40.

53. Vetter, No. 7, and cf. No. 11, 21; Hofmann, No. 7, and cf. No. 11, 21.

54. Vetter, No. 15; Hofmann, No. 15a.

55. Vetter, No. 2, 11, 40, 50, 61; Hofmann, No. 2, 11, 43, 44, 56.

56. Vetter, No. 43; Hofmann, No. 45.

57. Vetter, No. 23, 57, 60d; Hofmann, No. 23, 29, 48. Cf. Ozment.

58. Vetter, No. 57; Hofmann, No. 48.

59. Vetter, No. 44, and cf. No. 60d; Hofmann, No. 29, and cf. No. 49.

60. Vetter, No. 15; Hofmann, No. 15a.

61. Vetter, No. 38; Hofmann, No. 38.

62. Vetter, No. 64; Hofmann, No. 53.

63. Vetter, No. 65; Hofmann, No. 59.

64. Vetter, No. 43, 63; Hofmann, No. 42, 45.

65. Vetter, No. 7, 75; Hofmann, No. 7, 75.

66. Vetter, No. 24; Hofmann, No. 24.

XII. THE CLOUD OF UNKNOWING

1. John P. H. Clark, "Sources and Theology in the *Cloud of Unknowing*," *Downside Review*, 98 (1980), 108 ff.

2. Phyllis Hodgson, ed. *The Cloud of Unknowing and the Book of Privy Counselling*, EETS OS 218 (London, 1944) (= *Cloud*, H) Introduction, pp. lxxxii ff. I also refer to Dom Justin McCann, *The Cloud of Unknowing and Other Treatises* (London, 1952) (= *Cloud*, M).

3. Ibid., lxxvii ff.

4. *Cloud*, Prologue, H. pp. 2–3; M, p. 4.

5. *Stirrings*, in *Deonise Hid Diuinite and Other Treatises on Contemplative Prayer*, ed., Phyllis Hodgson, EETS OS 231 (London, 1955) (= D.H.D), p. 62.

6. Ibid., pp. 74–76.

7. *Cloud*, ch. 8, H, pp. 31 ff.; M, pp. 18 ff. For the teaching of Augustine and Gregory on the two lives, see C. Butler, *Western Mysticism*, 2nd ed. (London, 1926). Medieval theologians went beyond the earlier doctors in their definitions of "contemplation," and in tending to see it as, in principle, the prerogative of religious but not of those living in the world; they tightened the equation of "state" and "life." As noted, the *Cloud*'s author does not

make such an equation entirely; Walter Hilton makes a more definite break with it.

8. *Cloud*, ch. 8, H, p. 32; M, p. 19.

9. Cf. John P. H. Clark, "Action and Contemplation in Walter Hilton," *Downside Review*, 97 (1979), 258–74.

10. *Cloud*, chs. 18–19, H, pp. 48 ff.; M, pp. 32 ff.

11. *Book of Privy Counselling*, H, pp. 164 ff.; M, pp. 128 ff.

12. *Cloud*, ch. 4, H, p. 23; M, pp. 12 ff.

13. *Cloud*, ch. 60, H, pp. 111 ff.; M, p. 82 ff.

14. *Cloud*, ch. 60, H, p. 10; H. p. 82.

15. *Cloud*, ch. 68, H, pp. 121 ff.; M, pp. 90 ff.

16. *Cloud*, ch. 5, H, p. 24; M, p. 13.

17. *De Mystic, Theologia*, 1.3, PG 3a, 1001.

18. Ibid., 5, PG 3, 1048.

19. *De Divinis Nominibus*, 7.3, PG 3, 872.

20. *Cloud*, ch. 70, H, p. 125; M, p. 93.

21. *De Divinis Nominibus* 1.4, PG 3, 592. See V. Lossky, *The Vision of God* (London, 1963), p. 103.

22. Cf. John P. H. Clark, "The 'Lightsome Darkness'—Aspects of Walter Hilton's Theological Background," *Downside Review*, 95 (1977), 98 ff.

23. *Summa theologica* I q. 12.

24. *Cloud*, ch. 16, H, p. 46; M, p. 30.

25. *Cloud*, ch. 68, H, p. 122; M, p. 91.

26. *Cloud*, ch. 69, H, pp. 122 ff.; M, pp. 91 ff.

27. *Dark Night of the Soul*, 2.5.2 tr. Kavanaugh and Rodriguez (London, 1964).

28. *De Divinis Nominibus*, 1.6, PG 3, 596.

29. *Book of Privy Counsellling*, H, p. 143; M, pp. 110 ff.

30. *De Divinis Nominibus*, 4.13, PG 3, 712.

31. See the Latin sources of the English version of *Hid Divinity*, in *D.H.D.* Appendix A, and discussion in John P. H. Clark, "Sources and Theology in the *Cloud of Unknowing*," *Downside Review*, 98 (1980), 86, n. 14.

32. *Cloud*, ch. 6, H, p.26; M, p. 14.

33. *Cloud*, ch. 24, H, p. 58; M, p. 39.

34. *Summa Theologica* 1-2 q. 27 a 2 ad 2; 2-2, q. 27 a 4.

35. *Cloud*, ch. 4, H, p. 18; M, p. 9.

36. Clark, "Sources and Theology . . . ," 105 ff.

37. *Cloud*, ch. 6, H, p. 26; M, p. 14.

38. *Epistle of Discretion in Stirrings* in *D.H.D.*, p. 72.

39. *Explanatio in Lib. de Myst. Theol.*, M. Vatican Arch. Cap. S. Pietro D. 181, ff. 163r, cols. 1–2, cited in Clark, "Sources and Theology," 100 n. 68.

40. *Book of Privy Counselling*, H, p. 169; M, p. 133. Cf. note 54.

41. Étienne Gilson, *The Mystical Theology of St. Bernard* (New York, 1940; rpt. 1955), ch. 5.

42. John P. H. Clark, "Sources and Theology . . . ," 106, n. 95.

43. John P. H. Clark, "Walter Hilton and Liberty of Spirit," *Downside Review*, 96 (1978), 61–78.

44. *Cloud*, ch. 8, H, p. 32; M, p. 19.

45. *De Mystica Theologia*, c. 4, *PG* 3, 1040.
46. *Book of Privy Counselling*, H, p. 143; M, p. 110.
47. *Cloud*, ch. 3, H, p. 17; M, p. 8.
48. *Cloud*, ch. 4, H, p. 22; M, p. 12.
49. *Cloud*, ch. 24, H, p. 58; M, p. 40. After Augustine *De Doct. Christiana*. 3.10.16 (PL 34, 72).
50. Gilson, ch. 1.
51. *Cloud*, ch. 5, H, p. 25; M, p. 14.
52. *Cloud*, ch. 24, H, p. 58; M, p. 40.
53. *Ep. of Prayer*, in D.H.D., pp. 52 ff.
54. *Book of Privy Counselling*, H, p. 169; M, p. 133. (The context was referred to in note 40.)
55. *Cloud*, ch. 12, H, pp. 38 ff.; M, p. 24.
56. *Cloud*, ch. 31, H, p. 66; M, p. 46.
57. *Cloud*, ch. 32, H, pp. 66 ff.; M, pp. 46 ff.
58. *Cloud*, ch. 48, H, pp. 90 ff.; M, p. 66.
59. *Cloud*, ch. 50, H, pp. 93 ff.; M, pp. 68 ff.
60. *Cloud*, ch. 53, H, pp. 97 ff.; M, pp. 71 ff.
61. *Cloud*, ch. 55, H, pp. 103 ff.; M, p. 76.
62. *Cloud*, ch. 56, H, pp. 104 ff.; M, pp. 76 ff.
63. *Cloud*, chs. 13–14, H, pp. 40 ff.; M, pp. 25 ff.
64. *Cloud*, ch. 16, H, p. 46; M, p. 30.
65. John P. H. Clark, "Walter Hilton and 'Liberty of Spirit,'" 71 ff.
66. *Summa Theologica*, 1–2 q. 111 a 2.
67. *Cloud*, ch. 34, H, pp. 68 ff.; M, pp. 48 ff.
68. *Cloud*, ch. 5, H, p. 25; M, pp. 13 ff.
69. *Cloud*, ch. 7, H, p. 28; M, p. 16.
70. *Cloud*, ch. 4, H, p. 21; M, p. 11.
71. *Cloud*, ch. 17, H, p. 47; M, p. 31, after Richard of St. Victor, *Benjamin Major*, 1, c. 1.
72. *Book of Privy Counselling*, H, pp. 170 ff.; M, p. 134, referring to Augustine, *Sermo*, 143. See John P. H. Clark, "Sources and Theology . . . " p. 96.
73. *Book of Privy Counselling*, H, p. 159; M, p. 124.
74. *Book of Privy Counselling*, H, p. 154; M, p. 120.
75. *Cloud*, ch. 70, H, pp. 11 ff.; M, p. 92. Cf. note 17 above.
76. Expounded in e.g. E. W. Trueman Dicken, *The Crucible of Love* (London, 1963), chs. 8–9.
77. J. Orcibal, *S. Jean de la Croix et les Mystiques Rheno-Flamands* (Paris, 1966), pp. 113 ff.
78. John P. H. Clark, "The Lightsome Darkness—Aspects of Walter Hilton's Theological Background," *Downside Review*, 95 (1977), 95–109.
79. John P. H. Clark, "The *Cloud of Unknowing*, Walter Hilton and St. John of the Cross: a Comparison," *Downside Review*, 96 (1978), 281–98.
80. Ibid., 296 ff.
81. Gilson, ch. 5.
82. *Book of Privy Counselling*, H, pp. 167 ff.; M, pp. 131 ff.

83. John P. H. Clark, "The *Cloud of Unknowing* . . . a Comparison," 297 ff.

XIII. Nicholas of Cusa's The Vision of God

1. In a letter of 1453 to the abbot of the monastery at Tegernsee, Caspar Aindorffer, Nicholas says explicitly that he has not himself enjoyed the delights of the mystics: "If anything I write or say be uncertain, I have not yet tasted that the Lord is sweet." ("Ego si quid scripsero aut dixero incertum erit: nondum enim gustavi quoniam suavis est Dominus.") The whole of this letter and Nicholas' correspondence with Tegernsee may be found in E. Vansteenberghe, *Autour de la docte ignorance, Beiträge zur Geschichte der Philosophie und Theologie des Mittelalters* 14, 2–4 (1915). The quote above is from letter IV, p. 113, but the whole letter provides background and commentary on *The Vision of God.*

2. All translations of *The Vision of God* are taken from Emma Gurney Salter's translation of 1928, itself a reworking of Giles Randall's version of 1646, Nicholas of Cusa, *The Vision of God,* tr. E.G. Salter, intro. Evelyn Underhill (New York, 1978). These translations are referred to by the appropriate page number in Salter, followed by capital *E.* The Latin text is referred to by page number and capital *L;* here I refer to the Duprés' Latin text with its facing German translation—their text is based on the 1514 Paris edition (no critical edition of *The Vision of God* is available as yet): Nikolaus von Kues, *Philosophisch-theologische Schriften,* Dritter Band, übersetzt D. und W. Dupré (Herder, 1967), pp. 93–219.

3. On the introductory chapters of *The Vision of God,* see Ernst Hoffmann, "Gottesschau bei Meister Eckehart und Nikolaus von Cues," in *Festschrift Heinrich Zangger,* II. Teil (Zurich,1935), pp. 1040–45.

4. For an analysis of what *The Vision of God* contributes to Nicholas' teaching on the coincidence of opposites, see Kurt Flasch, *Die Metaphysik des Einen bei Nikolaus von Kues* (Leiden, 1973), pp. 194–204.

5. For a view of the metaphysics behind these chapters and its relation to earlier and later thinkers, see two papers by Werner Beierwaltes, "Visio absoluta: Reflexion als Grundzug des göttlichen Prinzips bei Nicolaus Cusanus," *Sitzungsberichte der Heidelberger Akademie der Wissenschaften* (1978), pp. 5–33; "Deus Oppositio Oppositorum (Nicolaus Cusanus De visione dei XIII)," *Salzburger Jahrbuch für Philosophie,* 8 (1964), 175–85.

6. For the connection between unfolding and enfolding and the coincidence of opposites, see Jasper Hopkins, *A Concise Introduction to the Philosophy of Nicholas of Cusa,* 2nd ed. (Minneapolis, 1980), pp. 16–30, and by the same author, *Nicholas of Cusa on Learned Ignorance* (Minneapolis, 1981), pp. 10–22.

7. Nicholas de Cusa, *Idiota de Mente: The Layman—About Mind,* tr. and intro. Clyde Lee Miller (New York, 1979), p. 65. For a contrast between *ratio* and *intellectus* and references to Nicholas' other works, see Theodorus Van Velthoven, *Gottesschau und Menschliche Kreativität* (Leiden, 1977), pp. 33–43.

8. Beierwaltes, "Deus Oppositio," esp. pp. 179–81.

9. Hopkins, *Concise Introduction*, p. 21; see Josef Stallmach, "Der 'Zusammenfall der Gegensatze' und der unendliche Gott," in *Nikolaus von Kues—Einführung in sein philosophisches Denken*, ed. Klaus Jacobi (Freiburg/München, 1979), pp. 56–73.

10. Aurelius Augustinus, *De Trinitate* viii, 10, 14. On Cusanus' doctrine of the Trinity, see Rudolf Haubst, *Das Bild des Einen und Dreieinen Gottes in der Welt nach Nikolaus von Kues* (Trier, 1952).

11. On the import of the third book of *On Learned Ignorance*, see Hopkins, *Nicholas on Learned Ignorance*, pp. 30–43; cf. also Rudolf Haubst, *Die Christologie des Nikolaus von Kues* (Frieberg, 1956).

XIV. SIXTEENTH CENTURY JEWISH MYSTICISM

1. Uriel Acosta, *A Specimen of Human Life* (New York, 1967). For general background on the Marranos, see Cecil Roth, *A History of the Marranos*, 4th ed. (New York, 1974).

2. See Salo Baron, *Social and Religious History of the Jews*, vol. 13 (New York and London, 1969).

3. Gershom Scholem, *Kabbalah* (Jerusalem, 1974), pp. 42–61; idem, *Major Trends in Jewish Mysticism*, 3rd ed. (New York, 1961), pp. 119–243; idem, *Ursprung und Anfänge der Kabbala* (Berlin, 1962).

4. Fritz Yitzhak Baer, *A History of Jews in Christian Spain*, vol. 1 (Philadelphia, 1961), pp. 243–305.

5. Scholem, *Kabbalah*, pp. 67–79.

6. Quoted by Abraham Azulai in *Or ha-Ḥamma* (Jerusalem, 1876), intro. See also Scholem, *Kabbalah*, p. 68.

7. Gershom Scholem, *Sabbatai Sevi: The Mystical Messiah, 1626–1676*, rev. English ed. (Princeton, 1973), chapter 1.

8. Moses Cordovero, *Sefer Gerushin* (Venice, 1602), p. 51a.

9. R. J. Z. Werblowsky, *Joseph Karo, Lawyer and Mystic* (London, 1962).

10. The best general survey of Safed in the period under discussion is still Solomon Schechter, "Safed in the Sixteenth Century," *Studies in Judaism*, 2nd ser. (Philadelphia, 1908), pp. 203–306.

11. The best study of Karo is Werblowsky, *Joseph Karo*.

12. Translated in Werblowsky, p. 17.

13. See Joseph Ben Shlomo's article in Scholem, *Kabbalah*, pp. 401–04. For a thorough discussion of Cordovero's philosophy, see Ben Shlomo, *Torat ha-Elohut shel Rabbi Moses Cordovero* (Jerusalem, 1965).

14. Moses Cordovero, *Shiur Koma* (Warsaw, 1883), par. 20, p. 98.

15. Idem, *Elima Rabbati* (Lvov, 1881), p. 24d. For a treatment of the problem of pantheism in the Kabbalah, see Scholem, *Kabbalah*, pp. 144–52.

16. For Luria's biography, see Scholem, *Kabbalah*, pp. 420–28. See also Meir Benayahu, *Sefer Toldot ha-Ari* (Jerusalem, 1967).

17. The best introduction to Luria's thought in English is Scholem, *Major Trends in Jewish Mysticism*, pp. 244–86.

18. *Etz Haim* (Jerusalem, 1930), 17–18. The *Etz Haim* was compiled by Haim Vital and Vital's son, Samuel. The core of the book was written down

between 1573 and 1576 but was not published in its complete form until the nineteenth century. See Scholem, *Kabbalah*, pp. 424–55.

19. The most thorough treatment of the complexities of creation in the Lurianic system is Isaiah Tishby's *Torat ha-Ra ve-ha-Klippah* (Jerusalem, 1942). Much of the present discussion is based on Tishby. See also Scholem, *Kabbalah*, pp. 128–44.

20. See Scholem, "Schöpfung aus Nichts und Selbstverschränkung Gottes" in his *Über einige Grundbegriffe des Judentums* (Frankfurt, 1970), pp. 53–89.

21. On the connection between Lurianic Kabbalah and the history of Jewish messianism, see Scholem, *Sabbatai Ṣevi*, pp. 8–66 and idem, *The Messianic Idea in Judaism* (New York, 1971), pp. 1–48.

22. Scholem, *Kabbalah*, pp. 344–50.

23. Solomon Alkabets, *Shoresh Yishai* (Constantinople, 1561), pp. 81a ff. The translation is Werblowsky's, p. 241.

24. Scholem, "Die Theologie des Sabbatianismus im Lichte Abraham Cardosos," in his *Judaica*, vol. 1 (Frankfurt, 1968), p. 146.

25. On the spread of Lurianic Kabbalah, see Scholem, *Sabbatai Ṣevi*, pp. 66–93.

26. Joseph Dan, *Sifrut ha-Musar ve-ha-Derush* (Jerusalem, 1975), pp. 202–29.

27. On the connection between Lurianic Kabbalah and Hasidism, see Scholem, *Major Trends*, pp. 325–50 and the still-definitive article by Isaiah Tishby and Joseph Dan, "Hasidism" (Hebrew) *Encyclopedia Hebraica*.

Index

ab(e)geschiedenheit: term in Eckhart, 243, 251; in Tauler, 260
"abstraction of senses": in Aquinas, 152, 154–56
Acosta, Uriel, 313
Active life, 38–39, 87, 151, 171, 253, 274–75. *See also* Contemplative life.
Adam, 205–06, 209, 301
Adam Kadmon, 324–25
Affections. *See* Will
aísthēsis, 55–58, 63–64, 70
Alacoque, Margaret Mary, 168
Albert the Great, 135, 137, 143, 146, 152–53
Albigensian movement, 140, 174
Alkabets, Solomon, 326
Allen, Hope Emily, 162, 174, 218, 228, 231, 233
Alice of Schaarbeek, 175
"all will be well", 205, 214
Ancrene Riwle, 196
Angela of Foligno, 178
Anima, Animus: in Neoplatonism, 54–58, 64–74
Aquinas, Thomas, 135–59; university controversies, 147; three apostolates, 148–54; in *Cloud of Unknowing,* 273, 277, 279. Works: *DeCaelo,* 155; *Catena Aurea,* 144; *On the Eternity of the World,* 153; *De generatione,* 155; *On the Perfection of the Spiritual Life,* 149; *O Salutaris Hostia,* 145; *Summa Contra Gentiles,* 144; *Summa Theologiae,* 138, 145–49, 245; *Tantum Ergo,* 145; *Those Who Prevent Young Men from Entering Religious Life,* 150; *On the Unicity of the Intellect Against the Averroists,* 153; *On Virtues and Vices,* 151
Aristotelian science, 322
Ascent of Soul, 67
Ascetic Practices, in Smaragdus, 44–46. *See also* Prayer
Audelay, John, 183
aufgehoben, term in Eckhart, 243
Augustine, 19–35; 148, 202, 209–10, 248, 277–79, 281, 288, 290, 294, 307, 310. Works: *Christian Doctrine,* 281; *Confessions,* 20–23, 27, 28; the *Trinity,* 29
Averroes, 152–53
Azikiri, Eliezer, 328

Bacharach, Naphtali, 328
Baker, Augustine, 180, 198
Bahir. See Sefer ha-Bahir
Bahya ben Asher, 106
Bartholomew of Capua, on Aquinas, 156–57
Beatrice of Nazareth, 175–76, 243
Beghards, 174, 240, 242–43, 255, 280
Beguines, 174, 240, 242–43, 245, 248, 255
Berav, Jacob, 318
Bernard of Clairvaux, 77–95, passim; 166, 176, 248, 281, 289
binah, 117–18, 120
Blake, William, 113
Blood of Christ, 202–03
Body, in Augustine, 32–33
Boehme, Jacob, 113, 323 (Böhme)
Boethius of Dacia, 147, 153

Bonavaenture, 135, 146, 149, 277, 310
Boniface VIII (Pope), 240
Book of Clarity. See Sefer ha-Bahir.
Book of Gostyle Grace (or The Maulde
    Boke), tr. of Mechthild of Hackeborn's
    Liber Spiritualis Gratiae, 168
Book of Privy Counselling. See Cloud-
    author
Bosse, Roberta Bux, 228–29; 231
brautmystik, 168, 171, 175, 177
Brethren of Common Life, 174
Bride (soil): in Bernard of Clairvaux, 93
Bride and Bridegroom, 74; in Zohar,
    123; in Hadewijch, 177; in Angela of
    Foligno, 180; 289
Birgitta of Sweden, 181–84
Brunham, John, 217
bullitio, 252
Butler, Dom Cuthbert, 24, 32, 248
Butler-Bowdon, W., 218

Canticle of Canticles, 77–95, passim; in
    Zohar, 107–08, 123–24; Midrash on,
    123
Catherine of Siena, 157; 184–91
Chambers, R. W., 227, 230
Chanson d'adventure, 83
Charity: in spiritual life, 149–50
Chesler, Phyllis, 232
Chesteron, G. K., 146
Cholmeley, Katherine, 228
Christ: as Bridegroom, 78, 86, 90; as
    mother, 206, 209–11; as Second
    Adam, 209; as hen, 210
Christine of St. Trond, 175
Christian Humanism, in Smaragdus, 38
Circle: image of, 54, 67–68
Clark, John P. H., 211
Clement V (Pope), 240
Cloud-author, 273–91, passim. Works:
    Book of Privy Counselling, 274, 276,
    281, 286, 289; Cloud of Unknowing,
    Denis' Hid Divinity, 274; Epistle of
    Discretion in Stirrings, 274; Epistle of
    Prayer, 274; Study of Wisdom, 274
"cloud of forgetting," idea of, 276, 282
"cloud of unknowing," idea of, 276–79
Coleman, T. W., 227
Colledge, Edmund [Eric], 183, 198, 228,
    246
Collis, Louise, 227
Compunction, in Smaragdus, 43, 47–48
Contemplation, in Smaragdus, 41–42;
    infused, 155
Contemplative life (see also Active life),
    39, 151, 253, 274–75
Contemplative Union, 81
Contemplatives of the devil, 283

Cotton, Sir Robert, 198
Cordovero, Moses, 316–22. Works:
    Pardes Rimonim, 319–20; Sefer
    Geneshin, 316
Councils: Chalcedon, 309; Fourth
    Lateran, 239; Second Council of
    Lyons, 156– , 239; Vienne, 242–43
Cressy, Dom Serenus, 198
Crucifixion, 83, 264

Daniel (prophet), 72
Dante, 208
Darkness: in Nicholas of Cusa, 298,
    311. See also "cloud of unknowing"
    and Dark Night.
Dark Night, 152, 180, 213, 269, 287–88
Dean Ruth, 161–62
de Chardin, Teilhard, 248
Delaney, Sheila, 232
Descent of Soul. See Fall of Soul.
Detachment: in Eckhart, 251
de Vidas, Elijah, 328
de Worde, Wynkyn, 218
Dillard, Annie, 219
din, 121–22
Divine Darkness, 61
Divine exile, 324–26
Divine Names, 61–63
"docta ignorantia" ('learned
    ignorance'), 294–95, 297, 299, 305,
    311
Dominicans, 140, 240–41; and women
    mystics, 172–73
Dorothea of Montau, 173–74
Dresnitz, Solomon Shlomel, 318
Dronke, Peter, 164
Dulcis Iesu Memoria, 87–91
durchbrechen, 251–53

Easton, Adam, 182–83
Ebner, Christine, 173
Ebner, Margaret, 173
Eckhart, 31, 170, 237–57 passim,
    259–60, 290, 294; and Aquinas, 244;
    influence of, 254–56; and
    Neoplatonism, 244; trial, 245–47.
    Works: brief notice of, 244–47; Book
    of Divine Consolation, 254; Counsels on
    Discernment, 248; On Detachment,
    251
Ecstasy: in Aquinas, 138; in Augustine,
    21–22; in Bernard of Clairvaux,
    86–87; in Eckhart, 248
Eliot, T. S., 214
Elizabeth of Schönau, 166–67
Emek ha Melekh, 328
Erickson, Carolly, 229
Eschmann, I. T., 148

Eucharist, 146
Eugenius III (Pope), 166
Eve: as anima, 65–66
Exoteric revelation, 100
Expulsion of Jews from Spain, 313, 315, 328
Eyn Sof, 115–17; 314, 316, 320–25

Fall: in Neoplatonic usage, 64–67
Fasts, 265
Fear of God, in *Cloud of Unknowing,* 284
Feminism, and Margery Kempe, 229–34
Flete, William, 183–84, 288
Fides quaerens intellectum, 137
Fournier, James, 246
Franklin, James, 170
Franciscans, 240
Frauenbewegung, 174, 241–43, 248
Frauenfrage, 174
Frauenmystik, 233
Free Spirit movement, 169, 179, 242, 255, 280, 283
Friends of God, 172, 174

Gabriel (angel), 109
Gallus, Thomas, 279–80
Gascoigne, Thomas, 183
Gauthier, R. A., 148
Gerard d'Abbeville, 147, 149, 153
Gerona, and kabbalistic circles, 103–05, 317
Gertrude the Great, 167, 170–72
Gertrude of Hackeborn, 167
Gerson, John, 183
Gifts of the Holy Spirit, 151–52
Gikatilla, Joseph, 106
gilgul, 326–27
Gilson, Etienne, 82, 87–88
God: as point, 207–09
Godfrey of St. Disibodenberg, 163
God's Birth in the Soul, 268
Gonsalvo of Spain, 244
Gordon, Mary, 215
Gnosticism, 53–54, 103, 112
Grace: in Aquinas, 136–37; in *Cloud of Unknowing,* 284–85; in Nicholas of Cusa, 297, in Tauler, 269–70
Great Mother within God, 119. *See also* Christ as mother
Greenhalgh, James, 273
Gregory the Great, 2, 39, 47, 248, 277–78, 288, 290
Gregory of Nyssa, 274
Ground of Soul, in Eckhart, 249–54; in Julian of Norwich, 199; in Tauler, 270–71
Grundmann, Herbert, 242, 243

Gudmarsson, Ulf, 181
Gui, Bernard, 154

Hadewijch, 175–77, 243
halakhah, 98, 113, 3129
halal ha-panui, 322–23
Hasidic movement, 319, 328
havurot, 319
hazelnut, image in Julian of Norwich, 207
Heavenly Jerusalem, 222
Hegel, 323
Hekhalot mysticism, 314
Henry of Halle, 168–69
Henry of Nordlingen, 169, 173
Henry of Virneburg, 245
hesed, 121
Hildegard of Bingen, 163–66
Hilton, Walter, 207, 273, 275–76, 281–82, 284, 288
Hirsh, John C., 227
hod, 128
hokhmah, 116–18
Holy Fear, in Catherine of Siena, 188
Holy Ghost (Spirit), 38, 267
Horowitz, Israel, 328
Horsley, Adam, 273
High of St. Victor, 279
Huxley, Aldous, 215
Hypostasis, 54

ibn Tabul, Joseph, 321, 323
Ignorance, in Neoplatonism, 56
Illumination (*see also* Three Stages), in Margery Kempe, 220
Imitatio Christi, 248–49, 264
"In agro dominico" (bull), 247
"In a valey of this restles mynde," analyzed, 82–87
Incarnation, 69–74, 79, 91, 145–46, 200, 202–10, 251–53
Imago Dei, 249–50
Improperia, 82–88
Inge, W. R., 19, 24, 92
Intelligence and revelation, 145
Isaac of Acre, 106
Isidore of Seville, 47

James of Vitry, 242
St. Jerome, 150
"Jhesu, swete in the love of thee," 91
John XXII (Pope), 158, 240, 246
St. John Chrysostom, 44
St. John of the Cross, 92, 215, 278, 286–87, 289
John of Marienwerder, 173
John of San Giuliano, 141–42
Johnstone, Fr. William, 208

Jordan of Quedlinburg, 255
Julian of Norwich, 195–216 passim; 229

Kabbalah, 105, 97–134 passim, 313–29
    passim
Kaf Ha-ketoreth, 315
Karo, Joseph, 313, 316–19
Katherine-group, 199
Kavvanot, 316, 326
Kawwanah, 103
Kelim, 324
Kempe, John, 217
Kempe, Margery, 174, 217–35 passim;
    and Julian of Norwich, 196–97, 220,
    227–28
kennesset yisra'el, 123
keter, 115–16
Kind (i.e. Nature), in Julian of Norwich,
    199
klippot, 324–25
Knowles, David, 227

Langland, William, 200
Langmann, Adelhard, 173
leiden, 263–65
Lewis of Bavaria, 240
Liberty, ascetical notion of, 68–69
Light, 22, 54, 62, 138, 157, 164–65,
    207, 299, 303, 307
Lilith, 125
St. Liutberga of Wendhausen, 178
"living without a why," (sunder
    warumbe), 253–54
Logic and Mysticism, 58–60
Lollard movement, 219, 221, 223,
    230–31, 280, 283
Lombard, Peter, 29
Lottin, Dom Odo, 148
Love, in Nicholas of Cusa, 308–09
Lucia of the Incarnation, 162, 185
Lull, Raymond, 294
Luria, Isaac, 315–17, 321–28
Lutgarde of Aywieres, 171, 175
Luther, Martin, 259

maggidism, 316–17
Maimonides, Moses, 98, 320
malkhut, 122
Manuscripts cited (all of Julian of
    Norwich): BL Addit. 37790, 197; BL
    Sloane 2499, 197–98; BL Sloane 3705,
    197; BN Fonds Anglais 40, 197;
    Colwich Abbey 18, 197; Upholland
    Ms., 197; Westminster Cathedral, 197
Marguerite d'Oingt, 178
Marranos, 313
Martha and Mary, 88, 230, 253, 266,
    275, 284, 286

Martindale, C. C., 167
Mary (Blessed Virgin), 203, 205
Mary. See Martha and Mary.
Mary of Oignies, 175, 224, 243
Masculine and Feminine, 162
matnitin, 111
Matter, E. Ann, 233
Mechthild of Hackeborn, 167–68
Mechthild of Magdeburg, 168–70; 243
Meditation, in Cloud of Unknowing, 285;
    in Smaragdus, 40–41
Mendicants, 140, 240–42
Messianism, 314–15, 327
Metheora, 155
Mind, nature of in Augustine, 31
Midrash, 98, 99, 109
Minnesang, 168–69
mitzvot, 325
Mixed life, 275. See Active life,
    Contemplative life
mizwot, 132
More, Dame Gertrude, 198
Moses, 25
Moses of Burgos, 105
Mystical Body, 187
Mystical contemplation, 138
Mystical Marriage, 84, 222, 248
Mystical Union, 25, 31, 61
Mysticism: as construct, 2; definitions,
    24–25; expulsion of the Jews and,
    315–16; Jewish Focus on redemption,
    317; in Julian of Norwich, 212–14;
    and Kabbalah, 118–19; in Margery
    Kempe, 227; problems in typologies,
    247; as reaction to scholasticism, 4; in
    Tauler, 266–67; as term for Aquinas,
    136–38; women's, 233–34

Nahmanides, Moses, 104, 114
"naked intent unto God," 280–81
Neoplatonism, 53, 104. See Platonism.
neshamah, 105
Newman, John Henry, 215
nezah, 128
Nicholas of Cusa, 255; 293–312 passim.
    Works: Layman: About Mind, 305– ;
    On Learned Ignorance, 309; The Vision
    of God, 294–310, (summarized) 311.
Nicholas of Strassburg, 246
nitzotzot, 324
Nous. See Animus.

O'Connell, John R., 228
The Orchard of Syon, 185
Origen, 79, 85

Pantheism, 249, 280, 322
Papacy: in High Middle Ages, 239–40

Parable of Lord and Servant: in Julian of Norwich, 201
Paradise: in Nicholas of Cusa, 301–04; St. Paul, 25, 47, 69, 79, 80, 148–49, 204, 229, 248, 276, 280, 282
Pecham, John, 149
Pelagianism, 265
Pelphrey, Charles Brant, 204–05
Pepwell, Henry, 217
Peter of Auvergne, 153
Peter of Skanninge, 182
Petitot, C. H., 157
Petroff, Elizabeth, 162
Philo, 112, 209
Platonism, in Augustine, 19–22, 26
Plotinus, 19, 64, 67
Poland, 328
Porete, Marguerite, 243
Prayer, in Smaragdus, 39–50 passim; in Catherine of Siena, 188; in Julian of Norwich, 205–06; in Tauler, 270
Proclus, 244, 293
Psalms, in Bernard, 94
Pseudo-Dionysius, 62, 77, 81, 143, 208, 274, 277–82, 293, 310
Psyche, 54–58. *See also* Anima.
Purgation: in Margery Kempe, 220. *See also* Three Stages.

"Quia amore langueo," refrain, 85–87
Quietism, 265

Rabbi Abraham ben David, of Posquieres, 102
Rabbi Moses De Leon, 106, 112–15
Rabbi Pinhas of Korzec, 106
Rabbi Simeon ben Yohai, 106
Ramirez, Santiago, 148
Raymond of Capua, 185
Raymond of Pennafort, 144
Real Presence, 241
Reason: and coincidence of opposites, 303; and God, 102; and seeing God, 300–01
Reginald of Piperno, 142, 144, 155–56
Riehle, Wolfgang, 233
reshimu, 323
Return to God, in Aquinas, 151
Reynolds, Sr. Anna Maria, 198
Richard, companion of Margery Kempe, 222
Richard of St. Victor, 274, 277
Roger of Ford, 167
Rolle, Richard, 92, 200, 273–74, 277, 282

Sabbatianism, 325, 327
Safed, 316, 317–19

Samael, 125
Sarracenus, John, 279
Sarug, Israel, 328
Satan, 125
Scholem, Gershom, 112, 314, 315, 326, 327
Schwester Katrei, 255
Scotus Eriugena, 293–94
Sefardic Jews, 317–18
Sefer Ha-Bahir, 98, 99
Sefir Ha-Meshiv, 315
sefirot, 103, 104, 109, 115–19, 314, 316, 321
Sensuality and Substance, in Julian of Norwich, 199
shekhinah, 108–09, 122–23, 316
shevirat ha-kelim, 324
Shivhei Ha-ari, 321
shorshei ha-dinim, 323
Siger of Brabant, 147, 153
Silesus, Angelus, 256
Simeon ben Yohai, 113
sitra ahra, 126
Smaragdus, 37–51 passim
Song of Songs. *See* Canticle of Canticles.
Soul, as bride, 86; entry of Spirit into, 263–64; erotic nature, 68; powers of in Eckhart, 238; purity of, 46; three parts of, 104
Southern, R. W., 175–75
Southfield, William, 220
Spinoza, Baruch, 313
Spiritual dryness, 189
Stagel, Elsbeth, 172–73
Stargardt, Ute, 174
Stigmata: invisible in Gertrude the Great, 170; in women mystics, 175; invisible in Catherine of Siena, 184
Stone, R. K., 227
Sudermann, Daniel, 255
Suso, Henry, 172–73, 249, 255, 259
Syon Abbey, 183–84, 217, 226

Tauler, John, 255, 259–72 passim, 284, 288, 290
Temple of Souls, 256
Ten utterances, 101
Teresa of Avila, 170, 186, 215
Thierry of Chartres, 294
Thirteenth Century, overview, 139–41
Thomas of York, 149
Thornton, Martin, 228
Three stages of illumination, 186, 212, 234, 268–69
tiferet, 128
tikkun, 325–27
Todros Abulafia of Toldeo, 105

Toledat Ha-Ari, 321
Tomer Devorah, 328
Trinity, 30–31, 63–64, 66, 69, 71–74,
  145–46, 165, 200–01, 210, 250, 253,
  285–86, 307–09
Twelfth Century Renaissance, 163
tzimtzum, 322–24

Ubertino da Casale, 179
Underhill, Evelyn, 24, 27, 161
Union, 70, 93–94, 177, 179, 186,
  190–91, 204, 269–70, 309–10. See also
  Mystical Union.
Universities, 140–41
Urban IV (Pope), 144

van Ruysbroeck, Jan, 172, 176, 255,
  284
Via negativa (see also Pseudo-Dionysius),
  77, 82, 92
Vices, 47, 49
Vigils, 265
Virginity, 229
Virtues, theological, 69
Visions: in Angela of Foligno, 179–81;
  in Aquinas, 138, 151; in Augustine,
  22–25, 32, 49; in the Cloud of
  Unknowing, 283; in Eckhart, 248; in
  Hildegard of Bingen, 164–65; in
  Julian of Norwich, 196, 202, 213–14;
  in Margery Kempe, 219; in Nichola
  of Cusa, 295–98, 311; in Tauler, 147
Vision of St. Paul, 157
Vita apostolica, 240–41, 253
Vitae sororum, 173

Vital, Haim, 317, 321, 326–27
Volmar, 163

Warrack, Grace, 198
Watkin, E. I., 228
Wemple, Suzanne, 178
Wenck, Johannes, 255
Werblowsky, R. J., Zvi, 316
Will, in Augustine, 28–30
William of St.-Amour, 143–44, 153
William of Moerbeke, 146, 153, 244
William of St. Thierry, 53–75 passim;
  176, 279
William of Tocco, 139, 144, 147
Wilson, R. M., 227
wirken, 263
Wisdom (Christ), 70–71
Wright, Wendy, 162

yesod, 121
yihud, 121

zaddih, 328
Zohar: anecdote of Rabbis Eleazar and
  Abba, 107, 109–11; anecdote of R.
  Hiyya, 121; anecdote of R. Simeon,
  120; anecdote of R. Simeon (on
  Torah), 130–31; and Cordovero, 320;
  dualism, 124–26; evil, 124–26; and
  "imitation of God," 131–32; man,
  nature and human life, 126–28; and
  Luria, 325; notion of creation, 116;
  notion of God, 115–16; origin of soul,
  127–28; and pantheism, 122; return
  of soul to God, 132–33; union, 29